Generative AI in the Social Sciences and Humanities

Generative AI is transforming how we learn, teach, and conduct research, reshaping the foundations of the social sciences and humanities. *Generative AI in the Social Sciences and Humanities* examines this profound shift, offering an accessible and authoritative guide for scholars, educators, and professionals navigating the opportunities and risks of AI in academic life.

Bringing together an international team of contributors from Poland, Italy, the UK, Ukraine, and Finland, this volume provides an interdisciplinary exploration of how generative AI is reshaping research practices, educational environments, and scholarly culture within SSH. The book covers a broad thematic landscape: from the evolution and taxonomy of AI, to its uses in disinformation studies, academic integrity, and specialised professional training. It includes empirical insights from focus groups and classroom research, detailed analyses of LLM-driven risks such as hallucinations, bias, and erosion of critical thinking, as well as practical applications like AI-enhanced tutoring and dataset governance. Combining theoretical perspectives with real-world examples, the monograph illuminates how AI tools are deployed, perceived, and negotiated in universities, research institutions, and digital public spheres.

The book is unique for its SSH-focused perspective, empirical depth, and strong ethical framing. It provides concrete guidelines and best practices for the responsible use of AI, enabling researchers, educators, and students to balance innovation with integrity. By bringing technical and humanistic perspectives into dialogue, the volume offers a vital roadmap for navigating AI's rapidly evolving place in academic life.

- First major volume fully dedicated to AI in the social sciences and humanities, not STEM
- Based on original empirical research (focus groups, classroom studies, and interviews)
- Offers practical guidelines for researchers, educators, and decision-makers

Rafał Olszowski is a social scientist specialising in research on collective intelligence, e-participation, the digital public sphere, political communication on social media, argument mining, AI ethics, e-government, and the history of political doctrines. He is affiliated with AGH University of Kraków. He is the author of two monographs: *Permanence and Change in the Political Thought of Edmund Burke* (2021) and *Collective Intelligence in Open Policymaking* (2024). In addition to his academic work, he is an experienced business consultant in new technologies, a designer of educational board games, and a manager of innovation-driven learning projects. Beyond his professional activities, he is actively involved in the non-governmental sector through the Aurea Libertas Institute Foundation.

Jakub Gomułka is a philosopher and computer scientist whose work centres on Ludwig Wittgenstein, Stanisław Lem, knowledge graph technology, and the applications of generative AI within the humanities. He is affiliated with the Faculty of Humanities at the AGH University of Kraków. He is the author of two monographs on Wittgenstein's philosophy and currently serves as the lead researcher in the development of the ongoing Lem Knowledge Graph project. In addition, he contributes to the Wittgenstein Ontology project conducted by the Wittgenstein Archives at the University of Bergen.

Generative AI in the Social Sciences and Humanities

Navigating Challenges and Opportunities in Research and Education

Edited by
Rafał Olszowski
and Jakub Gomułka

CRC Press
Taylor & Francis Group
Boca Raton London New York

CRC Press is an imprint of the
Taylor & Francis Group, an **informa** business

Designed cover image: Taylor & Francis

First edition published 2027
by CRC Press
2385 NW Executive Center Drive, Suite 320, Boca Raton FL 33431

and by CRC Press
4 Park Square, Milton Park, Abingdon, Oxon, OX14 4RN

CRC Press is an imprint of Taylor & Francis Group, LLC

ISBN: 978-1-041-14370-3 (hbk)
ISBN: 978-1-041-14794-7 (pbk)
ISBN: 978-1-003-67618-8 (ebk)

DOI: 10.1201/9781003676188

Typeset in Times
by SPi Technologies India Pvt Ltd (Straive)

Dedication

For my Parents, with gratitude for everything—Rafał Olszowski
For Nadia, my beloved wife—Jakub Gomułka

Contents

Contributors

Wasim Ahmed
Hull University Business School
University of Hull
Hull, UK

Mirosława M. Długosz
Faculty of Humanities
AGH University of Krakow
Krakow, Poland

Mirko Duradoni
Department of Human and Social Sciences,
Mercatorum University,
Rome, Italy

Manuela Farinosi
Department of Mathematics, Computer Science and Physics,
University of Udine
Udine, Italy

Paulina Gajoch
Faculty of Humanities
AGH University of Krakow
Krakow, Poland

Filip Gampel
Faculty of Humanities
AGH University of Krakow
Krakow, Poland

Jakub Gomułka
Faculty of Humanities
AGH University of Krakow
Krakow, Poland

Hasse Hällström
Independent Researcher

Mariann Hardey
Durham Business School
Durham University
Durham, UK

Alla Ishchuk
Dragomanov Ukrainian State University,
Faculty of Foreign Philology, Kyiv, Ukraine

Mykhailo Ishchuk
State Tax University,
Educational and Scientific Institute of Economic Security and Customs,
Irpin, Ukraine

Claudio Melchior
Department of Foreign Languages and Literature,
University of Udine
Udine, Italy

Filippo Mosca
University of Tor Vergata
Rome, Italy

Rafał Olszowski
Faculty of Humanities,
AGH University of Krakow
Krakow, Poland

Grzegorz Ptaszek
Faculty of Humanities,
AGH University of Krakow
Krakow, Poland

Karolina Rożek
Faculty of Humanities,
AGH University of Krakow
Krakow, Poland

Krzysztof Tomasz Stawarz
Faculty of Humanities,
AGH University of Krakow
Krakow, Poland

Maria Stojkow
Faculty of Humanities,
AGH University of Krakow
Krakow, Poland

Krzysztof Turek
Department of Philosophy,
Krakow University of Economics,
Krakow, Poland

Marcin Woźniak
Fundacja Optimum Pareto
Swarmcheck
Krakow, Poland

Dorota Żuchowska-Skiba
Faculty of Humanities,
AGH University of Krakow
Krakow, Poland

Acknowledgements

We are deeply grateful to the Faculty Authorities and our colleagues at the Faculty of Humanities, AGH University of Krakow, for fostering an environment of intellectual curiosity and cooperation. Special mention goes to the dean of our Faculty Jacek Gądecki, the administrative director Anna Kulpa, the vice-dean Dariusz Wojakowski, as well as Leszek Porębski, Tomasz Piróg, Marcin Pietroń, Grzegorz Swierk, and Kamil Jaszczyński.

Our deepest appreciation goes to our families and friends for their understanding, patience, and endless support. Their belief in our work and encouragement have been very helpful. Heartful thanks go to Natalia Olszowska, Janusz Batko, Rafał Lis, Karol Tatara, and Kay Łańcucki.

Special thanks to the editorial team at Taylor & Francis—CRC Press for their professionalism, patience, and guidance throughout the publication process.

We are profoundly grateful to the "Excellence Initiative – Research University" programme at AGH University of Krakow for its generous support of Application No. 9052, which contributed to funding part of the research and the proofreading of this monograph. This research was partially funded by Narodowe Centrum Nauki (National Science Centre, Republic of Poland), the research grant UMO-2023/49/B/HS5/01379.

Introduction

Rafał Olszowski and Jakub Gomułka

The launch of ChatGPT in November 2022 captured the attention of society at large and marked a turning point in public awareness of generative artificial intelligence (AI), vividly exposing both the promises and the pitfalls of the technology of large language models (LLMs). It quickly became apparent that LLM-based systems offer compelling opportunities for a broad range of users, including students, lecturers, and researchers. The capacity of generative AI to process complex language structures, generate reviews, and assist in text analysis represents a fundamentally new phenomenon, unmatched by tools available in the past. However, alongside these opportunities, significant concerns have emerged, particularly within educational contexts, regarding the potential misuse of such systems. A central issue is the challenge of maintaining academic integrity in university classrooms. For example, Noam Chomsky has argued that these systems enable 'basically high-tech plagiarism' and offer 'a way of avoiding learning' (Marshall 2023).

Situated at the intersection of technological innovation and cultural self-understanding, generative AI can be seen as not merely a tool, but a civilisational test for disciplines long tasked with interpreting meaning, context, and human agency in times of profound change. The emergence of generative AI can be read as yet another moment in a long sequence of technological ruptures that have repeatedly unsettled established epistemic practices. From the invention of writing and printing to the rise of mass media and later, social media, each transformation has provoked anxieties about authority, authenticity, and the conditions of knowledge production and distribution.

As Hannah Arendt warned in her reflections on modernity, moments of rapid technological and social change tend to erode established frameworks of judgement (Arendt, 1961, p. 204). By this, she did not mean a simple loss of norms or values, but a deeper disruption of the human capacity for judgement understood as the ability to think reflectively, to situate actions within shared worlds of meaning, and to distinguish between what is merely effective and what is meaningful or responsible. In works such as *The Human Condition*, Arendt described modernity as an historical situation in which instrumental rationality, concerned with optimisation, utility, and control, progressively displaces forms of thinking rooted in experience, plurality, and responsibility (Arendt, 1998, p. 4). As was pointed out by Arendt, understanding is increasingly reduced to operational competence, while the criteria for evaluating truth, significance, and moral consequence become blurred. Societies undergoing rapid technological transformation thus risk mistaking functional efficiency for genuine comprehension, and procedural success for judgement grounded in human experience and ethical reflection.

DOI: 10.1201/9781003676188-1

Generative AI confronts the social sciences and humanities with a similar, yet intensified, dilemma. It arrives as a promise of unprecedented acceleration, scalability, and accessibility in scholarly work, offering new forms of interaction that reshape how knowledge is produced and communicated. Through interactive dialogue, personalised feedback, and assistance in lecture preparation, LLMs expand the pedagogical repertoire, particularly in the articulation and transmission of complex ideas. At the same time, this technological promise unsettles long-standing assumptions about authorship, interpretation, expertise, and the moral economy of knowledge on which academic practice rests. The ease with which LLMs can generate human-like text, often indistinguishable from conventional scholarly writing, raises concerns about academic integrity, the erosion of critical thinking skills, and the growing difficulty of assessing the reliability and epistemic status of such content. What emerges, then, is not merely a technical challenge, but a deeper question about how education and research can preserve their formative and critical functions in an environment increasingly shaped by generative AI.

Understanding how LLMs generate their responses remains a complex challenge, owing to the opaque nature of their internal mechanisms. This lack of transparency complicates efforts to evaluate the accuracy and relevance of model-generated text. While generative AI can produce human-like linguistic expressions, it lacks understanding and reasoning in any strong sense, which in turn complicates the interpretation of the apparent justifications and confidence with which such responses are presented.

Nevertheless, despite these evident risks, it would be a mistake to restrict the use of AI-based technologies solely on the basis of concerns about academic integrity. These technologies have the potential to fundamentally transform the educational experience of students in the social sciences and humanities (SSH), as well as the knowledge and skills they acquire. Moreover, they hold considerable promise for streamlining and facilitating scholarly work, ensuring that technical obstacles do not unduly hinder research.

Observations of LLM use among both students and academic researchers illustrate how generative AI in academia has shifted from a peripheral innovation to a central, and increasingly contested, element of higher education's future. Given the capabilities of LLMs, students commonly use them for idea generation, summarising academic texts, clarifying difficult concepts, improving language and style, drafting outlines or preliminary versions of assignments, and supporting exam preparation. At the same time, students often display a tendency to overtrust AI-generated responses, despite growing evidence that LLMs can produce biased, inaccurate, or misleading content. Researchers, in turn, are already harnessing these tools for a wide range of tasks, from literature reviews and hypothesis generation to writing support and data processing. Such applications align closely with the discursive and interpretive character of SSH, offering tangible gains in efficiency and accessibility.

Responding to the growing potential of generative AI, this book explores the dimensions of this transformative technology that lecturers, researchers, and students perceive as most significant for the future of academia. As we worked on the material presented in this monograph, it became clear that there is an urgent need to systematically review current experiences, develop recommendations, establish best practices, and articulate practical guidelines for responsible use, so that academia can engage effectively with the challenges posed by generative AI. These issues are examined in this multi-author volume, which brings together contributions from an international group of researchers based in Poland, Italy, Ukraine, Finland, and the United Kingdom.

Chapter 1 provides the conceptual and historical groundwork for the volume by situating contemporary debates on generative AI within the longer intellectual trajectory of AI research. Rather than treating LLMs as an abrupt rupture, it reconstructs the successive paradigms symbolic, connectionist, and data-driven, which have shaped AI's development alongside the philosophical controversies that accompanied them. By tracing how questions of intelligence, understanding, and representation have been repeatedly redefined, the chapter equips the reader with a critical vocabulary necessary for engaging with later contributions. In doing so, it frames generative AI not as an isolated technological novelty, but as the latest expression of enduring tensions between formalisation and meaning, computation and interpretation—tensions that resonate throughout the subsequent chapters of the book.

Chapter 2, drawing mostly on focus group research, addresses several fundamental questions concerning how the difference between humans and contemporary generative AI technologies is understood. The authors employ the concept of myth both to engage with popular representations of the latter and to reveal the emotional climate surrounding it. They identify six of the most pervasive myths about AI: (1) that it will replace professionals; (2) that it is always infallible and objective; (3) that it is able to understand context in the same way as humans; (4) that it operates autonomously and independently; (5) that it poses a threat to privacy and security; and (6) that it can quickly provide answers to all problems. The researchers observe that these myths facilitate the anthropomorphisation of generative AI. Analysis of the focus group study, which involved 18 participants—scholars representing different disciplines within SSH—revealed that, within the academic community, three of the six identified myths are present: myths (1), (4), and (5). The authors suggest that the absence of myths (2), (3), and (6) indicates that scholars who are regular users of generative AI technologies are partly immune to the influence of prevailing media narratives.

Chapter 3 shifts the focus from conceptual and historical analysis to the lived experience of academia, offering an empirically grounded insight into how generative AI is perceived and negotiated by scholars and educators in the SSH. Drawing on focus group interviews, the chapter captures a landscape of pronounced ambivalence, in which hopes for efficiency, innovation, and accessibility coexist with concerns about epistemic reliability, academic integrity, institutional pressure, and the erosion of human-centred academic values. By foregrounding everyday practices and perceived risks alongside anticipated benefits, the chapter reveals generative AI as a catalyst of structural change, not merely a neutral technical aid. In doing so, it provides a crucial empirical anchor for the volume, illustrating how abstract debates about AI materialise in concrete academic contexts and institutional realities.

Chapter 4 focuses on the negative influence of generative AI on higher education students. The author points out to the fact that the new AI tools, including LLMs, are widely employed by students in the course of their academic tasks. Generated content is usually accepted uncritically, sometimes even despite a declared scepticism towards AI. Meanwhile, content produced by language models often contains incorrect information resulting from the phenomenon of AI hallucinations. The author emphasises the need to develop AI literacy, that is, a set of skills enabling the responsible use of LLMs.

Chapter 5 addresses one of the most critical epistemic risks associated with generative AI: the phenomenon of AI hallucinations. Moving beyond purely technical accounts, the chapter situates hallucinations at the intersection of model architecture, social trust, and academic communication. It demonstrates how seemingly plausible but fabricated outputs affect high-stakes domains and, more specifically, how they undermine scholarly practices through false citations, distorted summaries, and the uncritical automation of reviews. By linking hallucinations to mechanisms such as automation bias, the ELIZA effect, and weakened epistemic vigilance, the chapter frames this phenomenon as a systemic challenge for the SSH rather than a marginal technical flaw. In doing so, it reinforces the volume's central argument that responsible engagement with generative AI requires not only technical safeguards but also renewed forms of critical literacy, institutional accountability, and reflexive judgement within academia.

The authors of Chapter 6 examine the structure of current academic discourse on the use of generative AI in teaching within SSH. Drawing on an extensive review of recent literature available through the ERIC database of education-related publications, they describe an ongoing process of integrating generative AI into a complex educational ecosystem. Within this ecosystem, LLMs and other AI tools are portrayed as supporting key educational activities, including communication, critical thinking, collaboration, and the sharing of knowledge. At the same time, the authors identify a body of literature that highlights potential risks associated with the use of LLMs, such as embedded biases that may disadvantage certain groups of students. Despite these concerns, the overall stance of the reviewed sources is predominantly positive, with most authors emphasising the constructive role that generative AI can play in teaching.

Providing a systematic overview of how artificial intelligence is currently applied in research within the SSH, Chapter 7 positions AI not merely as a supporting tool but as an emerging research infrastructure. Drawing on a structured literature review and bibliometric analysis, it maps key methodological trends, thematic clusters, and domains of application, ranging from generative tools supporting research workflows to empirical modelling, digital humanities, and large-scale social data analysis. By identifying both technological-methodological and socio-normative axes of AI adoption, the chapter demonstrates how computational approaches are becoming increasingly integrated into SSH research practices, while simultaneously raising epistemological and ethical challenges. In doing so, it provides a panoramic synthesis that connects individual empirical and conceptual contributions of the volume, situating them within broader transformations of knowledge production, interdisciplinarity, and research governance in the age of AI.

Chapter 8 analyses the challenges involved in integrating artificial intelligence into Ukrainian higher education, with a particular focus on English philology and customs and commodity studies. The authors argue that the pace and form of AI adoption differ substantially across educational contexts and that the Ukrainian situation is shaped by acute resource shortages and the ongoing war, which has shifted institutional priorities from innovation to survival. These conditions create significant practical barriers to implementation: most universities lack the resources to provide systematic training for academic staff in the use of generative AI, resulting in a situation in which students often demonstrate greater practical competence than their teachers. Consequently, AI integration is driven largely by student initiative rather than by coordinated institutional planning. The chapter also raises pedagogical concerns, notably the risk that AI tools may be used to bypass learning processes and weaken critical thinking, as students tend to treat AI outputs as authoritative rather than as heuristic support. Levels of AI literacy are low among both students and staff, which is particularly problematic given the availability of AI tools that could effectively support teaching. The authors also highlight the absence of clear, field-specific institutional policies defining acceptable and unacceptable uses of AI, and stress the urgent need for such guidance.

Focusing on students as key stakeholders of academic transformation, Chapter 9 provides an empirically rich account of how generative AI is perceived, adopted, and contested within contemporary higher education. Drawing on a large-scale, multimethod research programme conducted among Italian university students, it reconstructs patterns of use, perceived benefits and risks, and expectations regarding the future role of generative AI in academia and beyond. By identifying distinct student profiles and highlighting the coexistence of personal optimism with broader societal concerns (the so-called 'proximity paradox'), the chapter demonstrates that students' attitudes towards generative AI are neither naïvely enthusiastic nor uniformly resistant. Instead, they reflect a nuanced demand for institutional clarity, ethical guidance, and governance frameworks that move beyond prohibition. In doing so, the chapter offers a crucial bottom-up perspective that complements the volume's theoretical and normative discussions, grounding debates on generative AI in the lived experiences and reflexive judgements of those most directly affected by its everyday use in higher education.

The authors of Chapter 10 examine an erosion of critical thinking observed among students who use generative AI, a phenomenon investigated within the TITAN project, funded by the European HORIZON programme. They attribute this development to the inherent opacity of current LLMs, which reinforces automation bias and encourages users to delegate cognitive effort to a 'black box', thereby diminishing critical engagement. Under such conditions, generative AI effectively comes to think for its users rather than with them. Paradoxically, the project's central aim—to cultivate critical thinking in order to strengthen citizens' capacity to recognise disinformation—is pursued through the very use of LLM technology. The project introduces a coaching chatbot designed to apply the Socratic method and to 'think with its users'. The deployment of a specialised language model proved effective in improving measurable indicators associated with critical thinking. Nevertheless, user reports reveal a degree of frustration, arising precisely from the system's critical-thinking-inducing mechanisms.

Chapter 11 develops a distinctly SSH-oriented perspective on AI ethics, shifting the focus from abstract moral principles to the concrete conditions under which AI intervenes in processes of interpretation, judgement, and institutional practice. Moving beyond a technology-centred understanding of ethics, the chapter locates responsibility firmly with human actors and governance structures, emphasising risks such as epistemic dependency, the erosion of critical engagement, and the reproduction of structural injustice. By critically examining major regulatory frameworks, including the EU AI Act, UNESCO's Recommendation, OECD Principles, and US regulatory initiatives, the chapter shows how ethical values are translated, with varying success, into legal and institutional arrangements. Drawing on examples from higher education, qualitative research, the labour market, and the legal system, it demonstrates how SSH scholarship plays a crucial role in operationalising ethical principles through institutional design, procedural safeguards, and democratic accountability. In this way, the chapter positions AI ethics not as a technical add-on, but as a core dimension of socially legitimate AI governance grounded in human meaning-making and responsibility.

The authors of Chapter 12 explore the transformative impact of AI-generated images on SSH research, moving beyond current applications to examine both radical innovations and profound philosophical implications. They try to demonstrate how AI image generation enables new research methodologies: visual algorithmic ethnography that synthesises community identities into composite portraits, dynamic visualisations of abstract theoretical concepts, and hermeneutic objects that allow researchers to 'see' complex historical and cultural data in tangible forms. Drawing on Foucault, Barthes, Hall, and psychoanalytic theory, they argue that AI images are not neutral tools but ideological artefacts that manifest the 'will' of prompters while amplifying collective biases encoded in training data. They notice that the technology destabilises traditional notions of authorship, copyright, and memory itself, enabling the creation of 'synthetic memories' that blur boundaries between past and fabrication. Most critically, the authors warn against the false dichotomy between 'AI' and 'human' creation, arguing instead that AI-generated images are hyper-human statistical remixes reflecting our collective aesthetics, desires, and prejudices.

Chapter 13 examines how LLMs are beginning to function as experimental research instruments within the humanities. Focusing on the development and scholarly testing of customised GPTs built on Ludwig Wittgenstein's *Tractatus* and selected parts of his digital Nachlass, the chapter offers a nuanced account of how domain-specific LLMs interact with established practices of interpretation, textual analysis, and philosophical inquiry. Instead of positioning these tools as substitutes for scholarly expertise, the analysis highlights their hybrid status: unreliable as sources of knowledge, yet potentially valuable as dialogical and exploratory aids that provoke questions, surface tensions, and stimulate critical reflection. By foregrounding scholars' situated experiences, including both the epistemic limitations and the heuristic affordances of customised GPTs, the chapter situates LLMs within SSH research as contested mediators of meaning—tools whose significance lies less in accuracy than in their capacity to reshape interpretative workflows and reflexive engagement with texts.

The final chapter offers a philosophical analysis of LLMs and their limitations. Its author draws explicitly on Cartesian notions of *mathesis universalis* and method in order to account for the AI hallucination phenomenon. According to him, embedding technology—the capacity to convert sequences of words into multidimensional vectors that are mathematically related to one another on the basis of statistical analyses of vast corpora of human-produced texts—provides language models with something akin to *mathesis universalis* but does not equip them with any internal commitment to the epistemic validation of their outputs. Such a capacity enables formal manipulation and pattern recognition, but it does not furnish any resources for assessing the truthfulness of linguistic expressions as claims about the world. In this sense, while generative AI may be said to embody Cartesian *mathesis universalis*, it lacks what Descartes designates as method, understood as a procedure for grounding and validating knowledge. In the absence of such a method, the author argues, these systems are structurally prone to hallucination and cannot, in principle, overcome this limitation.

Throughout the volume, generative AI emerges as neither a neutral tool nor an autonomous force, but as a contested element of contemporary academic practice whose meaning is negotiated in everyday use. By combining historical reflection, empirical research, methodological analysis, ethical inquiry, and concrete case studies, the book offers a multidimensional perspective on both the opportunities and the risks associated with AI-assisted scholarship. Our guiding premise is that meaningful engagement with generative AI requires neither uncritical enthusiasm nor defensive rejection, but a reflective, context-sensitive, and institutionally grounded approach that preserves the critical, interpretative, and formative functions of SSH in an AI-shaped academic landscape.

REFERENCES

Arendt, H. (1961). *Between Past and Future*. The Viking Press.

Arendt, H. (1998). *The Human Condition*. The University of Chicago Press.

Marshall, C. (2023). Noam Chomsky on ChatGPT: It's "Basically High-Tech Plagiarism" and "a Way of Avoiding Learning". *Open Culture*. https://www.openculture.com/2023/02/noam-chomsky-on-chatgpt.html (accessed: 19 December 2025).

1 The Evolution of AI
Bridging Technology and the Humanities

Filip Gampel, Jakub Gomułka, and Krzysztof Tomasz Stawarz

INTRODUCTION

The public release of generative models, particularly ChatGPT at the end of 2022, was undoubtedly a milestone in the development of artificial intelligence. It allowed AI to finally break out of the jargon and expert-technical environment and reach the masses, transforming it into a kind of socio-cultural phenomenon that influences millions of people's lives and decisions. What was once confined to academic and technological circles has now become part of everyday life, making AI a subject of mainstream public discourse and daily encounters for the general population.

From the perspective of the social sciences and humanities (SSH), this technological shift is particularly salient. SSH disciplines are fundamentally concerned with human experience and the nature of knowledge, the very questions that generative AI now directly engages with. Contemporary AI services raise non-trivial questions about the concepts of authorship, creativity, agency, and truth itself, ambiguously influencing social power structures and actively transforming the labour market and other domains of our lives. This makes AI a critical object of inquiry for SSH scholars. Simultaneously, AI is emerging as a powerful methodological instrument, creating a dual challenge for the disciplines.

This chapter aims to outline the history of AI and situate the current scholarly positions and debates within the SSH community. It begins with the philosophical foundations that inspired the field, traces the symbolic AI paradigm and its limitations, and explains the technological transition to neural architectures and large language models (LLMs). The rest of the article discusses the dual implications of AI for researchers and scholars in the SSH—both as a subject of research in itself and as a tool supporting academic career development.

PHILOSOPHICAL FOUNDATIONS OF AI

It is, in fact, difficult to determine how far back the roots of artificial intelligence—both as a technological practice and as a theoretical endeavour—can be traced. Much depends on how broadly one defines the concept. The first mathematical tools—counting rods and abacus—appeared several centuries BCE (Hodgkin, 2005: 79).

 DOI: 10.1201/9781003676188-2

In a very general sense, these were instruments through which certain mathematical operations could be performed externally to the human mind. At the same time, antiquity also witnessed the conceptual foundations of the 'mechanisation' of thought in the form of Euclid's axiomatic system and Aristotle's syllogistics (Russell & Norvig, 2010: 6).

The idea of automating basic arithmetical operations was already being implemented in the early modern period: among others, the philosopher and mathematician Blaise Pascal constructed the first mechanical calculators. Yet, due to their fragility, these devices remained more in the realm of curiosities than of practical instruments (Kistermann, 1998). Concurrently, Enlightenment thinkers began to envision more extensive algorithmic approaches to thought. Gottfried Wilhelm Leibniz—also the constructor of a mechanical calculating machine—proposed that it would be possible to build an automaton capable of algorithmically determining the truth or falsity of any mathematical proposition (Davis, 2001: 7). This ambition was part of a broader project to develop *scientia generalis*, a universal science, based on *characteristica universalis*, a universal formal language.[1] This language, according to Leibniz, was to meet three criteria: (1) a clearly defined set of primitive symbols, (2) rules for composing complex expressions from simpler ones, and (3) rules for transforming such expressions. In his view, all rational cognitive operations would consist in the application of transformations within a strict formal calculus; knowledge would be rendered free of error (save for mechanical mistakes), and any controversy could, in principle, be resolved—analogously to mathematics or syllogistics—through appropriate computation (Schneider, 1994).

In the nineteenth century, mathematicians and philosophers developed tools of formal logic that would, in the following century, become the theoretical foundations for the construction of digital computers. George Boole abstracted Aristotle's classical logic into an algorithmic algebraic form (Burris, 2024), and several decades later, Gottlob Frege introduced quantifiers and proposed the first axiomatic systems for propositional and predicate logic (Potter, 2000: 62). Frege was a proponent of logicism: a standpoint, according to which arithmetic could be derived from logic alone. The logicist project—rooted in Leibniz's ideas—gained substantial traction at the turn of the twentieth century, not only due to the aforementioned contributions of Boole, Frege, and other logicians, but also owing to the parallel efforts of nineteenth-century German mathematicians such as Karl Weierstrass, Richard Dedekind, and Georg Cantor, who sought to unify mathematics and ground it in the set theory.

The controversies and difficulties faced by logicism—most notably the paradoxes of what came to be called the 'naive set theory'—contributed to the emergence of analytic philosophy in the early twentieth century. Its founding figures—Bertrand Russell, Ludwig Wittgenstein, and indeed Frege himself—formulated new approaches to the philosophy of mathematics, logic, and, ultimately, language. Wittgenstein, in his influential, yet enigmatic, *Tractatus Logico-Philosophicus* (1922), proposed a conception of language whereby all meaningful propositions must be analysable into logical structures composed of elementary components. This amounted to a revival of Leibniz's idea of *characteristica universalis*. Shortly thereafter, the group of philosophers and scientists associated with the Vienna Circle—including Moritz Schlick, Rudolf Carnap, and Otto Neurath—building upon Wittgenstein's proposal, also returned to the idea of *scientia generalis*, advocating for a completely unambiguous and unified system of scientific knowledge based on a universal language. It is worth noting that such a conception of knowledge presupposes a particular view of reality as its condition of possibility: just like the symbolic system intended to describe it, the world itself must also consist of logical structures composed of certain irreducible, elementary components—as Wittgenstein himself stated in his *Tractatus* (1922).

The theoretical context from which key concepts in artificial intelligence emerged thus comprised the evolving relationship between mathematics and logic, as well as developments in the analytic philosophy of language. Within this context, Alan Turing formulated a set of ideas that proved foundational to the discipline. In his 1936 paper, 'On Computable Numbers, with an Application to the *Entscheidungsproblem*', Turing introduced the definition of a universal computing machine. His aim was to demonstrate the theoretical impossibility of the idea originally posed by Leibniz—algorithmically determining the truth-value of all mathematical statements—which had been problematised in the twentieth century by David Hilbert. This abstract model—later known as the Turing Machine—described a process of stepwise manipulation of symbols on an infinitely extendable tape divided into discrete cells, thereby formalising the notion of algorithmic computation.

Some fifteen years later, drawing on practical experience gained during the Second World War with computing machines at Bletchley Park, where he contributed to the deciphering of Nazi codes, Turing published the now-canonical paper 'Computing Machinery and Intelligence' (1950). There, he defended the view that, despite the theoretical limitations he had himself helped establish, the future development of digital computers—practical implementations of the Turing Machine—would eventually lead to a point at which their operations would rightfully be called 'thinking'. This article is widely regarded as the founding text of the research programme of artificial intelligence, formally initiated in 1956.

The AI Research Programme and the Symbolic Paradigm

Turing's theory of computation, along with Claude Shannon's foundational work on digital circuits, laid the foundation for the construction of the first general-purpose computing machines in the 1940s. A series of technological breakthroughs, culminating in the advent of field-effect transistors and integrated circuits, led to the first modern computers being built in the late 1950s and early 1960s. Advancements in neurology, spanning the late nineteenth to the first half of the twentieth century, revealed that the brain is an electrical network of neurons. This suggested that electrical machines may well be designed to reason the same way humans do. Although the concept of imitating biological structures with 'artificial neural networks' proved to be profoundly influential several decades later, the nascent field of artificial intelligence would pursue a different trajectory at first.

As computers became more commonplace in the 1950s, researchers realised that machines which manipulated numbers were also capable of manipulating symbolic expressions. Paired with the developments in logic and foundations of mathematics, this bore the idea that human reasoning could be emulated by computers, instructed properly on the rules of manipulating symbols. This paradigm, known as 'Symbolic

AI', would dominate the field well into the 1990s. Its first hallmark was the Logic Theorist, a program written in 1956 by Allen Newell, Herbert Simon, and Cliff Shaw (Newell & Simon, 1956). The program demonstrated its capacity for automated logical reasoning by proving 38 of the first 52 theorems presented in Chapter 2 of Russell and Whitehead's *Principia Mathematica*. In Simon's words, they 'invented a computer program capable of thinking non-numerically, and thereby solved the venerable mind-body problem, explaining how a system composed of matter can have the properties of mind' (Crevier, 1993: 46).

Newell and Simon presented their work at the Dartmouth workshop in 1956. This event, organised by John McCarthy, Marvin Minsky, Nathaniel Rochester, and Shannon, came to be recognised as the birthplace of the academic discipline of AI research (the very term 'artificial intelligence' was coined by McCarthy at the meeting). The official proposal of the workshop captures an atmosphere of exuberance:

> We propose that a 2-month, 10-man study of artificial intelligence be carried out during the summer of 1956 […]. The study is to proceed on the basis of the conjecture that every aspect of learning or any other feature of intelligence can in principle be so precisely described that a machine can be made to simulate it. […] We think that a significant advance can be made in one or more of these problems if a carefully selected group of scientists work on it together for a summer.
>
> *(McCarthy et al., 2006)*

Indeed, the following years saw the development of programs with capabilities regarded as amazing at the time: Newell and Simon generalised their work with the General Problem Solver (Newell et al., 1959), which was able to perform domain-independent reasoning; Herbert Gelernter's Geometry Theorem Prover (Gelernter et al., 1960) was able to solve geometry problems; James Slagle's Symbolic Automatic Integrator (Slagle, 1961) did so with calculus tasks. The STRIPS system developed at Stanford served as the software for the first general-purpose robot Shakey (Fikes & Nilsson, 1971). The main component was a planning algorithm, which allowed the robot to perform complex tasks (such as 'push the block off the platform') by breaking it down into smaller sub-goals and actions. Pioneering work was done in the field of natural language processing: Daniel Bobrow's STUDENT (Bobrow, 1964) solved word problems as found in high-school algebra text books; Joseph Weizenbaum's ELIZA (Weizenbaum, 1966) was the world's first chatbot, convincing many users of its intelligence, though it largely consisted of a keyword searching algorithm combined with a few grammatical rules to transform the user's input (the 'ELIZA effect'—see the chapter 'The Phenomenon of AI Hallucinations and Their Influence on Society and Academic Communication in SSH' in this volume). Minsky and Seymour Papert's research program postulated the development of AI systems for artificially simple micro-worlds (usually in the form of a 'blocks world', i.e. a virtual box filled with blocks of varying colour, shape, and size). This led to foundational work in computer vision by Gerald Sussman, Adolfo Guzman, David Waltz, and Patrick Winston. Terry Winograd's SHRDLU (Winograd, 1970) program allowed the user to query a block world and pass various instructions in natural language.

These first successes bore a wave of excessive optimism: Many of the prominent researchers mentioned above held that achieving a machine with human-level intelligence would be a matter of a few years or decades away at most. Paired with a large stream of funding by the newly founded Advanced Research Projects Agency (ARPA, later DARPA), the National Research Council, and the British government, it led to public expectations that could not be met. Essentially, all AI programs devised so far were built to deal with 'toy problems', and researchers did not appreciate how difficult it would be to generalise them to tackle real-world scenarios. This led to a cutback in funding in the 1970s, ushering in a period later called 'the first AI winter'.

Despite the setback, research in the field continued. A number of prominent laboratories continued to develop strictly deductive, logical systems. This led to the emergence of rule-based systems in the 1970s, in the form of logic programming (cf. the first logic programming language, Prolog (Colmerauer & Roussel, 1993)) and production systems, which consisted of a set of IF statements about conclusions or decisions to make, given some preconditions. Critics such as Hubert Dreyfus (see section 'Philosophical criticisms of the symbolic AI' in this chapter) pointed out that this fundamentally differed from the way humans solved problems, feeding into the debate of what it meant for a machine to be 'intelligent'. In any case, the approach failed in problems such as 'story understanding' or 'object recognition', which require commonsense knowledge and reasoning. For instance, when thinking about a bird, a human might assume that it flies or eats worms, despite the fact that this would not be true for all birds. The MIT school centred around Minsky, Papert, and Schank developed programs that aimed at capturing such imprecise and illogical assumptions. Such programs necessarily lacked high-level abstract definitions and would use task- and domain-specific instructions instead of arguments from first principles. This approach came to be known as 'scruffy', in contrast to the 'neat' logical and mathematical approaches developed at other leading laboratories. At the same time, the realisation that first-order logic 'lacks the expressive power to adequately represent the knowledge required for reasoning by default' (Reiter, 1978) led to theoretical advancements such as systems with a closed world assumption or non-monotonous logics.

The 1980s saw the rise of 'expert systems'. These were AI programs, which solved narrowly defined tasks using logical inference and an extensive knowledge database provided by human experts. Pioneering work in this domain was carried out by Edward Feigenbaum and his students: Dendral (1965) helped to identify chemical compounds from spectrometric readings; MYCIN (1972) identified bacteria and diagnosed blood diseases. The expert system R1 (1980) developed at CMU for the Digital Equipment Corporation assisted in computer system configuration based on customer requirements; it became a huge economic success. Overall, AI applications for the first time were doing something useful, which allowed the field to grow into a billion-dollar industry, with corporations setting up their own in-house AI departments. Likewise, the academic sector again attracted large government funding. In 1982, the Japanese government launched the ambitious Fifth Generation Computer Systems Project, which encompassed research into automated problem-solving, inference, natural language understanding, and knowledge-based architecture (Feigenbaum & Shrobe, 1993). Despite great contributions to the nascent field of concurrent logic programming, it did not deliver on many of its impressive goals (e.g. carry on a casual conversation, translate languages, interpret pictures, and reason like a human) and was halted in 1992. Likewise, beginning in the late 1980s, hundreds of AI companies were shut down or went bankrupt. Inflated expectations led to the formation of an economic bubble and the onset of another AI winter. Despite continued research (often under new names) and some hallmark achievements—like IBM's Deep Blue defeating world champion Garry Kasparov in a game of chess (1997)—the field would suffer from a poor reputation well into the twenty-first century.

The lesson of the 1980s, that intelligent systems required working with a large knowledge base, came to be known as the 'knowledge revolution'. It was only reluctantly accepted by the research community, as academic thought had been shaped by reductionism and the law of parsimony. However, many mundane tasks surprisingly still remained out of reach for AI systems. In the words of Hans Moravec: 'It is comparatively easy to make computers exhibit adult level performance on intelligence tests or playing checkers, and difficult or impossible to give them the skills of a one-year-old when it comes to perception and mobility' (Moravec, 1988, p. 15). The long-standing commonsense knowledge problem inspired the Cyc project (1984), which set out on the monumental task of constructing a database of everyday knowledge. But some researchers suspected that the issue lay within the symbolic approach itself. Building AI programs using sets of hand-crafted explicit rules for manipulating information stored in explicit knowledge databases ultimately proved to be fundamentally unsuited for many tasks in perception, robotics, or natural language processing. Yet another paradigm shift was needed to deliver long-awaited breakthroughs.

Artificial Neural Networks and Large Language Model Technology

Notions such as 'machine learning' or 'neural network' may nowadays seem inextricably linked with artificial intelligence. As we have seen, historically, this was not the case. In fact, until the 1980s, most AI textbooks would not mention machine learning at all. Yet, alternatives to the symbolic approach are essentially as old as the field itself.

Drawing on analogies between biological and technological systems, the 1940s and 1950s marked the onset of transdisciplinary inquiry into regulatory feedback in such systems: the birth of cybernetics. The field was pioneered by Arturo Rosenblueth, Norbert Wiener, and Julian Bigelow with the 1943 essay 'Behavior, Purpose and Teleology', and Warren McCulloch and Walter Pitts, who in the same year introduced the first mathematical model of a neural network. The original paper considered a single-layer network model, which was given the name 'perceptron'. Inspired by this work, Minsky and Dean Edmonds built the first neural net machine, the SNARC (1951). Another working realisation of McCulloch's and Pitts' idea was the Mark I Perceptron constructed by Frank Rosenblatt (1958). Despite embodying a rather simple statistical idea (linear regression), the machine, when plugged to visual sensors and properly trained, was able to recognise and classify certain figures like numbers and letters.

Early cybernetic research in the 1950s also led to the construction of robots such as the John Hopkins Beast or William Grey's 'turtles'. Like the first physical artificial neural networks, these employed bespoke, purely analogue circuitry with no digital electronics or symbolic reasoning.

The field continued to thrive in the early 1960s, with ADALINE (1960) and MADALINE (1962) having up to 1000 adjustable weights, and the US Army-funded MINOS I (1960) and II (1963) reaching 6600 synapses. The machines performed tasks like classifying symbols and handwriting, balancing an inverted pendulum, speech recognition, and weather forecasting. The most significant limitation at the time was the inability to train multilayer networks, as backpropagation was not known to the researchers in the field. Combined with competition from symbolic AI and an influential, critical book by Minsky and Papert (1969), research into perceptrons became practically suspended by the end of the decade, and the field saw virtually no progress in the following years.

The 1980s saw a revival with important theoretical work due to John Hopfield and Geoffrey Hinton. They showed that certain types of neural networks could learn, process information, and would probably converge given any external conditions. For these contributions, Hopfield and Hinton would be awarded the 2024 Nobel Prize in Physics. In 1986, Hinton and David Rumelhart rediscovered the backpropagation algorithm. Another important contribution was the rise of reinforcement learning—the idea of training intelligent agents using a reward model depending on how well they perform. This was explored by Richard Sutton and Andrew Barto beginning in the 1970s, which culminated in grounding the field in Markovian decision theory and introducing the temporal difference algorithm in the late 1980s. These developments brought great renewed attention to the field, which was dubbed 'connectionism'. They also sparked considerable debate with proponents of symbolic AI, who were still dominant at the time.

In the field of natural language processing (NLP), symbolic methods remained prevalent into the early 1990s. Apart from the historical context of AI research, here, the shift to statistical methods was also discouraged by the dominance of Chomskyan linguistic theories, which had only just started losing ground at the time. For instance, the prominent Transformational Grammar model held that all (and only) grammatical sentences within a language may be derived from a system of formal rules. Noam Chomsky argued that sentences similar in meaning and vocabulary derive from a common 'deep structure', linked by explicit transformational rules enabling one to be generated from the other (Chomsky, 1956). In contrast, the fundamental assumption of statistical NLP is to model human language using probability distributions. The occurrence of a word in a text is determined by a conditional probability with respect to all preceding words. In practice, such a distribution cannot be computed due to the vast number of possible combinations. One might therefore choose to consider only the last N words (N typically being a small number, like 1 or 2). The idea goes back to Andrey Markov's study of Pushkin's *Eugene Onegin* (Markov, 1913), but its realisation became possible only around that time with the availability of powerful computers and large language data due to the growth of the Internet. The so-called N-gram models formed the state of the art in NLP for roughly two decades, from the early 1990s to the early 2010s.

The next breakthrough was achieved with the seminal paper (Bengio et al., 2003), which applied the idea of neural networks to language modelling. The core innovation was to introduce what is now called *word embeddings*. The authors represented words as vectors in a D-dimensional 'feature' space. The number of features is significantly smaller than the size of the vocabulary (for the original paper, a typical choice was D=30 at a vocabulary size of 17,000). The representations were learned by the model using the aforementioned backpropagation algorithm. This allowed the solving of the data sparsity problem that plagued earlier attempts, since words with a similar role (semantically or syntactically) would have a (now well-defined) similar representation in feature space.

Whereas an N-gram model works in terms of discrete units that have no inherent relationship to one another, a continuous space model works in terms of word vectors where similar words are likely to have similar vectors. Thus, when the model parameters are adjusted in response to a particular word or word-sequence, the improvements will carry over to occurrences of similar words and sequences. (Mikolov et al., 2013c).

For instance, if the words 'apple' and 'orange' have a similar representation, the model would learn that 'The man eats an apple' and 'The man eats an orange' have similar probability, even though only one of the sentences would be present in the training data.

The impact of the concept would fully unwind only a decade later, as training neural networks at scale was technically challenging, and N-grams remained the method of choice. At the same time, the late twentieth and early twenty-first centuries saw rapid advancements in non-neural machine learning techniques, such as Support Vector Machines (Cortes & Vapnik, 1995), random forests (Breiman, 2001), and Gradient Boosting Machines (Friedman, 2001). These algorithms became foundational tools for classification and regression tasks due to their robustness and ability to handle high-dimensional data.

A watershed moment came in 2012 with the 'AlexNet paper', which introduced a novel model for image classification (Krizhevsky et al., 2012). It showed unrivalled performance in image classification benchmarks. Until that time, state-of-the-art computer vision models would largely use hand-crafted feature pipelines. In contrast, AlexNet was a deep convolutional neural network, which autonomously learned abstract, distributed representations of features. The approach was not conceptually new (cf. LeCun et al., 1989), but for the first time, it was done at scale, using GPUs and the very large ImageNet dataset (Deng et al., 2009).

The overwhelming success of AlexNet brought neural networks into the focus of the AI research community. The obvious goal was to transfer the approach from computer vision to other fields. In the case of NLP, two early and successful attempts were the studies cited herein (Mikolov et al., 2013a) and (Mikolov et al., 2013b). The two papers combined a number of (mostly previously established) modelling choices into a shallow neural network-based approach, which could scale Bengio's original idea and create the famous Word2vec embedding. Another influential method, GloVe (Global Vectors), combined global matrix factorisation with local context window analysis to embed words in a space that reflects their co-occurrence statistics (Pennington et al., 2014). Embedding techniques provided a means to encode linguistic patterns for tasks such as text classification, sentiment analysis, and named entity recognition, and they could be adapted to specialised domains through fine-tuning. They also contributed to advancements in transfer learning and multilingual models, demonstrating their utility in both research and applied contexts.

Word embeddings proved to be useful, but they still worked only for fixed-size windows limited to a few words, while many NLP applications clearly required modelling input of variable length. Around 2010, capturing long-range dependencies in sequential data (such as time series, text, or speech) was commonly attempted using Recurrent Neural Networks (RNNs), which allowed for sequential processing and the retention of previous input states. The foundation of such networks is the recurrent unit, which maintains a hidden state that is updated at each step of processing based on the previous hidden state and the current input state. This enables the network to learn while taking into account previous states in the sequence. Research into RNNs dates back as early as the 1990s (Elman, 1990; Jordan, 1997). A key issue with sequential processing in early RNNs was the vanishing gradient problem, which became more pronounced as the length of the processed sequence increased. In other words, for longer sequences, the backpropagation mechanism was no longer an effective method for training a network. A partial solution to this problem was augmenting RNNs with the Long Short-Term Memory (LSTM) module (Hochreiter & Schmidhuber, 1997). This architecture learns to retain information from a sequence that may be needed later and to discard information that can be forgotten. For instance, in NLP tasks, the network can learn grammatical dependencies between words in a sequence.

While simple LSTMs were, in principle, able to capture dependencies at arbitrary distances, they were limited in that they mapped input to output sequences of the same length. This was unsatisfactory for tasks like summarisation, question answering, or machine translation. The issue was tackled by sequence-to-sequence models, which use two neural networks trained end-to-end. The first encodes the input sequence using embeddings into a hidden *context vector* of fixed length, which is then decoded by the second network into the output sequence. The first such model was introduced by Kalchbrenner & Blunsom (2013), and quickly improved upon in Cho et al. (2014) and Sutskever et al. (2014). These approaches married the concept of word embeddings with existing architectures, but they all suffered from the same bottleneck: the fixed size of the context vector. This is why they ultimately still struggled with handling long-range dependencies.

The issue was first resolved in Bahdanau et al. (2014), which introduced the *attention mechanism* already known in computer vision (Larochelle & Hinton, 2010; Denil et al., 2012; Mnih et al., 2014). The model showed promising results:

> Perhaps more importantly, the proposed approach achieved a translation performance comparable to the existing phrase-based statistical machine translation. It is a striking result, considering that the proposed architecture, or the whole family of neural machine translation, has only been proposed as recently as this year.
>
> *(Bahdanau et al., 2014)*

> The following years saw many types of attention being explored in the context of NLP (Seo et al., 2016; Lin et al., 2017); however, none of them was able to clearly outperform the remaining variants, and attention itself was not yet recognised as a crucial component in model architecture.
>
> *(cf. Jozefowicz et al., 2016)*

The situation changed with the introduction of the Transformer architecture in the landmark paper 'Attention is all you need' (Vaswani et al., 2017). As the title suggests, the main innovation was to replace recurrent structures in the decoder and encoder with self-attention mechanisms (Vaswani et al., 2017). Positional encodings were used to represent the order of elements in the input, compensating for the lack of recurrence in the architecture. Dispensing with recurrence and convolutions was, in essence, a simplification that made it possible to process input sequences in parallel, rather than sequentially as in earlier models. This significantly reduced training times and unlocked the potential to use much larger training datasets. The model's encoder-decoder structure, with multi-headed attention and feed-forward layers, provided a versatile framework that could be applied to a variety of sequence-to-sequence tasks.

The Transformer proved to be a groundbreaking architecture, but in fact, the original model's size (2.13 million parameters) and training corpus (36 million sentences) were tiny by modern standards. The crucial next step was to develop techniques that would make it possible to train larger models on increasingly larger datasets. In 2018, OpenAI researchers proposed a training procedure split into two parts (Radford et al., 2018). In the first phase, called *generative pre-training* (giving the name to the company's flagship series GPT), the model is presented with large amounts of unlabelled data (unsupervised learning), which allows it to accurately predict tokens given a preceding sequence. However, for many use cases, this is unsatisfying: for instance, in the context of a conversational agent, for the input 'What are some important sights in Cracow?', the output might be: 'No idea, I am new to this town as well'. Given the training material and a model solely trained towards next word prediction, this might be a plausible response, but it is not helpful for the task at hand. Therefore, in the second phase, *discriminative fine-tuning*, which is a type of supervised learning, the model is presented with exemplary input-output pairs for various tasks.

As the technology matured, it quickly became commonplace to include a third training phase, *reinforcement learning*. This technique was introduced roughly at the same time as the Transformer (Christiano et al., 2017), and serves to align the model more closely with human values and preferences (i.e. one commonly expects the model not to lie or provide information that might be harmful to the user).

Pre-training language models left-to-right was a somewhat limiting approach, which is why Google's BERT (Bidirectional Encoder Representations from Transformers) expanded on the transformer framework by using masked language modelling and next-sentence prediction as training objectives (Devlin et al., 2019). This strategy enabled the model to learn bidirectional context, improving its applicability to various downstream NLP tasks with minimal fine-tuning requirements.

Shortly after BERT, other LLMs were built upon these ideas by scaling model size and training data, resulting in further performance gains in tasks like text generation, summarisation, and question answering (Radford et al., 2019; Brown et al., 2020). These models maintained the transformer's reliance on self-attention and parallel processing, allowing them to process complex linguistic patterns more effectively than earlier architectures.

The models that, over time, gained the most prominence and, in popular perception, became almost synonymous with language model technology—and AI in general—were the Generative Pre-trained Transformers (GPTs) series created by OpenAI. The company had been working on pre-training technology since 2018, when it developed the first version of GPT (Radford et al. 2018). According to data published by the creators, the GPT-1 network had 117 million parameters and was trained on 7,000 self-published indie ebooks. The next model developed by OpenAI in 2019, GPT-2, was based on the same solutions but scaled up tenfold: it contained 1.5 billion parameters and was trained on a dataset created from 8 million web pages (Hegde & Patil 2020). This model was already capable of generating coherent statements several paragraphs long. The following year, OpenAI scaled up the technology once again, this time by a factor of one hundred, releasing the GPT-3 model containing 175 billion parameters and trained on a correspondingly larger filtered dataset composed of diverse sources (scraped web pages, books, Wikipedia). This version of the transformer gained the ability to create simple programs written in languages such as Python, while its proficiency in generating longer natural language responses inspired both admiration and even fear among reviewers (Manjoo 2020).

On 30 November 2022, OpenAI launched its ChatGPT service based on the GPT-3.5 model, which, by January of the following year, had become the fastest-growing consumer software application in history, amassing over 100 million users in just two months and coming to epitomise modern AI for many. The chatbot was capable of engaging in longer conversations in various languages, adapting their content to the users' needs. Moreover, due to extended training on carefully curated data and the addition of the ability to search for additional information on the internet in the spring of 2023, ChatGPT began to serve as something akin to a general knowledge base.

In March 2023, OpenAI released another model, GPT-4, the technical details of which were not made public, although it is speculated to have surpassed its predecessor by another tenfold, containing 1.75 trillion parameters (Schneider, 2023). It became available to users both in the form of ChatGPT and via an API. Gradually, the company made the entire family of GPT-3 and GPT-4 models available to its users and continued to develop the latter by adding multi-modality. Simultaneously, due to their ability to generate functional code in various programming languages, GPT-3 and later GPT-4 were integrated into the GitHub Copilot service, providing users with an advanced tool for code completion and automatic programming.

In 2023, the GPT models released by OpenAI attracted significant interest among researchers as well. Alongside their capabilities, attention began to focus on their limitations and the phenomenon of generating imprecise or even incorrect information, referred to as AI hallucinations. The technique known as prompt engineering was also developed, as it became evident that the quality of the responses depended on how questions were formulated for the model.

In the spring of 2024, GPT-4o was introduced—a model capable of processing and generating textual, audio, and visual data. In September of the same year, a model named OpenAI o1 was launched, with its two weaker versions—o1-preview and o1-mini—made available to ChatGPT users. The company presented o1 as the first in a series of 'thinking' models, as it utilises a 'chain-of-thought' prompt algorithm during response generation. It was, in a sense, a response to critics pointing out the limitations of previous models, primarily their inability to perform seemingly simple cognitive operations, such as counting the occurrences of a specific letter in a word.

The successor to o1 was o3 (the name 'o2' was omitted, as it coincides with that of a British mobile network operator), which was released in December 2024. It is speculated that o3 represents a new generation of LLMs, characterised by a two-level operational structure: at the first level, the model identifies the appropriate method for solving a problem within the space of possible prompt algorithms (chains-of-thought). At the second level, the most optimal method is selected to generate the output. This approach is what enables o3 to achieve significantly better results in the ARC-AGI benchmark, which is used to evaluate generalisation and adaptation capabilities in new scenarios. However, the trade-off for this improvement is a dramatic increase in the number of tokens processed for a single prompt—requiring tens of millions—which makes the model economically inefficient (Chollet, 2025).

As with GPT-4, the sizes of these models and precise details of their training datasets remain unknown. It is speculated that OpenAI maintains an exponential trend in parameter growth. This means that the latest models offered by the company are becoming increasingly expensive—both to train and to use—raising concerns about the sustainability of this technology.

Despite its 'first-mover' advantage, OpenAI remains in fierce competition with several companies. Antropic, a company founded by former OpenAI employees, developed the Claude series of models centred around the idea of 'Constitutional AI' and safety. The 2024 Claude 3 Opus and Claude 3.5 Sonnet models were found superior to its GPT counterparts on several benchmarks measuring coding and reasoning ability. Google, having initially stumbled with the release of Bard in 2023, quickly reorganised its efforts. The Gemini family, launched in 2024, soon rose to be a leading language model, with an industry-leading context window size. Another competitor is the Grok series by xAI, an AI company founded in 2023 by Elon Musk, who was previously a co-founder of OpenAI.

In February 2023, Meta AI released the LLaMA model architecture under the GPLv3 license, making it free software. Although access to the pre-trained weights of this model was restricted, the weights were quickly leaked, leading to the rapid proliferation of language model technology and related tools. As a result, Meta embraced the open ecosystem: In 2023, Llama 2 was released on an open license that permitted commercial use. The release of Llama 3 followed the next year, with the largest model of the 3.1 family boasting a giant 405 billion parameters, and a performance rivalling top proprietary models. At the time of writing, Meta's most recent models are the Llama 4 family, released in 2025, featuring a mixture-of-experts architecture.

The open-weights policy of the Llama series marked a shift in the industry, with other top-tier models following suit and releasing open-source models. Most notably, the release of the Deepseek V3 in late 2024 and Deepseek R1 in early 2025 by a Chinese company garnered widespread public attention. The model proved to be competitive with leading proprietary American models, while being open-source, significantly more cost-effective, and trained on weaker AI chips due to the ongoing trade war between the US and China. Other notable examples of Chinese models include the Qwen series by e-commerce giant Alibaba, and the start-ups Moonshot AI and Z.ai with their flagship models Kimi K2 and GLM 4.5. The industry thus became a new front in the technological arms race between the US and China.

PHILOSOPHICAL CRITICISMS OF SYMBOLIC AI

The research programme of artificial intelligence has faced numerous philosophical critiques originating from various intellectual traditions. What follows is a presentation of those objections that were considered most significant by scholars directly involved in the development of AI—specifically, the criticisms advanced by Hubert Dreyfus and John Searle.

Dreyfus, a philosopher working within the phenomenological tradition and a specialist in the thought of Husserl, Heidegger, and Merleau-Ponty, was commissioned by the RAND Corporation—a United States government agency supporting AI research—to assess the state of progress in the field during the mid-1960s. This resulted in the publication of a highly critical assessment of AI, namely *Alchemy and Artificial Intelligence* (1965), the theses of which Dreyfus would go on to expand in subsequent works: *What Computers Can't Do* (1972) and *What Computers Still Can't Do* (1992).

At the core of Dreyfus's argument lies a critique of four assumptions which, in his view, underlie the AI program. The biological assumption claims that the brain processes information in a manner analogous to a digital system that manipulates symbols. The psychological assumption holds that the mind operates on discrete units of information—symbols—according to formal rules. The epistemological assumption posits that all knowledge can be formalised. Finally, the ontological assumption asserts that reality consists of discrete, independent facts that can be represented by equally independent symbols.

According to Dreyfus, all of these assumptions are false, which renders the goals of the symbolic AI paradigm fundamentally unachievable. In particular, he challenges the psychological assumption, arguing that even if the mind does at times manipulate symbols, the outcomes of such operations are context-dependent. They are influenced by other mental processes—often unconscious—that are neither symbolic in nature nor governed by rigid rules.

Dreyfus further elaborated his critique in *Mind over Machine* (1986), co-authored with his brother Stuart. Deepening their attack on the symbolic vision of AI, the Dreyfus brothers focused especially on algorithms for problem-solving. They employed the philosophical distinction between knowing-that and knowing-how. They argued that while knowing-that—explicit, propositional knowledge—can be effectively modelled using context-independent algorithms operating on symbols, knowing-how, which constitutes a far more substantial part of our everyday cognitive life, is based on trained intuitions and tacitly applied skills. This latter form of knowledge provides the background and context for all our conscious mental operations, yet AI researchers have not even acknowledged it as a legitimate object of inquiry.

In their view, symbolic algorithms are incapable of achieving the goal of reproducing the manner in which the human mind processes information about the world and generates knowledge.

In the early 1980s, another line of critique emerged, one that went further by arguing that artificial intelligence is not merely limited in its capabilities, but is in principle incapable of performing genuine mental operations. At best, it can only simulate them—imperfectly and superficially. A precursor to this line of attack can be found in Thomas Nagel's well-known article 'What Is It Like to Be a Bat?' (1974), which emphasised the significance of subjective experience—an indispensable aspect of mental states. Although Nagel's critique was directed primarily at reductive materialism in the philosophy of mind, rather than AI as such, it indirectly undermined the latter as well.

A more direct critique followed a couple of years later with John Searle's influential article 'Minds, Brains, and Programs' (1980), which introduced the well-known Chinese Room Argument. (It is worth noting that similar lines of reasoning had previously been developed by Anatoly Dneprov (1961) and Ned Block (1978), though they did not attract comparable attention.)

The Chinese Room Argument challenges the claim that the mind is essentially a system for processing symbolically represented information, and that replicating such processing in a different medium—such as a digital computer—amounts to creating an artificial mind. This claim, which Searle labelled the strong AI hypothesis, was tacitly accepted by most leading figures in the field (Crevier, 1993: 46). In contrast, Searle advocated for a weak AI hypothesis, according to which digital computers can merely simulate mental operations without truly performing them (Searle, 2009: 1).

Searle's argument takes the form of a thought experiment. A person, entirely unfamiliar with the Chinese language, is given a set of rules that allows them to manipulate Chinese symbols in such a way that they can produce coherent responses in Chinese. The point of the experiment is to show that understanding is not a necessary condition for symbol manipulation, provided one has access to a sufficient set of syntactic rules—that is, rules concerned only with the formal structure of the symbols, not their meaning. By analogy, Searle argues that a digital computer cannot be said to understand the information it processes, since its operations are based solely on syntactic rules.

Importantly, Searle's line of argument does not rule out the possibility of developing an AI system that mimics the human mind with extraordinary precision. His objection is rather to the idea that such a system would constitute a genuine subject of experience. In his view, even the most sophisticated AI would remain nothing more than a simulation.

LLMS AS THE SUBJECT OF RESEARCH IN SSH

Contemporary SSH research on LLMs and AI in general encompasses both theoretical and methodological approaches that examine these systems as complex sociotechnical phenomena. Since 2022, this scholarly attention has expanded across multiple SSH disciplines, generating debate about what these technologies are and what they mean for society (Bail, 2024; Davidson & Karell, 2025).

The question of whether LLMs demonstrate genuine understanding or merely execute sophisticated statistical pattern matching seems to be the main theme in today's SSH debate. The influential 'stochastic parrots' critique by Bender et al. (2021) argued that LLMs lack true comprehension, functioning instead as statistical systems that reproduce patterns without deeper semantic understanding. This perspective, challenging claims of emergent intelligence, suggests that superficially impressive performance may mask underlying mechanistic limitations. However, recent studies examining LLM capabilities in various reasoning tasks suggest that scale and training methodologies can produce behaviours resembling genuine understanding, even if the underlying mechanisms differ from human cognition (Aher et al., 2023; Ornstein et al., 2025). This still ongoing debate reflects deeper philosophical questions about the nature of intelligence and understanding that have long occupied SSH domains.

Some research investigates how LLMs can reproduce social biases present in training data. The survey by Gallegos et al. (2024) consolidates and formalises notions of social bias and fairness in LLMs, thus introducing three taxonomies covering bias evaluation metrics, evaluation datasets, and mitigation techniques. Their framework situates these contributions within the broader LLM development lifecycle, highlighting how social biases can arise and be addressed at different stages of model development. Moreover, UNESCO (2024) reports persistent gender bias in LLMs, including GPT-2 and LLaMA-2, showing that when prompted to describe people in different occupations, the models more often associate men with diverse and higher status jobs while frequently generating stereotypical and undervalued roles for women. Finally, the EU AI Act represents a significant policy response, establishing legal frameworks for 'high-risk' AI systems in employment, education, and public services. This regulatory approach emphasises the necessity for 'high-quality datasets' and mechanisms to 'minimise discriminatory outcomes', highlighting the intersection of technical and policy interventions (European Union, 2024).

SSH scholars have been developing frameworks for studying LLMs that extend beyond traditional computational approaches. The concept of 'synthetic ethnography' introduced by de Seta et al. (2024) bridges ethnographic methods with computational analysis and treats LLM as more of a cultural artefact, revealing underlying assumptions in training data. Model ethnography represents another methodological innovation, involving sustained qualitative engagement with LLMs to understand their behavioural patterns and limitations through extended interactions and systematically varied prompts. Discourse and corpus analysis methods examine linguistic patterns and stylistic tendencies in LLM results. These approaches create large datasets of model-generated text across varied prompts, applying both quantitative and qualitative analysis to identify recurring themes, strategies, and assumptions (Ziems et al., 2024; Jacomy & Borra, 2024).

The influence of LLMs on the educational sector has motivated substantial SSH research on academic integrity. Detection of AI-generated content still remains challenging and ethically problematic. Research indicates that while certain statistical signatures can sometimes identify LLM-generated text, these methods suffer from high false-positive rates and can be circumvented through alternative prompting strategies (Cotton et al., 2023; Perkins, 2023). This challenge has prompted discussions about changes to educational assessment. Educators explore approaches that integrate AI tools while maintaining fundamental learning objectives. Some propose shifting from product-based to process-based assessment by evaluating students' ability to work effectively with AI tools rather than excluding their use entirely (Davidson & Karell, 2025).

The phenomenon of AI 'hallucination' also represents an important concern for SSH researchers. Sun et al. (2024) propose a taxonomy of AI hallucination, distinguishing 8 first-level and 31 second-level error types, from overfitting and logical or factual errors to unfounded fabrications, including false academic information. A comprehensive treatment of this topic is provided in the present volume, in the chapter entitled 'The Phenomenon of AI Hallucinations and Their Impact on Society and Academic Communication in the Social Sciences and Humanities'.

SSH research increasingly examines governance frameworks for LLM development. Studies analyse the concentration of model development among a small number of technology companies, raising questions about democratic oversight and public accountability (Cheong, 2024). Research on algorithmic governance explores how LLMs might transform public administration and policy-making processes. While some studies suggest potential efficiency gains, others warn of risks, such as reduced transparency and erosion of human agency. Proposed solutions include AI auditing bodies, algorithmic impact assessments, and public advocacy roles to ensure that community interests are equally represented in AI governance structures (Novelli, 2023; Zhao, 2025).

LLMS AS A TOOL OF SSH

The adoption of LLMs as a research tool in SSH represents a methodological transformation comparable to the development of statistical software. This shift requires new frameworks for addressing these systems' probabilistic nature and potential limitations. Karjus (2025) proposes 'machine-assisted quantitising designs' that combine LLM automation with human expertise for large-scale qualitative analysis. This hybrid methodology neither fully automates qualitative analysis nor relies on traditional manual coding. Instead, it creates systematic workflows where LLMs handle repetitive tasks while human researchers focus on interpretation and contextual analysis. This division of labour potentially enables research questions previously constrained by cost and time limitations. Törnberg (2024) contributes methodological standards for LLM-based text annotation, proposing best practices for ensuring reliability and validity through systematic prompt testing and inter-annotator reliability assessment between human and machine coders.

LLMs have proved useful in content analysis tasks requiring semantic understanding beyond simple keyword matching. Research by Ziems et al. (2024) evaluates LLM performance in computational social science tasks, finding that while models achieve 'fair levels of agreement' with human annotators, they cannot entirely replace human judgement, particularly in taxonomic labelling and nuanced interpretation. The study emphasises that effective LLM workflows augment rather than replace human researchers. Large-scale multi-lingual analysis represents a particularly promising territory, enabling researchers to conduct comparative cultural analysis across dozens of languages simultaneously, opening research questions previously constrained by linguistic expertise and translation costs.

An innovative application involves using LLMs to simulate human responses in survey research and experimental settings. Studies by Argyle et al. (2023) and Park et al. (2024) explore whether LLMs can generate realistic 'silicon samples' that approximate human demographic groups' attitudes and behaviours. Early results suggest that LLMs can replicate certain population-level trends in survey responses, particularly on political attitudes and consumer preferences. The methodology raises important ethical questions about replacing human participation. While LLM simulation enables rapid hypothesis testing, researchers emphasise that it cannot substitute for genuine human engagement, particularly when studying marginalised communities or sensitive topics.

LLMs transform educational practices across SSH disciplines, serving as tutoring systems and assessment tools. Systematic reviews identify diverse applications such as personalised learning, including language learning support. However, educational applications raise significant ethical concerns about academic integrity, potential reduction in critical thinking development, and privacy issues related to student data (see the previous section). The most effective educational applications involve collaborative human-AI approaches rather than replacement models. For example, LLMs assist in creating differentiated learning materials, allowing instructors to focus on higher level discussion and collaborative activities with students (Davidson & Karell, 2025).

Using LLMs as research tools necessitates new validation frameworks ensuring research reliability and reproducibility. The probabilistic nature means identical prompts can yield different outputs, challenging traditional replicability notions. Proposed solutions include ‘Precise Boolean rubrics’ that break complex evaluations into binary questions, reducing subjective interpretation. Multiple-model approaches, where several LLMs analyse data with human arbitration, represent emerging practice (Bunt et al., 2025). Documentation standards are evolving to include detailed reporting of model versions, prompts, temperature settings, and other parameters influencing outputs. This transparency is essential for enabling replication and cumulative knowledge building.

CONCLUSION

One of the aims of this chapter has been to show that the research programme of artificial intelligence was, from the outset, entangled with the humanities and, in addition to its technological roots, was also shaped by ideological assumptions. Throughout its development in the second half of the twentieth century, it did not remain beyond the reach of critique: the achievements of engineers consistently drew the critical attention of SSH scholars. The sweeping technological transformation associated with transformer architecture has only deepened this engagement.

For researchers in SSH, LLMs call for a dual perspective. As studies reveal, they are far from neutral instruments: they embody and perpetuate social biases, cultural presuppositions, and institutional hierarchies. Ongoing debates over genuine understanding versus statistical pattern recognition underscore the uncertainty surrounding LLMs’ capabilities, an uncertainty with profound implications for their regulation and incorporation into social institutions.

As methodological tools, LLMs offer unprecedented possibilities for scaling analysis; yet, their responsible use requires rigorous validation, transparency, and ethical oversight. The challenges they pose are not merely technical. Meeting these demands requires interdisciplinary cooperation and a sustained commitment to equity and democratic governance.

Ultimately, the evolution of AI demonstrates that technological progress is inseparable from social transformation. The choices made in designing and deploying such systems both reflect and reshape cultural values and relations of power. For

SSH disciplines, this entails both an opportunity and a duty: to interrogate these technologies critically while helping to steer their development towards more just and beneficial ends.

ACKNOWLEDGEMENTS

During the preparation of this work, the authors used Claude 4.5 Sonnet in order to translate initial draft sections from Polish to English, paraphrase selected passages for improved readability, refine English syntax and grammar, and ensure adherence to academic writing conventions in English. After using these services, the authors reviewed and edited the content as needed and take full responsibility for the publication's content.

NOTE

1 The idea of *mathesis universalis* developed by Descartes was undoubtedly a source of inspiration for Leibniz. In this volume, Hasse Hällström discusses this concept in detail in the chapter titled '*Mathesis Universalis* without Method: Large Language Models Seen through a Cartesian Lens'.

REFERENCES

Aher, G. V., Arriaga, R. I., & Kalai, A. T. (2023). Using Large Language Models to Simulate Multiple Humans and Replicate Human Subject Studies. In A. Krause, E. Brunskill, K. Cho, B. Engelhardt, S. Sabato, & J. Scarlett (eds.), *Proceedings of the 40th International Conference on Machine Learning*, Vol. 202, PMLR, 337–371.

Argyle, L. P., Busby, E. C., Fulda, N., Gubler, J. R., Rytting, C., & Wingate, D. (2023). Out of One, Many: Using Language Models to Simulate Human Samples. *Political Analysis*, 31(3): 337–351. https://doi.org/10.1017/pan.2023.2

Bahdanau, D., Cho, K., & Bengio, Y. (2014). Neural Machine Translation by Jointly Learning to Align and Translate. ArXiv Preprint ArXiv:1409.0473.

Bail, C. A. (2024). Can Generative AI Improve Social Science? *Proceedings of the National Academy of Sciences*, 121(21): e2314021121. https://doi.org/10.1073/pnas.2314021121

Bender, E. M., Gebru, T., McMillan-Major, A., & Shmitchell, S. (2021). On the Dangers of Stochastic Parrots: Can Language Models Be Too Big?. In *Proceedings of the 2021 ACM Conference on Fairness, Accountability, and Transparency*, 610–623. https://doi.org/10.1145/3442188.3445922

Bengio, Y., Ducharme, R., Vincent, P., & Jauvin, C. (2003). A Neural Probabilistic Language Model. *Journal of Machine Learning Research*, 3: 1137–1155.

Block, N. (1978). Troubles with Functionalism. *Minnesota Studies in the Philosophy of Science*, 9: 261–325.

Bobrow, Daniel G. (1964). *Natural Language Input for a Computer Problem Solving System* (PhD). Massachusetts Institute of Technology.

Breiman, L. (2001). Random Forests. *Machine Learning*, 45 (1): 5–32.

Brown, T. B., Mann, B., Ryder, N., Subbiah, M., Kaplan, J., Dhariwal, P., Neelakantan, A., Shyam, P., Sastry, G., Askell, A., Agarwal, S., Herbert-Voss, A., Krueger, G., Henighan, T. J., Child, R., Ramesh, A., Ziegler, D. M., Wu, J., Winter, C., Hesse, C., Chen, M., Sigler, E., Litwin, M., Gray, S., Chess, B., Clark, J., Berner, C., McCandlish, S., Radford, A., Sutskever, I., & Amodei, D. (2020). Language Models are Few-Shot Learners. *Advances in Neural Information Processing Systems*, 33: 1877–1901.

Bunt, H. L., Goddard, A., Reader, T. W., & Gillespie, A. (2025). Validating the Use of Large Language Models for Psychological Text Classification. Frontiers. *Social Psychology*, 3, 1460277. https://doi.org/10.3389/frsps.2025.1460277

Burris, S. (2024). George Boole. In Edward N. Zalta & Uri Nodelman (eds.), *The Stanford Encyclopedia of Philosophy* (Summer 2024 Edition), https://plato.stanford.edu/archives/sum2024/entries/boole. Accessed November 25, 2025.

Cheong, B. C. (2024). Transparency and Accountability in AI Systems: Safeguarding Wellbeing in the Age of Algorithmic Decision-Making. *Frontiers in Human Dynamics*, 6, 1421273. https://doi.org/10.3389/fhumd.2024.1421273

Cho, K., Van Merriënboer, B., Gulcehre, C., Bahdanau, D., Bougares, F., Schwenk, H., & Bengio, Y. (2014). Learning Phrase Representations Using RNN Encoder-Decoder for Statistical Machine Translation. ArXiv Preprint ArXiv:1406.1078.

Chollet, F. (2025). OpenAI o3 Breakthrough High Score on ARC-AGI-Pub. *ABC Prize*. https://arcprize.org/blog/oai-o3-pub-breakthrough. Accessed November 25, 2025.

Chomsky, N. (1956). Three Models for the Description of Language. *IRE Transactions on Information Theory*, 2(3): 113–124.

Christiano, P. F., Leike, J., Brown, T., Martic, M., Legg, S., & Amodei, D. (2017). Deep Reinforcement Learning from Human Preferences. *Advances in Neural Information Processing Systems*, 30: 4299–4307.

Colmerauer, A., & Roussel, P. (1993). The Birth of Prolog. *ACM SIGPLAN Notices*, 28(3): 37–52. https://doi.org/10.1145/155360.155362

Cortes, C., Vapnik, V. (1995). Support-Vector Machines. *Machine Learning*, 20: 273–297.

Cotton, D. R. E., Cotton, P. A., & Shipway, J. R. (2023). Chatting and Cheating: Ensuring Academic Integrity in the Era of ChatGPT. *Innovations in Education and Teaching International*, 61(2): 228–239. https://doi.org/10.1080/14703297.2023.2190148

Crevier, D. (1993). *AI: The Tumultuous Search for Artificial Intelligence*. New York: Basic Books.

Davidson, T., & Karell, D. (2025). Integrating Generative Artificial Intelligence into Social Science Research: Measurement, Prompting, and Simulation. *Sociological Methods & Research*, 54(3): 775–793. https://doi.org/10.1177/00491241251339184

Davis, M. (2001). *Engines of Logic: Mathematicians and the Origin of the Computer*. New York & London: Norton.

de Seta, G., Pohjonen, M., & Knuutila, A. (2024). Synthetic Ethnography: Field Devices for the Qualitative Study of Generative Models. *Big Data & Society*, 11(4). https://doi.org/10.1177/20539517241303126

Deng, J., Dong, W., Socher, R., Li, L. -J., Li, K., & Fei-Fei, L. (2009). Imagenet: A Large-Scale Hierarchical Image Database. In *IEEE Conference on Computer Vision and Pattern Recognition*, 248–255.

Denil, M., Bazzani, L., Larochelle, H., & de Freitas, N. (2012). Learning Where to Attend with Deep Architectures for Image Tracking. *Neural Computation*, 24(8): 2151–2184.

Devlin, J., Chang, M.W., Lee, K. & Toutanova, K. (2019). Bert: Pre-Training of Deep Bidirectional Transformers for Language Understanding. In *Proceedings of the 2019 Conference of the North American Chapter of the Association for Computational Linguistics: Human Language Technologies*, Vol. 1, Minneapolis, MN: ACL, 4171–4186.

Dneprov, A. (1961). Игра [The Game]. Знание-сила, 5: 39–41.

Dreyfus, H. L. (1965). *Alchemy and Artificial Intelligence*. Santa Monica, CA: RAND Corporation.

Dreyfus, H. L. (1972). *What Computers Can't Do: A Critique of Artificial Reason*. New York: Harper & Row.

Dreyfus, H. L. (1992). *What Computers Still Can't Do: A Critique of Artificial Reason*. Cambridge, MA: MIT Press.

Dreyfus, H. L., & Dreyfus, S. E. (1986). *Mind Over Machine: The Power of Human Intuition and Expertise in the Era of the Computer*. New York: Free Press.

Elman, J. L. (1990). Finding Structure in Time. *Cognitive Science*, 14(2): 179–211.

European Union. (2024). Regulation (EU) 2024/1689 of the European Parliament and of the Council of 13 June 2024 Laying Down Harmonised Rules on Artificial Intelligence (Artificial Intelligence Act). *Official Journal of the European Union*. https://eur-lex.europa.eu/eli/reg/2024/1689/oj. Accessed November 25, 2025.

Feigenbaum, E., & Shrobe, H. (1993). The Japanese National Fifth Generation Project: Introduction, Survey, and Evaluation. *Future Generation Computer Systems*, 9(2): 105–117. https://doi.org/10.1016/0167-739x(93)90003-8

Fikes, R. E., & Nilsson, N. J. (1971). Strips: A New Approach to the Application of Theorem Proving to Problem Solving. *Artificial Intelligence*, 2(3–4): 189–208. https://doi.org/10.1016/0004-3702(71)90010-5

Friedman, J. H. (2001). Greedy Function Approximation: A Gradient Boosting Machine. *Annals of Statistics*, 29(5): 1189–1232.

Gallegos, I. O., Rossi, R. A., Barrow, J., Tanjim, M. M., Kim, S., Dernoncourt, F., Yu, T., Zhang, R., & Ahmed, N. K. (2024). Bias and Fairness in Large Language Models: A Survey. *Computational Linguistics*, 50(3): 1097–1179. https://doi.org/10.1162/coli_a_00502

Gelernter, H., Hansen, J. R., & Loveland, D. W. (1960). Empirical Explorations of the Geometry Theorem Machine. In *Papers Presented at the May 3–5, 1960, Western Joint IRE-AIEE-ACM Computer Conference*, ACM Press. https://doi.org/10.1145/1460361.1460381

Hegde, C., & Patil, S. (2020). Unsupervised Paraphrase Generation Using Pre-Trained Language Models. Arxiv Preprint. Arxiv:2006.05477.

Hochreiter, S. & Schmidhuber, J. (1997). Long Short-Term Memory. *Neural Computation*, 9(8): 1735–1780.

Hodgkin, L. (2005). *A History of Mathematics: From Mesopotamia to Modernity*. Oxford: Oxford University Press.

Jacomy, M., & Borra, E. (2024). Measuring LLM Self-consistency: Unknown Unknowns in Knowing Machines. *Sociologica*, 18(2): 25–65. https://doi.org/10.6092/issn.1971-8853/19488

Jordan, M. I. (1997). Serial Order: A Parallel Distributed Processing Approach. In *Advances in Psychology*, 121: 471–495.

Jozefowicz, R., Vinyals, O., Schuster, M., Shazeer, N., & Wu, Y. (2016). Exploring the Limits of Language Modeling. ArXiv Preprint. ArXiv:1602.02410.

Kalchbrenner, N., & Blunsom, P. (2013). Recurrent Continuous Translation Models. In *Proceedings of the 2013 Conference on Empirical Methods in Natural Language Processing*, 1700–1709.

Karjus, A. (2025). Machine-Assisted Quantitizing Designs: Augmenting Humanities and Social Sciences with Artificial Intelligence. *Humanities and Social Sciences Communications*, 12(1): 1–18. https://doi.org/10.1057/s41599-025-04503-w

Kistermann, F. (1998). Blaise Pascal's Adding Machine: New Findings and Conclusions. *IEEE Annals of the History of Computing*, 20(1): 69–76.

Krizhevsky, A., Sutskever, I., & Hinton, G. E. (2012). Imagenet Classification with Deep Convolutional Neural Networks. *Advances in Neural Information Processing Systems*, 25: 1097–1105.

Larochelle, H., & Hinton, G. E. (2010). Learning to Combine Foveal Glimpses with a Third-Order Boltzmann Machine. *Advances in Neural Information Processing Systems*, 23: 1243–1251.

LeCun, Y., Boser, B., Denker, J. S., Henderson, D., Howard, R. E., Hubbard, W., & Jackel, L. D. (1989). Backpropagation Applied to Handwritten Zip Code Recognition. *Neural Computation*, 1(4): 541–551.

Lin, Z., Feng, M., dos Santos, C. N., Yu, M., Xiang, B., Zhou, B., & Bengio, Y. (2017). A Structured Self-Attentive Sentence Embedding. ArXiv Preprint ArXiv:1703.03130.

Manjoo, F. (2020). How Do You Know a Human Wrote This? *The New York Times*, July 30, Section A: 22.

Markov, A. A. (1913). An Example of Statistical Investigation of the Text 'Eugene Onegin' Concerning the Connection of Samples in Chains. *Izvestiya Imperatorskoi Akademii Nauk (Series VI)*, 7, 153–162.

McCarthy, J., Minsky, M. L., Rochester, N., & Shannon, C. E. (2006). A Proposal for the Dartmouth Summer Research Project on Artificial Intelligence, August 31, 1955. *AI Magazine*, 27(4): 12.

Mikolov, T., Chen, K., Corrado, G., & Dean, J. (2013a). Efficient Estimation of Word Representations in Vector Space. ArXiv Preprint ArXiv:1301.3781.

Mikolov, T., Sutskever, I., Chen, K., Corrado, G. S., & Dean, J. (2013b). Distributed Representations of Words and Phrases and Their Compositionality. *Advances in Neural Information Processing Systems*, 26.

Mikolov, T., Yih, W.T. & Zweig, G. (2013c). Linguistic Regularities in Continuous Space Word Representations. In *Proceedings of the 2013 Conference of the North American Chapter of the Association for Computational Linguistics: Human Language Technologies*. Atlanta, GA: ACL, 746–751.

Minsky, M., Papert, S. (1969). *Perceptrons: An Introduction to Computational Geometry*. Cambridge, MA: MIT Press.

Mnih, V., Heess, N., Graves, A., & Kavukcuoglu, K. (2014). Recurrent Models of Visual Attention. *Advances in Neural Information Processing Systems*, 27: 2204–2212

Moravec, H. (1988), *Mind Children*. Cambridge, MA: Harvard University Press.

Nagel, T. (1974). What Is Like to Be a Bat? *Philosophical Review*, 83(4): 435–450.

Newell, A.; Shaw, J. C.; Simon, H. A. (1959). Report on a General Problem-Solving Program. In *Proceedings of the International Conference on Information Processing*.

Newell, A., & Simon, H. (1956). The Logic Theory Machine–A Complex Information Processing System. *IEEE Transactions on Information Theory*, 2(3): 61–79. https://doi.org/10.1109/tit.1956.1056797

Novelli, C. (2023). Legal Personhood for the Integration of AI Systems in the Social Context: A Study Hypothesis. *AI & Society*, 38(4): 1347–1359. https://doi.org/10.1007/s00146-021-01384-w

Ornstein, J. T., Blasingame, E. N., & Truscott, J. S. (2025). How to Train Your Stochastic Parrot: Large Language Models for Political Texts. *Political Science Research and Methods*, 13(2): 264–281. https://doi.org/10.1017/psrm.2024.64

Park, J. S., Zou, C., Shaw, A., Hill, B. M., Cai, C. J., Morris, M. R., Willer, R., Liang, P., & Bernstein, M. S. (2024). Generative Agent Simulations of 1,000 People. arXiv [Cs.AI]. Retrieved from http://arxiv.org/abs/2411.10109

Pennington, J., Socher, R. & Manning, C. D. (2014). Glove: Global Vectors for Word Representation. In *Proceedings of the 2014 Conference on Empirical Methods in Natural Language Processing (EMNLP)*, Doha: ACL, 1532–1543.

Perkins, M. (2023). Academic Integrity Considerations of AI Large Language Models in the Post-Pandemic Era: ChatGPT and Beyond. *Journal of University Teaching and Learning Practice*, 20(2): 1–24. https://doi.org/10.53761/1.20.02.07

Potter, M. (2000). *Reason's Nearest Kin: Philosophies of Arithmetic from Kant to Carnap*. Oxford: Oxford University Press.

Radford, A., Narasimhan, K., Salimans, T., Sutskever, I., & others. (2018). Improving Language Understanding by Generative Pre-Training. https://cdn.openai.com/research-covers/language-unsupervised/language_understanding_paper.pdf

Radford, A., Wu, J., Child, R., Luan, D., Amodei, D. & Sutskever, I. (2019). Language Models Are Unsupervised Multitask Learners. *OpenAI Blog*, 1(8): 9.

Reiter R. (1978). On Reasoning by Default. In *TINLAP '78: Proceedings of the 1978 workshop on Theoretical issues in natural language processing*, Urbana-Champaign, Illinois, ACL, 210–218

Rumelhart, D., Hinton, G. E., Williams, R. J. (1986). Learning Representations by Back-Propagating Errors. *Nature*, 323: 533–536.

Russell, S.J. & Norvig, P. (2010). *Artificial Intelligence: A Modern Approach* (3rd ed.). Upper Side River, NJ: Pearson.

Schneider, M. (1994). Leibniz' Konzeption der "Characteristica Universalis" zwischen 1677 und 1690. *Revue Internationale de Philosophie*, 48(188): 213–236.

Schneider, M. (2023). GPT-4 Architecture, Datasets, Costs and More Leaked. *The Decoder*. https://the-decoder.com/gpt-4-architecture-datasets-costs-and-more-leaked. Accessed November 25, 2025.

Searle, J. (1980). Minds, Brains, and Programs. *Behavioral and Brain Sciences*, 3 (3): 417–457.

Searle, J. (2009). Chinese Room Argument. *Scholarpedia*, 4 (8): 3100.

Seo, M., Kembhavi, A., Farhadi, A., & Hajishirzi, H. (2016). Bidirectional Attention Flow for Machine Comprehension. ArXiv Preprint ArXiv:1611.01603.

Slagle, James R. (1961), *A Heuristic Program that Solves Symbolic Integration Problems in Freshman Calculus: Symbolic Automatic Integrator (SAINT)* (PhD). Department of Mathematics: Massachusetts Institute of Technology.

Sun, Y., Sheng, D., Zhou, Z., & Wu, Y. (2024). AI Hallucination: Towards a Comprehensive Classification of Distorted Information in Artificial Intelligence-Generated Content. *Humanities and Social Sciences Communications*, 11(1): 1–14. https://doi.org/10.1057/s41599-024-03811-x

Sutskever, I., Vinyals, O., & Le, Q. V. (2014). Sequence to Sequence Learning with Neural Networks. *Advances in Neural Information Processing Systems*, 27: 3104–3112.

Törnberg, P. (2024). Best Practices for Text Annotation with Large Language Models. *Sociologica*, 18(2): 67–85. https://doi.org/10.6092/issn.1971-8853/19461

Turing, A. (1936). On Computable Numbers, with an Application to the Entscheidungsproblem. *Proceedings of the London Mathematical Society*, 2(42): 230–265.

Turing, A. (1950). Computing Machinery and Intelligence. *Mind*, 50: 433–460.

UNESCO. (2024). *Challenging Systematic Prejudices: An Investigation into Bias Against Women and Girls in Large Language Models*. UNESCO Publishing. https://ircai.org/wp-content/uploads/2024/03/IRCAI_UNESCO_Report_Challenging_Systematic_Prejudices_web_March2024.pdf. Accessed November 25, 2025.

Vaswani, A., Shazeer, N., Parmar, N., Uszkoreit, J., Jones, L., Gomez, A. N., Kaiser, Ł., & Polosukhin, I. (2017). Attention is All You Need. *Advances in Neural Information Processing Systems*, 30: 5998–6008.

Weizenbaum, J. (1966). ELIZA—A Computer Program for the Study of Natural Language Communication between Man and Machine. *Communications of the ACM*, 9(1): 36–45. https://doi.org/10.1145/365153.365168

Winograd, T. (1970). Procedures as a Representation for Data in a Computer Program for Understanding Natural Language. *MIT AI Technical Report* 235.

Wittgenstein, L. (1922). *Tractatus Logico-Philosophicus*. Trans. by C.K. Ogden & F.P. Ramsey. Kegan Paul: London.

Zhao, Z. (2025). SOTA Large Language Models' Contribution on the Design of Economic Policies. *Advances in Engineering Technology Research*, 14(1): 1569. https://doi.org/10.56028/aetr.14.1.1569.2025

Ziems, C., Held, W., Shaikh, O., Chen, J., Zhang, Z., & Yang, D. (2024). Can Large Language Models Transform Computational Social Science? *Computational Linguistics*, 50(1): 237–291. https://doi.org/10.1162/coli_a_00502

2 AI Myths and Realities
Separating Fact from Fiction

Mirosława M. Długosz, Maria Stojkow, and Dorota Żuchowska-Skiba

INTRODUCTION

Artificial Intelligence (AI) is a branch of information technology that has revolutionised the way daily tasks are performed, using machines to promote automated and intelligent behaviour with a minimum of human intervention (Ding et al., 2022). It can be defined as the capability of machines to imitate certain functions of human intelligence, such as perception, learning, reasoning, and problem solving. In the last few decades, AI has developed rapidly, changing human society on a deep level (Liu et al., 2022). However, despite its progress, many misunderstandings, myths, and erroneous convictions about AI have also emerged, often fuelled by sensational media reporting and science fiction. This distorts public perception, exaggerating the capacities and risks of AI (Cotino-Arbelo et al., 2025). This article uses the concept of myth as an analytical category to describe social perceptions, beliefs, and simplified narratives concerning AI. Classical sociological and anthropological approaches treated myth as an element of culture that organises collective ideas about the world by ordering oppositions such as good versus evil, the known versus the unknown, and the safe versus the threatening (Eliade, 1998; Lévi-Strauss, 2000). In the context of modern technology, myths do not disappear; rather, they change their subject from supernatural forces to highly complex, opaque technologies (Nye, 2004; Mosco, 2004). AI, being difficult to understand intuitively, becomes a particularly susceptible object of mythologisation. AI myths, therefore, concern not only the imaginary world but also have a real impact on how technology is designed, implemented, and socially accepted (Cave et al., 2018). In the literature on the subject, AI myths most often function as social misconceptions, oversimplified beliefs, or exaggerated narratives that overstate the technology's potential, ignore its limitations, or attribute human characteristics to it (Cave et al., 2020; Fast & Horvitz, 2017). In this sense, a myth does not completely distort reality, but rather, it selectively simplifies it, highlighting some aspects and downplaying others. In AI research, myths serve a dual analytical function. First, they allow us to identify dominant interpretive patterns in which AI is perceived as a threat, salvation, tool of control, or autonomous agent (Cave et al., 2018; Fast & Horvitz, 2017). Second, they enable the analysis of the emotional and normative dimensions of technology perception, revealing the accompanying fears, hopes, and tensions (Jasanoff, 2015). Here, myths are not just

 DOI: 10.1201/9781003676188-3

cognitive errors, but elements of broader cultural narratives that organise how we talk about the future of work, education, and human-technology relations. In this study, myths are treated as categories that organise social conversations about AI. Their analysis not only verifies the truth of beliefs but also reconstructs collective imaginaries, interpretive frameworks, and coping mechanisms for technological uncertainty. Understood in this way, myths are analytical tools that allow us to capture not only users' thoughts about AI, but also how they make sense of it and the consequences these interpretations have on their attitudes and professional practices. Understanding these myths and confronting them with reality is key to proper implementation and trust in AI technology (Bewersdorff et al., 2023).

Most frequently repeated myths versus reality:

1. **AI will replace humans at work, including teaching and the medical profession (Omrani et al., 2022)**
   There is a widespread belief that AI will fully replace humans in the workplace. However, current AI systems are primarily designed to support human labour by reducing effort, increasing efficiency, and promoting social welfare (Liu et al., 2022). In education, AI plays a complementary role: it assists teachers but cannot replace them, as it lacks empathy, emotional depth, and the ability to interpret human nuances that are essential for learning (Giray, 2024). In the healthcare sector, AI supports doctors in diagnosis and early detection of diseases, but its operation still requires human supervision (Ali et al., 2023).
2. **AI is infallible and always objective**
   The belief that AI is fully objective and error-free does not reflect reality. AI may reproduce biases present in its training data or model architecture. Examples include systems predicting recidivism risk or providing hiring recommendations that showed racial or gender bias (Liu et al., 2022). Algorithmic bias has been documented since the 1970s and is difficult to eliminate completely (White & Lidskog, 2021; Valle-Cruz et al., 2023). Explanations generated by AI may also influence perceptions of fairness, particularly when sensitive attributes are used in decision-making processes (Schoeffer et al., 2024).
3. **AI understands context like a human**
   Although AI effectively analyses data and recognises patterns, it does not possess human-like contextual understanding. It functions as a statistical system that generates responses based on correlations rather than true semantic understanding (Nabavi, 2025). It lacks common sense, full reasoning abilities, authentic creativity, and consciousness—all core elements of human intelligence. Moravec's Paradox shows that tasks easy for humans (e.g. perception and motor skills) remain difficult for machines, whereas computational tasks are relatively easy for AI (Korteling et al., 2021; Paraman & Anamalah, 2022).
4. **AI operates autonomously and independently**
   It is often assumed that AI systems function completely autonomously. In reality, they do not possess agency, intentionality, or autonomy comparable to human decision-making. Although advanced AI models often operate

as 'black boxes', making their internal processes difficult to understand, this opacity does not indicate independence. Explainable AI (XAI) aims to increase transparency, improve user trust, and facilitate error detection (Abusitta et al., 2024; Ali et al., 2023; Valle-Cruz et al., 2023; Ding et al., 2022).

5. **AI poses a threat to privacy and security**
   Concerns about privacy violations, economic inequality, and security risks are partly justified (Guenduez & Mettler, 2022; Zhao et al., 2025). However, the actual level of risk depends primarily on ethical implementation, regulation, and responsible human oversight (Giray, 2024). While many AI systems remain specialised, general-purpose AI models have rapidly expanded in recent years and are now widely integrated into various domains (Cotino-Arbelo et al., 2025). The aim is to develop trustworthy AI characterised by reliability, safety, and ethical behaviour (Afroogh et al., 2024).
6. **AI quickly solves any problem and provides perfect answers**
   A popular belief suggests that AI can instantly solve any problem and deliver perfect answers. In reality, AI capabilities are constrained by training data, model architecture, and the absence of true understanding. Errors, oversimplifications, and hallucinations remain frequent across AI systems. AI also offers applications far beyond STEM fields, including art, music, literature, and various aspects of humanities and social education (Bewersdorff et al., 2023).

Research results, including analysis of the six most frequently repeated myths about AI, demonstrate the complexity and multidimensional character of social perception of this technology (Paraman & Anamalah, 2022). Both media narratives and government attitudes cause AI to be viewed as two extremes—from techno-optimistic visions to, albeit rarely emerging, pessimistic scenarios—leading to simplification and polarisation of opinion (Kapania et al., 2022). These myths, in connection with baffling terminology, play a significant role in the process of anthropomorphisation of AI systems, meaning they are attributed human characteristics, which leads to erroneous understanding of their real abilities and limitations (Bewersdorff et al., 2023; Korteling et al., 2021). Such magical thinking about AI often sidesteps concrete mechanisms of operation and the costs involved.

In the context of AI politics, earlier observations emphasise the need to build social trust by ensuring transparency, responsibility, and explainability of system functioning (Laux et al., 2023; Haresamudram et al., 2023). A lack of understanding of AI mechanisms can lead to user frustration and lower trust in the technology (González-Arencibia et al., 2024). For this reason, the development of social awareness and education about AI remains key, facilitating conscious decision-making, limiting the influence of disinformation, and reducing unjustified anxiety (Bewersdorff et al., 2023). Shaping awareness of intelligence—meaning the capacity for realistic evaluation of the potential and limitations of AI, while considering its social and ethical consequences—helps promote rational and responsible use of this technology (Korteling et al., 2021).

The progressing development of AI technologies gives rise to new doubts and ambiguous challenges related to fundamental issues in SSH, such as human thinking, creativity, behaviour, and the shaping of social relationships. **The aim of this analysis is to present a deeper consideration and explanation of social perceptions and myths about AI**.

METHODOLOGY

This study had a qualitative character and was based on three focus group interviews (FGIs), including academic teachers and individuals linked to education. **The objective was to compare myths about AI, found in the literature on the subject, with real opinions and experiences of the respondents**.

A total of 18 people participated in the study, representing a balanced mix of humanities and social sciences disciplines, such as philosophy, cultural and religious studies, cultural anthropology, linguistics, visual arts, sociology, psychology, and security studies. Participants had diverse professional and academic experiences, ranging from students and doctoral candidates to early career researchers and senior academics with many years of practice. This diversity made it possible to capture a variety of perspectives on the application of AI in academic work.

Questions presented to the focus group were not asked directly in the context of identifiable myths about AI, which allowed the respondents to freely express their opinions and experiences. Thanks to this, it was possible to capture authentic convictions and to observe in what way the participants negotiated the meanings and shared different perspectives on the role of AI in academic work.

Analysis of data was carried out based on a deductive and inductive methodological approach.

In the first phase, predefined theoretical categories were used, the six most frequently repeated myths about AI, assigned codes M1–M6. For each myth, a set of keywords was prepared, and these reflected its meaning (see Table 2.1). This made it possible to conduct a preliminary search of interview transcripts in the MaxQDA program and the assignment of fragments of the answers to the relevant categories. In parallel, inductive encoding was carried out, allowing for the capture of additional opinions and threads appearing spontaneously in conversations, those which had not

TABLE 2.1
AI Myths and Corresponding Keywords

Code	AI Myths	Keywords
M1	AI will replace humans in the workplace	'replace', 'job loss', 'automation', 'robots taking jobs'
M2	AI is infallible and always objective	'no mistakes', 'fully objective', 'neutral', 'bias-free', 'accurate'
M3	AI understands context like a human	'understands', 'human-like reasoning', 'intuition', 'empathy'
M4	AI operates autonomously and independently	'independent', 'autonomous', 'self-', 'no human control'
M5	AI is a threat to privacy and security	'surveillance', 'tracking', 'data misuse', 'privacy threat'
M6	AI quickly solves any problem and provides perfect answers	'perfect answers', 'solves everything', 'quick solutions', 'ready-made solutions'

Source: Authors' own work.

Note: M5: AI poses a threat to privacy and security 'surveillance', 'tracking', 'data misuse', 'privacy threat'; M6: AI solves any problem and provides perfect answers: 'perfect answers', 'solves everything', 'quick solutions', 'ready-made solutions'.

been planned in the theoretical scheme. Such an approach allowed for the verification of existing concepts as well as considering the wide-ranging spectrum of the individual experiences and convictions of participants.

In the next phase, a comparative analysis was undertaken, looking at the presence of various myths in different focus groups and considering potential differences ensuing from gender, academic discipline, and length of employment of the respondents. Thanks to this, it was possible to capture common tendencies as well as a variety of perspectives in the context of their perceptions of the role of AI in academic work.

RESULTS

Analysis of the focus group interviews has demonstrated that, of the six myths identified in the literature on the subject, only three were clearly present in the participants' statements.

Myth 1: AI will replace humans at work
Myth 4: AI is too complex for the average user and
Myth 5: AI is a threat to schools and societies

The remaining three myths—the omnipotence of AI (Myth 2), its absolute objectivity (Myth 3), and restriction of application to STEM (Myth 6)—were not reflected in the material compiled, which suggests that these are not dominant factors in the way in which the participants interpret and judge technology.

Myth 1 (M1) appeared in interviews as an especially strong belief that AI can, in a few years, significantly reduce the need for human labour in numerous occupations. What is important is that these fears were not limited exclusively to technical or administrative professions—respondents also named professions requiring high qualifications and specialised knowledge. One of the participants noted that:

> "Gigantic number of professions will have a problem… translators…, drivers…, radiologists have already fallen… there will be less surgeons" (Focus 3), painting a picture of forthcoming changes as a mass, almost unavoidable reduction in professional roles.

In another group, fears took the form of a more pragmatic reflection on the pace of work—AI is seen not even as a 'time-saving' tool but a factor increasing productivity pressure:

> AI does not let you down tools… simply more work can be done in those eight hours.
> **(Focus 2)**

Both of these narratives demonstrate that for the respondents AI re-defines the sense and organisation of work, potentially increasing rather than decreasing demands on employees.

Myth 4 (M4) was not articulated directly through popular descriptions such as 'black box' but was present in the lack of certainty and control over the direction in which technology is developing. One of the participants said:

> I cannot imagine… in which direction it will go… I have a feeling that many things… will become an anachronism.
>
> **(Focus 3)**

This statement shows that the complexity of AI in the perception of the respondents is not exclusively a question of difficulty in understanding the way algorithms work, but more of a wider problem—concerning the prediction of the social, economic, and cultural results of its development.

Myth 5 (M5) appeared in the context of both micro- and macrolevels of the impact of AI. At the level of education, participants expressed anxiety that easy access to AI tools can lower students' motivation to work independently and negatively influence the development of their social competences. One of the respondents emphasised:

> There is a very high risk of threats… where certain things will come very easy… it's a trap for social competences of younger people.
>
> **(Focus2)**

On a global level, on the other hand, issues of infrastructure and environment were raised:

> Huge energy consumption… it can be a halting factor… it will change the labour market a lot.
>
> **(Focus3)**

In both cases, AI emerges as a technology which—if it is not implemented with sufficient protection—can lead to serious, long-term consequences.

During the inductive encoding, there appear threats which were not foreseen in the framework of the six myths but have considerable importance for the understanding of the social perception of AI. **The first was anthropomorphisation of AI**. There was a clear tendency in the answers to ascribe human characteristics to AI, such as empathy or the ability to 'understand' a conversation partner. One of the participants stated:

> This other side answers me with empathy sometimes greater than majority of people.
>
> **(Focus3)**

This shows that for some of the users interacting with AI can have an emotional and relational dimension, beyond the strictly instrumental use of technology.

The second thread was an ambivalence of opinions, simultaneously seeing potential benefits and threats ensuing from using AI. One of the respondents said:

> It gives us a chance for both paths… conscious being… or working ourselves to death.
> **(Focus2)**

This polarisation of judgement indicates that attitudes to AI and its reception are not unambivalent, and the line between the positive and negative impact of technology can be fluid, depending on both the context of application and the method of its implementation.

It demonstrates that, although a considerable number of the myths described in the literature are truly reflected in users' discussions, there are others, especially those concerning its omnipotence, objectivity, and limitations, which do not play a big part in their day-to-day thinking about technology. Instead, there emerge individual threads depending on context, such as personalisation of relations with AI or an ambivalence towards the judgement of its influence, and these may become the key to further studies on social perceptions and adaptations of artificial intelligence.

CONCLUSIONS

Analysis of the focus group discussions demonstrates that the perception of artificial intelligence by society is multidimensional and complex. Public narratives concerning AI, drawn from the media, including science fiction movies, as well as from political attitudes, are often polarised and extreme, which leads to the emergence of both excessive optimism and unfounded anxiety (Paraman & Anamalah, 2022; Kapania et al., 2022). Participants in this study demonstrated an inclination towards the anthropomorphisaton of AI, giving it human characteristics and emotions, confirming earlier observations in literature (Bewersdorff et al., 2023; Korteling et al., 2021). This 'magical thinking' frequently results in a miscalculation of the capacities of AI systems and sidestepping their limitations, including costs and social consequences.

Fears about the automation of labour, the complexity of technology, and threats to society (M1, M4, and M5) indicate that users' experiences are different and multidimensional. Anxiety concerning employment also included the direct risk of loss of work and more subtle forms of intensification of workload, while perception of AI complexity was related not only to its 'black box' but also to the difficulties of predicting wider ranging socio-economic effects. Perception of AI as a social threat touched on multiple aspects, including both the risk to students' social competence and motivation, as well as macroeconomic and environmental consequences.

The absence of myths M2, M3, and M6 in discussions suggests that everyday experiences with AI in professional and social practice decrease the influence of sensational media narratives. At the same time, the emergence of new themes, such as anthropomorphisation of AI and the ambivalence of attitudes, emphasises the emotional and psychological dimensions of contact with technology, including the mechanisms of trust and potential emotional dependency. Key in the context of these observations is the development of awareness and education on AI, which makes it possible to consciously use technology and make a rational judgement of its abilities and limitations (Bewersdorff et al., 2023; Korteling et al., 2021). Education should not only correct myths but also strengthen the ability for critical analysis of media narratives, understanding of ethical and social consequences, and prediction of practical after-effects of AI implementation. Furthermore, building trust in AI requires transparency, responsibility, and explainability of the way the systems operate, which decreases the risk of users' frustration and strengthens acceptance of technology (Laux et al., 2023; Haresamudram et al., 2023; González-Arencibia et al., 2024).

ACKNOWLEDGEMENTS

While preparing the article, the authors used NoteboookLM in the early stages of analysing source texts and Perplexity as an aid in literature research. In the final stage of their work, the authors used DeepL Write to perform linguistic corrections. After using this tool, the authors independently verified the content and bear full responsibility for the final version of the study.

REFERENCES

Abusitta, A., Li, M. Q., & Fung, B. C. (2024). Survey on explainable AI: Techniques, challenges and open issues. *Expert Systems with Applications*, 255, 124710. https://doi.org/10.1016/j.eswa.2024.124710

Afroogh, S., Akbari, A., Malone, E., Kargar, M., & Alambeigi, H. (2024). Trust in AI: Progress, challenges, and future directions. *Humanities and Social Sciences Communications*, 11(1). https://doi.org/10.1057/s41599-024-04044-8

Ali, S., Abuhmed, T., El-Sappagh, S., Muhammad, K., Alonso-Moral, J. M., Confalonieri, R., Guidotti, R., Del Ser, J., Díaz-Rodríguez, N., & Herrera, F. (2023). Explainable Artificial Intelligence (XAI): What we know and what is left to attain Trustworthy Artificial Intelligence. *Information Fusion*, 99, 101805. https://doi.org/10.1016/j.inffus.2023.101805

Bewersdorff, A., Zhai, X., Roberts, J., & Nerdel, C. (2023). Myths, mis- and preconceptions of Artificial Intelligence: A review of the literature. *Computers and Education Artificial Intelligence*, 4, 100143. https://doi.org/10.1016/j.caeai.2023.100143

Cave, S., Dihal, K., Dillon, S. (2020). *AI Narratives: A History of Imaginative Thinking about Intelligent Machines*. Oxford: Oxford University Press. https://doi.org/10.1093/oso/9780198846666.001.0001

Cave, S., et al. (2018). Portrayals and perceptions of AI and why they matter. *Nature Machine Intelligence*, 1(2), 74–79.

Cotino-Arbelo, A. E., González-González, C. S., & Molina-Gil, J. M. (2025). Youth expectations and perceptions of generative artificial intelligence in higher education. *International Journal of Interactive Multimedia and Artificial Intelligence* (In Press), 1–9. https://doi.org/10.9781/ijimai.2025.02.004

Ding, W., Abdel-Basset, M., Hawash, H., & Ali, A. M. (2022). Explainability of artificial intelligence methods, applications and challenges: A comprehensive survey. *Information Sciences*, 615, 238–292. https://doi.org/10.1016/j.ins.2022.10.013

Eliade, M. (1998). *Mit i rzeczywistość*. Warszawa: KR.

Fast, E., & Horvitz, E. (2017). Long-term trends in the public perception of artificial intelligence. In *AAAI Conference on Artificial Intelligence*, https://doi.org/10.1609/aaai.v31i1.10635

Giray, L. (2024). Ten myths about artificial intelligence in education. *Higher Learning Research Communications*, 14(2). https://doi.org/10.18870/hlrc.v14i1.1508

González-Arencibia, M., Ordoñez-Erazo, H., & González-Sanabria, J. (2024). Explainable artificial intelligence as an ethical principle. *Ingeniería*, 29(2), e21583. https://doi.org/10.14483/23448393.21583

Guenduez, A. A., & Mettler, T. (2022). Strategically constructed narratives on artificial intelligence: What stories are told in governmental artificial intelligence policies? *Government Information Quarterly*, 40(1), 101719. https://doi.org/10.1016/j.giq.2022.101719

Haresamudram, K., Larsson, S., & Heintz, F. (2023). Three levels of AI transparency. *Computer*, 56(2), 93–100. https://doi.org/10.1109/mc.2022.3213181

Jasanoff, S. (2015). *The Ethics of Invention: Technology and the Human Future*. New York: W. W. Norton.

Kapania, S., Siy, O., Clapper, G., Sp, A. M., & Sambasivan, N. (2022). Because AI is 100% right and safe: User Attitudes and Sources of AI Authority in India. In *CHI Conference on Human Factors in Computing Systems*. https://doi.org/10.1145/3491102.3517533

Korteling, J. E., Van De Boer-Visschedijk, G. C., Blankendaal, R. A., Boonekamp, R. C., & Eikelboom, A. R. (2021). Human- versus Artificial Intelligence. *Frontiers in Artificial Intelligence*, 4. https://doi.org/10.3389/frai.2021.622364

Laux, J., Wachter, S., & Mittelstadt, B. (2023). Trustworthy artificial intelligence and the European Union AI act: On the conflation of trustworthiness and acceptability of risk. *Regulation & Governance*, 18(1), 3–32. https://doi.org/10.1111/rego.12512

Lévi-Strauss, C. (2000). *Antropologia strukturalna*. Warszawa: KR.

Liu, H., Wang, Y., Fan, W., Liu, X., Li, Y., Jain, S., Liu, Y., Jain, A., & Tang, J. (2022). Trustworthy AI: A computational perspective. *ACM Transactions on Intelligent Systems and Technology*, 14(1), 1–59. https://doi.org/10.1145/3546872

Mosco, V. (2004). *The Digital Sublime: Myth, Power and Cyberspace*. Cambridge, MA: MIT Press.

Nabavi, E. (2025). Rethinking how we think about AI and common sense. *Journal of Science Communication*, 24(01). https://doi.org/10.22323/2.24010706

Nye, D. (2004). *American Technological Sublime*. Cambridge, MA: MIT Press.

Omrani, N., Rivieccio, G., Fiore, U., Schiavone, F., & Agreda, S. G. (2022). To trust or not to trust? An assessment of trust in AI-based systems: Concerns, ethics and contexts. *Technological Forecasting and Social Change*, 181, 121763. https://doi.org/10.1016/j.techfore.2022.121763

Paraman, P., & Anamalah, S. (2022). Ethical artificial intelligence framework for a good AI society: Principles, opportunities and perils. *AI & Society*, 38(2), 595–611. https://doi.org/10.1007/s00146-022-01458-3

Schoeffer, J., De-Arteaga, M., & Kühl, N. (2024). Explanations, fairness, and appropriate reliance in human-AI decision-making. In *Proceedings of the CHI Conference on Human Factors in Computing Systems (CHI'24)*. https://doi.org/10.1145/3613904.3642621

Valle-Cruz, D., García-Contreras, R., & Gil-Garcia, J. R. (2023). Exploring the negative impacts of artificial intelligence in government: The dark side of intelligent algorithms and cognitive machines. *International Review of Administrative Sciences*, 90(2), 353–368. https://doi.org/10.1177/00208523231187051

White, J. M., & Lidskog, R. (2021). Ignorance and the regulation of artificial intelligence. *Journal of Risk Research*, 25(4), 488–500. https://doi.org/10.1080/13669877.2021.1957985

Zhao, Q., Van Prooijen, J., Jiang, X., & Spadaro, G. (2025). Suspicious of AI? Perceived autonomy and interdependence predict AI-related conspiracy beliefs. *British Journal of Social Psychology*, 64(2). https://doi.org/10.1111/bjso.12883

3 Opportunities and Threats of AI in the Social Sciences and Humanities

Insights from a Focus Group Interview

Grzegorz Ptaszek, Rafał Olszowski, and Krzysztof Tomasz Stawarz

INTRODUCTION

Universities are implementing new educational technologies to improve the quality of education and adapt teaching methods and tools for a new generation of students who have grown up in a digital media environment. Although higher education institutions recognise the need for change in this area, academic staff are not adopting the technologies as readily or in the way their institutions anticipate (Liu, Geertshuis, Grainger, 2020). Access to appropriate infrastructure is not the only factor influencing the use of new technologies for teaching and research purposes, but the motivation of academic teachers is also important.

The emergence of new artificial intelligence-based technologies has revealed the importance of higher education keeping pace with technological progress, and the extent to which these technologies are changing the relationship between students and teachers, while also modifying the teaching and learning process. On the other hand, as Butson and Spronken-Smith (2024) point out, AI is not only increasing the pace of research but is also revolutionising our approach to scientific problems and data-processing methods, as well as the concept of knowledge itself. We are witnessing a breakthrough that challenges long-standing academic traditions. However, as Potkalitsky (2025) acknowledges, the fundamental tensions that AI introduces to the educational environment can be transformed from potential obstacles into powerful tools for promoting intellectual growth when used consciously.

The influence of Generative Artificial Intelligence technologies on academic practices—both research and teaching—within the humanities and social sciences forms the central concern of this volume. In one way or another, each of the chapters

DOI: 10.1201/9781003676188-4

addresses this overarching theme. In the present chapter, we turn our attention to the academic community itself: how do scholars and educators working in these disciplines perceive the opportunities and challenges posed by the growing presence of generative AI? Are their attitudes characterised more by optimism or by concern? How are existing GenAI tools being integrated into their everyday academic work? In what terms do they articulate the potential risks associated with the widespread adoption of such technologies? And crucially, what forms of institutional support do they regard as necessary in navigating this evolving landscape?

To explore these questions, we conducted a series of Focus Group Interviews with researchers and university teachers from a range of disciplines within the humanities and social sciences. The findings, which we present and analyse in the sections that follow, provide insight into how the academic world is beginning to respond—both practically and conceptually—to the emergence of generative AI. While not exhaustive, these insights offer a valuable glimpse into a field in transition, and into the ways in which academics are attempting to make sense of, and make use of, rapidly advancing technological tools.

LITERATURE REVIEW

The early debate on AI in academia, before the rise of generative LLMs, focused primarily on adoption frameworks and the readiness of institutions to implement AI. Chatterjee and Bhattacharjee's study (2020) is emblematic of this period. At that time, AI was envisioned as a set of functional tools—chatbots, adaptive platforms, or smart content systems—aimed at reducing workload and providing personalised learning. Notably, the emphasis lay less on epistemic risks and more on the organisational and behavioural determinants of AI adoption. This situates the year 2020 as a baseline, when AI was still seen through the lens of traditional technology acceptance models, rather than as a new dimension in academic work.

Building on this foundation, McGrath et al. (2023) expanded the topic by introducing ethical and responsibility-oriented dimensions. Their experimental study investigated how university teachers perceive institutional obligations to adopt AI in equitable ways. Teachers' intuitions varied significantly depending on student profiles: there was greater support for AI use when it served disadvantaged or first-generation students. This highlights a normative turn in the debate: AI was no longer just a question of efficiency, but also of responsibility and equity. The study revealed both scepticism and low AI literacy among faculty, yet it also pointed to a willingness to use AI when it could demonstrably reduce inequalities in learning outcomes. In doing so, the authors reframed AI adoption as a moral as well as pedagogical issue, anticipating many of the fairness debates that would intensify once generative AI became mainstream.

The arrival of LLMs transformed the landscape of academic work, both in research and in teaching, introducing a qualitatively new situation compared with earlier, narrowly functional AI systems. Whereas previous technologies automated routine processes, LLMs entered the domain of language, reasoning, and interpretation—the core territories of humanities and social sciences. This marked a qualitatively new situation, prompting researchers to investigate the implications for authorship, critical judgement, and the credibility of academic knowledge. One example is

Al-Zahrani and Alasmari's large-scale survey in Saudi Arabia (2024). With over a thousand diverse stakeholders, including university faculty and students, the study revealed a clear shift in attitudes: stakeholders increasingly recognised AI as a 'transformative force' in higher education, capable of personalising learning, automating administration, and fostering innovation. Yet, the concerns also became more complex, encompassing data privacy, algorithmic bias, and the epistemological consequences of automated decision-making. Unlike the Chatterjee and Bhattacharjee study (2020), where infrastructural adoption was central, here, the debate assumed widespread availability and instead focused on integration into teaching, the establishment of ethical safeguards, and the development of AI literacy. This suggests that after the diffusion of LLMs, the challenge lies not in whether AI will be adopted, but in how it can be regulated and embedded in responsible ways.

While Al-Zahrani and Alasmari's findings illustrate this shift within a specific national context, similar dynamics have been observed worldwide. Among the most recent studies, the *Digital Education Council Global AI Faculty Survey* (2025) provides a contemporary global snapshot of faculty attitudes. Drawing on responses from 1,681 academics across 28 countries, the survey shows that 61% have already used AI in teaching, most commonly for creating teaching materials and supporting administrative tasks. At the same time, 83% of respondents expressed concern about students' ability to critically evaluate AI outputs, and 82% feared over-reliance on such tools. Perhaps most revealing, 80% of faculty did not find their institutions' AI guidelines comprehensive, and only 6% reported satisfaction with available AI literacy resources. These results highlight a tension between optimism—65% of faculty view AI as an opportunity—and caution, with many calling for redesigned assessments, new approaches to academic integrity, and substantial investment in training and institutional support.

Academics are also increasingly incorporating AI into their research workflows on a weekly or even daily basis. According to Van Noorden & Perkel's (2023) survey of over 1,600 researchers worldwide, AI-based tools are becoming commonplace in scientific practice, and many believe that they will soon become integral to the research process. Researchers are already using large language models (LLMs) to assist with summarising and drafting academic papers, generating ideas, and writing code. Others are experimenting with generative AI in more specialised domains, such as designing novel protein structures, enhancing weather prediction models, and supporting medical diagnostics, illustrating the wide range of applications emerging across disciplines.

The *Nature* survey also highlighted widespread concerns among researchers regarding the potential negative impacts of AI on science. Among the risks identified, 69% of respondents warned that AI tools might encourage reliance on pattern recognition without true understanding; 58% pointed to the risk of reinforcing bias or discrimination embedded in datasets; 55% expressed concern that such tools could facilitate scientific fraud, and 53% noted that careless use of AI may lead to irreproducible results. Despite these concerns, more than a quarter of researchers who already use AI in their work believe that these tools will become *essential* in their field within the next decade (Van Noorden & Perkel, 2023).

Guidelines for researchers' use of AI are still far from standardised. For example, UNESCO's *Guidance for Generative AI in Education and Research* outlines various ways in which AI tools can enhance research processes, such as efficiently processing large datasets, supporting the development of analytical models, suggesting hypotheses, and even identifying new research directions. These capabilities, according to the report, can significantly broaden the application of knowledge (UNESCO, 2023).

Ongoing debates are shaping the development of such guidelines, including within the social sciences. One prominent example is the American Psychological Association (APA), which has issued a policy outlining key principles for the use of generative AI. Among its central positions is that AI tools cannot be credited as authors, but should instead be acknowledged in the methods section (or a comparable part of the manuscript). This acknowledgement should include the full prompt used and a reference specifying the AI tool, version, and other relevant details (Huff, 2024). According to APA leaders, LLMs are proving useful for tasks such as conducting literature reviews, formulating research questions, handling routine procedures, improving grammar, and streamlining time-intensive steps such as citation formatting and manuscript submission. However, they also note that the use of AI significantly increases the risk of plagiarism. While AI detection tools do exist, APA Style team members emphasise their unreliability. In one striking example, when the text of the US Constitution was submitted to such a detector, it returned a result claiming that 99% of the historic document had been AI-generated (Huff, 2024).

As both student use and scholarly adoption of AI continue to rise, academic institutions are beginning to respond through evolving policy frameworks, emphasising transparency, responsible use, and ethical safeguards. However, as the technology continues to outpace regulation, a key imperative emerges: to cultivate not only technical competence but also critical AI literacy, an ability to understand, question, and ethically engage with these tools, so that their integration strengthens, rather than weakens, the foundational values of academic inquiry.

MATERIALS AND METHODS

Research Design

To explore academic teachers' views and emotions on the use of GenAI tools in teaching and research, a study was conducted using focus group interviews (FGIs). This method enables participants to express their views on topics related to the study's purpose in a simulated real-life situation, and to respond to other group members' statements, ensuring a more in-depth exploration of the phenomenon.

The study employed a semi-structured group interview scenario to collect qualitative data. This consisted of three main parts: an introduction, a warm-up section, and the main section containing the key research questions. The introduction presented the study's purpose (exploring the use of AI tools in research and teaching), established the group discussion rules, and obtained consent for recording. The warm-up section contained demographic questions and a general discussion of AI technology, while the main section focused on specific aspects of AI use in three areas: scientific development, personal development, and academic teaching.

The study was approved by the Human Research Committee at the Faculty of Humanities of the AGH University of Krakow prior to the collection of data.

Participants

Recruitment for the study was conducted according to the principle of purposeful selection. Members of the research team contacted individuals from the academic community, representing a variety of humanities and social science disciplines, and invited them to participate.

Eighteen people participated in total. Eight took part in the first interview (P1–P8; FGI1), five in the second (P1–P5; FGI2), and five in the third (P1–P5; FGI3). They represented various scientific disciplines in the humanities and social sciences, with diverse professional and academic experience. The group included individuals at various stages of their academic careers, including one student planning an academic career, three doctoral students, several young assistant professors/postdocs, and seven researchers with many years of experience. A distinctive feature of the group was the significant number of individuals with interdisciplinary academic profiles, combining academic work with practical or commercial activities. The selection of participants ensured representation of various humanities disciplines (e.g. philosophy, cultural and religious studies, cultural anthropology, linguistics, and visual arts) and social science disciplines (e.g. sociology, psychology, and security studies), while also taking into account the perspectives of interdisciplinary practitioners and researchers, which was important for a comprehensive study of the use of AI technologies in academic work.

Procedure

As part of the study, three FGIs were conducted between September and November 2024. These took place in a focus room at the Faculty of Humanities of the AGH University of Science and Technology. Each interview lasted approximately 90 minutes and was conducted by a different moderator according to a prepared semi-structured scenario. Before the interview began, the participants were asked to give their informed consent to participate and to the audio recording of the interview. Each participant was also informed that they could withdraw their consent at any stage of the research process. Participants did not receive any remuneration for taking part in the study.

After recording the interviews on a digital device, they were transcribed using the Claude 3.5 Sonnet model (FGI1) and the TurboScribe.ai website (FGI2 and FGI3). The content of the automatic transcription was then thoroughly verified and corrected by the researcher. Any data that could identify participants were anonymised.

Data Collection and Analysis

The FGIs' transcribed data were subjected to thematic analysis, following the procedural guidelines of Braun & Clarke (2006). This approach was selected for its systematic and flexible framework for identifying and interpreting patterns in qualitative data. To ensure methodological rigour and reliability, a codebook was developed (MacQueen et al., 1998) following an initial data familiarisation phase, which involved repeated readings of the manually corrected transcripts. The coding process was iterative and primarily inductive, allowing themes to emerge directly from the data. This inductive approach was complemented by a deductive structure at the highest level of analysis, where categories reflected the chronological stages of the focus groups as delineated in the moderator's guide. The resulting three-level codebook comprised: (1) chronological categories, (2) broad thematic codes, and (3) granular, context-sensitive sub-codes. All coding and data management were carried out using the open-source software Taguette.

RESULTS

CONCEPTUALISING AI

In their attempts to comprehend AI, participants frequently described it as a 'neutral tool', the ethical implications of which are determined by the user. One participant articulated this common view:

> *For me, the concept of a tool is key. You can use a knife to make a sandwich or to kill someone. A tool is neutral—what matters is how people use it.*
>
> *(P6_FGI1)*

However, this 'neutral tool' paradigm was frequently challenged by the concept of operational opacity, or the 'black box' problem. Participants identified a critical tension between the idea of a simple tool and a system whose internal processes are not fully understood, even by its creators. One participant expressed this concern as follows:

> *What is more, the creators of artificial intelligence themselves claim that they do not fully control this algorithm. Therefore, no one will probably admit this openly. However, the truth is that it does seem to have taken on a life of its own, and we will only find out in time where it will go and in which direction. [...]*
>
> *(P5_FGI3)*

This lack of transparency was seen as fundamentally undermining the 'neutral tool' concept, as users cannot exercise full and informed control over a system whose decision-making logic is inaccessible. This highlights a conceptual conflict between AI as a controllable instrument and as a quasi-autonomous, inscrutable technology.

In addition, the discourse centred on the question of whether artificial intelligence (AI) truly exhibits genuine intelligence or merely mimics such capabilities, with the capacity for replication but not authentic creation. This distinction was central to understanding the technology's role and limitations:

> *Because ChatGPT seems creative to us, because it sometimes comes up with ideas that we don't come up with. But on the other hand, we know that it is reproductive, it is not something that it invented, but something that it analysed and spit back out, meaning it is something that someone else invented. [...]*
>
> *(P5_FGI3)*

This discourse between mimicry and authentic intelligence was further linked to the perceived erosion of uniquely human skills. Additionally, it was noted that media portrayals often generate 'information noise' by presenting a distorted or sensationalised image of AI's capabilities, which in turn influences user and public perception.

Perceptions and Attitudes Towards AI

One of the most pronounced emotions was a sense of bewilderment—not knowing how to keep up with AI developments. Participants frequently reported feeling lost or left behind. For example:

> *[…] I just can't keep up, I feel like I'm behind this development. For example, I don't know, or I look at my colleagues who are able to modify it somehow, to make it more useful. I haven't caught up with what's going on yet, right?*
>
> *(P4_FGI1)*

Alongside confusion, many respondents voiced fears and uncertainty about the long-term ramifications of AI. Concerns centred on misuse, rapid and unpredictable change, and possible harms to work, privacy, and social life. These worries often outweighed hopes about efficiency gains:

> *I think we are making a huge mistake by thinking of progress in such an enlightened way, as if it were some kind of providence guiding us. Nothing is guiding us. We are running somewhere, and so far we have been lucky that there has been no cliff.*
>
> *(P3_FGI2)*

A substantial number of participants expressed ambivalence. Echoing the earlier idea of AI as a 'neutral tool', they described it as a double-edged sword—potentially useful but also risky—and aimed to find a pragmatic middle ground between strong optimism and strong pessimism:

> *I see it as a great opportunity. Of course, I also see the risks that may be associated with it, but for me it is a fascinating tool, and observing its development, the changes, and the elements that I use myself, I find it very positive, with the assumption that, like any tool, it can also be misused.*
>
> *(P7_FGI1)*

> *[…] and my concern is that we look at technology only through the prism of this reward, of what will be in the future, without considering at all that the problems that may arise could potentially be permanent, […] so I would say that, in all of this, I am more concerned about people than the technology itself, in the sense of people who uncritically and unhesitatingly implement technology without any reflection.*
>
> *(P5_FGI2)*

Positive emotions such as curiosity and fascination did appear, though less frequently. When present, these were typically tied to AI's potential to improve efficiency or enable new possibilities. For example:

> *I am curious. I am curious. Curiosity, open-mindedness, and, let's say, a desire to explore this and see how I can use it to build myself and my students, because I am responsible for them, right?*
>
> *(P8_FGI1)*

Lastly, when discussing drawbacks and fears, a recurring theme was a kind of 'human-centred optimism'. Participants stressed trust in people, the irreplaceability of human-to-human relationships, and the belief that machines will not (and should not) replace core human roles. These views often tempered dystopian concerns and explained why many remained cautiously engaged with AI:

> *On the other hand, as sociologists, we know that humans are social beings and need social contact, so it seems to me that in some respects this can be replaced, but in others it absolutely cannot. And no simulation, no matter how sophisticated the tools developed, can replace this contact.*
>
> *(P5_FGI3)*

Opportunities and Positive Applications of AI in HE

Despite a pervasive sense of anxiety, members of academia have identified significant opportunities for AI to improve their work in research, teaching, and organisation.

Improving Scientific Research

Participants identified the primary benefit of AI as its ability to streamline the research process by automating tedious tasks. They regarded AI as a significant aid for conducting literature reviews, analysing qualitative and quantitative data, and supporting the writing and editing processes. As one academic stated:

> *Because I know that we generally spend a lot of time in scientific work reviewing literature and writing state-of-the-art papers. Artificial intelligence can do all of that for us.*
>
> *(P2_FGI1)*

It was also noted that this method is useful for conducting qualitative analyses:

> *For example, I use AI tools for thematic analysis, i.e. for analysing qualitative data […]*
>
> *(P6_FGI1)*

This automation was regarded as a means to free up researchers' time for more cognitively demanding tasks, such as formulating research questions and interpreting findings. Furthermore, the potential of AI tools to assist non-native English speakers in overcoming language barriers and promoting equity in global academic publishing was emphasised:

> *But it is also good for the development of science, because we will include people from non-English-speaking countries and make communication a little easier for them, for example in the most important journals, which until now have often been less favourable to people who speak English less fluently. So I think there are a lot of positives here too.*
>
> *(P4_FGI2)*

Innovative Teaching Methods

In the context of teaching, participants acknowledged the transformative capacity of AI to disrupt established pedagogical practices. The perception of these tools was that they functioned as instruments for the generation of a variety of teaching materials, including exercises and lesson plans. These materials were utilised for the personalisation of learning experiences for individual students and the creation of classroom activities that were more engaging and interactive. For instance, AI has the capacity to generate bespoke instructions for a student encountering difficulty with a particular concept, or to produce content for educational games. One participant shared the following observation:

> *The exam was taken on computers. I just figured out that they probably organised themselves into groups, made a single sheet or some kind of file from which they simply pull out the answers. They just solved it and did it mindlessly. So I had to do this. Suddenly increase the pool. So AI was super helpful. Make similar examples—I had 50 generated.*
>
> *(P4_FGI1)*

> *Recently, they played a board game, for example, so I had to generate some custom cards, which they then drew. Here, it speeds things up a lot, because all I have to do is enter the requirements I want, and I get a list to print out, and that's it.*
>
> *(P5_FGI3)*

Efficiency and the Productivity Paradox

Across all applications, the most consistently lauded benefit of AI was its potential for significant time savings. Participants noted that tasks that once took months or even a year could now be completed in days. This has led to the conclusion that AI could be utilised to complete the 'menial tasks', thereby allowing academics to focus solely on intellectual pursuits:

> *(...) I have come to the conclusion that 'Okay, so it will do the stupid work for us, and now we will only have to think'.*
>
> *(P7_FGI1)*

Nevertheless, this optimism was significantly moderated by concerns regarding a 'productivity paradox'. A pervasive fear was expressed that any efficiency gains would not result in increased leisure time or a reduction in working hours. Instead, it was anticipated that such gains would serve to perpetuate a culture of overwork, whereby institutional expectations of output would continue to rise. Contrary to the hypothesis that AI would alleviate the pressures of academic life, some believed that it could potentially exacerbate them:

> *You know, because if it is actually used, accelerated by machines, something that used to take a week will now take seven minutes. Well, that's great, but the question is whether that time will then be spent, for example, on wellness. Will that time be spent on self-development, on working with ourselves, with our families? All these humanistic and, let's say, these guidelines, these ecce homo guidelines. Will we devote this time to that, or will we devote it to producing, let's say, oh, I have seven days minus seven minutes left, so let's keep going. And here, it seems to me, there is such a big trap that at some point we will be chasing our own tails, right?*
>
> *(P1_FGI2)*

> *Something that is supposed to give us more time may in fact turn out not to do so at all, because compacting our work will result in us getting more of it to fill that time [...]*
>
> *(P3_FGI2)*

> *Well, in the past, let's say, if someone told you that you had to do a certain number of tasks according to the guidelines, and today, knowing that three-quarters of that can be suggested or helped by artificial intelligence, you'll get 200% more. And you will be much more efficient, you will have to be more efficient, because it is clear that you don't have to rely solely on your own efficiency, but rather you just need to use GPT chat properly and you will be able to generate, for example, not 10 tests for students during a semester, but 100 in an hour. Therefore, it's a clear profit for the employer.*
>
> *(P5_FGI3)*

Threats and Concerns Related to Using AI in HE

Participants voiced significant and wide-ranging concerns, spanning technological flaws and societal disruptions.

Technological Limitations and Risks

The most immediate risks identified were inherent to the technology itself. The propensity of AI to 'hallucinate' or generate fabricated information was a primary concern, engendering a substantial 'trust deficit' and eroding its reliability in an academic context where accuracy is paramount. One participant issued a warning:

> *It also happens that, for example, if I ask for suggestions regarding certain sources, these sources are imaginary, so you have to be very careful about that.*
>
> *(P1_FGI3)*

This requirement necessitates constant human verification, thereby negating some of the promised efficiency gains. Algorithmic bias, which has the potential to perpetuate societal stereotypes, and the substantial energy consumption of AI systems were also identified as significant technological challenges.

> *However, there is also a risk that, whatever you say, a language model that is, after all, trained on a given data set, may base this personalisation on stereotypes or outdated ideas, for example, and in my opinion, this is also a concern that, on the one hand, it kills creativity, and on the other hand, it may actually reinforce certain, I would say, bad practices or stereotypes from a social perspective.*
>
> *(P5_FGI2)*

Social and Market Threats

In addition to the technological aspects, members of the academic community articulated profound concerns regarding the societal implications of AI. Three themes were particularly prominent, representing the most frequently cited social and market anxieties discussed by the participants.

Firstly, participants expressed significant anxiety about the impact of AI on the labour market, fearing widespread job displacement and a fundamental transformation of professions. This creates a profound challenge for the higher education sector, which struggles to prepare students for an uncertain future with curricula that risk becoming rapidly obsolete:

> *Some people have to drift away, they have to find... The young people we educate may also work in professions that do not yet exist on the labour market. So they will also have to find their place. They will face challenges that we simply do not know about now and are unable to prepare them for.*
>
> *(P8_FGI1)*

> *We don't even think about it, but the question is to what extent we will be able to use the skills we have, because retraining, say, from a miner to a wind turbine technician when the energy model changes is relatively easy, but retraining from a miner to someone who will operate artificial intelligence algorithms is not necessarily so. Will a translator with excellent language skills be able to service machines? Not necessarily. So for many people, this could be a very serious change.*
>
> *(P5_FGI3)*

Secondly, the discussion highlighted the threat of corporate monopolies wielding a 'hidden form of power' through their control over AI technologies and data:

> *This is related to the power of those who do it, because they take control of the world, I'm saying this from the perspective of a thriller, but generally with a hidden form of power, because it is a hidden form of power, is it not? If they stimulate my thinking and I don't know how to think, then... they'll turn me into a zombie, right?*
>
> *(P2_FGI1)*

Concerns were raised about the potential for mass manipulation through disinformation, as well as the creation of a new digital divide where access to reliable, advanced tools is restricted to a wealthy elite:

> *And the question is, will this also lead to such a radical division of the world between those who have and those who do not have? [...]*
>
> *(P1_FGI2)*

Lastly, a recurring concern was the erosion of core human skills, as an over-reliance on AI tools may hinder the development of critical thinking, creativity, and independent problem-solving abilities:

> *However, it's a bit difficult when it comes to the teaching aspect you mentioned. In my case, when I'm preparing for research, for example, the first thing students do is not think about what questions to ask, but go to AI, type something in, and say they're ready. And you can see that these questions or things that are spit out are not personalised, they are more statistic, so to speak.*
>
> *(P2_FGI2)*

Participants feared that this intellectual dependency, likened to a muscle atrophying from disuse, would ultimately devalue the deep learning and rigour that foster genuine innovation. As one participant put it:

> *Relying on a prosthesis at some point causes us to lose our own muscle strength, doesn't it?*
>
> *(P2_FGI1)*

A notable distinction emerged in the manner in which academics viewed AI for their own work as opposed to its utilisation by students. It was widely held that, given the prior completion of arduous training and the attainment of fundamental competencies through 'trial and error', the utilisation of AI as a tool would be a judicious course of action. However, concerns have been raised that for students who have not yet developed these core competencies, the utilisation of AI merely serves as a shortcut, thereby undermining the entire learning process. One academic encapsulated this sentiment:

> *I don't know how to stop students who haven't yet acquired the skills to work independently, but just want to use this tool right away, and therefore can't really evaluate it. First of all, they're not developing themselves, right? And secondly, they can't evaluate the results that the tool spits out.*
>
> *(P4_FGI1)*

Adaptive Strategies and Visions for the Future

In response to these opportunities and challenges, participants proposed several adaptive strategies for the evolution of academia.

A recurrent theme pervading the discourse was the redefinition of the academic's role, a transformation that entailed moving from the conventional 'knowledge transmitter' to a more nuanced figure, such as a 'mentor', 'facilitator', or 'guide'. In this new role, the focus would shift to teaching higher order competencies such as critical thinking, ethical AI use, and creativity—skills that AI cannot replicate:

> *Our role as teachers is changing significantly. We are moving from being experts to being, I don't know, mentors, facilitators and so on, who show the way to certain things or teach critical thinking and analysis rather than knowledge, because with a phone in my pocket, I can beat a professor of quantum physics.*
>
> *(P5_FGI3)*

Some respondents noted that the changing role of the academic teacher brought about by AI may, as a consequence, lead to a departure from mass education in favour of more personal, individualised courses—with the shift towards educators acting as mentors necessitating a reduction in scale, given the limitations in staffing and resources:

> *And this is like the collapse of all mass education in the sense that we have many students who we have to quickly assess with a mass test in a short period of time, without digging into what they think. Because if we were to read their essays, for example, using some kind of tutoring method, then we would have to devote more time to them, which means that we would automatically have 10 students instead of 100. And paradoxically, a more personalised relationship between the teacher and the student begins.*
>
> (P2_FGI1)

According to the participants, this ongoing evolution in pedagogy necessitates the development of new assessment methods. As traditional written assignments become vulnerable to AI-generated plagiarism, they advocated for a shift towards methods that can reliably measure genuine understanding. In order to ensure academic integrity, greater emphasis is placed on oral exams and presentations, practical tasks, and supervised in-class writing:

> *We are approaching the end of bachelor's and master's theses, because they have been fictitious in many respects for a long time now.*
>
> (P5_FGI3)

> *In my opinion, when we have such humanities subjects, where reflection is, as it were, the core of this discipline, this family of sciences, let's call it that, I believe that it should be recommended more and more often to simply focus on oral exams or tests.*
>
> (P5_FGI2)

In conclusion, there was a compelling and impassioned appeal for institutional action. A pivotal demand was the provision of institutional support in the form of training and financial resources, catering to both staff and students. One participant articulated a prevalent sense of exasperation, which is a sentiment shared by many:

> *Firstly, I am a university employee, no one has trained me in this, and I can see that large organisations such as Scopus already have AI solutions. Secondly, no one has given me a budget to pay for it. I pay for ChatGPT 4 myself, out of my own pocket.*
>
> (P2_FGI1)

While there was a certain degree of scepticism regarding the question of whether regulations could ever keep pace with technological development, the consensus was that without proactive institutional investment in AI literacy, the potential benefits of AI would remain unrealised while its many risks would be amplified.

DISCUSSION

The study aimed to identify potential applications of generative AI in academic research and teaching practices within the social sciences and humanities. Three focus interviews were conducted with Polish academic teachers who had diverse experiences in various scientific disciplines within these fields.

The study revealed that Polish academic teachers perceive artificial intelligence as an imperfectly neutral tool, primarily due to a lack of user control over AI's decision-making processes. Emotionally, AI evokes feelings of confusion and the sense of falling behind, more often than fascination and curiosity among the respondents.

It is particularly important to emphasise that Polish academics openly discuss the productivity paradox. While AI may seemingly relieve teachers of routine tasks and speed up their performance, in reality, it reinforces the 'hustle culture' that promotes corporate efficiency over workers' well-being. This raises concerns that academic institutions will expect their employees to perform even better and faster, which will only increase stress. However, this shows that, as a tool designed to support academics, AI may become a de facto tool that further entrenches the corporate ethos of speed in academia (Berg and Seeber, 2016).

The interviewees also emphasise that integrating AI into education and research processes will transform the role of universities as we know them. In teaching, for instance, it will contribute to a shift from mass education to personalised learning. Teachers will become more like mentors, guides, and facilitators, using AI tools to develop students' critical thinking skills and teach them how to collaborate with AI to enhance their learning experience. Respondents in earlier studies also identified this type of change in the role of academics (Schmidt et al., 2025). However, this requires academic teachers to continuously improve their skills, and they must have at least an intermediate level of AI literacy (Chan & Colloton, 2024; Pretorius & Cahusac de Caux, 2025).

Building on these findings, our analysis shows that Polish academics adopt a predominantly ambivalent and cautious stance towards generative AI, echoing patterns reported in international research. For example, McGrath et al. (2023) found that university teachers often oscillate between curiosity and apprehension, with responsibility and fairness repeatedly raised as concerns. Similarly, Van Noorden and Perkel's (2023) global survey of researchers indicates that many scientists are already using AI tools, but with an undercurrent of distrust about transparency and bias. Our participants' feelings of being 'left behind' by rapid AI developments closely mirror this global ambivalence (Mohamed et al. 2025).

Another significant point was the perception that AI might widen inequalities and reinforce digital divides. Interviewees feared that privileged institutions and well-funded academics will gain disproportionate benefits from AI, while others risk exclusion. Al-Zahrani and Alasmari (2024) similarly emphasise that the digital divide is one of the most pressing social risks of AI in education. Liu et al. (2020) also found that academics' adoption of new technologies is highly uneven, influenced by institutional support, individual skills, and broader systemic inequalities. The Polish academics' fear of a 'binary world' therefore adds a distinctive voice to ongoing debates, underlining the urgency of addressing equity and access.

When discussing students' use of AI, our respondents consistently drew a boundary between faculty and learners. They felt that while academics could ethically integrate AI into their workflows, students should not rely on it to bypass the 'hard path' of learning. This stance reflects concerns reported in other contexts: Kim et al. (2025) document how educators worry that over-reliance on AI undermines students' critical thinking, creativity, and resilience. At the same time, other scholars argue that a carefully scaffolded use of AI could help students develop judgement and literacy in navigating algorithmic systems (Butson & Spronken-Smith, 2024). Our findings thus reflect a tension between protective instincts and the recognition that AI is likely to become a permanent feature of students' professional futures.

Finally, questions of regulation arose repeatedly in our focus groups. Participants doubted that legal frameworks could keep up with the speed of technological change. This scepticism corresponds with international debates about the 'pacing problem' in technology regulation (Marchant, Allenby, & Herkert, 2011). Respondents suggested that even if strict rules are introduced, workarounds such as VPNs or offshore tools will undermine enforcement. Such comments highlight the practical challenges of governing AI, reinforcing calls for multilevel strategies that combine regulation with institutional guidelines and professional norms (Butson & Spronken-Smith, 2024).

Overall, our focus-group results align with international research in portraying AI as both opportunity and threat. Yet, Polish academics particularly emphasised the importance of slowness, reflection, and well-being in contrast to narratives of speed and disruption. This focus enriches the global debate by centring humanistic and ethical concerns, offering a distinctive SSH perspective that foregrounds the values of critical thinking, equity, and creativity over efficiency at all costs.

CONCLUSION

The study reveals the complex and multifaceted nature of perceptions of AI in academia, where technological optimism collides with profound epistemological and social concerns. The findings point to fundamental tensions that could shape the future of higher education in the AI era, if we treat them as an opportunity for development.

Our findings confirm international trends showing that academics worldwide are intrigued, yet cautious, about AI. They see its potential to support teaching and research but fear its unintended consequences, such as undermining creativity, deepening inequalities, and reinforcing the culture of speed. At the same time, Polish academics offered a distinctive emphasis on human well-being and the value of slowing down—suggesting that responsible AI adoption requires not just technical literacy, but also cultural reflection.

The implications are clear: universities need to invest in AI literacy for both faculty and students, redesign assessments to foster critical engagement with AI, and implement guidelines that prioritise academic integrity and staff welfare. Future research should further investigate how these attitudes evolve as generative AI becomes embedded in everyday practice, and how institutional policies can balance innovation with equity and humanistic values (Table 3.1).

TABLE 3.1
The Full Codebook Created After the Familiarisation Phase and Used for Data Analysis

Category	Code	Sub-code
1. Perceptions and attitudes towards AI	1.1. Impressions and Emotions	1.1.1 Ambivalence 1.1.2. Positive emotions 1.1.3. Negative emotions
	1.2. Conceptualising AI	1.2.1. AI as a neutral tool 1.2.2. AI as an autonomous entity 1.2.3. The black-box problem 1.2.4. Defining intelligence and (re)creativity 1.2.5. Human optimism about AI 1.2.6. Inevitable, ongoing change 1.2.7. Overhyped; not a big deal 1.2.8. Media manipulation of AI's public image
	1.3. Cultural differences in perceptions of AI	1.3. Cultural differences in perceptions of AI
2. Opportunities and positive applications of AI	2.1. Improving scientific research	2.1.1. Automation of data analysis 2.1.2. Support for literature review 2.1.3. Assistance with writing and editing 2.1.4. Technical support 2.1.5. Inspiration and idea generation
	2.2. Innovations in pedagogy/teaching practice	2.2.1. Creation of instructional materials 2.2.2. Personalisation of teaching 2.2.3. Increased learner engagement 2.2.4. Student support services
	2.3. Organisational improvement and self-development	2.3.1. Personal assistant 2.3.2. Support for career development
	2.4. Efficiency and productivity	2.4.1. Time savings 2.4.2. The productivity paradox
3. Threats and concerns related to AI	3.1. Technological limitations and risks	3.1.1. Errors and hallucinations 3.1.2. Algorithmic bias 3.1.3. Resource-intensiveness 3.1.4. Data security and privacy
	3.2. Social and market threats	3.2.1. Transformation of the labour market 3.2.2. Erosion of human skills and competencies 3.2.3. Dehumanisation and erosion of interpersonal relationships 3.2.4. Issues of authorship and academic integrity 3.2.5. Digital exclusion 3.2.6. Corporate monopolies and covert control over information
	3.3. Individual costs and dilemmas	3.3.1. Cognitive and psychological burden 3.3.2. Financial costs 3.3.3. Personal ethical dilemmas
4. Adaptive strategies and visions for the future	4.1. Change in the role of the academic teacher	4.1. Change in the role of the academic teacher

(Continued)

TABLE 3.1 (Continued)

Category	Code	Sub-code
	4.2. Evolution of the educational process	4.2.1. Shift towards higher order competencies 4.2.2. Move away from mass education 4.2.3. New assessment methods
	4.3. Need for regulation and institutional action	4.3.1. Calls for regulation 4.3.2. Scepticism towards regulation 4.3.3. Need for training and support 4.3.4. Bottom-up/grassroots integration
	4.4. Concrete practices and tools	4.4. Concrete practices and tools

ACKNOWLEDGEMENTS

During the preparation of this work, the authors used Claude 3.5 by Anthropic for grammar and spelling check, paraphrase, and reword. After using these services, the authors reviewed and edited the content as needed and take full responsibility for the publication's content.

REFERENCES

Al-Zahrani, A. M., & Alasmari, T. M. (2024). Exploring the impact of artificial intelligence on higher education: The dynamics of ethical, social, and educational implications. *Humanities and Social Sciences Communications*, *11*, 912. https://doi.org/10.1057/s41599-024-03432-4

Berg, M., & Seeber, B. K. (2016). *The slow professor: Challenging the culture of speed in the academy*. University of Toronto Press.

Braun, V., & Clarke, V. (2006). Using thematic analysis in psychology. *Qualitative Research in Psychology*, *3*(2), 77–101. https://doi.org/10.1191/1478088706qp063oa

Butson, R., & Spronken-Smith, R. (2024). AI and its implications for research in higher education: a critical dialogue. *Higher Education Research & Development*, *43*(3), 563–577. https://doi.org/10.1080/07294360.2023.2280200

Chan, C. K. Y., & Colloton, T. (2024). *Generative AI in higher education: The ChatGPT effect*. Routledge. https://doi.org/10.4324/9781003459026

Chatterjee, S., & Bhattacharjee, K. K. (2020). Adoption of artificial intelligence in higher education: A quantitative analysis using structural equation modelling. *Education and Information Technologies*, *25*, 3443–3463. https://doi.org/10.1007/s10639-020-10159-7

Digital Education Council. (2025). *Global AI faculty survey 2025*. Digital Education Council. https://www.digitaleducationcouncil.com/form/ai-faculty-survey

Huff, C. (2024, October 1). *The promise and perils of using AI for research and writing*. American Psychological Association. https://www.apa.org/topics/artificial-intelligence-machine-learning/ai-research-writing

Kim, J., Klopfer, M., Grohs, J. R., Eldardiry, H., Weichert, J., Cox, L. A., II, & Pike, D. (2025). Examining faculty and student perceptions of generative AI in university courses. *Innovative Higher Education*. https://doi.org/10.1007/s10755-024-09774-w

Liu, Q., Geertshuis, S., & Grainger, R. (2020). Understanding academics' adoption of learning technologies: A systematic review. *Computers & Education*, *151*, 103857. https://doi.org/10.1016/j.compedu.2020.103857

MacQueen, K. M., McLellan, E., Kay, K., & Milstein, B. (1998). Codebook development for team-based qualitative analysis. *Field Methods*, *10*(2), 31–36. https://doi.org/10.1177/1525822X980100020301

Marchant, G. E., Allenby, B. R., & Herkert, J. R. (2011). *The growing gap between emerging technologies and legal-ethical oversight: The pacing problem*. Springer. https://doi.org/10.1007/978-94-007-1356-7

McGrath, C., Cerratto Pargman, T., Juth, N., & Palmgren, P. J. (2023). University teachers' perceptions of responsibility and artificial intelligence in higher education: An experimental philosophical study. *Computers and Education: Artificial Intelligence*, *4*, 100139. https://doi.org/10.1016/j.caeai.2023.100139

Mohamed, M. G., Goktas, P., Khalaf, S. A., Kucukkaya, A., Al-Faouri, I., Seleem, E. A. E. S., Ibraheem, A., Abdelhafez, A. M., Abdullah, S. O., Zaki, H. N., & Nashwan, A. J. (2025). Generative artificial intelligence acceptance, anxiety, and behavioral intention in the middle east: a TAM-based structural equation modelling approach. *BMC Nursing*, 24(1), 703. https://doi.org/10.1186/s12912-025-03436-8

Potkalitsky, N. (2025, May 21). Productive paradoxes: Navigating AI's contradictions in education. *LinkedIn*. https://www.linkedin.com/pulse/productive-paradoxes-navigating-ais-contradictions-potkalitsky-phd-x1oqc/?trackingId=Py9zcxy%2BSI%2BLgVchesQwyw%3D%3D

Pretorius, L., & Cahusac de Caux, B. (2025). *The AI literacy framework for higher education: A grounded theory exploration of the foundational, social, conceptual, ethical, and affective domains of AI literacy (Version 5)*. Monash University. https://doi.org/10.26180/25965178.v5

Schmidt, D.A., Alboloushi, B., Thomas, A., & Magalhaes, R. (2025). Integrating artificial intelligence in higher education: perceptions, challenges, and strategies for academic innovation, *Computers and Education Open*, *9*, 100274.

UNESCO. (2023). *Guidance for generative AI in education and research*. https://unesco.org.uk/site/assets/files/10375/guidance_for_generative_ai_in_education_and_research.pdf

Van Noorden, R., & Perkel, J. M. (2023). AI and science: What 1,600 researchers think. *Nature*, *621*(7981), 672–675. https://doi.org/10.1038/d41586-023-02980-0

4 Misinformation, Disinformation, and Critical Thinking in Academic Contexts
The Impact of AI

Grzegorz Ptaszek

INTRODUCTION

As a result of their popularity among ordinary users, GenAI tools were quickly adopted in higher education, becoming a widely used resource for both students and academics (Malik et al., 2023; Krause et al., 2025; Lee et al., 2024; Marshik et al., 2024). Recent international research involving over 48,000 participants from 47 countries found that 83% of students regularly use AI in their studies, with the majority relying on free, publicly available generative AI tools (Gillespie et al., 2025). However, attitudes towards these technologies vary depending on the field of study. The research of Bewersdorff et al. (2025) shows that 'cautious critics' of AI predominated among students of the humanities and social sciences, while 'AI advocates' predominated among engineering and technology students.

As newer GenAI models have emerged, the range of applications has expanded to include information retrieval, data analysis, solving complex tasks, processing content, etc. Research shows that students treat large language models (LLMs) as digital tutors, using these tools to improve their understanding of concepts, summarise texts, and prepare for exams (Paustian & Slinger, 2024; Krause et al., 2025). Additionally, LLMs are a valuable source of information and inspiration for students seeking ideas for projects and final papers (Common Sense Media, 2024; Our Future Foundation, 2023; Ravšelj et al., 2025), fostering creativity and supporting academic writing. However, this does not necessarily mean it is a shortcut to learning, as for many students, it does not reduce the time needed to study or prepare for exams (Our Future Foundation, 2023). According to researchers, AI-supported practices can provide effective personalised educational experiences and enable better learning outcomes than those achieved under conventional conditions (Dong et al., 2025).

Alongside several positive applications of GenAI tools in the learning and knowledge acquisition process for students (Hennekeuser, 2024), researchers have begun to

DOI: 10.1201/9781003676188-5

identify negative phenomena associated with dishonest practices, such as plagiarising term essays or theses (Cotton et al., 2023). There are also concerns about the risk of over-reliance on AI results without verification, which can weaken critical thinking skills (Zhai et al., 2024). Consequently, students are exposed to more false, misleading, biased, or harmful content, making them more susceptible to it, which may result in the formation of new false beliefs (Kidd & Birhane, 2023). As a result, higher education is facing a serious challenge: technologies that were intended to support the learning process may be undermining it, producing a generation of graduates with limited critical thinking skills who are susceptible to information manipulation.

This chapter will discuss the phenomenon of GenAI models generating false, biased, or distorted information, which negatively impacts students' critical thinking abilities. These phenomena necessitate a thorough reconsideration of GenAI's role in higher education, as well as the development of strategies to minimise its harmful impact on educational quality.

THE DEVELOPMENT OF AI TOOLS AND THE PHENOMENON OF MISINFORMATION, DISINFORMATION, AND BIAS

In discussions about the impact of GenAI tools on higher education, student learning, and knowledge acquisition, the dangers associated with AI models' misbehaviour are highlighted. These dangers include providing distorted information that perpetuates misconceptions, false or manipulated information, biased information, and a risk of producing completely fabricated data (Galaz et al., 2023; Mittelstadt et al., 2023).

Although the terms 'misinformation' and 'disinformation' appear to be synonymous, there is a fundamental difference between them. Misinformation is false or inaccurate information disseminated without the intention to mislead or manipulate. Disinformation, on the other hand, is false or manipulated information intended to elicit specific emotions and behaviours in the recipient. It is worth noting that, although some researchers define hallucinations as unintentional misinformation generated by LLMs (Chen & Shu, 2024), they are not always categorised as such. Some researchers view hallucinations as computer errors because they mainly occur when there is an inconsistency between the LLM's results and the user's guidelines (Huang et al., 2023) or between the source content and the generated result, which cannot be verified based on the source (Ji et al., 2023) (see Chapter 5).

Misinformation in an Educational Context

In education, misinformation can take particularly complex forms when it combines with students' existing misconceptions. According to Kendeou and Johnson (2024), misinformation in education can manifest at an individual level as naive beliefs or misconceptions that students hold before, or because of, learning. These can be classified into five categories: preconceived notions resulting from everyday experiences; non-scientific beliefs with religious or mythological origins; conceptual misunderstandings arising from improper teaching without confrontation with preconceived notions and non-scientific beliefs; vernacular misconceptions resulting from different meanings of words in colloquial and scientific contexts; and factual misconceptions, resulting from false information acquired at an early age and maintained without verification (National Research Council, 1997).

Today, these individual misconceptions can be reinforced further by GenAI-generated content that reproduces the misconceptions embedded within the data, creating a feedback loop between individual and AI-generated misinformation (Mittelstadt et al., 2023). These false or biased beliefs can relate to various issues, such as climate change (Galaz et al., 2023), mental health (Tiller et al., 2026), and characteristics such as nationality, gender, race, and religion (Shrawgi et al., 2024). They can also influence decisions and judgements. Furthermore, GenAI has the potential to mislead people by generating misleading explanations that appear reliable and convincing. For example, it can generate false scientific theories, suggesting a link between vaccination programmes and environmental changes, create viral educational materials for children that promote false concepts in an attractive way, and automatically provide incorrect medical advice that could influence health decisions (Danry et al., 2025).

Sources and Manifestations of Misinformation and Bias in LLMs

The problem of misinformation and disinformation generated by LLMs relates to the quality of the training data, the training process, and transparency (Huang et al., 2023). According to Weidinger et al. (2021), stereotypes and discrimination in LLMs stem from two main causes. First, training data reflect historical patterns of systemic injustice and social inequality, which are perpetuated by algorithms. Second, marginalised groups are underrepresented in the data. Additionally, LLMs can amplify even minor biases present in training data through a phenomenon known as 'bias amplification'. This issue was identified in research by Feng et al. (2023), who tested various LLMs for political bias in data. These analyses revealed fundamental differences in the political leanings and focus on social versus economic issues of LLMs. For example, BERT and its variants were more socially conservative than different versions of the GPT model. This can result in models producing different results for the same prompt, depending on the implemented worldview. Furthermore, research by Ma et al. (2024) showed that LLMs do not sufficiently consider the nuances of challenges specific to LGBTQ+ people when used as a mental health support tool. While chatbots expressed empathy towards users and provided a safe space for individuals experiencing social discrimination, their responses were impersonal and often based on general, politically correct statements.

Experiments conducted by Choi et al. (2025) identified a false consensus effect (FCE) in popular LLMs (GPT-4, Claude 3, LLaMA 2, and Mixtral). This effect consists of models overestimating the extent to which users share their beliefs. It can disrupt smooth communication between humans and machines by creating and reinforcing false beliefs. Research has revealed that the FCE is strongest when LLMs receive information that confirms their beliefs without requiring them to provide logical justification. However, a combination of opposing arguments and a multi-stage analysis process significantly reduces the effect. Therefore, the style of communication and the extent to which users engage in reflective thinking can significantly influence the behaviour of the model and weaken the false consensus effect.

Misinformation can influence not only students' beliefs but also their achievements, reducing the quality of education (Chan & Colloton, 2024). Conversely, biased information can reinforce students' false beliefs (Danry et al., 2025) and undermine teachers' knowledge, experience, and trust in learning (Fulsher et al., 2025).

ASSESSING THE CREDIBILITY OF INFORMATION AND BELIEF IN AI-GENERATED MISINFORMATION

Previous studies have shown that psychological factors play an important role in assessing the credibility of information. The main factors identified are cognitive factors relating to how information is processed and motivational and emotional factors influencing attitudes towards this process.

Two Models of Information Processing

Assessing the credibility of information is a complex process. Among the first researchers to address this issue were Shelly Chaiken and Serena Chen (1999). The heuristic-systematic model of information processing assumes that, depending on factors such as knowledge or time, people process information either systematically (focusing on the content and details of the information) or heuristically, in a simplified manner (relying on superficial cues and simple rules that allow for quick judgement without deep analysis). Researchers investigating the different types of credibility (information or source) use HSM assumptions to explain, for example, AI's impact on how users process and respond to misinformation in GenAI contexts (Shin et al., 2024). These studies have identified various heuristic cues, such as source expertise and social popularity, as well as systematic factors, such as the quality of arguments and the completeness of information, which influence credibility evaluation.

Another model that explains how information is analysed in the process of assessing its credibility is the 3S model of information trust (Lucassen & Schraagen, 2011, 2012). The three Ss represent semantics, surface, and source features or cues of information, which correspond to three distinct strategies which people employ when evaluating information credibility. Semantic cues refer to the content and meaning of information, its internal coherence, and consistency with existing knowledge. Surface cues relate to the presentation and format of information, i.e. its appearance, grammar, and technical quality, which influence the assessment of credibility. Source cues refer to the origin and authority of information, the credibility of the author, publisher, or platform. According to this model, depending on the familiarity with the subject matter (domain knowledge), readers will be guided in their assessment of the credibility of information either by semantic cues (high knowledge) or surface cues (low knowledge). In this model, previous experiences with a given source can serve as an indicator of the credibility of current information, such that if someone has had positive or negative experiences with a particular source, they will transfer this to an assessment of the credibility of the information (Lucassen & Schraagen, 2012).

These models are essential for understanding why users may believe misinformation generated by AI. Without domain knowledge, they rely on superficial cues, such as the quality of presentation and apparent professionalism, which AI can easily mimic. Furthermore, positive experiences with AI tools in the past can create a false sense of trust in all AI-generated content, thereby increasing the likelihood of accepting misinformation as credible.

Trust and Attitudes Towards Artificial Intelligence and Recognising Disinformation

According to research, on the one hand, trust in and a positive attitudes towards AI not only influence AI acceptance (Gillespie et al., 2025), but also how credible AI-generated information is perceived to be (Molina & Sundar, 2022), and the overall level of critical thinking about AI-generated information (Lee et al., 2025; Gerlich, 2025).

On the other hand, the novelty of AI as a technology (Lee, 2024) and greater scepticism towards AI-generated content can also affect the process of evaluating credibility for GenAI versus human-produced information.

Researchers also note that the mechanism of expectancy violation vis-à-vis generative AI platforms plays an important role in assessing the credibility of AI-generated content. This applies to situations when the quality and accuracy of the AI content do not align with readers' anticipated standards (Ou et al. 2024).

THE IMPACT OF USING GENAI TOOLS ON CRITICAL THINKING

Critical Thinking as the Foundation of Education and a Safeguard Against Misinformation

Critical thinking is one of the most important cognitive abilities of human beings, and fostering this ability has become a primary goal of education at all levels. By encouraging students to think and act more critically, teachers can help them understand the world around them and prepare them to act appropriately within it. Critical thinking involves recognising faulty arguments, generalisations, and unsubstantiated or truth claims based on unreliable authority or vague concepts (Burbules & Berk, 1999). It encourages students to explore opposing views, question assumptions, and develop well-reasoned arguments—a skill that is essential for problem-solving and decision-making (Melisa et al., 2025).

Critical thinking skills are linked to analytical thinking, and researchers have identified them as key to building resilience to disinformation and conspiracy theories. As Swami et al. (2014) demonstrated, adopting a conscious, deliberate, energetic, slow, emotionally neutral, and rule-based approach to thinking can reduce belief in conspiracy theories. In contrast, intuitive thinking is fast, automatic, and habit-driven. It is also prone to emotional reactions and difficult to consciously control. This type of thinking promotes belief in conspiracy theories. Therefore, analytical information processing can inhibit the biases that support the assimilation and acceptance of conspiracy theories. For instance, analytical thinking can counteract the effects of heuristics and biases known to influence belief in conspiracy theories.

Threats to Critical Thinking in the Era of Generative AI: From Excessive Dependence to Weakened Cognitive Skills

While some studies indicate that GenAI model use can positively impact critical thinking development in students (Xia et al., 2025; Essien et al., 2024), the focus in the context of misinformation and disinformation should be on phenomena related to critically evaluating results generated by AI systems. Understanding these phenomena hinges on grasping the way AI influences belief formation and decision-making processes. According to Kidd and Birhane (2023), LLMs significantly impact users' beliefs. People turn to AI in moments of uncertainty, when they are most open to new information. The model's immediate response reduces this uncertainty, closing openness to alternative perspectives. Consequently, the initial information from AI, even if incorrect, exerts a significant influence on beliefs, rendering subsequent corrections much less effective as the user is no longer in an initial state of uncertainty.

This vulnerability in belief formation is exacerbated by the phenomenon of over-reliance on AI (Passi and Vorvoreanu, 2024; Karamuk, 2025). It arises from the uncritical acceptance of GenAI suggestions, which can lead to poor decision-making, particularly when users are unable to properly assess the system's reliability or the level of trust they should place in it (Zhai, Wibowo & Li, 2024). Over-reliance on AI is closely related to trust in AI, occurring when users are unaware of the capabilities, performance, and workings of the AI system (Passi and Vorvoreanu, 2024). Important factors influencing over-reliance on AI include individual characteristics such as AI literacy, expertise, and familiarity with the task (Passi and Vorvoreanu, 2024). International surveys have shown that 52% of students who use AI tools in their studies check accuracy or consider the limitations of AI tools when making decisions based on output. At the same time, over 53% of AI users believe they cannot complete their academic work without AI assistance (Gillespie et al., 2025). The extent of this phenomenon suggests that over-reliance on artificial intelligence has become a widespread issue in education, which could undermine students' critical thinking skills and their ability to be academically independent.

Researchers analysing the cognitive effects of GenAI also point out that greater use of AI leads to more cognitive offloading, which in turn weakens critical thinking (Iqbal et al., 2025; Gerlich, 2025; Lee et al., 2024). Cognitive offloading occurs when individuals delegate cognitive tasks to external support tools—in this case, GenAI models—reducing their involvement in in-depth, reflective analysis (Risko & Gilbert, 2016). Overreliance on these models can weaken the ability to seek alternative solutions and influence decision-making, for example, by suggesting ready-made solutions. Furthermore, it creates a technological dependency that weakens cognitive resilience, making users more vulnerable to failure and less intellectually self-sufficient (Gerlich, 2025).

Despite these challenges, the research shows that using AI consciously and responsibly can preserve, and potentially enhance, critical thinking skills. A study by Acosta-Enriquez et al. (2024) found that students' beliefs about ChatGPT as a learning tool were linked to their responsible use of the model, as demonstrated by their verification of the information it generates. The study showed that students who verify information more thoroughly and use ChatGPT responsibly tend to perform better academically, confirming the positive impact of these behaviours. These results justify the incorporation of pedagogical interventions into academic practice, where students and lecturers collaborate using AI tools and critically and reflectively evaluate their effects, considering alternative perspectives, questioning assumptions, seeking evidence, and evaluating arguments (Essel et al., 2024).

THE IMPORTANCE OF AI LITERACY IN PREVENTING AI-GENERATED MISINFORMATION AND DISINFORMATION

Critical thinking skills, including the ability to critically analyse sources and information, are among the most important in academic education (Cottrell, 2008). As students increasingly use AI tools, the importance of critical GenAI literacy is growing. This includes understanding how GenAI tools are designed and work, and their role in the complex technological and ideological systems in which they operate (Chan & Colloton, 2024). From a socio-ethical perspective, these skills form part of AI literacy, relating to the impact of AI on individuals and society (Biagini, 2025).

AI literacy is also defined according to the scientific perspective and discipline (Biagini, 2025). However, not all definitions consider the critical evaluation of GenAI-generated content to be a key component. Some definitions mainly emphasise the effectiveness of using tools and strengthening user agencies in cooperation with machines (Kong, Cheung & Zhang, 2021). In an educational context, AI literacy, like media literacy, should be understood as the knowledge and skills necessary to understand, evaluate, and use artificial intelligence technologies responsibly in everyday life in the digital age (Mills et al., 2024). AI literacy can equip learners with the skills required for knowledge acquisition and development, which is essential for making informed decisions about the use of artificial intelligence beyond educational contexts. Pretorius and Cahusac de Caux (2025) distinguish five elements of AI literacy in academic education. The conceptual and emotional dimensions of this focus on developing skills that influence the critical and reflective evaluation of GenAI technology and its results (see Table 4.1).

These dimensions can be put into practice through activities such as 'spot the error' exercises with AI-generated content, or case studies in which students compare the results of different AI models on the same topic. This helps them develop an awareness of the limitations of AI.

Previous research shows that AI literacy is linked to assessing the credibility of content generated by AI systems and responding to unsatisfactory answers. Users with low AI literacy did not take action to address their dissatisfaction, whereas those with high AI literacy interacted with the system to correct errors in the responses they received (Kim et al., 2024). Furthermore, research indicates that AI literacy influences students' self-efficacy in utilising AI tools (Bewersdorff et al., 2025), potentially impacting their capacity to critically evaluate AI-generated content.

Another important factor identified in AI literacy research is the paradoxical relationship between expertise and susceptibility to algorithmic influence when it comes to recognising misinformation. Users with low levels of expertise demonstrate algorithmic susceptibility by accepting AI recommendations uncritically, which can lead to the acceptance of potentially erroneous information. Conversely, despite their declared aversion to algorithms and tendency to reject AI suggestions, users with

TABLE 4.1
Elements of AI Literacy in Higher Education

Foundational Dimension	Conceptual Dimension	Social Dimension	Ethical Dimension	Emotional Dimension
Deploying Specific Functionalities of the Generative AI Platforms	Locating Information	Dialogues with Customised Generative AI for Research Insights	Acknowledging AI Contributions	Emotional Aspects of Evaluating Generative AI Output
Familiarising Our Students with the Capabilities of the Platform	Organising Information	Generative AI as a Co-creator of Artistic Creations	Addressing Artistic Integrity and Environmental Impact	Emotional Reactions to Generative AI Data Analysis
Familiarising Ourselves with the Capabilities of the Platform	Evaluating Information	Generative AI as a Partner in the Learning Process	Ensuring Data Privacy and Informed Consent	Emotional Reactions to Generative AI Feedback
Selecting Appropriate Generative AI Platforms	Using Information	Using Generative AI as an Interlocutor	Transparency and Limitations of Generative AI	Reflection on Biases and Stereotypes
Understanding the Collaborative Role of Generative AI	Repurposing Information			

Source: Pretorius and Cahusac de Caux (2025).

high levels of expertise show significant reliance on AI in their decision-making processes (Passi and Vorvoreanu, 2024). This reliance may also influence their susceptibility to AI-generated misinformation, particularly when the content aligns with their expert expectations.

Global research findings emphasise the critical importance of AI literacy, showing that individuals with AI training are almost twice as likely to trust and accept AI technologies appropriately and more likely to engage critically with AI tools (Gillespie et al., 2025). As GenAI technologies are transforming learning and knowledge acquisition practices and creating new risks related to misinformation, AI literacy should become an integral part of study programmes, particularly in subjects such as the humanities and social sciences, where the ability to critically evaluate information is essential (Pretorius & Cahusac de Caux, 2025).

CONCLUSION

The development and widespread use of GenAI tools in higher education raises serious concerns about the quality of education and the development of students' critical thinking skills, given the false, distorted, and biased information that LLMs generate. Researchers emphasise the urgent need to develop strategies that balance the benefits of AI integration with the development of independent analytical skills, particularly in educational settings (Gerlich, 2025). It is important to recognise that AI technology should not be used unthinkingly, nor should it exempt people from critically evaluating AI-generated content. Rather, it should support the development of critical thinking by thoughtfully integrating these aspects into curricula and academic education.

Research shows that GenAI can improve skills if it is treated as a supporting tool and a human-machine collaboration method is implemented in teaching (Ju, 2023; Danry et al., 2025). Emphasising the importance of teaching methods of human-machine interaction is particularly important to build logical reasoning and critical thinking skills, strengthening resilience to false or manipulated content generated by artificial intelligence.

ACKNOWLEDGEMENTS

During the preparation of this work, the author used Claude 3.5 by Anthropic for grammar and spelling check, paraphrase, and reword. After using these services, the author reviewed and edited the content as needed and takes full responsibility for the publication's content.

REFERENCES

Acosta-Enriquez, B. G., Arbulú Ballesteros, M. A., & Huamaní Jordan, O. et al. (2024). Analysis of college students' attitudes toward the use of ChatGPT in their academic activities: Effect of intent to use, verification of information and responsible use. *BMC Psychology* 12, 255. https://doi.org/10.1186/s40359-024-01764-z

Bewersdorff, A., Hornberger, M., Nerdel, C., & Schiff, D. S. (2025). AI advocates and cautious critics: How AI attitudes, AI interest, use of AI, and AI literacy build university students' AI self-efficacy. *Computers and Education: Artificial Intelligence*, 8, 100340. https://doi.org/10.1016/j.caeai.2024.100340

Biagini, G. (2025). Towards an AI-literate future: A systematic literature review exploring education, ethics, and applications. *International Journal of Artificial Intelligence in Education*, 1–51. https://doi.org/10.1007/s40593-025-00466-w

Burbules N. C., & Berk R. (1999). Critical thinking and critical pedagogy: Relations, differences, and limits [w:] Critical theories in education. In T. S. Popkewitz & L. Fendler (eds.), *Changing Terrains of Knowledge and Politics* (pp. 45–66). New York: Routledge.

Chan, C. K. Y., & Colloton, T. (2024). *Generative AI in Higher Education: The ChatGPT Effect*. Routledge. https://doi.org/10.4324/9781003459026

Chen, C., & Shu, K. (2024). Combating misinformation in the age of LLMs: Opportunities and challenges. *AI Magazine* 45, 354–368. https://doi.org/10.1002/aaai.12188

Chen, S., & Chaiken, S. (1999). The heuristic-systematic model in its broader context. In S. Chaiken & Y. Trope (eds.), *Dual-Process Theories in Social Psychology* (pp. 73–96). Guilford Press. https://books.google.pl/books?id=5X_auIBx99EC&printsec=frontcover&hl=pl&source=gbs_ge_summary_r&cad=0#v=onepage&q&f=false

Choi, Junhyuk, Hong, Yeseon, & Kim, Bugeun. (2025). People will agree what I think: Investigating LLM's False Consensus Effect. In L. Chiruzzo, A. Ritter, & L. Wang (Eds.). *Findings of the Association for Computational Linguistics: NAACL* (pp. 95–126), Albuquerque, NM: Association for Computational Linguistics.

Common Sense Media (2024). *Teen and Young Adult Perspectives on Generative AI: Patterns of Use, Excitements, and Concerns*. https://www.commonsensemedia.org/research/teen-and-young-adult-perspectives-on-generative-ai-patterns-of-use-excitements-and-concerns

Cotton, D. R. E., Cotton, P. A., & Shipway, J. R. (2023). Chatting and cheating: Ensuring academic integrity in the era of ChatGPT. *Innovations in Education and Teaching International*, 61(2), 228–239. https://doi.org/10.1080/14703297.2023.2190148

Cottrell, S. (2008). *The study skills handbook* (3rd ed.). Palgrave Macmillan.

Danry, V., Pataranutaporn, P., Groh, M., & Epstein, Z. (2025). Deceptive explanations by large language models lead people to change their beliefs about misinformation more often than honest explanations. In *Proceedings of the 2025 CHI Conference on Human Factors in Computing Systems (CHI '25)* (Article 933, pp. 1–31). Association for Computing Machinery. https://doi.org/10.1145/3706598.3713408

Dong, L., Tang, X., & Wang, X. (2025). Examining the effect of artificial intelligence in relation to students' academic achievement: A meta-analysis. *Computers and Education: Artificial Intelligence*, 8, 100400. https://doi.org/10.1016/j.caeai.2025.100400

Essel, H. B., Vlachopoulos, D., Essuman, A. B., & Amankwa, J. O. (2024). ChatGPT effects on cognitive skills of undergraduate students: Receiving instant responses from AI-based conversational large language models (LLMs). *Computers & Education: Artificial Intelligence*, 6, 100198. https://doi.org/10.1016/j.caeai.2023.100198

Essien, A., Bukoye, O. T., O'Dea, X., & Kremantzis, M. (2024). The influence of AI text generators on critical thinking skills in UK business schools. *Studies in Higher Education*, 49(5), 865–882. https://doi.org/10.1080/03075079.2024.2316881

Feng, S., Park, C. Y., Liu, Y., & Tsvetkov, Y. (2023). From pretraining data to language models to downstream tasks: Tracking the trails of political biases leading to unfair NLP models. arXiv. https://doi.org/10.48550/arXiv.2305.08283

Fulsher, A., Pagkratidou, M. & Kendeou, P. (2025). GenAI and misinformation in education: A systematic scoping review of opportunities and challenges. *AI & Society*, 1–13. https://doi.org/10.1007/s00146-025-02536-y

Galaz, V., Metzler, H., Daume, S., Olsson, A., Lindström, B., & Marklund, A. (2023). AI could create a perfect storm of climate misinformation. (arXiv:2306.12807). arXiv. https://doi.org/10.48550/arXiv.2306.12807

Gerlich, M. (2025). AI tools in society: Impacts on cognitive offloading and the future of critical thinking. *Societies*, 15(1), 6. https://doi.org/10.3390/soc15010006

Gillespie, N., Lockey, S., Ward, T., Macdade, A., & Hassed, G. (2025). *Trust, Attitudes and Use of Artificial Intelligence: A Global Study 2025 [Report]*. The University of Melbourne. https://doi.org/10.26188/28822919.v1

Hennekeuser, D., Vaziri, D. D., Golchinfar, D., Schreiber, D., & Stevens, G. (2024). Enlarged education—Exploring the use of generative AI to support lecturing in higher education. *International Journal of Artificial Intelligence in Education*, 35, 1–33.

Huang, L., Yu, W., Ma, W., Zhong, W., Feng, Z., Wang, H., Chen, Q., Peng, W., Feng, X., Qin, B., & Liu, T. (2023). A survey on hallucination in large language models: Principles, taxonomy, challenges, and open questions. arXiv. https://doi.org/10.48550/arXiv.2311.05232

Iqbal, J., Hashmi, Z. F., Asghar, M. Z. et al. (2025). Generative AI tool use enhances academic achievement in sustainable education through shared metacognition and cognitive offloading among preservice teachers. *Scientific Reports*, 15, 16610. https://doi.org/10.1038/s41598-025-01676-x

Ji, Z., Lee, N., Frieske, R., Yu, T., Su, D., Xu, Y., Ishii, E., Bang, Y. J., Madotto, A., & Fung, P. (2023). Survey of hallucination in natural language generation. *ACM Computing Surveys*, 55(12), 248. https://doi.org/10.1145/3571730

Ju, Q. (2023). Experimental evidence on the negative impact of generative AI on scientific learning outcomes. arXiv, arXiv:2311.05629

Karamuk, E. (2025). The automation trap: Unpacking the consequences of over-reliance on AI in education and its hidden costs. In M. B. Garcia, J. Rosak-Szyrocka, & A. Bozkurt (eds.), *Pitfalls of AI Integration in Education: Skill Obsolescence, Misuse, and Bias* (pp. 147–170). IGI Global. https://doi.org/10.4018/979-8-3373-0122-8.ch007

Kendeou, P., & Johnson, V. (2024). The nature of misinformation in education. *Current Opinion in Psychology*, 55, 101734. https://doi.org/10.1016/j.copsyc.2023.101734

Kidd, C., & Birhane, A. (2023). How AI can distort human beliefs. *Science*, 380(6651), 1222–1223. https://doi.org/10.1126/science.adi0248

Kim, Y., Lee, J., Kim, S., Park, J., & Kim, J. (2024). Understanding users' dissatisfaction with ChatGPT responses: Types, resolving tactics, and the effect of knowledge level. In *Proceedings of the 29th International Conference on Intelligent User Interfaces* (pp. 385–404). Association for Computing Machinery. https://doi.org/10.1145/3640543.3645148

Kong, S.-C., Cheung, W. M.-Y., & Zhang, G. (2021). Evaluation of an artificial intelligence literacy course for university students with diverse study backgrounds. *Computers and Education: Artificial Intelligence*, 2, 100026. https://doi.org/10.1016/j.caeai.2021.100026

Krause, S., Panchal, B. H., & Ubhe, N. (2025). Evolution of learning: Assessing the transformative impact of generative AI on higher education. *Frontiers of Digital Education*, 2, 21. https://doi.org/10.1007/s44366-025-0058-7

Lee, D., Arnold, M., Srivastava, A., Plastow, K., Strelan, P., Ploeckl, F., Lekkas, D., & Palmer, E. (2024). The impact of generative AI on higher education learning and teaching: A study of educators' perspectives. *Computers and Education: Artificial Intelligence*, 6, 100221. https://doi.org/10.1016/j.caeai.2024.100221

Lee, E-J. (2024). Minding the source: toward an integrative theory of human–machine communication, *Human Communication Research*, 50(2), 184–193. https://doi.org/10.1093/hcr/hqad034

Lee, H.-P. (Hank), Sarkar, A., Tankelevitch, L., Drosos, I., Rintel, S., Banks, R., & Wilson, N. (2025). The impact of generative AI on critical thinking: Self-reported reductions in cognitive effort and confidence effects from a survey of knowledge workers. In *CHI Conference on Human Factors in Computing Systems (CHI'25)*. ACM. https://doi.org/10.1145/3706598.3713778

Lucassen, T., & Schraagen, J. M. (2011). Factual accuracy and trust in information: The role of expertise. *Journal of the American Society for Information Science and Technology*, 62(7), 1232–1242. https://doi.org/10.1002/asi.21545

Lucassen, T., & Schraagen, J. M. (2012). Propensity to trust and the influence of source and medium cues in credibility evaluation. *Journal of Information Science*, 38(6), 566–577. https://doi.org/10.1177/0165551512459921 (Original work published 2012)

Ma, Z., Mei, Y., Long, Y., Su, Z., & Gajos, K. Z. (2024). Evaluating the experience of LGBTQ+ people using large language model based chatbots for mental health support. In *Proceedings of the 2024 CHI Conference on Human Factors in Computing Systems* (pp. 1–15). Association for Computing Machinery. https://doi.org/10.1145/3613904.3642482

Malik, T., Hughes, L., Dwivedi, Y. K., & Dettmer, S. (2023). Exploring the transformative impact of generative AI on higher education. In Janssen, M., et al. *New Sustainable Horizons in Artificial Intelligence and Digital Solutions. I3E 2023*. Lecture Notes in Computer Science, vol. 14316. Cham: Springer. https://doi.org/10.1007/978-3-031-50040-4_6

Marshik, T., McCracken, C., Kopp, B., & O'Marrah, M. (2024). Student and instructor perceptions and uses of artificial intelligence in higher education. *Teaching of Psychology*, 52(3), 339–346. https://doi.org/10.1177/00986283241299745

Melisa, R., Ashadi, A., Triastuti, A., Hidayati, S., Salido, A., Ero, P. E. L., Marlini, C., Zefrin, Z., & Fuad, Z. A. (2025). Critical thinking in the age of AI: A systematic review of AI's effects on higher education. *Educational Process: International Journal*, 14, e2025031. https://doi.org/10.22521/edupij.2025.14.31

Mills, K., Ruiz, P., Lee, K., Coenraad, M., Fusco, J., Roschelle, J., & Weisgrau, J. (2024). *AI Literacy: A Framework to Understand, Evaluate, and Use Emerging Technology*. Digital Promise.

Mittelstadt, B., Wachter, S. & Russell, C. (2023). To protect science, we must use LLMs as zero-shot translators. *Nature Human Behaviour* 7, 1830–1832. https://doi.org/10.1038/s41562-023-01744-0

Molina, M. D., & Sundar, S. S. (2022). When AI moderates online content: effects of human collaboration and interactive transparency on user trust. *Journal of Computer-Mediated Communication*, 27(4). https://doi.org/10.1093/jcmc/zmac010

National Research Council. (1997). *Science Teaching Reconsidered: A Handbook*. Washington, DC: The National Academies Press. https://doi.org/10.17226/5287

Ou, M., Zheng, H., Zeng, Y., & Hansen, P. (2024). Trust it or not: Understanding users' motivations and strategies for assessing the credibility of AI-generated information. *New Media & Society*, 28(2), 507–529.

Our Future Foundation (2023). *Transformacyjne trendy kształtujące szkolnictwo wyższe*. https://coopernicus.pl/pl/raporty

Passi, S., & Vorvoreanu, M. (2024). Overreliance on AI: Literature review [Technical report]. *Microsoft*. https://www.microsoft.com/en-us/research/wp-content/uploads/2022/06/Aether-Overreliance-on-AI-Review-Final-6.21.22.pdf

Paustian, T., & Slinger, A. (2024). Students are using large language models and AI detectors can often detect their use. *Frontiers in Education*, 9, 1374889. https://doi.org/10.3389/feduc.2024.1374889

Pretorius, L., & Cahusac de Caux, B. (2025). *The AI Literacy Framework for Higher Education: A Grounded Theory Exploration of the Foundational, Social, Conceptual, Ethical, and Affective Domains of AI Literacy*. Monash University. https://doi.org/10.26180/25965178.v5

Ravšelj, D., Keržič, D., Tomaževič, N., Umek, L., Brezovar, N., Iahad, N. A., Abdulla, A. A., Akopyan, A., Aldana Segura, M. W., AlHumaid, J., & Allam, M. F. (2025). Higher education students' perceptions of ChatGPT: A global study of early reactions. *PLOS One*, 20(2), e0315011. https://doi.org/10.1371/journal.pone.0315011

Risko, E. F., & Gilbert, S. J. (2016). Cognitive offloading. *Trends in Cognitive Sciences* 20(9), 676–688. https://doi.org/10.1016/j.tics.2016.07.002

Shin, D., Koerber, A., & Lim, J. S. (2024). Impact of misinformation from generative AI on user information processing: How people understand misinformation from generative AI. *New Media & Society*, 27(7), 4017–4047. https://doi.org/10.1177/14614448241234040

Shrawgi, H., Rath, P., Singhal, T., & Dandapat, S. (2024). Uncovering stereotypes in large language models: A task complexity-based approach. In *Proceedings of the 18th Conference of the European Chapter of the Association for Computational Linguistics* (Vol. 1: Long Papers) (pp. 1841–1857). Association for Computational Linguistics. https://doi.org/10.18653/v1/2024.eacl-long.111

Swami V., Voracek M., Stieger S., Tran U. S., & Furnham A. (2014). Analytic thinking reduces belief in conspiracy theories. *Cognition*, 133, 572–585. https://doi.org/10.1016/j.cognition.2014.08.006

Tiller, N. B., Marcon, A. R., Zenone, M., et al. (2026). Generative artificial intelligence-driven chatbots and medical misinformation: An accuracy, referencing and readability audit. *BMJ Open*, 16, e112695. https://doi.org/10.1136/bmjopen-2025-112695

Weidinger, L., Mellor, J., Rauh, M., Griffin, C., Uesato, J., Huang, P.-S., Cheng, M., Glaese, M., Balle, B., Kasirzadeh, A., Kenton, Z., Brown, S., Hawkins, W., Stepleton, T., Biles, C., Birhane, A., Haas, J., Rimell, L., Hendricks, L. A., Isaac, W., Legassick, S., Irving, G., & Gabriel, I. (2021). Ethical and social risks of harm from language models. arXiv. https://doi.org/10.48550/arXiv.2112.04359

Xia, Q., Zhang, P., Huang, W., & Chiu, T. K. F. (2025). The impact of generative AI on university students' learning outcomes via Bloom's taxonomy: A meta-analysis and pattern mining approach. *Asia Pacific Journal of Education*, 1–31. https://doi.org/10.1080/02188791.2025.2530503

Zhai, C., Wibowo, S. & Li, L. D. (2024). The effects of over-reliance on AI dialogue systems on students' cognitive abilities: A systematic review. *Smart Learning Environments*, 11, 28. https://doi.org/10.1186/s40561-024-00316-7

5 The Phenomenon of AI Hallucinations and Their Influence on Society and Academic Communication in SSH

Paulina Gajoch, Filip Gampel, and Jakub Gomułka

INTRODUCTION

Proponents of language models—and of generative artificial intelligence more broadly—emphasise their wide-ranging potential across various domains, including the creative industries, cultural activities, and academic research. However, a major limitation to their broader and more reliable adoption is the phenomenon commonly referred to as AI hallucination. This term denotes the generation of content that is inaccurate, misleading, or, in some cases, entirely fabricated, despite appearing plausible or well-formed.

In this chapter, we undertake a comprehensive analysis of this challenge, focusing on its nature, its societal implications, and its specific impact on academic communication. We begin by defining AI hallucination, offering a more precise description and a typology of its various forms, and outlining the technical and conceptual reasons why such errors occur. In the second part, we examine how these hallucinations can negatively affect society—particularly by undermining trust in digital information, automating misinformation, and exacerbating epistemic uncertainty. Thirdly, we turn to the academic context, showing how the use of generative AI in research and publishing may compromise scholarly standards and distort the transmission of knowledge. The chapter concludes by considering strategies for mitigating the harmful consequences of AI hallucinations.

UNDERSTANDING AI HALLUCINATIONS

The first matter to be discussed in this chapter is the meaning of the term AI hallucination. We will present commonly used classifications of this phenomenon, as well as the mechanisms behind its occurrence.

DOI: 10.1201/9781003676188-6

Definition and Typology

The term 'hallucination' originates from psychiatry, where it signifies a wakeful, sensual perception, which is perceived as real, but occurs in the absence of an appropriate, external stimulus (El-Mallakh & Walker, 2010). In the field of artificial intelligence, it has been adapted to signify generated content that seems plausible but is non-factual (Huang et al., 2025) or otherwise 'unfaithful' to the task at hand. Hallucinated content is misleading since it appears as coherent and grounded in the source content, which is why it may be hard to capture, in analogy to psychological hallucinations, which are hard to tell apart from sensations of the real world.

There is some ambiguity in what would be defined as 'source content' and thus a hallucination depends on various common natural language generation tasks (Ji et al., 2023). For instance, consider (1) translation, (2) text summarisation, (3) data-to-text tasks—that is, tasks where structured data such as tables or knowledge graphs are to be converted into human-readable text in natural language—and (4) information retrieval—that is, retrieving information from a corpus of unstructured data such as the internet or a collection of documents. In these contexts, any factual deviation from the sources provided by the user would be considered a hallucination, and tolerance for such behaviour would be very low. On the other hand, for dialogue systems such as ChatGPT, the source content would be the conversation history, and because of the open-endedness of possible use-cases, hallucinations—understood as unfaithfulness to this context—might have a somewhat higher tolerance threshold. Such open-domain dialogue systems are usually optimised not only for faithfulness but also for user engagement. Therefore, it may be, for instance, desired for the system to introduce to the discussion a relevant fact that was not present in the user input. Finally, the mechanisms behind hallucinations have been considered as desirable or even essential for creative tasks (Jiang et al., 2024).

It should be noted that the concept of hallucinations has been applied within all major fields of generative AI, including image, video, and audio generation (Sahoo et al., 2024). In what follows, we will discuss only the case of natural language generation, as the most relevant to social sciences and humanities, though most of our remarks will be readily generalisable to other areas.

We begin by providing a more detailed breakdown of the taxonomy of hallucinations in natural language generation as proposed in existing literature.

One common and general categorisation of hallucinations distinguishes between two main types, intrinsic and extrinsic (Maynez et al., 2020; Huang et al., 2021; Dziri et al., 2021).

Intrinsic hallucinations are direct contradictions in the output with reference to the source content. For instance, the user might ask the system to summarise a text which contains the information: 'Lem published his first book in 1951', but the output would erroneously state that this happened in 1915.

Extrinsic hallucinations refer to outputs that are neither supported nor contradicted by the source. In the above example, the system might add that 'Lem finished his first book in 1948, but it was not published until later', even though this information would not be supported by the user's input. Note that extrinsic hallucinations—as in this example—may be factually correct, based on some external knowledge of the system. Nevertheless, they might be problematic in many use cases.

The above categorisation is mostly applicable to traditional task-specific natural language generation tools. With the rise of large language models (LLMs), researchers realised the need for more nuanced taxonomies. Zhang et al. (2023b) propose dividing hallucinations into three types:

- **Input-conflicting** hallucinations contradict or are unfaithful with reference to the user's input.
- **Context-conflicting** hallucinations refer to inconsistencies within the generated output, i.e. the LLM contradicting itself.
- **Fact-conflicting** hallucinations are false or unverifiable claims with reference to established world knowledge.

A more granular taxonomy is found in Huang et al. (2025). Based on some specific errors commonly made by LLMs, the authors distinguish between **factuality hallucinations**, related to real-world information, and **faithfulness hallucinations**, related to various inconsistencies of the generated content.

Factuality hallucinations are further divided into:

- **Factual contradictions**, where generated content directly conflicts with information on *entities* or *relations* within the real world
- **Factual fabrications**, where generated text contains either non-existent or entirely unverifiable claims (*unverifiability hallucination*), or claims which are not universally valid due to a lack of consensus, or because they are a matter of subjective assessment (*overclaim hallucination*)

Faithfulness hallucinations fall into three types:

- **Instruction inconsistency**, where the LLM is unintentionally unfaithful to the user's instructions. This excludes intentional refusal for safety reasons or ethical guidelines.
- **Context inconsistency** refers to unfaithfulness to the input data provided by the user (not to be confused with the task or instruction)
- **Logical inconsistency** refers to internal logical errors in the LLM's output. A typical example would be a reasoning task where the subsequent step is not implied by the previous one.

There exist various other categorisation attempts in the literature, most of which roughly follow the lines of the above-mentioned (Li et al., 2024; Sahoo et al., 2024).

Mechanisms Behind the Phenomenon

Recent studies uncovered a great diversity of reasons why LLMs tend to manifest hallucinations, most of which are intimately related to these models' architecture and training process. We can broadly distinguish causes of hallucinations related to training data, the training process itself, and the inference mechanism. In the following section, we shall briefly review these three areas.

Hallucinations from Training Data

The quality and breadth of data used in training of an LLM remain a major source of hallucinations. We may distinguish between data used for pre-training, which accounts for most of the model's world knowledge and its general capabilities, and data used during alignment, which serves to enable the model to better follow human instructions and preferences.

State-of-the-art LLMs use giant amounts of data for pre-training. The ever-increasing demand for training data necessitates automatic or semi-automatic data collection methods, which leads to deteriorating data quality. Misinformation is introduced into the corpora, e.g. in the form of fake news. Paired with LLM's remarkable memorisation capabilities (Carlini et al., 2022), it increases the likelihood of reproducing such false statements in the form of hallucinations ('imitative falsehood'). It has also been noted that societal biases present in pre-training data also contribute to hallucinations, particularly in relation to gender (Paullada et al., 2021) and nationality (Ladhak et al., 2023; Narayanan Venkit et al., 2023). As a common example, the model might assume that a person working as a nurse is a female, even though the user did not provide this information.

As a further source of hallucinations, reviews on the subject commonly discuss the 'knowledge boundary' of LLMs, which refers to the limits of world knowledge present in the training data. Typically, LLMs excel at shallow, general, and encyclopedic-type knowledge, but struggle with domain-specific long-tail knowledge, since such data are much more scarcely present in the training corpus. Another inherent limit is the temporal boundary—knowledge of recent events beyond a training cut-off will not be present in the model. Likewise, the model's knowledge might become outdated with time. Finally, legal restrictions impose boundaries on potentially valuable material for training LLMs, such as copyrighted scientific publications and literary works. In any of the above-mentioned cases, LLMs tend to produce hallucinations regarding information outside their knowledge boundary.

Finally, inferior data used during the supervised fine-tuning phase of model training may encourage hallucinations. As shown in Gekhman et al. (2024), this happens in particular when the alignment data contain new knowledge not present in the pre-training dataset. Likewise, using task-specific alignment instructions that are focused on task format learning, as well as overly complex instructions, tends to increase hallucinations (Li et al., 2024).

Hallucinations from Training

The different training stages of present-day LLMs have all been found to contain pitfalls that increase the likelihood of hallucinations. Some of these are related to the very architecture of transformer-based models. The foundational ability of these models to predict subsequent tokens based on previous ones is learned during pre-training as a unidirectional, left-to-right process. This inherently limits their ability to capture more subtle contextual dependencies (Li et al., 2023). Similarly, the soft-attention mechanism of the transformer has been linked to an impairment of capturing context at different ranges for longer sequences (Chiang & Cholak, 2022, Hahn, 2020). Another major source of hallucinations is termed 'exposure bias'. It refers to the persistent disparities between the training data and data seen during inference. This is a particularly problematic issue, since a single erroneously generated token may thus cause a snowball effect, where the error is propagated throughout the following sequence.

The supervised fine-tuning stage of training serves to 'unlock' the model's knowledge learned during pre-training. This is usually achieved by forcing the model to respond to queries provided by the user. However, this becomes problematic if the task is related to information outside the model's knowledge boundary: it commonly lacks the means to adequately express incertitude or ignorance (Yang et al., 2023; Zhang et al., 2023a).

During the Reinforced Learning from Human Feedback (RLHF) phase, human feedback is used to align the model's output more closely with human preferences. This improves user experience, at the risk of encouraging a behaviour known as sycophancy—the tendency to generate untruthful content for the sake of appealing to the user. This effect was confirmed by linking the truthfulness of a response to certain patterns in the activation of the underlying neural network (Azaria & Mitchell, 2023).

Hallucinations from Inference

During inference, the LLM creates output by predicting tokens based on the preceding context. Quite surprisingly, selecting the most probable sequence often results in low-quality text, a phenomenon known as the likelihood trap (Meister et al., 2020). For this reason, various decoding strategies have been developed, introducing randomness into the picture. As a fundamental trade-off, generation at higher temperatures (that is, sampling more low-frequency tokens) increases the likelihood of hallucination (Aksitov et al., 2023).

Another source of hallucinations at the inference level is overconfidence, which signifies an excessive focus on partially generated output. Such models tend to prioritise fluidity over faithfulness, i.e. they lose focus on the broader context. Furthermore, using a softmax as the final layer in conjunction with a word embedding (a very common choice) leads to the *softmax bottleneck*, which was found to limit expressivity of the model (Yang et al., 2017). This issue is particularly severe for multimodal output distributions (Chang & McCallum, 2022). Finally, limited reasoning capabilities have been associated with hallucinations in tasks that require the model to form multiple associations within the provided context (Zheng et al., 2023).

SOCIETAL IMPACTS OF HALLUCINATING AI MODELS

In this section, we explore the social impact of AI hallucinations. Firstly, we examine how the phenomenon manifests in selected high-stakes contexts, namely in finance, medicine, transportation, the energy sector, and law. Secondly, we discuss two phenomena that enhance the negative impact of AI hallucinations by weakening our ability for critical thinking—the ELIZA effect and the automation bias. Thirdly, we focus on epistemic trust and vigilance, and the changes they must undergo because of the pervasiveness of generative AI.

Hallucinations in High-Stakes Contexts

Legal systems are grounded in precision, precedent, and the interpretation of normative acts. AI systems used in this context must therefore exhibit the highest possible factual reliability. Yet, there are documented cases in which AI has invoked non-existent court decisions, misinterpreted statutes, or attributed quotations to the wrong sources.

A flagship example is Mata v. Avianca, Inc., a widely discussed 2023 case in the United States in which two attorneys used ChatGPT to prepare arguments before a federal court. The model generated six citations to non-existent cases that were mistakenly incorporated into official filings. The court fined the lawyers five thousand dollars. In its reasoning, the court wrote that there is nothing inherently improper about using artificial intelligence to draft briefs; however, doing so does not relieve counsel of the duty to meticulously verify the content produced (Merken, 2023).

In medicine, the harms from hallucinations can be even greater: a single erroneous statement can mean the difference between life and death. Patients often use language models to generate descriptions of symptoms, interpret test results, and even seek suggestions regarding diagnosis and treatment. Although these models often provide accurate and useful information, the risk of diagnostic hallucination is real and documented.

A striking example is a case described in the medical literature of a 60-year-old man who presented to the emergency department with worsening paranoia and hallucinations despite having had no prior health problems (Eichenberger et al., 2025). Laboratory testing revealed profound electrolyte disturbances, including hypophosphatemia, metabolic alkalosis, and pseudohyperchloremia. While on the ward, the man was markedly thirsty yet refused water offered to him, citing dietary restrictions and noting that he distilled his own water at home. During the hospitalisation, it was determined that, for several months, he had been replacing table salt with sodium bromide purchased online, following a recommendation obtained from ChatGPT. Seeking to 'eliminate chlorides from his diet', he introduced a toxic substance, leading to severe bromide poisoning manifested by psychiatric and metabolic disturbances. Only after intensive inpatient care with electrolyte repletion and temporary antipsychotic treatment did his condition improve. His serum bromide concentration reached levels many times the normal range (1700 mg/L versus a reference range of 0.9–7.3 mg/L).

This case illustrates how easily unverified information generated by a language model can be treated as health advice and lead to behaviours with dramatic clinical consequences. As in legal practice, medicine likewise demonstrates the need for rigorous verification of AI-generated content, especially in situations where it may influence decisions affecting patient health and safety.

In financial markets, hallucinations by language models can also be highly consequential because investment and supervisory decisions rely on precise, auditable data. Generative systems used to summarise reports, communicate with clients, or extract data from prospectuses can 'invent' numbers, confuse sources, and produce seemingly credible narratives. When such outputs enter decision processes, automation bias, discussed in the next section, plays its role. With broad adoption, the risk of correlated errors and herd effects with systemic potential increases.

These concerns are not purely theoretical. In May 2023, a manipulated image of an explosion near the Pentagon—reportedly showing telltale signs of AI generation—spread on social media and triggered a brief drop in US stock indices before the rumour was disproven (Marcelo, 2023).

Generative-AI hallucinations are not a 'bug' in the classical technical sense; they stem from the structural properties of predictive models, which operate by forecasting the most probable sequence of tokens rather than by verifying facts. In high-risk contexts such as law, medicine, and finance, this seemingly innocuous behaviour can have real and dangerous consequences.

Technical measures—such as retrieval-augmented generation (RAG), fact-checking systems, or human-in-the-loop workflows—can mitigate part of the problem, but they cannot replace user awareness and competence in interpreting generated content. Regulatory, educational, and ethical responsibility are likewise crucial. Ultimately, AI hallucinations are less of a problem than the uncritical trust that artificial intelligence is often afforded.

Automation Bias and Atrophy of Critical Thinking

Automation bias is a well-documented phenomenon that has been the subject of scholarly interest for many years. It denotes the human tendency to give credence to information provided by machines rather than that from other sources, even when the latter is demonstrably correct (Skitka et al., 1999). Researchers have linked this psychological mechanism to another bias, namely the preference for information originating from other people over that conveyed by inanimate objects (Bruner & Tagiuri, 1954; Madhavan & Wiegmann, 2007). Automation bias can have serious, potentially catastrophic consequences in domains such as aviation and medicine (as demonstrated in the previous section), where even highly trained professionals may place undue trust in electronic decision-support systems, which are inherently fallible and prone to various failures.

In the context of language models and chatbots built upon them, automation bias is often discussed alongside another phenomenon (Strauß 2018), known as the ELIZA effect (Hofstadter, 1979, p. 596). The problem was discussed first by Joseph Weizenbaum (1977, pp. 188–191), the creator of the ELIZA system, which was designed to parody the stereotypical structure of psychotherapy. Although ELIZA's functioning relied on a simple script containing a set of rules for processing user input so that the responses would mimic those of a psychotherapist during a session, people interacting with the system frequently succumbed to the illusion of conversing with someone who genuinely understood them. The hypothetical psychological mechanism proposed by Weizenbaum to explain the ELIZA effect includes factors that are likely also responsible for automation bias: it was 'clothed in the magical mantle of Science and all of Science's well-known powers may be attributed to it' (Weizenbaum, 1977, p. 191).

The co-occurrence of automation bias and the ELIZA effect may lead to perceiving language models, on the one hand, as understanding agents and, on the other, as fully reliable sources of information. The latter tendency is reinforced by the specific form of linguistic communication characteristic of such models: a kind of neutrality resulting from generating responses based on content that represents the full spectrum of diverse perspectives, attitudes, and emotional tones, as well as a certain authoritativeness and clear overconfidence—the absence of any trace of hesitation in their style of expression (Chhikara, 2025).

In addition to the obvious risks associated with emotional involvement in a para-relationship with a model, the two phenomena described above may also lead to a weakening of higher order cognitive functions, in particular, the capacity for information retention and the ability to adopt a critical stance towards the information provided (Zhai et al., 2024; Gerlich, 2025). In its extreme form, this may manifest as dependence on an LLM and an inability to function independently without continuous prompts from the system. However, atrophy of the capacity for critical engagement need not take such a radical form to pose a serious threat, both to the individuals affected and to the functioning of democratic society as a whole.

In the context of these negative tendencies, the problem of AI hallucinations becomes all the more serious, as users are increasingly inclined to regard models as infallible and universally competent advisors, thereby relieving them of an ever-greater share of intellectual work. In this way, they lose the ability to recognise even those hallucinations that involve internal inconsistencies and that, to sufficiently critical observers, would appear obvious. It can therefore be reasonably argued that the proliferation, within the social circulation of information, of false or flawed content resulting from model hallucinations will intensify.

Hallucinations and Epistemic Vigilance

The exchange of information between people is the fundamental benefit of language. It allows us to acquire knowledge that would otherwise remain beyond our reach. Yet, the expansion of knowledge through interpersonal communication depends on the assumption that the source of information is reliable. In other words, we must adopt an attitude of epistemic trust. Philosophical analysis presents epistemic trust as a three-part relation, involving two agents—the truster and the trustee—as well as a belief in propositional content (McCraw, 2015). For such a relation to arise, the trustee must intentionally provide information: they must communicate the belief to which the trust refers. Otherwise, we are not dealing with a relation of trust, but rather with the formulation of hypotheses based on another person's behaviour. Epistemic trust involves both the truster's dependence on the trustee and the truster's belief (or disposition to believe) that the trustee is a reliable source of information. Some scholars associate epistemic trust with a particular feeling (Zagzebski, 2012), while others argue that feelings do not play a decisive role (McCraw, 2015).

Researchers studying epistemic trust also note its close connection with epistemic vigilance—a set of practices and dispositions that allow trusters to monitor, at least to some extent, the reliability of trustees. This vigilance enables them to detect situations in which trustees either lack sufficient competence to make their claims credible or are simply not telling the truth (Sperber et al., 2010; Origgi, 2014). The form such vigilance takes depends on cultural context as well as on the technologies used by a community. It manifests differently in the traditional societies of the Amazon, in small English towns, and in contemporary academic environments.

A growing number of researchers, including Alvarado (2023) and Messeri & Crockett (2024), argue that language models—due to the AI hallucination phenomenon—are not worthy of epistemic trust. Nevertheless, as has been pointed out in the previous section, they are in practice widely treated as reliable sources of information. Moreover, the AI industry and the associated research communities put their effort into implementing mechanisms that help maintain epistemic trust in the models, even when hallucinations reveal a lack of reliability (Kim et al., 2025). The problem of AI hallucinations, therefore, presents a serious challenge for epistemic vigilance: society needs to develop an appropriate set of practices—responses to model outputs—that can provide at least partial resistance to their influence. One such practice might be the careful verification of automatic translations; another could be the use of two or more different models in order to compare their responses.[1]

Yet, adequate epistemic vigilance against hallucinatory models is likely to be limited to the most educated and technologically competent segments of society. This suggests the emergence of a new form of stratification, and even of exclusion: reliable knowledge, free from the distortions of AI hallucinations, may become a good of which a significant part (perhaps even the majority) of society will be deprived.

AI HALLUCINATIONS AND ACADEMIC COMMUNICATION

The issue of AI hallucination and its impact on academic work involves several aspects, which will be discussed in this section. In addition to the most visible concern—fabricated bibliographic references—we also address the problematic practice of automatically generating reviews, as well as content distortions that may occur when language models summarise longer texts.

Fabricated Citations and Sources

Given their ability to process large portions of text, LLMs appear as a natural tool to be used in academia. Obvious use cases include the review of existing literature and scientific writing. A long-standing issue in these contexts is the prevalence of hallucinations. A 2024 study (Chelli et al., 2024) found hallucination rates of 29% (GPT 4), 40% (GPT 3.5), and 91% (Bard), respectively, given the task to list studies on various medical topics. The models struggled in fulfilling additional criteria provided by the researchers (such as 'randomised study', 'systematic review'). Still, for non-hallucinated research papers, the GPT models showcased a significant efficiency in retrieving accurate bibliographic information.

A similar study (Walters & Wilder, 2023) evaluating the capabilities of GPT 3.5 and GPT 4 found that when prompted to produce scientific writing with citations, 55%/18% of the generated references were hallucinated. Out of the non-fabricated cited works, 43%/24% contained one or more substantive citation errors.

AI has been found to facilitate unethical behaviour in academia, ranging from malpractices to outright fraud. A 2025 case study (Spinellis, 2025) analysed 53 articles published over several years in a research journal. The selection criterion was a small number of in-text citations, which was assumed to be a feature of AI-fabricated writing. The publications were further analysed with respect to other characteristic features, such as words and formulations typical of LLMs or a lack of empirical evidence. As a result, 48 of the articles appeared to be AI-generated. Several articles have been found to be misattributed to real authors from prestigious institutions. This was likely motivated by the objective of inflating the standing of the journal to attract authors looking to inflate their publication record.

In another study, Al-Sinani and Mitchell (2025) identified clusters of questionable research papers uploaded to preprint repositories. These research papers exhibited 'minimal technical content, repetitive structure, unverifiable authorship, and mutually reinforcing citation patterns among a recurring set of authors'. The authors identified a repetitive pattern: the fraudulent publications feature a first author with an unfamiliar, likely fictitious name, and a second author with a publication history, who frequently is also the uploader of the article, likely with the intention of boosting his or her publication metrics. The authors of the study conducted a controlled experiment in which they uploaded an entirely fabricated publication to one repository. The fake research paper remained online as of the time of writing of the study and attracted a number of citations within 24 hours.

Reviewers' Bad Practices

With the growing adoption of artificial intelligence in the scientific peer-review process, we are witnessing both its benefits and drawbacks. AI can assist reviewers in evaluating text quality, detecting plagiarism, and analysing statistical results. However, concerning practices are emerging, including uncritical reliance on AI tools, copying AI-generated evaluations, generating hallucinated citations, and a lack of transparency regarding the use of language models. This issue is escalating due to increasing publication pressure and the lack of robust ethical standards in academic journals.

One of the most troubling phenomena related to the use of language models in peer review is AI hallucination—the generation of false citations, non-existent articles, or distorted source data by language models. This is far from a marginal issue. According to a corpus created by Mugaanyi et al. (2024), hallucinated references may account for up to 27.3% of all citations produced by ChatGPT. Such unverifiable hallucinations can lead to unwarranted criticism or, conversely, to praise based on inaccurate premises. Latona et al. (2024) reported a 14.4% increase in the likelihood of higher review scores in favour of AI-assisted reviews. Regardless of the score outcome, reviews may include statements like: 'The authors should address the seminal work of *X* et al. (2021), published in *Nature*', despite no such publication ever existing.

Interestingly, as Agrawal et al. (2023) have shown, when prompted appropriately, ChatGPT-4 is able to distinguish between real and fake references with 92.7% probability, assigning higher credibility to genuine citations. This suggests that models are often able to expose their own hallucinations, and a follow-up question may suffice to prevent the use of fabricated sources.

Another growing concern is that many AI-assisted reviews contain no disclosure of AI usage. This could be due to journal policies prohibiting language model use in peer reviews, or fears that admitting to such use could harm a reviewer's reputation.

This lack of transparency means that journal editors and authors may be unaware that their manuscript evaluations were partially or entirely generated by AI.

According to Liang et al. (2024), between 6.5% and 16.9% of peer reviews submitted to major AI conferences may have been significantly modified by language models, beyond basic spell-checking or minor editing.

Even more revealing are the circumstances under which AI-generated content is more prevalent. This occurs when reviewers report lower confidence in their assessment, when reviews are submitted close to the deadline, and when reviewers are less likely to respond to author rebuttals or replies. These patterns raise a deeper question: is AI being used to mask a lack of competence or to bypass proper critical engagement, or are these trends symptomatic of systemic reviewer overload? While the answer may not be clear-cut, one revealing statistic published in *Nature* shows that just 20% of reviewers are responsible for 94% of all peer reviews (Kovanis et al., 2016). This concentration of responsibility may lead to reviewer burnout, declining ethical and scholarly quality, and greater reliance on AI as cognitive offloading.

Lack of transparency undermines the principles of openness and accountability in peer review. Failure to disclose AI use can conceal factual inaccuracies, misinterpretations, or unjustified evaluations, and can impact editorial decisions in uncontrolled ways. The consequences are foreseeable: a flawed manuscript may be accepted due to an AI-generated review, while a carefully crafted research paper could be rejected, demotivating the researcher unfairly affected.

Importantly, the use of AI itself is not inherently unethical. The core issue lies in the fact that AI-generated reviews often appear fluent, concise, and readable, yet are frequently generic, vague, and disconnected from the content of the research paper under review. Donker (2023) documented cases in which editors received AI-generated reviews that neatly summarised the methodology and findings, but the seemingly constructive comments did not relate to the actual data or were factually incorrect. Submitting such content, especially when copied verbatim from models like ChatGPT, can mislead authors and result in unnecessary and misguided changes to manuscripts.

In summary, one of the most pressing ethical issues is the lack of clarity about responsibility for the content of AI-assisted reviews. If a review contains factual errors, hallucinations, or biased judgements, who is accountable? The reviewer? The editor? Or the creators of the language model? As Mollaki (2024) emphasises, as of 2024, 8 out of 10 high-impact academic journals have introduced formal policies regulating the use of AI in both article writing and peer review. Yet, further development of these frameworks remains essential to uphold scholarly integrity.

Gaps in responsibility arise when humans rely on AI for decision-making without assuming full accountability. This can lead to a lack of consequences for erroneous evaluations, thereby eroding trust in the peer-review system—the cornerstone of modern scientific advancement.

Distorted Interpretations

One of the ways language models are being used in academic settings is as interactive interfaces for engaging with large texts. The simplest form of this practice involves generating summaries, abstracts, or lists of key points from a given work. A more advanced version employs retrieval-augmented generation (RAG) technology, allowing users to upload a chosen text and create an artificial interlocutor that possesses knowledge of its content. While some commentators have enthusiastically claimed that such practices represent a new and previously unattainable stage in the development of science (Duch, 2023; Wang et al., 2023; Grossmann et al., 2023), it is important to highlight the potentially serious risks they pose to scholarly communication and to the humanities and social sciences more broadly.

As shown in the work of Devaraj et al. (2022) and more recently, Peters & Chin-Yee (2025), even the most advanced language models consistently tend to oversimplify the texts they summarise. They often fail to identify all the key arguments and are prone to making substantive errors. In essence, all these problems can be understood as more or less subtle forms of model hallucination. Contrary to the dominant techno-optimistic narrative, the tendency towards oversimplification actually increases with the size and sophistication of the models. Moreover, attempts to counter this effect by adding explicit instructions for faithfulness to the prompt have proven counter-effective (Peters & Chin-Yee, 2025).

One might argue, paradoxically, that it is not the most severe forms of hallucinations that pose the greatest threat to the future of the humanities and social sciences. While major factual errors can indeed lead to cascading misunderstandings and disrupt scholarly communication, such mistakes are relatively easy to detect and correct. The situation is quite different with oversimplification: when the output of a language model contains no obvious mistakes, but instead misrepresents a work by placing emphasis on a relatively unimportant point while ignoring one of its central tenets, or by presenting cautious hypotheses as firmly held views, then efforts to correct the output may be resisted. Human users, affected by automation bias, may argue that the generated content is justified by the source text. This kind of reasoning is psychologically plausible, given the human tendency to prefer explanations that are 'simple, broad, reductive, and quantitative' (Messeri & Crockett, 2024). As a result, entire schools of interpretation may emerge that promote deviant and distorted readings of both classical and contemporary theories.

It is the theoretical branches of the humanities and social sciences that are especially vulnerable to these effects, as their reasoning is not grounded in hard experimental data but in speculation. In the natural sciences, oversimplification ultimately amounts to a lack of fidelity to numerical data and can, in principle, be eradicated through existing mechanisms of self-correction. In contrast, the humanities have traditionally relied on the sensitivity and intelligence of individual scholars, and on the cultivated art of interpretation developed through a *Bildung*—attentiveness to subtle distinctions in meaning, and openness to alternative perspectives (Gadamer, 1989). It should also be noted that some areas of the humanities, such as philosophy, have long struggled with a lack of mutual understanding between parallel research traditions. Debates between these traditions often take the form of cognitively unproductive battles for recognition. Nevertheless, there have been developmental tendencies within these traditions that now face the risk of disappearing entirely due to the dangers described above.

MITIGATING THE INFLUENCE OF HALLUCINATIONS

This section, which functions as a conclusion to our chapter, considers potential strategies for addressing the negative consequences of AI hallucinations. We conclude with somewhat pessimistic reflections on the challenges such efforts are likely to face.

Critical Thinking and Disseminating Reliable Knowledge of LLMs

Large language models are a technology surrounded by numerous myths, raising unrealistic expectations and, at times, fears. One of the main reasons for this is the previously mentioned ELIZA effect: the imitative abilities of LLM-powered chatbots far exceed the simple rule-based text-processing system created by Weizenbaum. Many users find it impossible to believe that these models operate purely through a series of essentially simple operations on vectors and matrices. Instead, they tend to assume that the models possess some form of subjectivity. This false belief is reinforced by official narratives promoted by developers and tech influencers, who speak of artificial agents and use language typically reserved for beings who have minds: terms such as 'thinking', 'decision-making', or 'understanding'. Interestingly, the notion of 'hallucination', discussed in this chapter, is part of that same trend. As argued by Slater and Humphries (2025), as well as Förster and Skop (2025), the idea of a 'hallucinating AI' is a deliberate misuse of language, meant to suggest the presence of some kind of artificial subjectivity. Language models do not hallucinate in the way humans do: they have no internal states or beliefs. In fact, as has been already pointed out here, what we call 'hallucinations' in this context are not even malfunctions: they are the correct output of a system, shaped by its architecture, training data, and prompting. The real issue lies in the way we attempt to use these tools: 'AI hallucinations' are in the eyes of beholders.

Contrary to popular assumptions and to the promotional rhetoric of the developers, simply making the models larger is not the solution to the problem of hallucination. Research shows that in some respects, the problem may even become worse as LLMs grow in size and complexity (Peters & Chin-Yee, 2025). At its root lies the simple fact that language models are not knowledge bases. At best, they are statistical simulations of the latter, built from processing vast amounts of text. In this sense, again, the fault lies partly with the users: their unrealistic expectations and overly trusting attitude towards the outputs generated by LLMs. This, in turn, stems from a lack of understanding.

It can therefore be said that the most basic remedy for the hallucination problem is the spread of accurate knowledge about language models, how they work, and the possibilities and limitations that follow from this. In particular, it is important to stress that the main goal of an LLM is not to provide true information but to generate output that best matches the given prompt. It is equally important to raise awareness of the psychological mechanisms that lead us to anthropomorphise models and place excessive trust in them.

A sound understanding of how these models function and can be used should go hand in hand with fostering a critical attitude among users. The point is not to stop using these tools altogether—they are very useful in many applications, including those involving knowledge—but to maintain a certain distance and epistemic vigilance when dealing with their output. Above all, this means resisting the psychological tendencies described earlier: the ELIZA effect and automation bias. It means developing habits of critically assessing the reliability of the information generated by models and routinely verifying their outputs, including translations.

Defeatist Ending: Where to Find Robust Sources? Tech Bros Propaganda

Proper education concerning the use of LLMs, as well as a critical approach to their outputs, may, however, face certain obstacles. The first relates to the deliberate exaggeration of these models' capabilities and an overly optimistic view of their potential applications, promoted by model developers—mainly owners and employees of leading tech companies—as well as other techno-enthusiasts, such as influencers and, regrettably, some researchers involved in the development of artificial intelligence. All of these actors have a vested interest in maintaining the hype around AI technologies, as it leads to increased investment in the sector and directly contributes to their own financial gain. As noted earlier in this chapter, research has even been published on effective strategies for sustaining (excessive) trust in language models. Unfortunately, due to the immense capital at their disposal, the dominant voice in public discourse about AI technologies is that of Big Tech propaganda. Analyses have already been produced on the hype culture surrounding the LLM sector and the risks it entails (Bohner & Vertesi, 2025).

The second obstacle concerns the issue of reliable sources of information. The emergence of language models has, in a relatively short period of time, contributed to the 'pollution' of various areas of the public sphere with information of questionable epistemic value. The first result now returned by Google search typically comes from a language model. LLMs also 'assist' writers producing content for popular news websites and social media. As a result, previous methods of evaluating information (such as simply 'googling' something) are becoming less effective: fact-checking is increasingly demanding. It would be inaccurate to place the full responsibility for this growing difficulty in accessing trustworthy information solely on LLMs, as we have for years observed a range of developments that contribute to the rising noise in the information environment. These include poorly moderated social media platforms, algorithms that create information bubbles, strong political polarisation that undermines shared epistemic standards, and the declining influence and quality of traditional media.

NOTE

1 New forms of deception made possible by AI technologies (speech generators and language models) also compel societies to modify their practices of epistemic vigilance. However, this broader problem lies beyond the scope of the present discussion.

REFERENCES

Agrawal, A., Suzgun, M., Mackey, L., & Kalai, A. T. (2023). Do Language Models Know When They're Hallucinating References? arXiv preprint arXiv:2305.18248.

Aksitov, R., Chang, C.-C., Reitter, D., Shakeri, S., & Sung, Y. (2023). Characterizing Attribution and Fluency Tradeoffs for Retrieval-Augmented Large Language Models (Version 2). arXiv. https://doi.org/10.48550/ARXIV.2302.05578

Al-Sinani, H. S., & Mitchell, C. J. (2025). From Content Creation to Citation Inflation: A GenAI Case Study (Version 1). arXiv. https://doi.org/10.48550/ARXIV.2503.23414

Alvarado, R. (2023). AI as an Epistemic Technology. *Science and Engineering Ethics*, 29, 32. https://doi.org/10.1007/s11948-023-00451-3

Azaria, A., & Mitchell, T. (2023). The Internal State of an LLM Knows When It's Lying (Version 2). arXiv. https://doi.org/10.48550/ARXIV.2304.13734

Bohner, J., & Vertesi, J. (2025). Towards a Socioeconomics of Hype: Hype Dynamics and Symbolic Boundary Work Within the Speculative AI Bubble. *Social Science Computer Review*. https://doi.org/10.1177/08944393251361935

Bruner, J. S., & Tagiuri, R. (1954). The Perception of People. In: *Handbook of Social Psychology* (vol. 2), edited by G. Lindzey. Reading, MA: Addison-Wesley, 634–654.

Carlini, N., Ippolito, D., Jagielski, M., Lee, K., Tramer, F., & Zhang, C. (2022). Quantifying Memorization Across Neural Language Models (Version 3). arXiv. https://doi.org/10.48550/ARXIV.2202.07646

Chang, H.-S., & McCallum, A. (2022). Softmax Bottleneck Makes Language Models Unable to Represent Multi-mode Word Distributions. In *Proceedings of the 60th Annual Meeting of the Association for Computational Linguistics (Volume 1: Long Papers)* (pp. 8048–8073). Association for Computational Linguistics. https://doi.org/10.18653/v1/2022.acl-long.554

Chelli, M., Descamps, J., Lavoué, V., Trojani, C., Azar, M., Deckert, M., Raynier, J.-L., Clowez, G., Boileau, P., & Ruetsch-Chelli, C. (2024). Hallucination Rates and Reference Accuracy of ChatGPT and Bard for Systematic Reviews: Comparative Analysis. *Journal of Medical Internet Research*, 26, e53164. https://doi.org/10.2196/53164

Chhikara, P. (2025). Mind the Confidence Gap: Overconfidence, Calibration, and Distractor Effects in Large Language Models. ArXiv preprint: arXiv:2502.11028.

Chiang, D., & Cholak, P. (2022). Overcoming a Theoretical Limitation of Self-Attention. In *Proceedings of the 60th Annual Meeting of the Association for Computational Linguistics (Volume 1: Long Papers)* (pp. 7654–7664). Association for Computational Linguistics. https://doi.org/10.18653/v1/2022.acl-long.527

Devaraj, A., Sheffield, W., Wallace, B. C., & Li, J. J. (2022). Evaluating Factuality in Text Simplification. ArXiv preprint: arXiv:2204.07562v1.

Donker T (2023). The Dangers of Using Large Language Models for Peer Review. *Lancet Infectious Diseases* 23(7): 781.

Duch, W. (2023). Artificial Intelligence and the Limits of the Humanities. ArXiv preprint: arXiv:2310.19425.

Dziri, N., Madotto, A., Zaïane, O., & Bose, A. J. (2021). Neural Path Hunter: Reducing Hallucination in Dialogue Systems via Path Grounding. In *Proceedings of the 2021 Conference on Empirical Methods in Natural Language Processing*. Association for Computational Linguistics. https://doi.org/10.18653/v1/2021.emnlp-main.168

Eichenberger, A., Thielke, S., & Van Buskirk, A. (2025). A Case of Bromism Influenced by Use of Artificial Intelligence. *Annals of Internal Medicine: Clinical Cases*, 4(8), e241260.

El-Mallakh, R. S., & Walker, K. L. (2010). Hallucinations, Psuedohallucinations, and Parahallucinations. *Psychiatry: Interpersonal and Biological Processes*, 73(1), 34–42. https://doi.org/10.1521/psyc.2010.73.1.34

Förster, S., & Skop, Y. (2025). Between Fact and Fairy: Tracing the Hallucination Metaphor in AI Discourse. *AI & Society*. https://doi.org/10.1007/s00146-025-02392-w

Gadamer, H.-G. (1989). *Truth and Method*. New York: Continuum.

Gekhman, Z., Yona, G., Aharoni, R., Eyal, M., Feder, A., Reichart, R., & Herzig, J. (2024). Does Fine-Tuning LLMs on New Knowledge Encourage Hallucinations? (Version 3). arXiv. https://doi.org/10.48550/ARXIV.2405.05904

Gerlich, M. (2025). AI Tools in Society: Impacts on Cognitive Offloading and the Future of Critical Thinking. *Societies*, 15(1): 6. https://doi.org/10.3390/soc15010006

Grossmann, I., Feinberg, M., Parker, D. C., Christakis, N. A., Tetlock, P. E., & Cunningham, W. A. (2023). AI and the Transformation of Social Science Research. *Science*, 380(6650): 1108–1109.

Hahn, M. (2020). Theoretical Limitations of Self-Attention in Neural Sequence Models. *Transactions of the Association for Computational Linguistics*, 8, 156–171. https://doi.org/10.1162/tacl_a_00306

Hofstadter, D. R. (1979). *Gödel, Esher, Bach: An Eternal Golden Braid*. New York: Basic Books.

Huang, L., Yu, W., Ma, W., Zhong, W., Feng, Z., Wang, H., Chen, Q., Peng, W., Feng, X., Qin, B., & Liu, T. (2025). A Survey on Hallucination in Large Language Models: Principles, Taxonomy, Challenges, and Open Questions. *ACM Transactions on Information Systems*, 43(2), 1–55. https://doi.org/10.1145/3703155

Huang, Y., Feng, X., Feng, X., & Qin, B. (2021). The Factual Inconsistency Problem in Abstractive Text Summarization: A Survey (Version 3). arXiv. https://doi.org/10.48550/ARXIV.2104.14839

Ji, Z., Lee, N., Frieske, R., Yu, T., Su, D., Xu, Y., Ishii, E., Bang, Y. J., Madotto, A., & Fung, P. (2023). Survey of Hallucination in Natural Language Generation. *ACM Computing Surveys*, 55(12), 1–38. https://doi.org/10.1145/3571730

Jiang, X., Tian, Y., Hua, F., Xu, C., Wang, Y., & Guo, J. (2024). A Survey on Large Language Model Hallucination via a Creativity Perspective (Version 1). arXiv. https://doi.org/10.48550/ARXIV.2402.06647

Kim, H., Seo, S., & Lee, S. W. (2025). When Generative AI Messes Up: How Politeness and Attribution Shape User Reactions to Hallucinations. *International Journal of Information Management*, 85. https://doi.org/10.1016/j.ijinfomgt.2025.102958

Kovanis, M., Porcher, R., Ravaud, P., & Trinquart, L. (2016). The Global Burden of Journal Peer Review in the Biomedical Literature: Strong Imbalance in the Collective Enterprise. *PloS One*, 11(11), e0166387.

Ladhak, F., Durmus, E., Suzgun, M., Zhang, T., Jurafsky, D., McKeown, K., & Hashimoto, T. (2023). When Do Pre-Training Biases Propagate to Downstream Tasks? A Case Study in Text Summarization. In *Proceedings of the 17th Conference of the European Chapter of the Association for Computational Linguistics*. https://doi.org/10.18653/v1/2023.eacl-main.234

Latona, G. R., Ribeiro, M. H., Davidson, T. R., Veselovsky, V., & West, R. (2024). The AI Review Lottery: Widespread AI-Assisted Peer Reviews Boost Paper Scores and Acceptance Rates. arXiv preprint arXiv:2405.02150.

Li, J., Chen, J., Ren, R., Cheng, X., Zhao, X., Nie, J.-Y., & Wen, J.-R. (2024). The Dawn After the Dark: An Empirical Study on Factuality Hallucination in Large Language Models. In *Proceedings of the 62nd Annual Meeting of the Association for Computational Linguistics (Volume 1: Long Papers)* (pp. 10879–10899). https://doi.org/10.18653/v1/2024.acl-long.586

Li, Z., Zhang, S., Zhao, H., Yang, Y., & Yang, D. (2023). BatGPT: A Bidirectional Autoregessive Talker from Generative Pre-trained Transformer (Version 2). arXiv. https://doi.org/10.48550/ARXIV.2307.00360

Liang, W., Izzo, Z., Zhang, Y., Lepp, H., Cao, H., Zhao, X., … & Zou, J. Y. (2024). Monitoring AI-Modified Content at Scale: A Case Study on the Impact of ChatGPT on AI Conference Peer Reviews. arXiv preprint arXiv:2403.07183.

Madhavan, P., & Wiegmann, D. A. (2007). Similarities and Differences between Human–Human and Human–Automation Trust: An Integrative Review. *Theoretical Issues in Ergonomics Science*, 8(4): 277–301.

Marcelo, P. (2023). *Fact Focus: Fake Image of Pentagon Explosion Briefly Sends Jitters Through Stock Market.* Associated Press. https://apnews.com/article/pentagon-explosion-misinformation-stock-market-ai-96f534c790872fde67012ee81b5ed6a4?utm_source=chatgpt.com (date of visit 19.08.2025).

Maynez, J., Narayan, S., Bohnet, B., & McDonald, R. (2020). On Faithfulness and Factuality in Abstractive Summarization. In *Proceedings of the 58th Annual Meeting of the Association for Computational Linguistics*. https://doi.org/10.18653/v1/2020.acl-main.173

McCraw, B. (2015). The Nature of Epistemic Trust. *Social Epistemology*, 29(4): 413–430.

Meister, C., Cotterell, R., & Vieira, T. (2020). If Beam Search Is the Answer, What Was the Question? In *Proceedings of the 2020 Conference on Empirical Methods in Natural Language Processing (EMNLP)* (pp. 2173–2185). Association for Computational Linguistics. https://doi.org/10.18653/v1/2020.emnlp-main.170

Merken, S. (2023). New York Lawyers Sanctioned for Using Fake ChatGPT Cases in Legal Brief. *Reuters.* https://www.reuters.com/legal/new-york-lawyers-sanctioned-using-fake-chatgpt-cases-legal-brief-2023-06-22/ (date of visit 19.08.2025).

Messeri, L. & Crockett, M. J. (2024). Artificial Intelligence and Illusions of Understanding in Scientific Research. *Nature*, 627: 49–58. https://doi.org/10.1038/s41586-024-07146-0

Mollaki, V. (2024). Death of a Reviewer or Death of Peer Review Integrity? The Challenges of Using AI Tools in Peer Reviewing and the Need to Go Beyond Publishing Policies. *Research Ethics*, 20(2), 239–250.

Mugaanyi, J., Cai, L., Cheng, S., Lu, C., & Huang, J. (2024). Evaluation of Large Language Model Performance and Reliability for Citations and References in Scholarly Writing: Cross-Disciplinary Study. *Journal of Medical Internet Research*, 26, e52935.

Narayanan Venkit, P., Gautam, S., Panchanadikar, R., Huang, T.-H., & Wilson, S. (2023). Nationality Bias in Text Generation. In *Proceedings of the 17th Conference of the European Chapter of the Association for Computational Linguistics* (pp. 116–122). Association for Computational Linguistics. https://doi.org/10.18653/v1/2023.eacl-main.9

Origgi, G. (2014). Epistemic Trust. In: *Information Evaluation*, edited by P. Capet & T. Delavallade. London: ISTE & Wiley, 35–54.

Paullada, A., Raji, I. D., Bender, E. M., Denton, E., & Hanna, A. (2021). Data And its (Dis) contents: A Survey of Dataset Development and Use in Machine Learning Research. *Patterns*, 2(11), 100336. https://doi.org/10.1016/j.patter.2021.100336

Peters, U., & Chin-Yee, B. (2025). Generalization Bias in Large Language Model: Summarization of Scientific Research. *Royal Society Open Science*, 12: 241776. https://doi.org/10.1098/rsos.241776

Sahoo, P., Meharia, P., Ghosh, A., Saha, S., Jain, V., & Chadha, A. (2024). A Comprehensive Survey of Hallucination in Large Language, Image, Video and Audio Foundation Models (Version 4). arXiv. https://doi.org/10.48550/ARXIV.2405.09589

Skitka, L. J., Mosier, K. L., & Burdick, M. (1999). Does Automation Bias Decision-Making? *International Journal of Human-Computer Studies*, 51(5): 991–1006.

Slater, J., & Humphries, J. (2025). Another Reason to Call Bullshit on AI "Hallucinations". *AI & Society*. https://doi.org/10.1007/s00146-025-02346-2

Sperber, D., Clément, F., Heintz, C., Mascaro, O., Mercier, H., Origgi, G., & Wilson, D. (2010). Epistemic Vigilance. *Mind & Language*, 25(4): 359–393.

Spinellis, D. (2025). False Authorship: An Explorative Case Study around an AI-Generated Article Published under My Name. *Research Integrity and Peer Review*, 10(1). https://doi.org/10.1186/s41073-025-00165-z

Strauß, S. (2018). From Big Data to Deep Learning: A Leap Towards Strong AI or 'Intelligentia Obscura'? *Big Data and Cognitive Computing*, 2(3): 16. https://doi.org/10.3390/bdcc2030016

Walters, W. H., & Wilder, E. I. (2023). Fabrication and Errors in the Bibliographic Citations Generated by ChatGPT. *Scientific Reports*, 13(1). https://doi.org/10.1038/s41598-023-41032-5

Wang, H., Fu, T., Du, Y. et al. (2023). Scientific Discovery in the Age of Artificial Intelligence. *Nature*, 620: 47–60. https://doi.org/10.1038/s41586-023-06221-2

Weizenbaum, J. (1977). *Computer Power and Human Reason: From Judgement to Calculation*. New York & San Francisco: Freeman and Company.

Yang, Y., Chern, E., Qiu, X., Neubig, G., & Liu, P. (2023). Alignment for Honesty (Version 2). arXiv. https://doi.org/10.48550/ARXIV.2312.07000

Yang, Z., Dai, Z., Salakhutdinov, R., & Cohen, W. W. (2017). Breaking the Softmax Bottleneck: A High-Rank RNN Language Model (Version 4). arXiv. https://doi.org/10.48550/ARXIV.1711.03953

Zagzebski, L. (2012). *Epistemic Authority: A Theory of Trust, Authority, and Autonomy in Belief*. OUP: Oxford & New York.

Zhai, C., Wibowo, S., & Li, L. D. (2024). The Effects of Over-Reliance on AI Dialogue Systems on Students' Cognitive Abilities: A Systematic Review. *Smart Learning Environments*, 11: 28. https://doi.org/10.1186/s40561-024-00316-7

Zhang, H., Diao, S., Lin, Y., Fung, Y. R., Lian, Q., Wang, X., Chen, Y., Ji, H., & Zhang, T. (2023a). R-Tuning: Instructing Large Language Models to Say 'I Don't Know' (Version 3). arXiv. https://doi.org/10.48550/ARXIV.2311.09677

Zhang, Y., Li, Y., Cui, L., Cai, D., Liu, L., Fu, T., Huang, X., Zhao, E., Zhang, Y., Xu, C., Chen, Y., Wang, L., Luu, A. T., Bi, W., Shi, F., & Shi, S. (2023b). Siren's Song in the AI Ocean: A Survey on Hallucination in Large Language Models (Version 3). arXiv. https://doi.org/10.48550/ARXIV.2309.01219

Zheng, S., Huang, J., & Chang, K. C.-C. (2023). Why Does ChatGPT Fall Short in Providing Truthful Answers? (Version 3). arXiv. https://doi.org/10.48550/ARXIV.2304.10513

6 Teaching Applications of AI in Social Sciences and Humanities

An Overview

Mirosława M. Długosz, Maria Stojkow, and Dorota Żuchowska-Skiba

INTRODUCTION

In recent years, generative AI (GenAI) has become a key element of transformations in education, opening new opportunities to support learning processes, develop critical thinking, and co-create knowledge (Sanabria-Navarro et al., 2023). Owing to its capacity to stimulate complex aspects of intelligence and cognitive processes, artificial intelligence (AI) is increasingly functioning not only as a tool but also as an integral component of social and cognitive interactions in educational practices (Sharples, 2023; Veletsianos et al., 2024). In this context, technology enhances both individual cognitive processes and social forms of cooperation, creating spaces for dialogue, reflection, and collective knowledge-building (Sharples, 2023; Dornauer et al., 2024; Filiz & Gür, 2025; Oliveira et al., 2025).

Within the humanities, GenAI is not limited to assisting with text or narrative analysis but also facilitates creative expression and the development of reflective skills in students and teachers (Joubin, 2024; Phillips et al., 2023; Fleischmann, 2024). This potential underscores the need for a responsible and ethical approach to AI implementation in pedagogy, aimed at building trust in these technologies and maximising their educational impact (Joubin, 2024). Consequently, AI becomes an indispensable component of educational transformation, integrating technologies into social and cognitive processes and reshaping traditional teaching and learning models (Sanabria-Navarro et al., 2023; Pradana et al., 2023).

Increasingly, AI is no longer perceived as a separate, autonomous system but as an integral part of the set of tools used in day-to-day didactic work and educational processes. Research indicates that AI-driven tools are becoming progressively embedded in educational practice, supporting teachers and students in writing, content analysis, and task organisation (Sabzalieva & Valentini, 2023; Sharples, 2023; Filiz & Gür, 2025). This trend is exemplified by emerging solutions such as Microsoft 365 Copilot and Google Vertex AI, which offer advanced functionalities

DOI: 10.1201/9781003676188-7

for automating educational tasks, personalising learning, and facilitating data analysis (Microsoft Education Team, 2025; Google Cloud, 2025).

To date, studies have primarily focused on user interaction with AI within the question-and-answer framework characteristic of generative language models. However, broader implementation of AI in integrated digital ecosystems and social media is transforming patterns of communication and collaboration in educational environments, opening new research perspectives regarding the relationships between technology and social practices (Alasadi & Baiz, 2023; Ifenthaler et al., 2024; Cavalcanti et al., 2024). AI has the potential to act as an active participant in educational communities, supporting both individual learning and cooperation among students and teachers (Ottenbreit-Leftwich et al., 2023; Ifenthaler et al., 2024). It can moderate discussions, assist in team project design, and foster new forms of collaboration (Sharples, 2023). At the same time, careful consideration of ethical aspects is essential to ensure that AI supports the development of social competencies and critical thinking rather than replacing significant human interactions (Sabzalieva & Valentini, 2023; Williams et al., 2023; Escotet, 2024). In this way, generative AI becomes an integral part of a complex educational ecosystem in which technological and social dimensions intertwine, creating new opportunities for educational engagement and cooperation (Sabzalieva & Valentini, 2023; Linderoth et al., 2024).

The model of educational interaction with AI is evolving from simple, individual queries to more complex socio-cognitive forms of cooperation. Sabzalieva and Valentini (2023) suggest that the future of educational applications of GenAI may involve the development of social-generative AI, in which AI systems actively participate in learner interactions, supporting communication, collaboration, and the construction of shared knowledge (Sharples, 2023; Suliman et al., 2024). This transformation is also reflected in scholarly literature. A bibliometric analysis by Tao, Denga, and Songa (2025), based on over 900 publications from 2022 to 2025, confirms a rapid increase in interest in AI in education, particularly in higher education, social sciences, and humanities. Dominant research areas include ethical use of AI, personalisation of teaching, integration of generative tools with didactic methods, and the development of critical and ethical competencies (Tao et al., 2025).

This period of growth coincided with the intense transformation of education following the COVID-19 pandemic, when educational institutions implemented AI-based solutions not only as a temporary response to the crisis but also as a lasting component of educational innovation (Bittencourt et al., 2024). These technologies played a particularly significant role in remote education, supporting personalised learning and facilitating interaction among students, for example, through intelligent peer-support recommendation systems (Li et al., 2022). Reviews of research confirm the growing importance of AI in online higher education, demonstrating its influence on course design, student support, and overall learning effectiveness (Ouyang, Zheng & Jiao, 2022).

Alongside the increased use of AI, attention has also focused on fairness and equity in access to knowledge. Studies show that educational algorithms can reinforce existing inequalities if they are not properly designed or tested for bias (Idowu, 2024; Poornesh, 2024). Bias is particularly critical in systems that predict educational outcomes, evaluate student progress, or recommend materials, as even subtle prejudice can systematically disadvantage certain student groups (Idowu, 2024). Consequently, researchers recommend specific methods to detect and mitigate algorithmic bias, aiming to increase equality of opportunity in AI-supported educational systems (Poornesh, 2024). In parallel, conceptual frameworks outlining ethical boundaries have emerged to guide responsible design and use of generative AI in education, taking social, cultural, and pedagogical values into account (Swindell et al., 2024). It has also been emphasised that the design of educational technologies can either exacerbate or reduce existing inequalities, necessitating an ethically informed approach (Close et al., 2024).

The aim of this review is to examine how AI, particularly generative AI, transforms teaching and learning in the social sciences and humanities by personalising education, supporting interactive learning, and fostering critical thinking, while highlighting challenges associated with integrating AI into existing curricula.

METHODOLOGY

In this review of literature, it has been decided to use ERIC database, maintained by the Institute of Education Sciences at the U.S. Department of Education (ERIC.ed.gov). This is due to its specialised profile, the high quality of the publications indexed, and precise subject-matching to the range of research carried out. ERIC is one of the most important sources of academic literature from the field of education, pedagogy, and interdisciplinary research connecting technology, didactics, and social sciences (Institute of Education Sciences, n.d.).

This database includes over 1.5 million bibliographical records and fully comprehensive documents, including peer-reviewed scholarly articles, research reports, doctoral theses, and institutional studies. It is characterised by a stringent selection of content and systematic thematic indexing based on the Thesaurus of ERIC Descriptors, which facilitates a high search accuracy of results/hits (ERIC, n.d.). This database also offers a series of tools facilitating the search for data essential for one's academic objective (Hertzberg and Rudner, 1999).

In the context of research on the use of AI and machine learning in higher education, especially in SSH, ERIC offers a rich database of publications concerning subjects such as personalisation of education, AI literacy, didactic design with the use of AI, and ethical aspects of technology in education. Moreover, the use of one strongly specialised database has allowed, to a large degree, the avoidance of the problems of record duplication and has limited the inclusion of materials of low accuracy, which is a frequent problem when linking multiple general-index databases. Because of this, the narrowing of the search exclusively to the ERIC database ensures cohesion and high quality of the methodological review, at the same time eliminating the risk of gathering sources that are irrelevant in terms of subject matter (Dagenais Brown, 2003; Strayer, 2008).

The decision to select the time span of the literature review to include the years 2022–2025 has been made deliberately. This range represents a period of particularly dynamic development of AI tools and increased interest in their employment in education, especially in the social sciences and humanities (Durak, et al., 2024). The inclusion of earlier years could have led to the inclusion in the analysis of solutions that are out of date and technologically inadequate. This period is characterised by especially intense changes in technology and perception in the context of the employment of AI in higher education. Amongst the principal factors supporting this choice is the important breakthrough that occurred in 2022–2023 within the development of generative AI. At that time, access to such tools as ChatGPT, Bing AI, Claude, or Google Gemini had been made widely available, and these tools rapidly gained recognition in scholarly and educational circles, becoming an integral part of didactic practice and academic research (see Chapter 7) (Sharples, 2023).

This review of literature has been carried out based on the outlines of PRISMA 2020 (Preferred Reporting Items for Systematic Reviews and Meta-Analyses), which are the international standards assembled to improve transparency, reliability, and methodological quality of the systematic academic reviews (Page et al., 2021). The structure of PRISMA relies on the stringent documentation of each phase of the process, from identification of the sources through selection, and all the way to analytical synthesis and conclusions. Thanks to this, it is possible to obtain high accuracy and replicability of the results, and a limitation of the risk of errors in selection or publication.

In the context of the rapid development of AI tools and their increasing presence in didactics and academic research, especially in the social sciences and humanities, the use of PRISMA was the key to ensuring methodological coherence and the quality of source information.

The process of searching for literature items included combinations of keywords representing three main areas:

- technological ('artificial intelligence', 'AI', 'machine learning')
- educational ('teaching', 'pedagogy', 'education')
- specific fields ('humanities', 'social sciences', 'social studies')

Amongst the phrases searched, the following keywords were used: 'artificial intelligence in education', 'AI and pedagogy', 'teaching with AI' AND 'humanities' OR 'social sciences'. The search strategy has been formulated in accordance with methodological recommendations for carrying out systematic reviews, where the precision of selection of keywords and employment of multidimensional search combinations are regarded as the key to limiting interference and increasing the quality of results (Cooper et al., 2013).

Such specific phrasing helps avoid results from beyond the research boundaries, for example, those concerning AI in education in science or technology, which are not the subject of the present analysis. Thanks to this approach, the literature review also includes wide-ranging research on AI in education, and more detailed analyses on its use in humanities and social didactics, which is essential to achieving the chosen objective.

The filters used narrowed down the results to:

- peer-reviewed publications
- documents such as scholarly articles and research reports (e.g. Journal articles)

In accordance with PRISMA guidelines, the selection process of sources has been carried out in two phases:

1. Screening (identification and preliminary qualification): On the basis of analysis of titles and summaries, **472 records were identified**, of which, after removal of duplicates and initial evaluation, **467 were chosen as potentially fitting the objectives of the review**.
2. Full-text evaluation (qualification for the quality analysis): Subsequently, a precise analysis of full texts was carried out, using the criteria of inclusion and exclusion. This analysis included only those publications which:
   - relate directly to education
   - included an element of AI/ML use in didactic practices, in the educational process, and in widely understood education
   - included the empirical, conceptual, or ethical dimension

At the end, 43 publications were approved for the final analysis.

The use of PRISMA 2020 guidelines ensured the transparency and reliability of the literature review process. A precisely formulated search strategy, logical criteria of inclusion and exclusion, and the systematic selection of sources contributed to the selection of high-quality research material, focusing on the use of AI in the didactics of humanities and social sciences.

NETWORK OF THEMATIC CONNECTIONS AND ANALYSIS OF KEYWORDS

Following the phase of preliminary selection, in which 467 publications were identified as potentially significant for the review, a thematic mapping was carried out, based on the co-occurrence of keywords. The generated map (Figure 6.1) shows the **co-occurrence of keywords in scholarly publications on the applications of AI in SSH**. It was created based on bibliometric data after cleaning and standardising the terminology (e.g. 'AI' and 'Artificial Intelligence (AI)' were unified under 'Artificial Intelligence'). Only relationships between keywords that co-occurred at least 4 times (weight ≥ 4) were included. In total, 47 strong connections were identified out of the original 1,776 edges, which helped avoid excessive clutter and better highlight the main trends. The map revealed the structure of relationships among the most frequently occurring terms in the ERIC database.

In this structure, the central place was occupied by terms such as AI, educational technology, technology use in education, and higher education, which constituted the thematic core of the literature on the subject. From this core, there radiated links to more detailed terms, which allowed identification of the principal directions for research and practices oriented to the use of AI in education. Around this dominant technological axis (including, for example, artificial intelligence, technology integration, and educational technology) emerged clear thematic vectors, indicating the specialised areas of interest.

The presence of phrases such as ChatGPT, natural language processing, and intelligent tutoring systems suggests that interest is growing in specific tools of generative

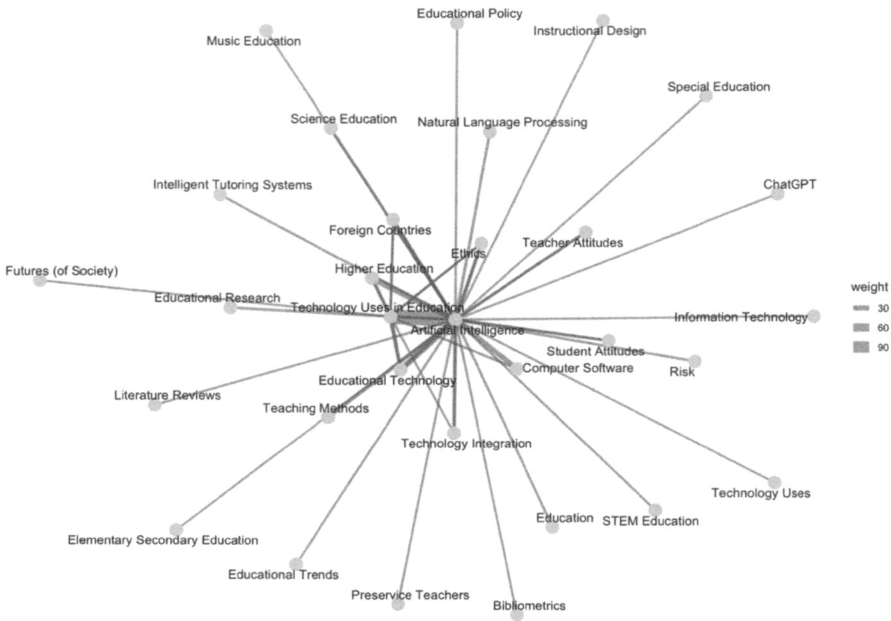

FIGURE 6.1 Map of co-occurrence of keywords in research on AI in education.

(Authors' own research.)

AI and their role in the personalisation of education and support for didactic interaction. On the other hand, terms such as ethics, risk, or teacher attitudes have created a socio-ethical continuum of issues, strongly connected with the technological terminology, which indicates that a process of reflection on the responsible use of technology is an integral part of contemporary discourse.

Furthermore, the strong presence of an institutional component can be noted—represented by terms such as educational policy, instructional design, or pre-service teachers—which indicates a growing interest in AI not only as a didactic tool but also as a factor influencing the shaping of educational systems as a whole. The emergence of these concepts demonstrates that there is a need to implement system and legislation changes, including the adaptation of educational programmes for teachers and the updating of educational policies.

In addition, categories such as foreign countries, elementary, secondary, or higher education emphasise the contextual variety of different educational systems. Convergent with this are demands to unify terminology and analytical frameworks, formulated in meta-academic review publications.

It is also worth noting that there has emerged a network of terms such as education and music education. Although at first sight these may appear disconnected from the main current of research on AI in education, their presence reflects the wider character of this field. The issues concerning learning and teaching in various subjects, scientific as well as artistic, are inextricably linked to questions of didactic strategies, models of interaction, evaluation of progress, and the development of students' competencies. At the same time, research anchored in the field of specific school disciplines contributes significantly to a reflection on the use of AI in education as a whole, and especially on this level, which is typical for SSH (disciplines focused on educational processes).

Thus, a map of the keywords has been developed, and it not only identifies dominant thematic axes, linked to the technological uses of AI, ethics, personalisation, or teacher competencies, but also shows their mutual relationships and points of cross-referencing. From that analysis emerges a dynamically developing field of study, which integrates perspectives from various areas, from technical sciences to pedagogics and psychology, to social sciences and humanities. Mutual influencing of these dimensions indicates the need for holistic approaches, taking into account both micro- as well as macrolevels of technology implementation—from didactic practice to educational policies.

This area is characterised by a high degree of dynamic and growing complexity. Its further development depends on the capacity to integrate various scholarly traditions, analytical tools, and contextual conditioning. Tendencies to systematise knowledge, build common conceptual frameworks, and undertake research are growing stronger and stronger, and this indicates that it is a maturing field of increasing importance for the future of education.

Based on the co-occurrence analysis of keywords, six main thematic categories were identified, which served as the framework for qualitative coding of full-text publications. The network of keywords revealed clear clusters and vectors, indicating the relationships between technological, socio-ethical, institutional, and disciplinary aspects of AI in education. These clusters informed the selection and justification of the following thematic categories:

1. **Use of AI in teaching and learning design**: This category reflects the central technological cluster in the keyword map, linking terms such as AI, educational technology, and instructional design. It represents research focused on integrating AI tools into didactic processes and designing flexible learning environments.
2. **Challenges and attitudes towards AI in education**: Emerging from the socio-ethical vector connected to the central technological cluster, this category encompasses studies examining perceptions, trust, barriers, and digital readiness, highlighting the importance of human factors in AI adoption.
3. **Ethical and social considerations**: Closely related to the previous cluster, this category corresponds to the ethical and institutional terms observed in the map, emphasising human-centric implementation, algorithmic transparency, bias, responsibility, and trust.
4. **Personalisation and adaptive learning tools**: Connected to technological terms such as ChatGPT, intelligent tutoring systems, and adaptive platforms, this category reflects the focus on tailoring learning pathways to individual needs, including inclusive education and support for learners with specific cognitive or communication challenges.

5. **AI in social sciences and humanities**: Represented by discipline-specific keywords extending from the central technological cluster, this category highlights research on AI applications in higher education and SSH disciplines, including literary analysis, history, ethics, political science, and the development of critical thinking.
6. **Meta-scientific reflections and systematic reviews**: Corresponding to keywords related to bibliometric and methodological analyses, this category captures studies reviewing trends, methods, and discrepancies between declared goals and practical implementation, demonstrating the field's growing systematisation and maturity.

The identification of these six categories demonstrates that research on AI in education is **multidimensional**, combining technological innovation, socio-ethical reflection, pedagogical practices, disciplinary applications, and meta-scientific evaluation. Each category directly links to specific clusters and thematic vectors in the keyword network, providing a **coherent framework for subsequent analysis**. In the next chapter, these categories will guide a detailed presentation of results, illustrating how AI is applied, perceived, and reflected upon across the social sciences and humanities.

DIRECTIONS OF RESEARCH ON AI IN EDUCATION

The first and central thematic category is the **use of AI in the didactics and design of learning**. Research in this area focuses on the integration of AI tools, such as chatbots, recommendation systems, or NLP models, with educational methods and the design of learning environments (Duran, 2024; Zhang et al., 2025a; Phillips et al., 2023), particularly highlighting the potential of AI to create adaptable and responsive learning spaces that support both teachers and students in the didactic process. Conceptual models (e.g. instructional design using AI) and empirical case studies illustrate how these technologies can be applied to personalise educational materials, automate grading and assessment (AI-powered marking), and provide tutoring tailored to individual needs (Létourneau et al., 2025). Adaptive learning systems and intelligent educational support platforms demonstrate significant effectiveness in improving student progress and increasing engagement (Ouyang et al., 2022). Additionally, attention has been drawn to the potential of tools such as ChatGPT in the context of lifelong learning, as AI technologies can provide continuous support for individualised, personalised learning in higher education (Rawas, 2024).

The second category is challenges and attitudes towards AI in education. Authors in this area analyse how teachers, students, and decision-makers perceive technology, focusing on aspects such as trust in AI, concerns about misuse, barriers to implementation, and users' levels of digital readiness (Bende, 2024; Giray, 2024). They emphasise the importance of teacher training and the development of digital competencies as prerequisites for effective AI integration in educational settings (Tsimpanis et al. 2023; Montenegro-Rueda et al., 2023). Mah, Lee, and Fung (2025) highlight the growing need to include AI literacy in educational programmes, understood as a combination of technological, critical, and ethical competencies necessary for conscious use of AI. Their research demonstrates that integrating AI education into mainstream curricula is key to effective programme reforms and better preparation of students and teachers to operate in digital environments (Mah et al., 2025).

The third category is ethical and social considerations. Literature increasingly emphasises the need for human-centric strategies when implementing AI in education (Sarı et al., 2024). This includes responsibility, algorithmic transparency, risk management, data privacy, and trust in technology (Nguyen et al., 2023). Empirical studies show that students' trust in AI systems is closely linked to the quality and transparency of information produced by these systems, directly affecting motivation and acceptance (Conijn et al., 2023). Ethical awareness among students and teachers, especially in secondary education, is becoming a key component of modern technological education (Er & Demirbilek, 2023). In this context, promoting reflection on algorithmic bias, designer accountability, and the socio-cultural consequences of AI use in education is essential (Idowu, 2024).

The fourth category is personalisation and adaptive learning tools, a theme frequently analysed in the literature. AI enables tailoring the teaching process to individual student needs, including learners with special educational needs (SEN). Tools such as intelligent tutoring systems, educational chatbots (e.g. ChatGPT), and adaptive teaching platforms allow the creation of individualised learning paths, particularly important in inclusive education (Hopcan et al., 2023; Marino et al., 2023). In recent years, research has increasingly focused on AI applications supporting students with communication and cognitive challenges, including the education of deaf students (Coy et al., 2025) and children with speech difficulties, through analyses linking pronunciation accuracy and language indicators in narratives (Case & Hallin, 2024).

The fifth category is AI in social sciences and humanities, which is slightly more specialised. Publications in this area focus on AI applications in teaching humanities and social studies subjects, particularly in higher education. These include literary text analysis, AI-supported history teaching, ethics, political sciences, and the development of critical thinking and argumentation skills using generative tools (Airaj, 2024; Coy et al., 2025; Joubin, 2024; Oliveira et al., 2025). Cultural, international, and institutional contexts play a critical role in shaping the implementation and acceptance of AI in academic environments (Alasadi & Baiz, 2023; Zhang et al., 2025a; Durak et al., 2024).

The sixth category is meta-scientific reflections and systematic reviews, which focus on research on the field of AI in education itself. Bibliometric and systematic literature analyses allow for the identification of dominant research trends, methodological evolution, and discrepancies between stated objectives and real-life implementation of AI in educational practice (Alasadi & Baiz, 2023; Durak et al., 2024; Montenegro-Rueda et al., 2023; Munaye et al., 2025; Zhang et al., 2025b; Qin & Zhang, 2025).

CONCLUSIONS

The results of the research clearly show that the discussion on AI in education is structured around distinct thematic areas, which reflect both **technological possibilities and broader educational, ethical, and social concerns** (Bittencourt et al., 2024; Chounta et al., 2022; Ifenthaler et al., 2024; Durak et al., 2024; Qin & Zhang, 2025).

This field integrates various perspectives, from technological science to pedagogy and psychology, to social sciences and humanities (Veletsianos et al., 2024). Such merging of disciplines indicates the necessity of a holistic approach, which includes the detailed aspects of didactic practices as well as wide frameworks of educational policy. In this way, research on AI in education applies also to **micro- and macrolevels of technology implementation** (Zhang et al., 2025a; Li et al., 2022).

What is noticeable in this dynamically developing area of study is the growing complexity of issues, which requires the putting together of various research traditions, analytical tools, and taking into account the specific context conditioning. Aspiration for the systematic ordering of knowledge, the creation of common terminological and conceptual frameworks, and the undertaking of comparative analyses is a clear sign of the **maturing of this scholarly field and the growing importance of research on AI in education** (Zhang et al., 2025b).

In addition, the range of researchers' interests has changed in recent years. Next to the questions of effectiveness and functionality of tools, growing attention is being paid to the **social, ethical, and cultural implications of AI in education**. Increasingly, a **person—user, beneficiary, co-creator of educational systems anchored in artificial intelligence—becomes the centre of attention** (Airaj, 2024; Sharples, 2023; Williams et al., 2023). This shift in research focus underlines the need to design solutions that will not only be technologically effective but also socially responsible (Poornesh, 2024; Idowu, 2024).

The **interdisciplinary character, dynamic development, and complexity of topics** demonstrate that the future of research on AI in education will require further integration of a variety of approaches and the creation of solutions suited to the **complex needs of contemporary education** (Bende, 2024; Mah et al., 2025; Montenegro-Rueda et al., 2023).

ACKNOWLEDGEMENTS

While preparing the article, the authors used tools built into the ERIC database, including functions supporting search, filtering, and metadata analysis (including AI-based tools available in the database interface). These solutions were used exclusively at the stage of initial record selection and search result organisation. All subsequent stages of the review, full-text analysis, coding, categorisation, and interpretation were carried out manually.

At a later stage, DeepL Write was also used for spell checking and language correction. After using these tools, the authors independently verified and edited the text and bear full responsibility for the content of the publication.

REFERENCES

Airaj, M. (2024). Ethical artificial intelligence for teaching-learning in higher education. *Education and Information Technologies*, *29*(13), 17145–17167.

Alasadi, E. A., & Baiz, C. R. (2023). Generative AI in education and research: Opportunities, concerns, and solutions. *Journal of Chemical Education*, *100*(8), 2965–2971.

Bende, I. (2024). Preparedness for artificial intelligence in education. *Acta Didactica Napocensia*, *17*(2), 29–36.

Bittencourt, I. I., Chalco, G., Santos, J., Fernandes, S., Silva, J., Batista, N., Hutz, C., & Isotani, S. (2024). Positive artificial intelligence in education (P-AIED): A roadmap. *International Journal of Artificial Intelligence in Education*, *34*(3), 732–792.

Case, J., & Hallin, A. E. (2024). The relationship between speech accuracy and linguistic measures in narrative retells of children with speech sound disorders. *Journal of Speech, Language, and Hearing Research*, *67*(9S), 3340–3358.

Cavalcanti, A. P., Mello, R. F., Gašević, D., & Freitas, F. (2024). Towards explainable prediction feedback messages using BERT. *International Journal of Artificial Intelligence in Education*, *34*(3), 1046–1071.

Chounta, I. A., Bardone, E., Raudsep, A., & Pedaste, M. (2022). Exploring teachers' perceptions of artificial intelligence as a tool to support their practice in Estonian K-12 education. *International Journal of Artificial Intelligence in Education*, *32*(3), 725–755.

Close, K., Warr, M., & Mishra, P. (2024). The ethical consequences, contestations, and possibilities of designs in educational systems. *TechTrends*, *68*(1), 186–194.

Conijn, R., Kahr, P., & Snijders, C. (2023). The effects of explanations in automated essay scoring systems on student trust and motivation. *Journal of Learning Analytics*, *10*(1), 37–53. https://doi.org/10.18608/jla.2023.7801

Cooper, H. M., Patall, E. A., & Lindsay, J. J. (2013). Research synthesis and meta-analysis. In L. Bickman & D. J. Rog (Eds.), *The SAGE handbook of applied social research methods* (2nd ed., pp. 344–370). SAGE Publications, Inc. https://doi.org/10.4135/9781483348858

Coy, A., Mohammed, P. S., & Skerrit, P. (2025). Inclusive deaf education enabled by artificial intelligence: The path to a solution. *International Journal of Artificial Intelligence in Education*, *35*(1), 96–134.

Dagenais Brown, J. (2003). The ERIC database: A comparison of four versions. *Reference Services Review*, *31*(2), 154–174.

Dornauer, V., Netzer, M., Kaczkó, É., Norz, L. M., & Ammenwerth, E. (2024). Automatic classification of online discussions and other learning traces to detect cognitive presence. *International Journal of Artificial Intelligence in Education*, *34*(2), 395–415.

Durak, G., Çankaya, S., Özdemir, D., & Can, S. (2024). Artificial intelligence in education: A bibliometric study on its role in transforming teaching and learning. *International Review of Research in Open and Distributed Learning*, *25*(3), 219–244.

Duran, V. (2024). Analyzing teacher candidates' arguments on AI integration in education via different chatbots. *Digital Education Review*, *45*, 68–83.

Er, E., & Demirbilek, M. (2023). AI ethics: An empirical study on the views on middle school students. In M. Demirbilek, M. S. Ozturk, & M. Unal (Eds.), *Proceedings of ICSES 2023—International conference on studies in education and social sciences* (pp. 334–350). Antalya, Turkey: ISTES Organization.

ERIC. (n.d.). *ERIC thesaurus. Institute of education sciences*. U.S. Department of Education. Retrieved April 27, 2026, from https://eric.ed.gov/?ti=ERIC+Thesaurus

Escotet, M. Á. (2024). The optimistic future of Artificial Intelligence in higher education. *Prospects*, *54*(3), 531–540.

Filiz, A., & Gür, H. (2025). Students' perceptions and applications of metacognitive awareness levels in problem solving with ChatGPT. *Educational Process: International Journal*, *14*, e2025063.

Fleischmann, K. (2024). Generative artificial intelligence in graphic design education: A student perspective. *Canadian Journal of Learning and Technology*, *50*(1), 1–17.

Giray, L. (2024). Ten myths about artificial intelligence in education. *Higher Learning Research Communications*, *14*(2), 1–12.

Google Cloud. (2025, February 27). Introducing new GenAI features in Vertex AI to support education and research. *Google Cloud Blog*. https://cloud.google.com/blog/products/ai-machine-learning/vertex-ai-genai-updates-education

Hertzberg, S., & Rudner, L. (1999). Quality of researchers' searches of the ERIC database. *Education Policy Analysis Archives*, *7*, 25.

Hopcan, S., Kuo, Y.-C., & Hwang, G.-J. (2023). Artificial intelligence in special education: A systematic review. *Journal of Educational Computing Research*, *61*(1), 3–28. https://doi.org/10.1080/10494820.2022.2067186

Idowu, J. A. (2024). Debiasing education algorithms. *International Journal of Artificial Intelligence in Education*, *34*(4), 1510–1540.

Ifenthaler, D., Majumdar, R., Gorissen, P., Judge, M., Mishra, S., Raffaghelli, J., & Shimada, A. (2024). Artificial intelligence in education: Implications for policymakers, researchers, and practitioners. *Technology, Knowledge and Learning*, *29*(4), 1693–1710.

Institute of Education Sciences. (n.d.). About ERIC. U.S. Department of Education. Retrieved April 27, 2026, from https://ies.ed.gov/use-work/education-research-database-eric

Joubin, A. A. (2024). Enhancing the trustworthiness of generative artificial intelligence in responsive pedagogy in the context of humanities higher education. In *General aspects of applying generative AI in higher education* (pp. 203–217). https://phys.org/news/2025-02-rethinking-ai-higher-professor-foster.html

Létourneau, A., Deslandes Martineau, M., Charland, P., Karran, J. A., Boasen, J., & Léger, P. M. (2025). A systematic review of AI-driven intelligent tutoring systems (ITS) in K-12 education. *NPJ Science of Learning*, *10*(1), 29.

Li, C., Xing, W., & Leite, W. L. (2022). Toward building a fair peer recommender to support help-seeking in online learning. *Distance Education*, *43*(1), 30–55.

Linderoth, C., Hultén, M., & Stenliden, L. (2024). Competing visions of artificial intelligence in education—A heuristic analysis on sociotechnical imaginaries and problematizations in policy guidelines. *Policy Futures in Education*, *22*(8), 1662–1678.

Mah, D. K., Lee, T., & Fung, H. (2025). Perspectives of academic staff on AI in higher education: Implications for instructional design and digital literacy. *Frontiers in Education*, *10*. https://doi.org/10.3389/feduc.2025.1484904

Marino, M. T., Vasquez, E., Dieker, L., Basham, J., & Blackorby, J. (2023). The future of artificial intelligence in special education technology. *Journal of Special Education Technology*, *38*(3), 404–416.

Microsoft Education Team. (2025, January 15). How Microsoft 365 Copilot transforms teaching and learning. *Microsoft Education Blog*. https://educationblog.microsoft.com/en-us/2025/01/microsoft-365-copilot-teaching-learning

Montenegro-Rueda, M., Fernández-Cerero, J., Fernández-Batanero, J. M., & López-Meneses, E. (2023). Impact of the implementation of ChatGPT in education: A systematic review. *Computers*, *12*(8), 153.

Munaye, Y. Y., Admass, W., Belayneh, Y., Molla, A., & Asmare, M. (2025). ChatGPT in education: A systematic review on opportunities, challenges, and future directions. *Algorithms*, *18*(6), 352.

Nguyen, A., Ngo, H. N., Hong, Y., Dang, B., & Nguyen, B. P. T. (2023). Ethical principles for artificial intelligence in education. *Education and Information Technologies*, *28*(4), 4221–4241.

Oliveira, L., Tavares, C., Strzelecki, A., & Silva, M. (2025). Prompting minds: Evaluating how students perceive generative AI's critical thinking dispositions. *Electronic Journal of E-Learning*, *23*(1), 1–18.

Ottenbreit-Leftwich, A., Glazewski, K., Jeon, M., Jantaraweragul, K., Hmelo-Silver, C. E., Scribner, A., … & Lester, J. (2023). Lessons learned for AI education with elementary students and teachers. *International Journal of Artificial Intelligence in Education*, *33*(2), 267–289.

Ouyang, F., Zheng, L., & Jiao, P. (2022). Artificial intelligence in online higher education: A systematic review of empirical research from 2011 to 2020. *Education and Information Technologies*, *27*(6), 7893–7925.

Page, M. J., McKenzie, J. E., Bossuyt, P. M., Boutron, I., Hoffmann, T. C., Mulrow, C. D., … & Moher, D. (2021). The PRISMA 2020 statement: an updated guideline for reporting systematic reviews. *BMJ*, 372.

Phillips, T. M., Saleh, A., & Ozogul, G. (2023). An AI toolkit to support teacher reflection. *International Journal of Artificial Intelligence in Education*, *33*(3), 635–658.

Poornesh, M. (2024). Through a teacher's lens: Combating bias in AI-powered education for a just future. *Clearing House: A Journal of Educational Strategies, Issues and Ideas*, *97*(4), 119–124.

Pradana, M., Elisa, H. P., & Syarifuddin, S. (2023). Discussing ChatGPT in education: A literature review and bibliometric analysis. *Cogent Education*, *10*(2), 2243134.

Qin, Q., & Zhang, S. (2025). Visualizing the knowledge mapping of artificial intelligence in education: A systematic review. *Education and Information Technologies*, *30*(1), 449–483.

Rawas, S. (2024). ChatGPT: Empowering lifelong learning in the digital age of higher education. *Education and Information Technologies*, *29*(6), 6895–6908.

Sabzalieva, E., & Valentini, A. (2023). ChatGPT and artificial intelligence in higher education: Quick start guide. https://unesdoc.unesco.org/ark:/48223/pf0000385146

Sanabria-Navarro, J. R., Silveira-Pérez, Y., Pérez-Bravo, D. D., & de-Jesús-Cortina-Núñez, M. (2023). Incidences of artificial intelligence in contemporary education. *Comunicar: Media Education Research Journal*, *31*(77), 93–103.

Sarı, T., Nayir, F., & Bozkurt, A. (2024). Reimagining education: Bridging artificial intelligence, transhumanism, and critical pedagogy. *Journal of Educational Technology and Online Learning*, *7*(1), 102–115.

Sharples, M. (2023). Towards social generative AI for education: Theory, practices and ethics. *Learning: Research and Practice*, *9*(2), 159–167.

Strayer, J. J. (2008). ERIC database alternatives and strategies for education researchers. *Reference Services Review*, *36*(1), 86–96.

Suliman, Z., Mohale, N. E., Maphoto, K. B., & Sevnarayan, K. (2024). The interconnectedness between Ubuntu principles and generative artificial intelligence in distance higher education institutions. *Discover Education*, *3*(1), 188.

Swindell, A., Greeley, L., Farag, A., & Verdone, B. (2024). Against artificial education: Towards an ethical framework for generative artificial intelligence (AI) use in education. *Online Learning*, *28*(2), n2.

Tao, L., Deng, H., & Song, Y. (2025). Generative artificial intelligence in education: A topic-based bibliometric analysis. *Educational Technology & Society*, *28*(2), 327–347.

Tsimpanis, K., Avouris, N. M., Chounta, I. A., Daskalaki, S., Dimitriadis, Y. A., Gari, C. M., Kalouptsoglou, A., Ortega-Arranz, A., & Balaouras, P. (2023). Implementing a data-driven framework for measuring digital readiness across European universities. In *EUNIS* (pp. 129–139).

Veletsianos, G., Houlden, S., & Johnson, N. (2024). Is artificial intelligence in education an object or a subject? Evidence from a story completion exercise on learner-AI interactions. *TechTrends*, *68*(3), 411–422.

Williams, R., Ali, S., Devasia, N., DiPaola, D., Hong, J., Kaputsos, S. P., & Breazeal, C. (2023). AI+ ethics curricula for middle school youth: Lessons learned from three project-based curricula. *International Journal of Artificial Intelligence in Education*, *33*(2), 325–383.

Zhang, F., Wang, X., & Zhang, X. (2025a). Applications of deep learning method of artificial intelligence in education. *Education and Information Technologies*, *30*(2), 1563–1587.

Zhang, J., Jantakoon, T., & Laoha, R. (2025b). Meta-analysis of artificial intelligence in education. *Higher Education Studies*, *15*(2), 189–210.

7 Research Applications of AI in the Social Sciences and Humanities

An Overview

Mirosława M. Długosz, Maria Stojkow, and Dorota Żuchowska-Skiba

INTRODUCTION

The development of artificial intelligence (AI) has, in recent years, been regarded as one of the most groundbreaking phenomena in contemporary science (Hajkowicz et al., 2023).

Dynamic progress in the field of machine learning, generative language models, and processing of semantic data not only changes the way many disciplines function but also re-defines relationships between technology and cognitive process, and reshapes structures, practices, and organisational models within contemporary scientific research (Bianchini et al., 2022; Bloom et al., 2020; Boeing & Hünermund, 2020).

At the outset, the development of AI was focused primarily within the boundaries of science and technological sciences, such as robotics, engineering, or applied mathematics (Klinger et al., 2020; Xu et al., 2021; Nolan, 2024). However, over time, this technology has grown to be a part of paradigms characteristic of social sciences and humanities (SSH). The evidence for this is the increasing number of studies reflecting on its role in the analysis of social, cultural, and communication phenomena (Farber, 2025; Gorenc, 2025). This is accompanied by the development of dedicated methodologies such as the ethical framework of AI-netnography (Cheah, 2025) or philosophical reflections on the cognitive state of machines and their relation to human intelligence (Edmond & Lehmann, 2021; Irwin, 2025).

Humanities and social science (HSS), traditionally rooted in interpretation, hermeneutics, and qualitative methods of exploration, increasingly treat artificial intelligence not only as a tool of automatisation but also as a co-creator of the research process. Literature on the subject points to new evidence regimes and digital interpretation practices, which transform the way analysis is carried out and the results are interpreted (Edmond, 2020; Ma et al., 2024; Munk et al., 2022). In this context, dynamic development of generative models transforms the methodological approach and publication procedures, including reviewing and editing practices (Nguyen-Trung, 2025; Bijker et al., 2024).

DOI: 10.1201/9781003676188-8

At the same time, AI expansion in SSH is linked to important challenges such as epistemological restrictions, lack of full transparency of models, dependence on the quality of training data, and the risk of reproduction of existing prejudice and cultural stereotypes (Mittelstad et al., 2016; Birhane, 2021; D'Ignazio & Klein, 2020). In addition, doubts arise in relation to the seizure by AI of those capacities hitherto seen as exclusively human, such as interpretation of sense, analysis of social context, or creative synthesis, giving rise to questions on the boundaries of delegation of understanding technology (Floridi, 2019; Bender & Koller, 2020).

On the other hand, from a global perspective, there appears to be a problem of epistemological inequalities. These inequalities primarily concern the sphere of scientific research—including differences in the ability to conduct data-intensive studies, implement advanced computational tools, and participate in the global circulation of knowledge (Xu et al., 2024; Bassanelli et al., 2025). Unequal access to research infrastructure and digital resources affects not only the pace of development within academic institutions but also their capacity to contribute to shaping international research agendas (Arancio, 2023).

It is important to emphasise that this introduction aims only to outline the scope of the literature review rather than to present all possible aspects of artificial intelligence. Its purpose is to highlight the key conceptual, methodological, and ethical issues developed in the subsequent sections, particularly those related to transformations in science, modes of knowledge production, and the role of AI in research processes (Bircan, & Özbilgin, 2025).

In light of these challenges and possibilities, there exists a need to systematically analyse the state of knowledge on the application of AI in SSH. The aim of this study is to provide a review of academic literature spanning 2022–2025, which will allow the identification of dominant directions of research, principal practical uses, and also epistemological and ethical tensions shaping the development of this dynamically evolving field.

METHODOLOGY

Literature review on the application of artificial intelligence (AI) in social sciences and humanities (SSH) has been carried out according to guidelines by PRISMA 2020 (Page, et al., 2021), which ensured the transparency of this study.

The identification phase included a literature search in the Scopus database for the period of 2022–2025. This particular database was chosen because of its interdisciplinary character, the high quality of sources reviewed, and the possibility of employing bibliometric tools (Falagas et al., 2008; Wang & Waltman, 2016; Donthu et al., 2021). The search included publications, in English, of the following document types: academic articles, literature reviews and academic reports, with the use of a combination of phrases combining technological and socio-humanities contexts, e.g. 'artificial intelligence' AND 'social sciences', 'machine learning', AND 'humanities', 'natural language processing' AND sociology, 'AI applications' AND 'SSH', 'algorithmic bias' OR 'data ethics' AND 'social research'. The selection of the time span of 2022–2025 was justified by the rapid development of generative artificial intelligence in that period and an increase in interest in its application in academic communication, research, and data analysis (OpenAI, 2023; Koo, 2025). At that stage, **703 publications** had been identified.

Cleansing and standardisation of data were carried out as the next step. This included the unification of terminology (e.g. 'AI', 'Artificial Intelligence (AI)', 'Artificial Intelligence') and the removal of duplicates, enabling the preparation of data for bibliometric analysis and the development of a map showing the co-occurrence of key words, where only relations fulfilling the condition weight ≥4 were taken into account. As a result, amongst the first 10,774 edges, 36 **strong links** were extracted, allowing identification of the principal thematic areas and facilitating connection of the publications to categories supporting the subsequent phases of the review.

The second phase of the selection process included a review of titles and summaries, as a result of which publications not relevant in terms of subject matter, repetitiveness, or non- fulfilment of formal criteria were removed. As a result, **126 publications** were selected and subjected to full-text analysis. During the **qualification** phase, qualitative coding of full texts was undertaken in order to ascribe them to thematic categories that had been selected inductively. These categories included, among others, research methodology, ethics and epistemology, language/translation/narrative, digital humanities, society/media/politics, human-AI interaction, education management, and the practical application of AI. This phase allowed for the selection of **42 publications** that have become the representative corpus for further analysis, making it possible to move to the phase of synthesis, during which a characteristic of each category was put together, key trends and re-occurring motifs were identified, and methodological and theoretical contexts were discussed.

CONNECTIONS BETWEEN AREAS OF STUDY OF AI IN SOCIAL SCIENCES AND HUMANITIES

The map of co-occurrence of key words (Figure 7.1) discloses a stable **network structure** of research, where 'Artificial Intelligence' and 'Machine Learning' are the methodological core of the whole network. Two mutually completing axes coming out of this centre can be identified: technological-methodological and socio-normative.

The technological-methodological axis incorporates terms such as 'Natural Language Processing', 'Deep Learning', 'Generative AI', 'large language models', and 'ChatGPT'. The closeness of those terms to the centre points to a shift from general declarations of AI application to precisely defined analytical practices, encompassing automatic transcription, information extraction, predictive modelling, and discourse analysis. The peripheral position of 'neural networks' signals historic, generic naming, while 'LLMs' and 'ChatGPT' represent the latest phase of application—task-based and anchored in textual data currents.

The socio-normative axis is formed by the nodes 'Social Sciences', 'Digital Humanities', and 'Computational Social Science', which fulfil the role of bridges between technology and social and cultural meaning. Through these nodes, there flow AI applications for the analysis of communication practices, knowledge circulation, or the dynamics of group attitudes. The presence of nodes such as 'AI ethics' and 'ethics' indicates that reflection on algorithmic bias, transparency, and responsibility forms an intrinsic part of all projects using AI in SSH, while ethical discussions influence the method of tools' implementation.

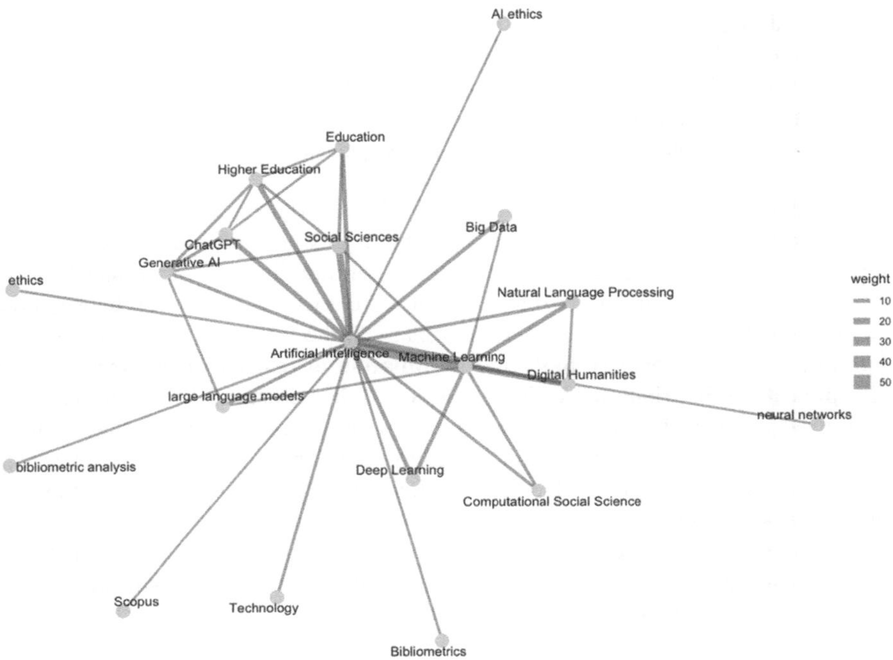

FIGURE 7.1 Map of connections of key terms in research on artificial intelligence and social sciences.

(Authors' own work.)

The map also distinguishes the **meta-scientific module** ('Bibliometrics', 'bibliometric analysis', and 'Scopus'). Links to the centre suggest that AI serves not only as a tool for studying society but also the science itself: tracking trends, cartography of research fields, and evaluation of the dynamics of disciplines.

The nodes 'Big Data' and 'Technology' create the implementation and technological context. Education is discussed separately here (see Chapter 6), which allows for a focus on analytical mechanisms, practical applications of AI, and ethical reflection.

In this text, we apply the following distinctions: AI refers to artificial intelligence in general, ML to machine learning techniques, and LLM to large language models used in generative AI.

On the basis of the analysis of the network, the publications were assigned five new analytical codes as follows:

1. **Conceptual and theoretical models**—literature reviews and theoretical frameworks defining the AI field in the area of SSH.
2. **Generative tools and automation of research processes**—uses of NLP, LLM, ChatGPT, automation of data processing, and analysis of information in research.
3. **Digital humanities and calculation methods**—digitisation, stylometry, machine translation, reconstruction of cultural masterpieces, and analysis of textual content.

4. **Challenges and ethics**—FATE (Fairness, Accountability, Transparency, Ethics), algorithmic bias, transparency, responsibility, and social risks.
5. **Empirical applications of AI in social research**—Predictive modelling, sentiment analysis, natural language processing in demographic, urbanistic, health, and financial studies, supporting expert and institutional decisions.

The analysis indicates that AI in SSH is evolving from the exploration phase to the institutionalisation process in which technologies are becoming an element of research infrastructure, and ethical and meta-scientific discourse continues to form the framework for their further development. To clarify the distinction between the analytical categories, particularly clusters 2 and 5, the following designations were introduced: **(2) 'Generative tools and automation of research processes'** and **(5) 'Empirical applications of AI in social research'**. Cluster 2 refers primarily to tools used by researchers during the research workflow, such as text generation, automated coding, data processing, and the organisation of research materials. Cluster 5, in contrast, captures instances in which artificial intelligence functions as a **method of data analysis** applied in empirical studies, for example, in predictive modelling, sentiment analysis, or the processing of large-scale social datasets. The key difference is that cluster 2 concerns tools supporting the **conduct of research**, whereas cluster 5 concerns the **use of AI as an analytical method** applied directly to social phenomena.

ARTIFICIAL INTELLIGENCE IN SOCIAL SCIENCES AND HUMANITIES

Categories isolated in the process create the point of departure for the systematic analysis of principal trends and directions in research on the application of AI in SSH. On the basis of those, it is possible to outline the characteristics of the key tools, practices, and ethical issues, as well as indicate the areas of use, which best reflect contemporary application of artificial intelligence in SSH.

The first research category is the conceptual and theoretical model in which artificial intelligence (AI) is used primarily for the automation processes of literature review, identification of research trends, and classification of academic disciplines. Systems based on AI support researchers in the exploration of a wide range of data, facilitating effective management of knowledge repositories and the development of recommendation systems, which make orientation in an ever-changing academic landscape much easier (Epstein, 2023; Castillo et al., 2024; Kasih et al., 2024).

Thanks to this, it is possible to streamline the processes of creation, evaluation, and distribution of scientific knowledge, which significantly affects the quality and transparency of research (Cox & Thelwall, 2025). AI tools allow for automatic analysis of quotations, identification of influential authors and publications, and discovery of new research areas. Systems analysing quotation networks facilitate visualisation of links between disciplines, and automated indexing and creation of databases allow for the rapid identification of important information when encountering a high density of publications (Chowdhury, 2023; Van Hooland & Coeckelbergs, 2022). The management of science also includes changes in the process of knowledge creation, reviews, evaluation of research, and creation of knowledge repositories. AI supports literature reviews, bibliometric analyses, and the development of recommendation systems for publication management (Cox & Thelwall, 2025).

Dominant in this category are works devoted to the application of AI in the processing of large sets of data, both qualitative and quantitative. Artificial intelligence finds its application in the automation of encoding processes, exploration of semantic patterns, and stylometry. The development of hybrid methodological approaches, merging elements of classical research methods with techniques of computational social sciences, is also emphasised (Bryda & Costa, 2023; Andreev, et al., 2025; De Paoli, 2024).

Practical Implementation and Generative Tools in SSH

Generative artificial intelligence (GenAI), using language models based on deep learning, is gaining significance in academic research, supporting such processes as creating literature reviews, generating hypotheses, or constructing theories (Schryen et al., 2025; Lim et al., 2023; Cook et al., 2025). Artificial intelligence technologies are increasingly used in academic writing, including the automation of text creation, summarisation of information, and supportive writing, and the structuring of academic work (Glickman & Zhang, 2024; Liebling et al., 2025; Khalifa & Albadawy, 2024). Large Language Models support the production of summaries of articles, literature reviews, academic translations, and the creation of research plans and grant projects, significantly shortening the time required for preliminary preparation of documentation (Khalifa & Albadawy, 2024).

Jarvenpaa and Klein (2024) point to the potential of GenAI in supporting the formulation of theories in the field of information systems, while Benbya et al. (2024) discuss the possibilities of GenAI application in the process of knowledge creation and creative work. However, integration of LLMs and systems such as ChatGPT in research practices requires the compilation of relevant ethical and procedural guidelines, which will ensure transparency, reliability, and responsibility in the application of AI in science (Berry, et al., 2025; Qiu et al., 2025).

Despite its potential benefits, the application of generative AI (GenAI) is associated with certain challenges. Susarla (2023) highlights the risk of 'model hallucination', meaning that generative AI models may produce fabricated or inaccurate information. Bender et al. (2021) critique GenAI for lacking a genuine understanding of the content generated, describing these models as 'stochastic parrots' that merely reconstruct sentences based on pre-trained sequences without true comprehension. While the 'stochastic parrots' metaphor (Bender et al., 2021) has been influential, some scholars note that it oversimplifies the emergent capabilities of contemporary generative models. The literature emphasises the need for critical evaluation of generated materials and the implementation of quality control mechanisms and plagiarism prevention to ensure credibility and the responsible application of GenAI tools in academic work (Berry et al., 2025).

Digital humanities and methods of calculation include digitisation, stylometry, machine-supported translations, reconstruction of cultural works, and the analysis of textual content (Alvero et al., 2025; Bolt et al., 2025; Harisanty et al., 2024,

Pavlidis, 2022). AI is used for analysis of cultural texts, generation and analysis of texts, automatic classification and comparison of texts, exploration of semantic models, stylometry, and digital hermeneutics (Fiedler & Döpke, 2025; Kurzynski, 2025; Nielsen & Zhou, 2025; Leong, 2025; Alvero et al., 2025; Moreno-Ortiz, 2024).

In cultural research, AI supports the analysis of art, literature, and philosophy. Tools based on machine learning make it possible to classify images, process manuscripts, and map cultural contexts in source data (Shahi et al., 2025; Leong, 2025; Meinecke et al., 2022). These technologies allow for modelling and exploration of complex narrative structures, tracing how ideas and cultural practices change and discovering hitherto inaccessible information in source materials (Kurzynski, 2025; Qian & Xie, 2026; Leong, 2025; Alvero et al., 2025).

AI also supports the development of academic research in social sciences and humanities, including the digitisation of cultural heritage, stylometry, and machine-supported translations. It facilitates the mapping of complex cultural contexts, classification and reconstruction of artworks, and the analysis of literature, history, and philosophy, opening up new research possibilities and allowing for more thorough interpretations of data which had, thus far, been inaccessible (Alvero et al., 2025; Sebastian et al., 2025).

The integration of AI with digital humanities enables the processing of large sets of data and support for qualitative and quantitative research, including narrative analysis, simulation of social behaviours, and decision-making in cultural studies (Gupta et al., 2025; Kozlowski & Evans, 2025; Qiu et al., 2025; Pavlidis, 2022). Such an approach leads to the emergence of new academic paradigms linking the humanities, social sciences, and digital technologies, facilitating a deeper understanding of language and culture (Friese, 2025).

Practical Application in SSH

The practical application of AI in social sciences includes predictive modelling, analysis of sentiment, and processing of natural language in demographic, urbanistic, health, and financial studies. These technologies support classification and predictive processes, increasing precision and effectiveness of expert and institutional decisions (Gohr et al., 2025; Khan & Almulhem, 2025; Do et al., 2024). As part of social, political, and media-narrative-centred analysis, researchers focus on the influence of AI on public communication, opinion polarisation, the spreading of disinformation and shaping of public debates, taking into account issues of propaganda, systemic racism, algorithmic bias, and the reception of political conflicts (Duridi et al., 2025; Pavlović & Hafner Fink, 2024).

Equally essential are studies on human interaction with AI, which concentrate on cooperation, trust, and mutual decision-making between humans and AI systems. Particular emphasis is placed on the human-centred AI, collective intelligence, and modelling of social agents in experimental conditions (Farber, 2025). These studies have practical implications and are directed towards finding solutions to real-life social and economic challenges with the use of effective methods of data analysis and prediction (Gohr et al., 2025; Khan & Almulhem, 2025; Liu et al., 2024).

CONCLUSIONS

Our analysis demonstrates that the five identified analytical categories, conceptual models, generative and practical tools, digital humanities, ethical challenges, and empirical applications, together form a coherent framework that reveals how AI is becoming structurally embedded in SSH research practices. In particular, we argue that the most dynamic transformations occur at the intersection of generative tools and empirical modelling, where automation and large-scale text analysis reshape methodological conventions. This intersection also illustrates how the methodological landscape of SSH is shifting towards hybrid human-AI research workflows, increasingly reliant on computational capacities previously unavailable within traditional qualitative and interpretative paradigms.

The application of artificial intelligence in SSH is characterised by a high degree of interdisciplinary input and thematic complexity. Integration of methods and theories ensuing from social sciences, humanities, and computer technologies facilitates a multidimensional approach to research issues and creates a wide range of possibilities for practical applications of AI in various academic contexts (Leong, 2025). What appears especially significant is an improvement of processes linked to knowledge management, such as bibliometric analysis or literature reviews, leading to an increase in the quality of research work and more effective creation and evaluation of academic knowledge (Cox & Thelwall, 2025; Khalil et al., 2025). Our findings confirm that the growing use of computational techniques does not replace established qualitative traditions, but instead creates new forms of complementarity between interpretative and algorithmic approaches.

At the same time, the development of AI tools generates ethical and regulatory challenges. Problems related to algorithmic bias, restricted transparency, and the lack of unambivalent responsibility in the use of AI require the compilation of consistent legislative and ethical frameworks. Especially important in the context of generative language models is the introduction of mechanisms limiting risks of abuse and ensuring the integrity of research processes (Raman, 2025; Gorenc, 2025; Ashruf, 2026). These concerns are amplified in LLMs, which operate as probabilistic systems capable of producing plausible, yet fabricated, outputs, thereby raising questions about authorship, data provenance, and reproducibility in research.

Generative tools, including LLMs, significantly transform day-to-day research practices, influencing text generation, summarising of materials, and analysis of data (Zhang et al., 2025). Integration of those models in SSH allows for a more effective processing of large sets of data and supports the development of digital humanities by machine translation and digitisation of cultural heritage (Leong, 2025; Alvero et al., 2025). At the same time, their application requires a critical approach and systematic verification of results, because generative models may generate imprecise or fabricated content not reflecting the author's intention (Zhang et al., 2025). This necessitates the development of discipline-specific validation protocols to ensure accuracy, reliability, and transparency in computationally assisted outputs.

Application of LLMs in the analysis of text data, such as thematic analysis or theme modelling, streamlines interdisciplinary research, facilitating the scaling of analysis of large amounts of source materials (Glickman & Zhang, 2024; Ali et al., 2024).

In digital humanities, AI supports the development of advanced methods of text analysis, machine translation, and digitisation of cultural heritage, which opens up new research perspectives and facilitates the protection and popularisation of cultural resources (Leong, 2025; Alvero et al., 2025). Across these domains, computational tools extend the scope of what can be examined, enabling new empirical insights and methodological experimentation that would be difficult to achieve through manual analysis alone.

The practical application of AI in applied sciences, such as demography, urban planning, or public health, has a measurable impact on the making of social and economic decisions, emphasising the role of AI as a tool supporting the analysis and solving of complex social problems (Gohr et al., 2025; Khan & Almulhem, 2025). From the perspective of further research, it is key to both deepen the interdisciplinary approach and systematically create and update regulations and ethical standards relevant to the specifics of SSH. A conscious and critical integration of AI tools in research processes remains a necessary measure ensuring reliability, methodological cohesion, and academic responsibility. Our analysis highlights that this integration must proceed with awareness of the epistemic traditions of SSH, ensuring that computational tools amplify rather than distort established interpretative practices.

Based on the reviewed literature, we conclude that the next stage of AI integration in SSH will require not only methodological innovation but also conscious normative work: the development of ethical standards, transparent reporting procedures, and interpretative frameworks appropriate for hybrid human-AI research environments. We emphasise that responsible adoption—critical, reflective, and methodologically aware—is essential to ensuring scientific integrity and maintaining the distinctive epistemic value of SSH. This includes developing conventions for documenting AI involvement in research, clarifying authorship boundaries, and establishing shared expectations regarding verification of AI-assisted analyses.

Finally, we argue that AI should be seen not merely as a technological instrument but as a transformative research infrastructure whose influence reshapes the ways knowledge is produced, validated, and disseminated in SSH. As AI systems become increasingly embedded in everyday research routines, their infrastructural role will continue to shape epistemic norms, research agendas, and the organisation of academic labour.

LIMITATIONS

This study has several limitations. First, the literature analysed is drawn primarily from Scopus, which overrepresents English-language research and publications from the Global North. As a result, scholarship from the Global South remains underrepresented, and some regional perspectives may not be fully reflected.

Second, the rapid development of AI technologies creates a recency bias: research published after 2022 reflects fast-moving trends, making it difficult to capture developments that have emerged only in the most recent years.

Third, the terminology used across the reviewed literature is inconsistent. Terms such as 'AI', 'LLM', and 'generative tools' are often used interchangeably, which complicates classification and affects conceptual clarity.

Finally, although our analytical categories provide a useful overview of current research directions, they represent only one possible way of organising a rapidly evolving field and may require further refinement as new methodologies and applications emerge.

ACKNOWLEDGEMENTS

While preparing the article, the authors used tools available in the Scopus database, including advanced search functions, citation analysis, and AI-powered insights. These tools were used during the initial literature review carried out as part of a broader research project.

The solutions available in Scopus only supported the first stage of record selection and meta-data review. All further stages of the analysis, including full-text evaluation, data synthesis, and interpretation of results, were performed manually.

At the final stage of the work, DeepL Write was used for linguistic correction. After using this tool, the authors independently verified the content and bear full responsibility for the final version of the study.

REFERENCES

Ali, D., Milleville, K., Verstockt, S., Van de Weghe, N., Chambers, S., & Birkholz, J. M. (2024). Computer vision and machine learning approaches for metadata enrichment to improve searchability of historical newspaper collections. *Journal of Documentation*, *80*(5), 1031–1056. https://doi.org/10.1108/jd-01-2022-0029

Alvero, A. J., Sedlacek, Q., León, M., & Peña, C. (2025). Digital accents, homogeneity-by-design, and the evolving social science of written language. https://doi.org/10.1017/S0267190525000042

Andreev, H., Pericleous, K., & Kosmas, P. (2025). Expanding the frontiers: Revolutionizing quantitative data analysis in social sciences with AI. In W. P. A. Christou (red.), *Artificial intelligence (AI) in social research* (pp. 37–47). Routledge. https://doi.org/10.1079/9781800626607.0004

Arancio, J. (2023). From inequalities to epistemic innovation: Insights from open science hardware projects in Latin America. *Environmental Science & Policy*, *150*, 103576.

Ashruf, C. (2026). Artificial intelligence through the eyes of Hannah Arendt: Fear, alienation, and empowerment. *AI & Society*, *41*, 455–462.

Bassanelli, S., Kinyanjui, C., & Turchetti, S., (2025). Mapping inequalities in the global availability of physics data over time. *Nature Reviews Physics 7*, 168–170. https://doi.org/10.1038/s42254-025-00821-9

Benbya, H., Strich, F., & Tamm, T. (2024). Navigating generative artificial intelligence promises and perils for knowledge and creative work. *Journal of the Association for Information Systems*, *25*(1), 23–36.

Bender, E. M., Gebru, T., McMillan-Major, A., & Shmitchell, S. (2021, March). On the dangers of stochastic parrots: Can language models be too big?. In *Proceedings of the 2021 ACM conference on fairness, accountability, and transparency* (pp. 610–623).

Bender, E. M., & Koller, A. (2020). Climbing towards NLU: On meaning, form, and understanding in the age of data. *Proceedings of the 58th Annual Meeting of the Association for Computational Linguistics*, 5185–5198. https://doi.org/10.18653/v1/2020.acl-main.463

Berry, K., Kumar, S., Kaushik, R., & Shukla, A. (2025). Convergence of AI and metaverse: Pioneering new frontiers in scientific research. In M. H. Al Aqad, A. S. Azar, A. Albattat, & A. Singh (eds.), *Navigating AI and the metaverse in scientific research* (pp. 77–98). IGI Global.

Bianchini, S., Müller, M., & Pelletier, P. (2022). Artificial intelligence in science: An emerging general method of invention. *Research Policy*, *51*(10), 104604.

Bijker, R., Schmit, C., Khalafi, R., Stassen, P., & Tummers, P. (2024). ChatGPT for automated qualitative research: Content analysis of online health communities. *Journal of Medical Internet Research*, *26*, e59050.

Bircan, T., & Özbilgin, M. F. (2025). Unmasking inequalities of the code: Disentangling the nexus of AI and inequality. *Technological Forecasting and Social Change*, *211*, 123925.

Birhane, A. (2021). Algorithmic injustice: A relational ethics approach. *Patterns*, *2*(2), 100205. https://doi.org/10.1016/j.patter.2021.100205

Bloom, N., Jones, C. I., Van Reenen, J., & Webb, M. (2020). Are ideas getting harder to find?. *American Economic Review*, *110*(4), 1104–1144.

Boeing, P., & Hünermund, P. (2020). A global decline in research productivity? Evidence from China and Germany. *Economics Letters*, *197*, 109646.

Bolt, T. J., Adams, E. D., Adramerinas, Z., Burns, P. J., Dasgupta, T., Deng, A., … & Dexter, J. P. (2025). Stylometric criticism of latin literature: From exploratory data analysis to close reading. *TAPA*, *155*(1), 205–250.

Bryda, G., & Costa, A. P. (2023). Qualitative research in the digital era: Innovations, methodologies and collaborations. *Social Sciences*, *12*(10), 570.

Castillo, V. S., Zapata, R. E., & Gamboa, A. J. P. (2024, November). Artificial intelligence and writing: Trends and future directions in the social sciences. In *The International Conference on Artificial Intelligence and Smart Environment* (pp. 488–497). Springer Nature Switzerland.

Cheah, C. W. (2025). AI-augmented netnography: Ethical and methodological frameworks for responsible digital research. *International Journal of Qualitative Methods*, *24*, 16094069251338910.

Chowdhury, K. P. (2023). Nonparametric functional analysis under joint estimation with applications for identifying highly cited papers. *Journal of Informetrics*, *17*(4), 101446.

Cook, D. A., Ginsburg, S., Sawatsky, A. P., Kuper, A., & D'Angelo, J. D. (2025). Artificial intelligence to support qualitative data analysis: Promises, approaches, pitfalls. *Academic Medicine: Journal of the Association of American Medical Colleges*, https://doi.org/10.1097/ACM.0000000000006134

Cox, A., & Thelwall, M. (2025). *AI for knowledge*. CRC Press.

De Paoli, S. (2024). Performing an inductive thematic analysis of semi-structured interviews with a large language model: An exploration and provocation on the limits of the approach. *Social Science Computer Review*, *42*(4), 997–1019.

D'Ignazio, C., & Klein, L. F. (2020). *Data feminism*. MIT Press. https://mitpress.mit.edu/books/data-feminism

Do, S., Ollion, É., & Shen, R. (2024). The augmented social scientist: Using sequential transfer learning to annotate millions of texts with human-level accuracy. *Sociological Methods & Research*, *53*(3), 1167–1200. https://doi.org/10.1177/00491241221134526

Donthu, N., Kumar, S., Mukherjee, D., Pandey, N., & Lim, W. M. (2021). How to conduct a bibliometric analysis: An overview and guidelines. *Journal of Business Research*, *133*, 285–296. https://doi.org/10.1016/j.jbusres.2021.04.070

Duridi, T., Atwe, L., Jaber, A., Daraghmi, E., & Martínez, P. (2025, April). Detection of propaganda and bias in social media: A case study of the israel-gaza war (2023). In *2025 International Conference on New Trends in Computing Sciences (ICTCS)* (pp. 204–210). IEEE.

Edmond, J. (2020). Introduction: Power, practices, and the gatekeepers of humanistic research in the digital age. In J. Edmond (Ed.), *Digital technology and the practices of humanities research* (pp. 1–20). Open Book Publishers. https://doi.org/10.11647/OBP.0333

Edmond, J., & Lehmann, J. (2021). Digital humanities, knowledge complexity, and the five 'aporias' of digital research. *Digital Scholarship in the Humanities*, *36*(Supplement_2), ii95–ii108.

Epstein, J. M. (2023). Inverse generative social science: Backward to the future. *Journal of Artificial Societies and Social Simulation: JASSS*, *26*(2), 9.

Falagas, M. E., Pitsouni, E. I., Malietzis, G. A., & Pappas, G. (2008). Comparison of PubMed, Scopus, web of science, and google scholar: Strengths and weaknesses. *The FASEB Journal*, *22*(2), 338–342. https://doi.org/10.1096/fj.07-9492LSF

Farber, S. (2025). Comparing human and AI expertise in the academic peer review process: Towards a hybrid approach. *Higher Education Research & Development*. https://doi.org/10.1080/07294360.2024.2445575

Fiedler, A., & Döpke, J. (2025). Do humans identify AI-generated text better than machines? Evidence based on excerpts from German theses. *International Review of Economics Education*, *49*, 100321.

Floridi, L. (2019). *The logic of information: A theory of philosophy as conceptual design*. Oxford University Press. https://doi.org/10.1093/oso/9780198833635.001.0001

Friese, S. (2025). Generative AI: A catalyst for paradigmatic change in qualitative data analysis. In *Artificial intelligence (AI) in social research* (pp. 71–83). CABI. Digital Library. https://doi.org/10.1079/9781800626607.0007

Glickman, M., & Zhang, Y. (2024). AI and generative AI for research discovery and summarization. *Harvard Data Science Review*, *6*(2). https://doi.org/10.1162/99608f92.7f9220ff

Gohr, C., et al. (2025). Artificial intelligence in sustainable development research. https://doi.org/10.1038/s41893-025-01598-6

Gorenc, N. (2025). AI embedded bias on social platforms. *International Review of Sociology*, 1–20. https://doi.org/10.1080/03906701.2025.2489056

Gupta, P., Nguyen, T. N., Gonzalez, C., & Woolley, A. W. (2025). Fostering collective intelligence in human–AI collaboration: Laying the groundwork for COHUMAIN. *Topics in Cognitive Science*, *17*(2), 189–216.

Hajkowicz, S., Sanderson, C., Karimi, S., Bratanova, A., & Naughtin, C. (2023). Artificial intelligence adoption in the physical sciences, natural sciences, life sciences, social sciences and the arts and humanities: A bibliometric analysis of research publications from 1960–2021. *Technology in Society*, *74*, 102260. https://doi.org/10.1016/j.techsoc.2023.102260

Harisanty, D., Obille, K. L. B., Anna, N. E. V., Purwanti, E., & Retrialisca, F. (2024). Cultural heritage preservation in the digital age, harnessing artificial intelligence for the future: A bibliometric analysis. *Digital Library Perspectives*, *40*(4), 609–630.

Irwin, R. (2025). Stiegler and Butler on AI and the evolution of intelligence. *Educational Philosophy and Theory*, 57(5), 473–488.

Jarvenpaa, S., & Klein, S. (2024). New Frontiers in Information Systems Theorizing: Human-gAI Collaboration. *Journal of the Association for Information Systems*, *25*(1), 37–181.

Kasih, E. N. E. W., Indriyanto, K., & Putra, A. V. L. (2024). Artificial intelligence for literature class: Trends and attitude. In *2024 10th International Conference on Education and Technology (ICET)* (pp. 142–148). IEEE.

Khalifa, M., & Albadawy, M. (2024). Using artificial intelligence in academic writing and research: An essential productivity tool. *Computer Methods and Programs in Biomedicine Update*, *5*, 100145.

Khalil, M., Liu, Q., & Jovanovic, J. (2025). AI for data generation in education: Towards learning and teaching support at scale. *British Journal of Educational Technology*, *56*(3), 993–998.

Khan, M. R. A., & Almulhem, A. (2025). Behavioral and propagation-based analysis of APT attacks for effective attack attribution. In *2025 13th International Symposium on Digital Forensics and Security (ISDFS)* (pp. 1–8). IEEE. https://doi.org/10.1109/ISDFS65363.2025.11012042

Klinger, J., Mateos-Garcia, J., & Stathoulopoulos, K. (2020). A narrowing of AI research?. *arXiv preprint arXiv:2009.10385*.

Koo, M. (2025). ChatGPT research: A bibliometric analysis based on the web of science from 2023 to June 2024. *Knowledge*, 5(1), 4. https://doi.org/10.3390/knowledge5010004

Kozlowski, A. C., & Evans, J. (2025). Simulating subjects: The promise and peril of artificial intelligence stand-ins for social agents and interactions. *Sociological Methods & Research*, *54*(3), 1017–1073.

Kurzynski, M. (2025). Poly-temporal, multi-layered: A techno-cognitive theory of narrative experience in literature. *International Journal of Humanities and Arts Computing*, *19*(1), 33–48.

Leong, W. Y. (2025, January). AI-powered color restoration of faded historical paintings. In *2025 Joint International Conference on Digital Arts, Media and Technology with ECTI Northern Section Conference on Electrical, Electronics, Computer and Telecommunications Engineering (ECTI DAMT & NCON)* (pp. 623–627). IEEE.

Liebling, D. J., Kane, M., Grunde-Mclaughlin, M., Lang, I., Venugopalan, S., & Brenner, M. (2025, May). Towards AI-assisted academic writing. In *Proceedings of the 1st Workshop on AI and Scientific Discovery: Directions and Opportunities* (pp. 31–45).

Lim, W. M., Gunasekara, A., Pallant, J. L., Pallant, J. I., & Pechenkina, E. (2023). Generative AI and the future of education: Ragnarök or reformation? A paradoxical perspective from management educators. *The International Journal of Management Education*, *21*(2), 100790.

Liu, C.-L., Chang, W.-T., Chu, C.-T., & Zheng, T.-Y. (2024). Machine learning and data analysis for word segmentation of classical Chinese poems: Illustrations with Tang and Song examples. *Digital Scholarship in the Humanities*, *39*(1), 228–241. https://doi.org/10.1093/llc/fqad073

Ma, R., Dedema, M., & Cox, A. (2024). A dancing bear, a colleague, or a sharpened toolbox? The cautious adoption of generative AI technologies in digital humanities research. https://arxiv.org/abs/2404.12458

Meinecke, C., Hall, C., & Jänicke, S. (2022). Towards enhancing virtual museums by contextualizing art through interactive visualizations. *ACM Journal on Computing and Cultural Heritage*, *15*(4), 1–26.

Mittelstadt, B. D., Allo, P., Taddeo, M., Wachter, S., & Floridi, L. (2016). The ethics of algorithms: Mapping the debate. *Big Data & Society*, *3*(2), 2053951716679679.

Moreno-Ortiz, A. (2024). Making sense of large social media corpora: Keywords, topics, sentiment, and hashtags in the Coronavirus Twitter corpus. In *Making sense of large social media corpora* (pp. 1–18). Palgrave Macmillan. https://doi.org/10.1007/978-3-031-52719-7_1

Munk, A. K., Olesen, A. G., & Jacomy, M. (2022). The thick machine: Anthropological AI between explanation and explication. *Big Data & Society*, *9*(1), 20539517211069891.

Nguyen-Trung, K. (2025). ChatGPT's potential in qualitative content analysis. *Quality & Quantity*. https://doi.org/10.1007/s11135-025-02165-z

Nielsen, R. A., & Zhou, A. Y. (2025). Integrating social science research across languages with assistance from artificial intelligence. *Dædalus*, *154*(2), 51–67.

Nolan, A. (2024). Artificial intelligence in science: Challenges, opportunities and the future of research. https://www.oecd.org/en/publications/artificial-intelligence-in-science_a8d820bd-en/full-report/artificial-intelligence-in-science-overview-and-policy-proposals_c1489d23.html?utm_source=chatgpt.com

OpenAI. (2023). *GPT-4 technical report*. https://openai.com/research/gpt-4

Page, M. J., McKenzie, J. E., Bossuyt, P. M., Boutron, I., Hoffmann, T. C., Mulrow, C. D., & Moher, D. (2021). The PRISMA 2020 statement: An updated guideline for reporting systematic reviews. *BMJ*, 372, n71. https://doi.org/10.1136/bmj.n71

Pavlidis, G. (2022). AI trends in digital humanities research. *Trends in Computer Science and Information Technology*, *7*(2), 26–34. https://doi.org/10.17352/tcsit.000048

Pavlović, P., & Hafner Fink, M. (2024). New ethnographic perspective on relational ethics in the field of artificial intelligence. *Quality & Quantity*, *58*(1), 1–19. https://doi.org/10.1007/s11135-023-01751-3

Qian, P., & Xie, X. (2026). Task–technology fit leads to conflict: The double-edged-sword effect of generative artificial intelligence on scientific creative performance in humanities and social sciences research. *International Journal of Human–Computer Interaction*, *42*, 1867–1891.

Qiu, S., Tang, Y., Yu, H., Xie, H., Dreher, J. C., Hu, Y., & Zhou, X. (2025). Toward a computational understanding of bribe-taking behavior. *Annals of the New York Academy of Sciences*, *1545*(1), 5–15.

Raman, R. (2025). Transparency in research: An analysis of ChatGPT usage acknowledgment by authors across disciplines and geographies. *Accountability in Research*, *32*(3), 277–298.

Schryen, G., Marrone, M., & Yang, J. (2025). Exploring the scope of generative AI in literature review development. *Electronic Markets*, *35*(1), 13.

Sebastian, R., Kottekkadan, N. N., Thomas, T. K., & Niyas K. K. (2025). Generative AI tools (ChatGPT*) in social science research. *Journal of Information, Communication and Ethics in Society*, *23*(2), 284–290.

Shahi, M., Rajabi, R., & Masoumzadeh, F. (2025). CNN-based classification of Persian miniature paintings from five renowned schools. *Digital Applications in Archaeology and Cultural Heritage*, *36*, e00397.

Susarla, A., Gopal, R., Thatcher, J. B., & Sarker, S. (2023). The Janus effect of generative AI: Charting the path for responsible conduct of scholarly activities in information systems. *Information Systems Research*, *34*(2), 399–408.

van Hooland, S., & Coeckelbergs, M. 2022. Exploring large-scale digital archives–opportunities and limits to use unsupervised machine learning for the extraction of semantics. In *Handbook of digital public history* (pp. 517–530). De Gruyter Oldenbourg.

Wang, Q., & Waltman, L. (2016). Large-scale analysis of the accuracy of the journal classification systems of Web of Science and Scopus. *Journal of Informetrics*, *10*(2), 347–364.

Xu, R., Sun, Y., Ren, M., Guo, S., Pan, R., Lin, H., Sun, L., & Han, X. (2024). AI for social science and social science of AI: A survey. *Information Processing & Management*, *61*(6), 103665. https://doi.org/10.1016/j.ipm.2024.103665

Xu, Y., Liu, X., Cao, X., Huang, C., Liu, E., Qian, S., & Zhang, J. (2021). Artificial intelligence: A powerful paradigm for scientific research. *The Innovation*, *2*(4), 100179.

Zhang, S., Xu, J., & Alvero, A. J. (2025). Generative AI meets open-ended survey responses: Research participant use of AI and homogenization. *Sociological Methods & Research*, *54*(3), 1197–1242.

8 AI in Specialised Education and Professional Training

Alla Ishchuk and Mykhailo Ishchuk

INTRODUCTION

The integration of artificial intelligence in higher education presents complex challenges for specialised professional training programmes worldwide. Universities all around the world are experimenting with AI-tutoring systems, automated grading, and administrative tools. But adoption looks different everywhere. Humanities departments move more slowly than others, testing AI for language teaching and text analysis while wrestling with basic questions about what this technology actually does to learning.

This technological adoption raises critical questions about educational integrity. This reflects concerns Chen (2025) raises about AI potentially bypassing learning processes—something we see when students submit AI-generated writing without doing the underlying research or critical thinking. The same dilemmas surface across teaching contexts: distinguishing helpful AI use from academic shortcuts, evaluating work that may be machine-generated, and preserving critical thinking when AI provides seemingly definitive responses. When does AI help become an academic crutch? How do we evaluate work that might be partly machine-written?

When AI gives confident-sounding answers, critical thinking becomes much harder to maintain. These concerns extend beyond theoretical considerations. Our daily teaching experiences in Ukrainian universities reveal both AI's educational potential and its significant limitations within resource-constrained environments where unreliable infrastructure, connectivity issues, and competing institutional priorities complicate technology integration.

These contextual factors make systematic examination essential. This study adopts a comparative approach to investigate responsible AI integration within Ukrainian higher education, focusing on pedagogical rather than technological considerations. Rather than evaluating specific software solutions, we address fundamental questions: How might AI enhance authentic learning? Where does it pose risks to educational processes? How can institutions preserve educational humanistic values while adapting to technological change?

 DOI: 10.1201/9781003676188-9

Ukrainian universities face distinctive implementation challenges compared to international counterparts already deploying comprehensive AI systems and established usage policies. Most Ukrainian universities still rely on traditional teaching methods and basic digital tools. This is not just institutional conservatism—it reflects deeper problems with resources and infrastructure.

The ongoing war has forced universities to focus on survival rather than innovation. When buildings are damaged and students and faculty are displaced, keeping basic education running takes priority over investigating new technologies.

Other problems compound these challenges. Faculty often lack technical knowledge or training support for AI integration. University budgets, already tight due to economic pressures, rarely include funding for AI software or training. Internet access varies significantly between urban and rural areas, limiting some students' ability to use AI tools reliably. Even when educators show interest, practical obstacles make implementation difficult. Students typically know these technologies better than their professors—ChatGPT awareness is slightly higher among students (73%) than teachers (69%) (Kononova et al., 2024; Dovgyi et al., 2024: 211).

However, these constraints may offer unexpected advantages. Ukrainian educators' extensive experience with resource limitations has fostered adaptability and pragmatic problem-solving approaches. This background encourages selective technology adoption based on genuine pedagogical value rather than novelty, potentially yielding more educationally sound integration strategies.

We examine AI's role in specialised education through a comparative analysis of English Philology and Customs Education in Ukrainian universities. By combining direct classroom observations from these diverse fields, we identify shared challenges and discipline-specific variations in AI adoption. This analysis examines both theoretical frameworks and practical implementation issues in university-level professional training, grounding recommendations in local educational realities while addressing broader questions facing educators considering AI integration.

Our objective is to provide realistic guidance that balances technological capabilities with pedagogical requirements and institutional constraints.

This chapter is based on reflective classroom observations conducted by the two co-authors during 2023–2025 in two Ukrainian universities: Dragomanov Ukrainian State University in Kyiv (English Philology case) and the State Tax University in Irpin (Customs and Commodity Science case). The observations draw on 83 class sessions in English Lexicology and English Stylistics (166 academic hours) and 90 in Customs Studies and Customs Management (180 academic hours), supported by teaching notes and pedagogical reflections. Rather than using formal qualitative coding, the study employs a reflective comparative approach grounded in first-hand teaching experience. Each author contributed insights from their own teaching field, identifying recurring patterns and discipline-specific contrasts in AI integration.

The comparison focuses on several dimensions: student-faculty technological gaps, ethical and pedagogical dilemmas, absence of institutional policy, assessment challenges, and professional readiness. This reflective, practice-based foundation enables the chapter to connect conceptual analysis with the lived realities of Ukrainian specialised education under war-related and infrastructural constraints.

THE CASE OF ENGLISH PHILOLOGY

Programme Context and Student-Led AI Integration

English Philology programmes in Ukraine train the next generation of teachers, translators, and linguists through coursework in language, literature, and applied linguistics. Students enrolled in the 'English Language and World Literature as a Second Language' Bachelor's programme take courses such as English Lexicology and Stylistics. Yet, something unexpected is reshaping these traditional programmes: artificial intelligence. Unlike many Western institutions that have rolled out formal AI policies, Ukrainian programmes lack institutional frameworks for AI integration. Students are driving AI adoption in these programmes, using tools like ChatGPT for writing support, Grammarly for editing, and DeepL for translation assistance. Faculty responses vary. Some see value in these technologies, while others raise concerns about maintaining academic standards and ensuring students develop core skills rather than relying on automated solutions.

Ukrainian English Philology programmes face a curious reality: AI integration happens primarily through student initiative rather than institutional planning. Future teachers, translators, and linguists experiment with these technologies while faculty struggle to keep pace.

Students increasingly turn to ChatGPT for complex linguistic questions—etymology, semantic change, cognitive linguistics, and stylistics. We observe them confidently citing AI responses during seminars, particularly in online classes, without consulting traditional academic sources. This creates a troubling pattern where AI outputs gain unwarranted authority in academic discussions. The appeal is obvious: instant answers versus lengthy research processes.

Meanwhile, everyday AI tools proliferate across our classrooms. Grammarly corrects grammar, DeepL handles translations, and ContextReverso provides contextual examples. Faculty experiment with platforms like Twee for generating exercises and lesson plans. Students practise vocabulary through chatbots and language apps. When used thoughtfully, these tools genuinely enhance learning. The challenge lies in defining 'thoughtful use' and ensuring that students do not bypass essential cognitive processes. However, they also highlight disparities in pedagogical integration. While AI is present in the classroom, it is often introduced without institutional guidance or systematic support.

Pedagogical and Institutional Challenges of Unmediated AI Adoption

Several pressing challenges emerge from this landscape that go beyond tool usage. The erosion of the writing process represents one of the most immediate concerns. Students who use AI to generate complete responses or polished texts often skip cognitively demanding stages: brainstorming, drafting, revising, and struggling with language. This 'productive struggle' is essential in foreign-language acquisition and in developing academic and communicative competencies needed in professional language careers. AI-generated writing appears fluent but lacks personal style, critical reflection, and authentic language development. This means students miss key opportunities to build rhetorical awareness and writing resilience. This depth loss becomes especially visible in repeated classroom patterns.

In the English Stylistics seminars, students were asked to provide examples of metaphors, euphemisms, or idiomatic expressions. A striking number—eight out of ten—chose the phrase *'to kick the bucket'*. This example is linguistically valid, but the overwhelming frequency suggests reliance on the same AI-generated content. Indeed, querying ChatGPT produced identical results, confirming the source. The issue was not limited to academic dishonesty, but rather a broader loss of variation, creativity, and engagement with course materials.

Instead of exploring diverse examples drawn from context, culture, or personal interpretation, students defaulted to pre-packaged outputs. This phenomenon illustrates how uncritical AI use can flatten student responses and reduce opportunities for developing analytical thinking and expressive nuance—key competencies in language education.

In one instance, during an English Lexicology seminar, a student was asked to explain the concept of a paradigm in relation to words. Instead of addressing the lexicological meaning—such as the notion of lexical consistency and grammatical variability, or the two major approaches to paradigms as either systems of forms or as patterns for word formation—the student began confidently discussing *'paradigm'* as a philosophical and psychological concept. He cited paradigms as conceptual frameworks for thought or scientific revolutions, delivering a fluent, well-structured monologue clearly sourced from an AI tool. When asked how this explanation related to word forms, the student was unable to respond and abruptly left the Zoom session.

This incident illustrates a broader pattern of uncritical AI use: students often present AI-generated content without recognising whether it is relevant to the academic context. Rather than using AI tools as heuristic aids, they treat them as authoritative sources, even when the output is unrelated or misleading. A similar issue occurred when another student attempted to explain the semantic evolution of the word broadcast but relied entirely on ChatGPT, which incorrectly defined the term as originally digital in nature. These examples show how AI over-reliance produces confident, yet incorrect, responses and disconnects students from their discipline's core knowledge. This pattern of accepting AI explanations regardless of context supports Zhai et al.'s (2024) findings: students struggle to assess AI output quality and relevance, which weakens both critical thinking and conceptual understanding. AI literacy among faculty is another core problem.

Many instructors do not understand how AI works or recognise its limitations (Ivanytska et al., 2024). They remain cautious about incorporating these tools thoughtfully into coursework. Students often explore these technologies on their own. Teachers, however, may not feel equipped to evaluate AI-generated output or set appropriate boundaries. This generational and professional knowledge gap contributes to uneven implementation. Moreover, most Ukrainian universities offer no formal training for instructors on AI integration, which further limits the potential for structured, ethical use.

The absence of institutional policy presents a related challenge. Official guidelines defining acceptable AI use in student work are often missing. Instructors must therefore make individual decisions about what to allow, creating inconsistency across departments and institutions. Assessment methods have not kept pace with technological change. Many educators struggle to determine whether students or AI generated particular texts. This lack of clarity can lead to unequal treatment of students, particularly when some use AI tools frequently while others avoid them altogether.

Re-imagining English Philology Education in an AI Era

AI education discussions rarely address cultural and linguistic relevance. AI language models focus heavily on American and British English, but their cultural references often miss the mark for Ukrainian learners. When students ask about American idioms, they get examples like *'tailgating parties'* that require cultural knowledge they lack. This creates real problems in our intercultural communication courses. Students might learn that Americans say *'How's it going?'* as a greeting, but AI examples rarely explain that this requires only a brief response, not a detailed life update. We see students confused about contextual appropriateness—they know the words but miss the social rules. When students rely too heavily on AI explanations, they often struggle with the pragmatic aspects of communication that native speakers take for granted. They also encounter fewer regional variations, which limits their ability to understand English as a truly global language.

These developments raise important questions about professional preparation. English Philology students train to become language teachers, linguists, or translators—professions now undergoing rapid AI-driven transformation. Students who rely too heavily on AI during university may struggle to teach language independently, explain linguistic concepts clearly, or produce nuanced translations without digital help. Translation professionals are already working with post-editing workflows and AI-generated content. This reality requires universities to rethink their curricula. Students need preparation beyond simply using AI tools—they must learn to evaluate these systems critically and adapt to working with them in their professional work.

AI technologies still hold promise for transforming English Philology education productively when implemented thoughtfully. Tools offering adaptive learning, discourse analysis, or role-play simulations can provide powerful resources when paired with pedagogical strategies promoting critical thinking and learner autonomy. AI-supported discourse tools can help students analyse stylistic features, ideological framing, or tone across texts. Well-designed simulated intercultural conversations can offer safe environments for developing pragmatic skills. Tools like Twee allow instructors to differentiate tasks and develop custom content quickly, improving curriculum planning flexibility and responsiveness. As Dou et al. (2025) note, AI can also help reveal learner behaviour patterns and bridge language education access gaps, which proves important in the Ukrainian context.

Realising this potential requires institutions to move beyond simply allowing or banning AI use. Clear academic integrity policies, structured faculty development, and revised assessment practices are urgently needed. More importantly, educators must cultivate AI literacy among students, teaching not only effective tool usage but also when and why to question, adapt, or reject outputs. AI can thus serve as an educational partner rather than a shortcut, supporting rather than undermining humanity's core values.

Ukrainian universities should consider several urgent measures to support responsible AI integration in English Philology and related fields. Universities need clear guidelines about AI use in student work that fit each discipline. Faculty members should help create these rules to match their fields' standards. Students and teachers both need training on how AI tools work, what they cannot do, and when using them raises ethical concerns. Traditional assessment strategies need revision. Oral examinations, annotated writing drafts, and reflective commentaries can better verify student understanding. State and institutional funding must support faculty development and provide access to vetted AI tools. Without such investment, innovation risks exacerbating educational inequality. With such infrastructure, AI can integrate as thoughtful language education enhancement rather than a shortcut.

THE CASE OF CUSTOMS EDUCATION

Programme Context and Student Engagement with AI

Customs and Commodity Science is a specialised field focused on the management of customs operations, trade procedures, and commodity classification, combining legal, economic, and technological knowledge. In Ukraine, this discipline is taught in both Bachelor's and Master's programmes, such as Management of Customs Affairs and Customs Management, covering subjects like customs procedures, risk management, trade operations, and the use of management information systems. Students gain theoretical understanding and practical skills necessary for careers as customs inspectors, clearance agents, or specialists in international trade management. While AI and advanced digital systems like ARMS play an increasing role in professional customs work, these systems are closed and inaccessible during formal education. Students, therefore, rely on reflective learning, simulations, and general-purpose AI tools to develop critical skills and understanding before entering professional practice.

In some academic fields, AI is increasingly present in both student and faculty practices (UNESCO, 2023; Wang et al., 2024). However, the use of artificial intelligence in Customs and Commodity Science education remains limited and somewhat scattered. The situation at Ukrainian universities illustrates this well. Faculty members teaching Customs and Commodity Science have indeed begun incorporating digital tools into their practice (Razumei, 2023), yet most of these implementations fall short of genuine AI integration. Instructors commonly turn to AI-assisted platforms when designing case studies, organising course syllabi, or generating topics for student assignments and final projects. These applications, while useful, remain confined to pedagogical support rather than substantive engagement with the discipline's specialised content—the complexities of customs procedures, trade law frameworks, and commodity classification systems.

This gap between accessible AI tools for students and restricted professional systems highlights the challenge of preparing learners for real-world customs practice while ensuring that they acquire foundational knowledge and critical thinking skills.

Challenges in Teaching, Learning, and Access to Professional AI Tools

In this field, the educational process is closely tied to large-scale data environments. Customs and Commodity Science involves vast volumes of structured data: customs declarations, trade statistics, commodity classification under the Harmonised System (World Customs Organization, n.d.), and national customs tariffs. Both instructors and students work with a range of automated information systems intended to organise and interpret these data. However, despite their technical sophistication, most of these systems do not actually involve any AI components. Tools commonly used in Ukrainian classrooms for classification or tariff reference are rule-based systems rather than adaptive or predictive AI models (for a comparison of rule-based and large language model (LLM) systems, see TeckNexus, 2025). One such example is the Unified Automated Information System of Ukrainian customs (often referred to by its Ukrainian acronym, ЄАІС), which operates based on predefined rules and procedures rather than machine learning or adaptive algorithms.

Faculty members in this field show limited engagement with AI technologies. Students, in contrast, actively seek out these tools. Students routinely use ChatGPT for explanations, employ machine translation services, and turn to various platforms when working on assignments—behaviours common across university disciplines (Almassaad et al., 2024; Nechyporenko et al., 2025). The contrast reveals something important: students and faculty operate with very different levels of AI familiarity and comfort. On the one hand, students experiment with generative AI to simplify complex concepts or draft essays; on the other, teachers may lack the technical background or institutional training to address AI use critically, let alone integrate it meaningfully into course content. As in other domains, this creates both opportunities and risks—students may benefit from rapid feedback and expanded resources, but also risk bypassing the rigorous analytical training that customs education demands.

Students often accept AI-generated information without questioning its accuracy, creating significant problems. Consider a common scenario: students analysing Ukraine's customs service efficiency routinely cite outdated statistics about multiday processing times. Current reality tells a different story. Average customs clearance now takes approximately 80 minutes for imports and just 25–30 minutes for exports (State Customs Service of Ukraine, 2025a). Where do these incorrect figures come from? AI systems scrape outdated sources or generate data without consulting real-time official statistics—information readily available through the State Customs Service. Students will present conclusions that sound reasonable but miss the mark entirely. This pattern exposes both the limitations of current AI systems and students' need for better data verification skills.

Stepping beyond the university context, however, we observe that AI is already influencing professional customs practice, particularly in line with international trends highlighting AI's increasing role in public sector operations, including tax and customs administrations (Aslett et al., 2024). Ukrainian customs authorities rely heavily on the Automated Risk Management System (ARMS, or АСУР in Ukrainian). This system identifies potential violations and flags high-risk shipments. ARMS analyses data from import/export declarations and predicts irregularities before goods reach the border (State Customs Service of Ukraine, 2024). The system includes machine learning modules that continuously refine risk profiles. This ongoing refinement improves both accuracy and efficiency in customs control. Take a concrete case: a shipment from Poland that unexpectedly routes through Romania and Moldova would trigger ARMS to flag it for closer inspection. These automated mechanisms achieve two goals simultaneously—they streamline border processing and strengthen both national security and regulatory compliance. ARMS operates through dynamic risk profiles—algorithmic combinations that weigh factors like product type, declared value, country of origin, and transportation route. The system analyses these parameters to spot anomalies and potential threats before goods physically arrive at the border. Recent updates confirm that ARMS integrates multiple AI-driven modules, including risk indicator generation, personal data verification, and automated commodity classification, reflecting a broader push towards intelligent automation in Ukrainian customs operations (State Customs Service of Ukraine, 2025b).

However, ARMS maintains important limitations. The system does not make final decisions on its own. Customs officers must still interpret its alerts and carry out actual inspections. This human oversight proves essential. Automated judgements alone create too much risk in a regulatory environment where mistakes carry serious legal and financial penalties.

ARMS remains a closed system with restricted access. Students cannot use it, nor can businesses. This limitation stems from the system's sensitive functions: revenue collection, public safety, and national security operations. Even during internships, students are allowed only to observe the system's interface, without the opportunity to interact with it. No training or simulation version currently exists, and new customs officers are instead trained on-site, under mentor supervision. Students graduate without practical exposure to the tools they will eventually need in their careers.

Other professions that integrate AI technology take a different approach. They commonly use scenario-based learning and provide sandbox environments for hands-on training. This gap leaves customs students at a disadvantage. Without an educational analogue to ARMS, students must rely on abstract understanding. Students do use AI for general purposes—ChatGPT for summaries or drafts, for example. But these tools frequently mix up historical data with current conditions. The same system can produce contradictory answers that both sound reasonable. Students often lack the specialised knowledge to spot these inconsistencies. This makes learning even more challenging.

Customs operations integrate AI cautiously for good reasons. Officials must modernise and speed up trade procedures while protecting national, economic, and environmental security. This balancing act demands carefully designed systems and strict policies. It explains why tools like ARMS stay closed to public access and why educational exposure remains restricted.

Systems like ARMS have not yet made their way into university curricula. But their role in professional customs work highlights something important: academic training needs to include AI awareness. Future customs officers will work with these systems. They need more than just operational knowledge. They must learn to interpret outputs, question underlying assumptions, and recognise system limitations. This shifts how we think about AI in customs work. It is no longer just a technological tool—it becomes part of the regulatory and decision-making framework itself.

Future Directions for AI Integration in Customs Education

The educational gap between current university teaching and the realities of AI-driven customs operations poses a clear challenge. Educational programmes in Customs Education and Customs Management require significant changes. Students need hands-on experience with simulated AI systems. Case studies focused on data-driven decisions would give them a practical understanding. They should also receive training that combines legal, economic, and technological viewpoints. Instructors face their own challenges. They need professional development opportunities to grasp how AI tools actually function in practice. They must also figure out how to introduce these tools responsibly into their classrooms.

While progress has been slow, the integration of AI into customs education is both possible and necessary. Educational institutions have several options for moving forward. They could develop hybrid modules introducing students to risk assessment algorithm logic. They might offer practical training using real-world datasets through sandbox versions of ARMS or similar tools. These approaches would prepare graduates who understand AI vocabulary and can work effectively with AI systems. More importantly, students would learn to critically assess outcomes and maintain their profession's legal and ethical standards.

The customs education example reveals something broader about specialised training today. Programmes must prepare students for rapidly changing professional environments. At the same time, they must preserve disciplinary integrity and critical thinking skills. As with language education, success will depend not on the tools themselves, but on how we choose to teach them.

CROSS-DISCIPLINARY COMPARISON: AI INTEGRATION IN UKRAINIAN SPECIALISED EDUCATION

The experiences from English Philology and Customs Education reveal both convergent patterns and discipline-specific variations in how AI integration unfolds within specialised professional training contexts marked by infrastructural constraints and institutional gaps.

Both disciplines demonstrate a student-faculty technology gap that manifests similarly across fields. In English Philology, students confidently present AI-generated content about paradigms without recognising contextual mismatches, while in Customs Education, students cite outdated AI-generated statistics about processing times. This pattern suggests that students across disciplines treat AI as authoritative rather than as tools requiring critical evaluation. Faculty in both areas lack institutional support for AI integration, leaving them to navigate challenges individually.

The absence of institutional policy creates parallel problems. English Philology instructors make individual decisions about acceptable AI use in writing, while Customs Education faculty struggle with students presenting unverified AI-generated trade analyses. Neither discipline has clear guidelines for distinguishing productive AI assistance from problematic over-reliance, creating inconsistent standards.

Both cases reveal assessment vulnerabilities. Traditional evaluation methods—essays in English Philology and case studies in Customs Education—prove inadequate for detecting AI-generated content or evaluating comprehension when AI provides ready answers. The result: instructors question whether they assess student learning or AI capability.

Despite shared patterns, each field faces distinct challenges shaped by professional requirements. English Philology grapples with process-oriented learning concerns—when students use AI for complete texts, they bypass cognitive work essential for future teachers, translators, and linguists. The discipline's emphasis on creativity and individual expression makes AI over-reliance particularly problematic.

Customs Education faces accuracy and timeliness challenges. While AI-generated creative writing may lack a personal voice but remain academically acceptable, AI-generated customs statistics can be factually wrong and professionally dangerous. The field's reliance on current, precise data means AI hallucinations create serious consequences for professional practice.

The professional preparation gap differs between fields. English Philology students may enter careers where AI tools become collaborative partners, requiring evaluation and adaptation skills. Customs professionals will work with specialised, restricted systems like ARMS that students cannot access during education, creating unique preparation challenges. These implementation challenges acquire particular significance within resource-constrained educational contexts. Limited infrastructure makes AI's accessibility especially valuable; yet, these constraints make institutional guidance harder to provide. The necessity of selective adoption, rather than wholesale technology integration, may ultimately lead to more pedagogically grounded approaches.

The comparative analysis reveals that successful AI integration requires discipline-sensitive approaches rather than institution-wide policies. While both fields need clear guidelines for acceptable AI use, specific content must reflect each field's learning objectives and professional requirements. Faculty development represents the most critical intervention, requiring discipline-specific rather than generic AI literacy training.

Both cases demonstrate that adaptive assessment strategies become essential when traditional evaluation proves inadequate. Each discipline needs approaches that verify student understanding while acknowledging that AI tools may legitimately support certain professional work aspects.

CONCLUSIONS

This comparative analysis of AI integration in English Philology and Customs Education reveals fundamental patterns in specialised professional training. While both disciplines face similar challenges—student-faculty technology gaps, absent institutional policies, and inadequate assessment practices—the implications differ markedly. Language education risks losing essential cognitive processes, while data-driven fields confront potentially dangerous factual errors.

The central finding is clear: effective AI integration demands discipline-sensitive approaches rather than generic institutional policies. Limited resources in Ukrainian universities have created selective approaches to AI adoption. Educators focus on pedagogy rather than technology for its own sake. Financial and infrastructure constraints push them towards tools that actually improve student learning rather than simply adopting the latest innovations.

Our analysis identifies ***five critical lessons for specialised professional training***:

1 **Discipline-sensitive policy frameworks are essential**: Generic institutional mandates fail to address field-specific risks. Language education must protect cognitive processes; data-driven fields must ensure factual accuracy. Policy development

requires input from faculty who understand both professional requirements and pedagogical needs.

2 **Faculty development must be field-specific**: Generic digital literacy training proves insufficient. Instructors need discipline-focused preparation addressing how AI functions within their specific domains and what limitations matter most for their students' professional futures.
3 **Assessment strategies require fundamental revision**: Traditional evaluation methods cannot detect AI assistance or verify authentic learning. Each discipline needs approaches appropriate to its knowledge construction methods: process documentation for language learning, data verification protocols for customs education.
4 **Student initiative outpaces institutional response**: Without guidance, students treat AI as an authoritative source rather than as a tool requiring critical evaluation. Universities must move from reactive to proactive frameworks.
5 **Resource constraints can drive pedagogical innovation**: Limited infrastructure encourages selective, purposeful adoption over novelty-driven expertise while respecting disciplinary differences.

By implementing discipline-sensitive approaches, institutions can transform AI from a source of uncertainty into a collaborative educational partner. The Ukrainian case suggests that thoughtful, constraint-driven innovation may prove more pedagogically sound than resource-rich but unfocused adoption—insights relevant for specialised professional training across diverse educational contexts. These findings invite further cross-institutional dialogue and comparative research across European professional training contexts.

REFERENCES

Almassaad, A., Alajlan, H., Alebaikan, R. (2024). Student Perceptions of Generative Artificial Intelligence: Investigating Utilization, Benefits, and Challenges in Higher Education. *Systems*, 12 (10), 385. https://doi.org/10.3390/systems12100385

Aslett, J., Hamilton, S., Gonzalez, I., Hadwick, D., Hardy, M.A. (2024). Understanding Artificial Intelligence in Tax and Customs Administration. *IMF Staff Discussion Notes*, 2024 (006), 1–40. https://doi.org/10.5089/9798400290435.005

Chen, Z. (2025, March 14). The Humanities in an AI World: Personal Reflections from SXSW EDU 2025. *Ithaka Blog*. https://about.jstor.org/blog/the-humanities-in-an-ai-world-personal-reflections-from-sxsw-edu-2025/

Kononova, N., Berbyuk Lindström, N., Panchuk, A. (2024). Teaching and Learning amid War Crisis: Perceptions of Ukrainian Academic Staff and Students on Online Education. *IBIMA Business Review*, 2024, 465847. https://doi.org/10.5171/2024.465847

Dovgyi, S., Babiichuk, S., Davybida, L., Biletska, M. (2024). Teachers' and Students' Attitudes towards the Use of Artificial Intelligence: All-Ukrainian Research. *Information Technologies and Learning Tools*, 104 (6), 197–215. https://doi.org/10.33407/itlt.v104i6.5890

Dou, A., Xu, W., Li, X., Zhang, S., Zhang, J. (2025). Artificial Intelligence in Language Learning: Bridging Gaps, Revealing Patterns, and Charting the Future. *International Journal of Distance Education Technologies (IJDET)*, 23 (1), 1–24.

Ivanytska, N., Koliasa, O., Kovalevska, T., Matsera, O., Tkachuk, T. (2024). Analyzing the Possibilities of Implementation of AI and Social Networks in Teaching Foreign Language Students: Ukrainian Universities Case Study. *Arab World English Journal (AWEJ)* Special Issue on ChatGPT. https://ssrn.com/abstract=4814759

Nechyporenko, V., Hordiienko, N., Pozdniakova, O., Pozdniakova-Kyrbiatieva, E., Siliavina, Y. (2025). How Often Do University Students use Artificial Intelligence in Their Studies? *WSEAS Transactions on Information Science and Applications*, 22, 203–214. https://doi.org/10.37394/23209.2025.22.18

Razumei, M.M. (2023). Artificial Intelligence in Risk Management and Determinations of Control Objects for Customs Audit. *Public Administration in the Field of National Security and Customs Affairs*, 2 (37), 83–89. https://doi.org/10.32782/2310-9653-2023-2.11

State Customs Service of Ukraine. (2024). The State Customs Service Integrated AI and BI into ASUR to Improve Risk Management Efficiency. *State Customs Service of Ukraine*. February 7, 2024. https://customs.gov.ua/news/it-transformatsiia-62/post/derzhmitsluzhba-integruvala-shi-ta-bi-v-asur-dlia-pidvishchennia-efektivnosti-upravlinnia-rizikami-2016

State Customs Service of Ukraine. (2025a). Ukrainian Customs: Development Despite the War in Q1 2025 [Report]. *Ministry of Finance of Ukraine*. https://mof.gov.ua/uk/news/mitnii_ogliad_ukrainska_mitnitsia_rozvitok_popri_viinu_za_i_kvartal_2025_roku_prezentatsiia-5118

State Customs Service of Ukraine. (2025b). Implementation of AI-Driven Modules in the Automated Risk Management System (ARMS) [Official Report]. *Ministry of Finance of Ukraine*. https://customs.gov.ua/news/it-transformatsiia-62/post/derzhmitsluzhba-vprovadzhuie-shtuchnii-intelekt-dlia-sproshchennia-mitnogo-oformlennia-avto-2025

TeckNexus. (2025, February 3). Rule-Based vs. LLM-Based AI Agents: A Side-by-Side Comparison. https://tecknexus.com/rule-based-vs-llm-based-ai-agents-a-side-by-side-comparison/

UNESCO. (2023). *Harnessing the Era of Artificial Intelligence in Higher Education: A Primer for Higher Education Stakeholders*. UNESCO Digital Library. https://unesdoc.unesco.org/ark:/48223/pf0000386670

Wang, S., Wang, F., Zhu, Z., Wang, J., Tran, T., Du, Z. (2024). Artificial Intelligence in Education: A Systematic Literature Review. *Expert Systems with Applications*, 252, 124167. https://doi.org/10.1016/j.eswa.2024.124167

World Customs Organization. (n.d.). *What Is the Harmonized System (HS)?* World Customs Organization. https://www.wcoomd.org/en/topics/nomenclature/overview/what-is-the-harmonized-system.aspx

Zhai, C., Wibowo, S., Li, L.D. (2024). The Effects of Over-Reliance on AI Dialogue Systems on Students' Cognitive Abilities: A Systematic Review. *Smart Learning Environments*, 11, 28. https://doi.org/10.1186/s40561-024-00316-7

9 Understanding University Students' Perspectives on Generative AI

Manuela Farinosi and Claudio Melchior

INTRODUCTION

The rapid development and widespread adoption of Generative Artificial Intelligence (GenAI), particularly large language models (LLMs) such as OpenAI's ChatGPT, have sparked substantial debate across academic, professional, and public domains (e.g. Popenici, 2023). These sophisticated technologies, capable of generating human-like text, synthesising complex information, and performing advanced cognitive tasks, are rapidly becoming integral to academic life, fundamentally challenging established pedagogical frameworks and institutional practices while transforming how knowledge is accessed, processed, and applied (Rahiman & Kodikal, 2024).

University students occupy a unique position in this technological transformation. As early adopters of these technologies, they serve not merely as end-users but as central and critical stakeholders who shape how GenAI tools are integrated into academic contexts. Their perceptions, adoption patterns, and resistance mechanisms provide essential insights for understanding the educational implications of these technologies and for developing evidence-based institutional policies, ethical guidelines, and pedagogical strategies.

Despite the growing scholarly attention to AI in education (Bond et al., 2024; Holland & Ciachir, 2024; Wang et al., 2025), significant empirical gaps persist, particularly regarding student perspectives in specific national contexts. The Italian higher education landscape, characterised by its distinctive institutional structures and cultural approaches to learning, remains notably underexplored in GenAI research.

To address this critical gap, this chapter synthesises the most significant findings that emerged from a series of studies conducted as part of a larger inter-departmental research project on artificial intelligence (AI) at the University of Udine. Our comprehensive multimethod research programme examined Italian university students' perceptions and experiences with ChatGPT and similar tools through a sequential and complementary approach.

The research programme evolved through distinct phases, from local to national scope. Beginning with an initial mixed-methods study at the University of Udine, we

 DOI: 10.1201/9781003676188-10

subsequently expanded both quantitatively—through a national survey—and qualitatively—through interviews extending across Northeast Italy. This iterative approach enabled us to build comprehensive insights while maintaining methodological rigour. Our investigation ultimately comprised four complementary studies:

- Institutional pilot study: Questionnaires (N = 531) combining fixed and open-ended items with University of Udine students
- Local qualitative exploration: Semi-structured interviews (N = 60) with University of Udine students
- Regional qualitative extension: Semi-structured interviews (N = 137) with students from Northeast Italian universities
- National survey: Large-scale questionnaire involving 1,366 students across 24 Italian universities

These studies were designed to address three fundamental research questions:

RQ1: What is the current state of GenAI familiarity and usage patterns among Italian university students across personal and academic domains?

RQ2: How do students perceive the integration of GenAI tools in university contexts, and what benefits and risks do they identify for teaching and learning processes?

RQ3: What are students' expectations regarding the future role of GenAI in higher education and professional contexts?

By synthesising the most significant findings from our multisite investigation, this chapter contributes empirically grounded insights to current debates on AI integration in academic settings. Given the nature of this edited volume, findings are presented through a discursive approach that distils the essential insights emerging from years of systematic investigation on this topic. For detailed statistical analyses, methodological specifications, and comprehensive data presentations, readers are referred to the individual papers previously published in international peer-reviewed journals. Here, we present the core understanding that has emerged from our engagement with Italian students' experiences of GenAI in higher education.

The chapter is structured in four sections. Following this introduction, we present a comprehensive literature review synthesising current theoretical frameworks and empirical findings on student perspectives regarding GenAI in higher education. The third section details our key findings, highlighting distinctive patterns in Italian students' perceptions and practices. The final section discusses implications for educational policy, institutional strategy, and future research directions in the Italian and broader international context.

LITERATURE REVIEW

Although the widespread use of GenAI in education is a relatively recent phenomenon, scholarly interest in and research on the application of AI in learning environments has a long-standing history. Earlier investigations primarily centred on adaptive learning systems, intelligent tutoring platforms, and the implementation of AI for personalised instruction (Chiu et al., 2023). However, the current landscape has undergone a notable transformation with the public release of LLMs such as ChatGPT, prompting a paradigmatic shift in how AI technologies are conceptualised and implemented in academic contexts (Deng et al., 2025; Montenegro-Rueda et al., 2023). These new-generation tools elicit both enthusiasm and scepticism, thus raising pressing pedagogical and ethical questions.

At the heart of this debate are concerns about the integration of AI into core educational practices as well as its long-term implications for teaching roles, student autonomy, and academic integrity. A central issue is whether GenAI functions primarily as a support mechanism that enhances cognitive engagement or whether it risks diminishing students' independent learning capacities (Zhang, 2024). As these tools become increasingly accessible and embedded in academic settings and routines, understanding students' perceptions is vital for constructing a balanced, evidence-informed approach to their appropriate use.

Theoretical frameworks, such as the Technology Acceptance Model (TAM), originally introduced by Davis (1989), offer useful lenses for interpreting student engagement with AI tools. According to TAM, two key constructs—Perceived Usefulness (PU) and Perceived Ease of Use (PEOU)—shape user attitudes towards new technologies. PU relates to the belief that a given tool will improve performance, while PEOU reflects the degree to which the technology is seen as straightforward and user-friendly. Studies have applied this framework to educational contexts, finding that positive perceptions of usefulness and usability are strong predictors of technology adoption (Lai et al., 2023; Liu & Zhang, 2024; Ma et al., 2024; Saif et al., 2024; Yilmaz et al., 2023).

Students' willingness to integrate emerging technologies into their academic routines is often influenced by several interrelated factors, including technological self-efficacy, compatibility with pre-existing learning habits, and alignment with pedagogical goals (Pinho et al., 2021). These factors vary across disciplines. For example, students in fields such as engineering and architecture typically report higher affinity for digital innovation compared to peers in the humanities and social sciences (Huedo-Martínez et al., 2023). Such disparities underscore the roles of technological familiarity and disciplinary culture in shaping engagement patterns. Additionally, global differences in cultural norms, regulatory policies, and educational values demand context-specific analyses of students' attitudes (Acosta-Enriquez et al., 2024; Roberts et al., 2023).

Despite the novelty of GenAI in educational contexts, a growing number of empirical studies have begun to explore how students perceive these tools. Overall, the literature presents a complex picture, with perceived benefits of the technologies often expressed alongside substantial concerns. On the positive side, ChatGPT and other similar tools are widely viewed as valuable aids for learning enhancement, motivation, and personalisation (Cotton et al., 2024; Karakose & Tülübaş, 2023). These applications offer students immediate access to information and clarification, thereby enabling them to navigate complex topics at their own pace and in their preferred learning style (Holmes & Tuomi, 2022). Additionally, GenAI tools are praised for their capacity to provide continuous feedback, generate recommendations tailored to individual learning paths, and support knowledge retention (Chan & Hu, 2023).

Notably, non-native speakers have leveraged GenAI to improve academic writing by refining grammar, structure, and coherence (Erito, 2023; Hasanein & Sobaih, 2023). Beyond linguistic support, many students use GenAI tools for brainstorming, summarising, and alleviating writer's block—functions that contribute to reduced cognitive load and greater productivity (Al-Obaydi et al., 2023). GenAI support appears to foster learner autonomy and self-directed study, especially in contexts where immediate human support may be unavailable.

Several studies have emphasised the role of AI in cultivating analytical and metacognitive skills. By facilitating the evaluation of information, prompting reflective thinking, and modelling inquiry-based approaches, GenAI has been argued to foster deeper forms of engagement (Kosmyna et al., 2025). Moreover, many students report viewing AI literacy as essential for future employment, advocating for its formal integration into university curricula (Abdelwahab et al., 2022; Lee et al., 2022).

However, the increasing reliance on GenAI introduces a range of pedagogical, ethical, and psychological challenges. A key area of concern is the potential erosion of interpersonal interaction in educational settings. Several studies indicate that students are apprehensive about the diminished role of instructors and the weakening of peer and teacher–student relationships, which are crucial for emotional engagement and cognitive development (Bisdas et al., 2021; Idroes et al., 2023; Seo et al., 2021). These concerns reflect broader anxieties surrounding the dehumanisation of education and the possible substitution of human insight with algorithmic reasoning.

Equally significant are concerns related to academic integrity. GenAI tools can generate content that is indistinguishable from student-written work, raising alarms about plagiarism, authorship, and intellectual honesty (Rawas, 2024; Sullivan et al., 2023). Without proper guidance and enforcement, students may use these tools to complete assignments in ways that contravene institutional policies or ethical norms. Additional risks include technical issues related to misinformation and errors. Large language models have been found to fabricate sources or produce content that is plausible but inaccurate, thus undermining scholarly reliability and contributing to the spread of misinformation (Famaye et al., 2024; Farrokhnia et al., 2024; Rudolph et al., 2023).

Furthermore, the underlying data that train LLMs may contain cultural or linguistic biases, leading to the perpetuation of stereotypes and discriminatory outputs (Yu, 2024). The potential consequences of such models, including their ability to reinforce biases and stereotypes, can be especially harmful in multicultural learning environments and among under-represented student populations. Concerns have also been raised about overdependence on AI tools, which may limit students' ability to cultivate original thought and undermine their creativity and critical reasoning (Kayali et al., 2023; Ngo, 2023). In some cases, students have reported increased stress when these tools become inaccessible, even temporarily, suggesting the emergence of psychological dependency (Ajlouni et al., 2023).

While students' attitudes towards GenAI vary considerably, a recurring theme is the demand for institutional transparency and support. Numerous studies emphasise that students seek clearer guidance from universities regarding the acceptable use of AI tools as well as structured opportunities for training in ethical and effective use (Tierney et al., 2025). Many students are also unaware of whether such policies already exist at their institutions (Malmström et al., 2023).

Finally, beyond educational concerns, the adoption of GenAI intersects with broader societal concerns about automation and labour market transformations. Students frequently express uncertainty about their future career prospects given the rapid integration of AI into professional domains, fearing job displacement as well as increased demand for highly specialised skills (Ghotbi et al., 2022).

In summary, the literature reveals that GenAI tools such as ChatGPT present dual potential in higher education: they offer opportunities for enhancing learning experiences, autonomy, and skill development, but pose significant challenges regarding accuracy, ethics, equity, and cognitive development. As these technologies evolve, it is crucial to critically examine their integration into educational settings by foregrounding students' voices, as they are key indicators of both the promise and risks of GenAI.

MAIN FINDINGS

The Diffusion of Generative AI in Italian Higher Education

The findings of our research indicate a clear transformation occurring within the Italian university system. Drawing on a multimethodological approach involving over two thousand students, with quantitative and qualitative techniques, a complex picture emerges of the integration of GenAI into academic and everyday practices. Our research documents the rapid dissemination of these tools among the student population, which occurred just over a year after the launch of ChatGPT. These tools have begun to transform the manner in which students study, conduct research, and produce academic work. However, it appears that Italian universities have not yet fully comprehended these changes, nor have they established regulations to address them.

The initial key finding is that, between 2023 and 2024, approximately four out of ten students reported utilising GenAI systems for directly related academic purposes, while almost seven out of ten reported using them for personal interests and projects. To be more precise, in a national survey of 1,366 students (with data collected between October 2023 and March 2024), 38.7% of respondents stated that they used GenAI for activities related to their university studies, while 69.2% said that they used it for personal and informal purposes.

This result is also confirmed by the 'local' research carried out with students from the University of Udine, which involved 531 students through a quantitative questionnaire. The data (collected at the end of 2023) revealed that 69.7% of respondents reported utilising GenAI for personal endeavours, constituting approximately two-thirds of the sample. Conversely, 40.9% of respondents indicated that their engagement with GenAI was for academic purposes. The substantial overlap of the percentages with the national sample reinforces the consistency of the picture that emerged: although GenAI was not yet widely used for study activities, at the time of the surveys, it was already a widespread and not marginal practice.

If the analysis is limited solely to self-declarations collected through the medium of questionnaires, it can be concluded that the starting value approximates 40% of students who were already using AI for university purposes at the time. However, a more in-depth analysis, conducted through the use of indirect control questions and by triangulating the results obtained with different methods and samples, suggests that the actual estimate should be raised to at least around 50%. In the national quantitative questionnaire, following the initial direct question on self-reported AI use, students were asked how they usually used ChatGPT (or similar tools) when completing assignments, exams, or other university-related activities. The response options encompassed the potential for declaring partial utilisation, characterised by responses indicating the execution of only specific components of the work (42.6% of responses); more extensive usage, designated by responses indicating the completion of the majority of the assignment (5.9%); and total utilisation, indicated by responses specifying the completion of the assignment with AI without the incorporation of checks or modifications (0.3%). The fourth response option to this question enabled students to reiterate: 'I do not use ChatGPT (or similar systems) for university activities'.

In comparison to the 38.7% of respondents who explicitly stated in the initial question that they used GenAI for university purposes, the responses to this indirect question returned a significantly higher percentage: 48.8% of the sample 'admitted', in one of the three ways described above, to having used GenAI for academic activities. This figure represents an increase of more than ten percentage points compared to the direct question. These questions were posed in the same manner in the questionnaire for the local sample from our university, and the pattern that emerges from the data is consistent. In this case too, the total number of users emerging from the control question stands at 49.2% (8.3 percentage points above the initial self-declaration).

Furthermore, additional research conducted by us in the immediate aftermath (data collected between April and May 2024) using qualitative methods on a small sample of 137 students showed that, in that context characterised by peer interviews,[1] more than half of the respondents (53.2%) acknowledged some form of GenAI use in their university practice. For these reasons, it is reasonable to assume that the figure of approximately 38–40% of users who spontaneously declared themselves in direct questions in quantitative surveys should be interpreted as a minimum threshold, below which it is unrealistic to place the phenomenon, while the estimate of around 50% (again referring to the period October 2023–May 2024) is closer to the actual reality.

We posit that the discrepancy between the explicit and the indirect estimations can be attributed to two primary factors. The first of these is associated with the consequences of social desirability mechanisms on responses. It is not irrelevant if the question comes from an official academic context (as was the case in the two quantitative studies, national and local), especially if the student has to decide to attribute to themselves practices that may be perceived as illegitimate in response to a questionnaire distributed by their university.[2] This is further compounded by a perceived lack of confidence in the efficacy of anonymisation procedures, despite the assurances provided and the implemented anonymisation practices. The second factor that may explain this discrepancy lies in the actual lack of a clear institutional regulatory framework. At the time of our research, almost no Italian university had rules or guidelines for the use of AI in academia. The absence of guidance pertaining to the utilisation of these tools, including the manner, location, and temporal context for their implementation, may have influenced the responses obtained. This issue will be revisited at the end of the chapter.

Demographic and Disciplinary Differences in Technological Adoption

The analysis of generative AI adoption patterns reveals systematic differences. The findings of the research consistently demonstrate a substantial correlation between gender and AI utilisation, with a statistically significant advantage observed in male students. In the use of GenAI for personal projects, there is a 24.8% disparity in favour of males over females (79.7% vs. 54.9%),[3] while in use for university activities, the difference stands at 17.3% (46.1% vs. 28.8%).[4] Local research data lend further credence to this finding; the utilisation of GenAI for personal activities is observed to be employed by 83.4% of males in comparison to 73.3% of females, while its application in academic contexts is used by 31.8% of males in contrast to 27.6% of females.[5]

Furthermore, a close correlation is observed between digital skills and the utilisation of Generative AI. In order to assess this relationship, a 'digital competence index' was constructed in the national survey by adding together the values of the responses relating to the self-assessment of one's level of digital skills with those relating to the use of smartphones, personal computers, and search engines (the digital devices and services most used by the sample).

Statistical analysis revealed that the digital competence index exhibited a significant positive correlation with the utilisation of generative AI in both personal projects ($\tau b = .211$, $p = .000$) and university activities ($\tau b = .137$, $p = .000$). This pattern is also confirmed in local research, where there is a strong direct association between ChatGPT use and self-reported digital competence.[6] These results suggest that the adoption of generative AI is not a random phenomenon, but is instead influenced by students' pre-existing digital skills. Specifically, students with stronger technological skills appear to be more inclined to experiment with and utilise these novel tools.

Consistently, a higher average use of GenAI emerges among students in STEM disciplines. However, the data reveal some interesting surprises: in the national survey, the highest percentage of students who report using GenAI for academic tasks is among students of political, social, and communication sciences (61.1%), followed only by their colleagues in computer science and ICT (52.7%), art and design (47.1%), industrial and information engineering (47.1%), and architecture and civil engineering (45%). Conversely, students in the humanities are the least inclined to use generative AI for university activities.[7]

Student Profiles in Relation to GenAI

The data reported thus far characterise the general trends that have been identified. However, when considering these data, it is important to remember that these overall trends emerge as a statistical summary of rather different attitudes. Consequently, an analysis of the national data was conducted, utilising clustering procedures.[8] This analysis enabled the identification of four distinct student profiles, which diverge in terms of their digital skills and their attitudes towards generative AI.

Approximately one-fifth of the student sample, labelled as 'the Indifferent' due to their specific characteristics, appear largely detached from the technological issues under discussion. These students (18.9% of the total), characterised by the lowest levels of self-reported digital skills, may have experimented with AI out of curiosity, but they perceive these tools as distant from their daily practices and educational needs. The demographic profile of this group is evenly distributed between males and females, and they show the least support for the regulation of AI in universities.

A comparable percentage of respondents, designated as 'the Fearful' (21.3%), express considerable concern regarding the development of GenAI. This group has intermediate digital skills and is the only cluster in which females outnumber males. They tend not to use GenAI (only 20.6% of them use it for university activities) and frequently express critical views on the subject. They argue that AI distorts the traditional educational relationship, compromises the quality of education, and essentially constitutes 'fraud' that penalises deserving students. They are the most convinced that the use of AI in universities is 'morally wrong' and that universities should prohibit its use.

The remaining part of the sample (which, in our case, was still biased towards students who were more digitally skilled and therefore attracted to and familiar with the topic) frequently uses all the main technological devices and GenAI for various university-related activities. Sharing these common characteristics, this group of students was subsequently divided into two distinct subgroups, differentiated by their underlying attitudes.

Those who have been defined as 'Enthusiasts' (30.3% of the sample) hold a wholly positive view of AI in universities and at social and work levels. They are convinced that this technology will enhance all human capabilities and express no concerns or fears, either on a personal or social level.

Conversely, 'Pragmatics' (29.5%), while utilising AI to the same extent as the Enthusiasts, diverges from the latter in that, in addition to the positive aspects, they do not neglect to critically evaluate the potential negative implications. For instance, 21.8% of Pragmatics express strong concern about the negative prospects of AI on society, compared to only 2.9% of Enthusiasts. Pragmatics, therefore, represents a more balanced and thoughtful approach to technology. While utilising it extensively, they recognise its usefulness without falling into the uncritical enthusiasm that seems to characterise the Enthusiasts.

Uses of GenAI in the University Context

Once a framework for the level of use and the different underlying attitudes towards AI has been defined, it becomes crucial to ask: what do the students who employ GenAI for their university activities actually do with it? The qualitative research, conducted through semi-structured interviews with a sample of 137 Italian university students, helps to address this question.[9] The qualitative analysis of usage practices reveals a diverse range of applications. Our data identify nine main categories of generative AI use in universities. The most frequently cited category is *support for understanding and individual study*. AI is employed by students as a form of personalised tutoring, with the capacity to deliver immediate explanations tailored to their level of comprehension. As one student reports: 'It's like having a professor who is always available and can explain things in different ways until you understand them'. This use of AI transforms it into an interactive study companion, capable of adapting to individual learning rhythms and styles. The second most important aspect is the *search for information and academic sources*. Students particularly appreciate AI's ability to quickly synthesise information from different sources and suggest directions for research. 'I used it for research for my thesis because, rather than searching for information on different websites, when you search for something on ChatGPT, it gives you all the information', explains one interviewee.

However, a certain degree of awareness also emerges regarding the limited reliability of the sources suggested by AI. The practice of *writing and revising academic texts* is a more controversial but widespread use. AI is utilised by students to enhance the structure of their academic papers, to identify more suitable wording, and to overcome writer's block. It is important to note that the majority of students emphasise (perhaps for social desirability?) that they use AI only as a starting point, after which they independently develop their own work.

The *preparation of presentations and examination materials* is a particularly appreciated pragmatic use. AI is utilised for the structuring of content, the suggestion of layouts, and the support of the organisation of ideas. *Translations and language support* are applications that are of particular value to students who are not native Italian speakers or to those who have to work with texts in foreign languages. Finally, less frequently mentioned are the *generation and modification of multimedia content*, specifically for students of creative and communicative disciplines, and *programming and code writing* for students of computer science disciplines. In general, across all types of students, AI is used for the automation and optimisation of practical activities, in particular to simplify repetitive and 'tedious' processes, such as the organisation of notes and files, or the creation of personalised productivity tools.

Perceived Risks and Disadvantages

The perception of the risks associated with the use of AI in universities, once more based on our qualitative data, reveals a significant critical awareness on the part of students, which is somewhat unexpected. The *loss of learning and skills* is the most frequently expressed concern. It is a concern that the excessive use of AI could potentially compromise the development of critical thinking, problem-solving skills, and independent research skills among students. Their words speak for themselves: 'The skills required for the task are not developed'; 'Students risk not acquiring the critical skills necessary for their educational path'. As one interviewee summarises: 'The risk is becoming mentally lazy and no longer developing the ability to think for oneself'.

Dependence on tools constitutes the second group of concerns. Students recognise the risk of developing a dependent relationship with these tools, losing confidence in their own abilities and becoming unable to work independently: 'It could create a dependency, resulting in an inability to work without them'; 'Risk of always depending on ChatGPT to do homework'; and 'You no longer learn to do things on your own'. This awareness is particularly developed among the more experienced users, who evidently speak from direct experience.

After that, a very interesting aspect for our research emerges, namely *ethical issues and academic dishonesty*. The students raise questions regarding the distinction between 'legitimate support' and 'misconduct', emphasising the necessity for institutions to establish explicit guidelines: 'It's like cheating: using artificial intelligence is not fair when taking exams or doing homework'; 'It's a form of dishonesty towards those who work without these tools'; and 'It could distort assessments and make the system less fair'. This aspect of students' requests for clear guidelines from institutions emerged, as mentioned above, in all the surveys we conducted with different samples and methods.

Finally, the students' responses emphasise the potential dangers associated with *content standardisation* ('All work risks looking the same'; 'Originality in assignments disappears, everything becomes standard'; 'Answers become similar among students'), which could result in uniformity of thought, and the risk of *plagiarism and a lack of originality* ('There might be more plagiarism or copy-and-paste'). Irrespective of whether they use AI or not, students consistently display an awareness of a fundamental technical limitation: the restricted *reliability and accuracy of GenAI*, a constraint of which they appear generally cognisant.

Perceptions of Future Impact: The 'Proximity Paradox'

A particularly salient finding from our research pertains to students' perceptions of the impact that generative AI systems will have on the future, both on a personal and on a social level. A paradoxical, yet consistent, pattern has been identified: students predict a lesser expectation of significant impact in cases where the focus is immediate and personal, and a greater expectation of major change in cases where the focus is more general and social.

On a personal level, when it comes to their future studies and work, students show substantial optimism, or at least do not express particular concerns, about their individual paths. The national research data provide a clear confirmation of this hypothesis: a mere 6.9% of students express significant concern regarding the impact of AI on their education, while the vast majority (77.9%) demonstrate no apprehension in this regard. Personal concerns regarding their professional future are also minimal, with only 11.2% expressing strong concern about their career. A mere 23% of students believe that AI is influencing their future study choices, and only 6.4% perceive this influence on their career.

This confidence in their ability to navigate technological change is in stark contrast to the concerns expressed about the overall social impact. When the focus of the questions shifts to more abstract and distant issues, as many as 66.1% of students express concern about 'the impact of AI on society in general', with 28% expressing strong concern (a figure four times higher than the percentage expressing personal concerns about their own education). In a similar way, 68% of respondents predict that AI will eliminate many jobs in the long term, with 26.3% of them expressing a strong conviction of this prospect.

Many students posit that AI will have a negative impact on critical thinking in society as a whole, fear negative consequences for art and culture, and predict significant disruption to the labour market.

They also express broader concerns for 'society as a whole' (including issues related to the quality of democracy, the concentration of power, and even dystopian visions), suggesting a perception of far-reaching systemic transformations.

In summary, the concerns raised relate to society in general (the impact of AI on 'others') rather than to students' own personal experiences (educational or professional futures). This apparent contradiction between 'personal optimism' and 'social pessimism' can be interpreted through different theoretical lenses. On the one hand, it reflects the typical optimism bias (Rothman et al., 1996), which leads individuals to underestimate risks for themselves while overestimating them for others. On the other hand, it may indicate a genuine confidence in their own ability to adapt and critically engage with technology, accompanied by concern for the systemic effects that may affect less prepared and less aware segments of the population.

The Call for Clarity and Regulation

As previously mentioned, all samples strongly call for regulatory clarity. The students' demands are not so much for the implementation of bans as for the establishment of shared rules. In the national sample, 81.4% of students expressed support for explicit regulation of GenAI use (with 37% expressing a strong preference), while 81% believed that universities should not prohibit the use of AI tools. In the Udine sample, the proportions are essentially identical: 80.4% in favour of regulation, 37.3% strongly in favour, and 80.5% opposed to total bans.

Even in the qualitative research conducted through interviews, the demand for regulatory clarity emerges consistently. Two-thirds of AI users express the need for regulation rather than outright bans: 'In my opinion, they should be regulated, because they exist now anyway, so it's worth using them'; 'Regulate them, because it's the future and you can't go against the future'; 'It will be necessary to regulate them, to prevent students from even writing their theses with AI'. These data demonstrate that students perceive regulation as a tool for fairness and transparency, rather than as a threat to their freedom. This request was found to be consistent across all of the samples that were surveyed, thereby confirming the hypothesis that regulatory uncertainty is a problem perceived by the majority of the student population, both among those who use these tools and those who do not. In light of this complex and pressing demand from students, the response of Italian universities currently appears inadequate and largely absent. At the time of our research, Italian universities had done very little in terms of developing specific regulations for the use of generative AI. With regard to professors, the conclusions are similar: data from our quantitative studies show that faculty members acted only to a limited extent, and in a spontaneous and fragmented manner. The most striking finding is that nearly 85% of students perceived no active response from their professors on this issue. Only 6% of faculty reported using ChatGPT in the classroom. Beyond this, the few reactions that did occur were ambiguous: some professors prohibited its use in their courses, while others encouraged experimentation with it. However, these responses remain clearly marginal: ignoring the issue seems to have been the most widespread form of reaction.

This institutional vacuum results in a fragmentation of experiences, whereby the same behaviour may be considered lawful or unlawful depending on the course or the instructor. For students, the absence of clarity or established regulations on an issue that has become integral to their daily study practices constitutes a fundamental impediment that must be addressed. These shortcomings are not merely technical issues; they reflect a lack of strategic vision and educational leadership on the part of Italian universities at a time of profound technological transformation. Institutions that should serve as hubs of innovation and pedagogical experimentation appear to have been caught unprepared by the speed with which students have adopted these tools.

CONCLUSION: IMPLICATIONS FOR POLICY AND PRACTICE

This comprehensive investigation of Italian university students' perspectives on generative AI provides crucial empirical evidence for addressing the fundamental question: what can we do with these data?

Our findings reveal that approximately half of Italian students are already integrating GenAI tools into their academic practices, despite the absence of clear institutional guidelines. Students represent one of the most critical stakeholders in higher education, serving not merely as passive recipients but as active agents who shape institutional culture and pedagogical innovation. Their perspectives provide invaluable insights that must inform evidence-based policy development, particularly given their role as early adopters experiencing both benefits and limitations firsthand.

The research demonstrates sophisticated student awareness of GenAI complexities. Their recognition of risks, including dependency, erosion of critical thinking, and ethical concerns, alongside appreciation of benefits such as personalised learning support, suggests nuanced understanding that transcends simple enthusiasm or resistance. The 'proximity paradox', where personal optimism coexists with broader social concerns, indicates mature thinking about technological transformation.

Most significantly, over 80% of students support explicit regulation while opposing outright bans. This preference for structured guidelines rather than prohibition indicates recognition that GenAI integration is inevitable and that the primary need is for ethical, transparent implementation frameworks.

Several strategic recommendations emerge for higher education institutions. Universities must develop comprehensive GenAI policies that distinguish between legitimate educational support and academic misconduct, establishing clear boundaries that preserve learning objectives. Institutions should invest in AI literacy programmes addressing concerns about dependency and critical evaluation. Faculty development initiatives are essential to ensure that educators can guide appropriate GenAI use effectively (Zhang et al., 2025).

The documented gender disparities and disciplinary variations demand targeted interventions to ensure equitable access and prevent amplification of existing digital divides. Policy frameworks must be flexible enough to accommodate different fields while maintaining institutional coherence.

By taking student perspectives seriously and incorporating their insights into policy development, Italian universities can position themselves at the forefront of thoughtful GenAI integration. The path forward requires collaborative engagement among students, faculty, and administrators to develop institutional responses that reflect the complexity revealed in student experiences with these transformative technologies.

ACKNOWLEDGEMENTS

We gratefully acknowledge the support of the Interdepartmental Research Project 'AI – Artificial Intelligence' at the University of Udine for funding this study. We would also like to thank our colleague Adriano Cirulli for his invaluable assistance in data collection.

NOTES

1 The interviews were conducted by master's students in Integrated Communication for Enterprises and Organisations at the University of Udine, as part of a participatory research activity embedded in teaching. After specific methodological training and the collective design of the interview guide, each student carried out 4–6 face-to-face interviews with peers from different degree programmes, recruited through personal networks. This peer-to-peer approach likely reduced social desirability bias, fostering a context in which respondents felt less judged when discussing potentially controversial academic practices. The final sample consisted of 137 students, mostly from Northeastern Italy, with generative AI usage rates (53.2%) consistent with estimates from the quantitative survey.
2 In both quantitative surveys, participation requests were distributed through the Public Relations Offices (URP) of the universities involved: the University of Udine for the local study and 24 different universities for the national study.
3 In both surveys, respondents could select 'male', 'female', or 'other'. The 'other' option was chosen by 1.7% of students in the national sample and 2.3% in the local sample. While socially and symbolically relevant, these proportions were too small to be treated as statistically significant in our models; we therefore conducted a binary correlation considering only the two interpretable categories.
4 These associations are statistically significant. Personal use – Gender: χ^2 (2, N = 1,366) = 100.504, $p < .001$, $\phi c = .192$. Academic use – Gender: χ^2 (2, N = 1,366) = 41.242, $p < .001$, $\phi c = .174$.
5 These associations are statistically significant: Personal use – Gender: χ^2 (2, N = 531) = 10.845, $p = .004$, $\phi c = .143$. Academic use – Gender: χ^2 (2, N = 531) = 25.633, $p < .001$, $\phi c = .155$.
6 Statistically significant difference in the use of AI both for personal activities (χ^2 (1, N = 531) = 31.372, $p < .001$, $\phi c = .243$) and for academic activities (χ^2 (1, N = 531) = 18.736, $p < .001$, $\phi c = .188$).
7 The use of AI for university-related tasks is significantly associated with the field of study, with an effect size estimated by Cramer's V of $\phi c = .280$.
8 The cluster analysis was conducted using the K-means multivariate method, a non-hierarchical partitioning approach, set to identify four groups. The main characteristics of each cluster were then examined through cluster variable cross-tabulations. All percentages reported in this section are statistically significant, as estimated with SPSS 21 using the chi-square test ($\alpha = .05$).
9 The sample consisted of 137 students (85 female, 51 male, 1 non-binary), mostly from Northeastern Italy and enrolled in bachelor's, master's, or single-cycle programmes. Participants, recruited through interpersonal networks, included full AI users (73), personal-only users (29), and non-users (35). Interviews were conducted between April and May 2024 and analysed through manual coding with MaxQDA.

REFERENCES

Abdelwahab, H.R., Rauf, A., & Chen, D. (2022). Business students' perceptions of Dutch higher education institutions in preparing them for artificial intelligence work environments. *Industry and Higher Education*, *37*(1), 22–34. https://doi.org/10.1177/09504222221087614

Acosta-Enriquez, B.G., Arbulú Ballesteros, M.A., Huamaní Jordan, O., García-Betances, R.I., Armas-Aguirre, J., & Meneses-La-Riva, M.E. (2024). Analysis of college students' attitudes toward the use of ChatGPT in their academic activities: Effect of intent to use, verification of information and responsible use. *BMC Psychology*, *12*(1), 255. https://doi.org/10.1186/s40359-024-01764-z

Ajlouni, A., Abd-Alkareem Wahba, F., & Salem Almahaireh, A. (2023). Students' attitudes towards using ChatGPT as a learning tool: The case of the University of Jordan. *International Journal of Interactive Mobile Technologies*, *17*(18), 99–117. https://doi.org/10.3991/ijim.v17i18.41753

Al-Obaydi, L.H., Pikhart, M., & Klimova, B. (2023). ChatGPT and the general concepts of education: Can artificial intelligence-driven chatbots support the process of language learning? *International Journal of Emerging Technologies in Learning*, *18*(21), 39–50. https://doi.org/10.3991/ijet.v18i21.42593

Bisdas, S., Topriceanu, C.C., Wong, K.T., Subhash, J., Rehani, B., Kudiyirickal, M.G., Patel, K.T., Yip, S., Mellor, T.K., Holsgrove, D., Adeoye, J., Penington, C., Thomson, P., Brennan, P.A., & Lechner, M. (2021). Artificial intelligence in medicine: A multinational multi-center survey on the medical and dental students' perception. *Frontiers in Public Health*, *9*, 795284. https://doi.org/10.3389/fpubh.2021.795284

Bond, M., Khosravi, H., De Laat, M., Bergdahl, N., Negrea, V., Oxley, E., Pham, P., Chong, S.W., & Siemens, G. (2024). A meta systematic review of artificial intelligence in higher education: A call for increased ethics, collaboration, and rigour. *International Journal of Educational Technology in Higher Education*, *21*(1), 4. https://doi.org/10.1186/s41239-024-00444-7

Chan, C.K.Y., & Hu, W. (2023). Students' voices on generative AI: Perceptions, benefits, and challenges in higher education. *International Journal of Educational Technology in Higher Education*, *20*(1), 43. https://doi.org/10.1186/s41239-023-00411-8

Chiu, T.K.F., Xia, Q., Zhou, X., Chai, C.S., & Cheng, M. (2023). Systematic literature review on opportunities, challenges, and future research recommendations of artificial intelligence in education. *Computers and Education: Artificial Intelligence*, *4*, 100118. https://doi.org/10.1016/j.caeai.2022.100118

Cotton, D.R.E., Cotton, P.A., & Shipway, J.R. (2024). Chatting and cheating: Ensuring academic integrity in the era of ChatGPT. *Innovations in Education and Teaching International*, *61*(2), 228–239. https://doi.org/10.1080/14703297.2023.2190148

Davis, F.D. (1989). Perceived usefulness, perceived ease of use, and user acceptance of information technology. *MIS Quarterly*, *13*(3), 319–340. https://doi.org/10.2307/249008

Deng, R., Jiang, M., Yu, X., Lu, Y., & Liu, S. (2025). Does ChatGPT enhance student learning? A systematic review and meta-analysis of experimental studies. *Computers & Education*, *227*, 105224. https://doi.org/10.1016/j.compedu.2024.105224

Erito, S.N.P. (2023). Exploring ESP students' perception toward the potential of artificial intelligence to promote students' self-efficacy in English writing skill. *Journal of English Language Learning*, *7*(2), 459–466. https://doi.org/10.31949/jell.v7i2.7598

Famaye, T., Adisa, I.O., & Irgens, G.A. (2024). To ban or embrace: Students' perceptions towards adopting advanced AI chatbots in schools. In G. Arastoopour Irgens & S. Knight (Eds.), *Advances in quantitative ethnography: ICQE 2023* (pp. 140–154). Springer. https://doi.org/10.1007/978-3-031-47014-1_10

Farrokhnia, M., Banihashem, S.K., Noroozi, O., & Wals, A. (2024). A SWOT analysis of ChatGPT: Implications for educational practice and research. *Innovations in Education and Teaching International*, *61*(3), 460–474. https://doi.org/10.1080/14703297.2023.2195846

Ghotbi, N., Ho, M.T., & Mantello, P. (2022). Attitude of college students towards ethical issues of artificial intelligence in an international university in Japan. *AI & Society*, *37*(1), 283–290. https://doi.org/10.1007/s00146-021-01168-2

Hasanein, A.M., & Sobaih, A.E.E. (2023). Drivers and consequences of ChatGPT use in higher education: Key stakeholder perspectives. *European Journal of Investigation in Health, Psychology and Education*, *13*(11), 2599–2614. https://doi.org/10.3390/ejihpe13110181

Holland, A.A., & Ciachir, S. (2024). AI in education: A global perspective on ChatGPT and other generative AI tools in higher education. *Computers and Education Open*, *5*, 100167. https://doi.org/10.1016/j.caeo.2024.100167

Holmes, W., & Tuomi, I. (2022). State of the art and practice in AI in education. *European Journal of Education*, *57*(4), 542–570. https://doi.org/10.1111/ejed.12533

Huedo-Martínez, S., Molina-Carmona, R., & Llorens-Largo, F. (2023). Study on the attitude of young people towards technology. In P. Zaphiris & A. Ioannou (Eds.), *Learning and collaboration technologies: Learning and teaching* (pp. 26–43). Springer. https://doi.org/10.1007/978-3-031-34411-4_3

Idroes, G.M., Noviandy, T.R., Maulana, A., Irvanizam, I., Suhendrayatna, S., Sari, S.A., Khairan, K., & Kusumo, F. (2023). Student perspectives on the role of artificial intelligence in education: A survey-based analysis. *Jurnal Pendidikan Progresif*, *13*(2), 494–515.

Karakose, T., & Tülübaş, T. (2023). How can ChatGPT facilitate teaching and learning: Implications for contemporary education. *Educational Process International Journal*, *12*(4), 7–16. https://doi.org/10.22521/EDUPIJ.2023.124.1

Kayali, B., Yavuz, M., Balat, Ş., Çakır, R., & Karataş, A. (2023). Investigation of student experiences with ChatGPT-supported online learning applications in higher education. *Australasian Journal of Educational Technology*, *39*(5), 20–39. https://doi.org/10.14742/ajet.8915

Kosmyna, N., Hauptmann, E., Tong Yuan, Y., Situ, J., Liao, X., Beresnitzky, A.V., Braunstein, I., & Maes, P. (2025). Your brain on ChatGPT: Accumulation of cognitive debt when using an AI assistant for essay writing task. *arXiv preprint*. https://doi.org/10.48550/arXiv.2506.08872

Lai, C.Y., Cheung, K.Y., & Chan, C.S. (2023). Exploring the role of intrinsic motivation in ChatGPT adoption to support active learning: An extension of the technology acceptance model. *Computers and Education: Artificial Intelligence*, *5*, 100178. https://doi.org/10.1016/j.caeai.2023.100178

Lee, Y.F., Hwang, G.J., & Chen, P.Y. (2022). Impacts of an AI-based chatbot on college students' after-class review, academic performance, self-efficacy, learning attitude, and motivation. *Educational Technology Research and Development*, *70*(5), 1843–1865. https://doi.org/10.1007/s11423-022-10142-8

Liu, Q., & Zhang, Y. (2024). Student acceptance of AI writing tools: An extended technology acceptance model perspective. *Computers & Education*, *196*, 104815. https://doi.org/10.1016/j.compedu.2023.104815

Ma, J., Wang, P., Li, B., Gao, S., Zhang, M., & Zhao, G. (2024). Exploring user adoption of ChatGPT: A technology acceptance model perspective. *International Journal of Human–Computer Interaction*, *40*(11), 2731–2746. https://doi.org/10.1080/10447318.2024.2314358

Malmström, H., Stöhr, C., & Ou, A.W. (2023). *Chatbots and other AI for learning: A survey of use and views among university students in Sweden* (Chalmers Studies in Communication and Learning in Higher Education No. 1). Chalmers University of Technology. https://doi.org/10.17196/cls.csclhe/2023/01

Montenegro-Rueda, M., Fernández-Cerero, J., Fernández-Batanero, J.M., & López-Meneses, E. (2023). Impact of the implementation of ChatGPT in education: A systematic review. *Computers*, *12*(8), 153. https://doi.org/10.3390/computers12080153

Ngo, T.T.A. (2023). The perception by university students of the use of ChatGPT in education. *International Journal of Emerging Technologies in Learning*, *18*(17), 4–19. https://doi.org/10.3991/ijet.v18i17.39019

Pinho, C., Franco, M., & Mendes, L. (2021). Application of innovation diffusion theory to the e-learning process: Higher education context. *Education and Information Technologies*, *26*(1), 421–440. https://doi.org/10.1007/s10639-020-10269-2

Popenici, S. (2023). *Artificial intelligence and learning futures: Critical narratives of technology and imagination in higher education*. Taylor & Francis. https://doi.org/10.4324/9781003424727

Rahiman, H.U., & Kodikal, R. (2024). Revolutionizing education: Artificial intelligence empowered learning in higher education. *Cogent Education*, *11*(1), 2293431. https://doi.org/10.1080/2331186X.2023.2293431

Rawas, S. (2024). ChatGPT: Empowering lifelong learning in the digital age of higher education. *Education and Information Technologies*, *29*(6), 6895–6908. https://doi.org/10.1007/s10639-023-12114-8

Rudolph, J., Tan, S., & Tan, S. (2023). ChatGPT: Bullshit spewer or the end oftraditional assessments in higher education? *Journal of Applied Learning & Teaching*, *6*(1), 342–363.

Roberts, H., Babuta, A., Morley, J., Lai, C.K., Cowls, J., Taddeo, M., & Floridi, L. (2023). Artificial intelligence regulation in the United Kingdom: A path to good governance and global leadership? *Internet Policy Review*, *12*(2), 1–30. https://doi.org/10.14763/2023.2.1709

Rothman, A.J., Klein, W.M.P., & Weinstein, N.D. (1996). Absolute and relative biases in estimations of personal risk. *Journal of Applied Social Psychology*, *26*(14), 1213–1236. https://doi.org/10.1111/j.1559-1816.1996.tb01778.x

Saif, N. et al. (2024). ChatGPT; validating technology acceptance model (TAM) in education sector via ubiquitous learning mechanism. *Computers in Human Behavior*, *154*, 108097. https://doi.org/10.1016/j.chb.2023.108097

Seo, K., Tang, J., Roll, I., Fels, S., & Yoon, D. (2021). The impact of artificial intelligence on learner–instructor interaction in online learning. *International Journal of Educational Technology in Higher Education*, *18*(1), 54. https://doi.org/10.1186/s41239-021-00292-9

Sullivan, M., Kelly, A., & McLaughlan, P. (2023). ChatGPT in higher education: Considerations for academic integrity and student learning. *Journal of Applied Learning & Teaching*, *6*(1), 31–40. https://doi.org/10.37074/jalt.2023.6.1.17

Tierney, A., Peasey, P., & Gould, J. (2025). Student perceptions on the impact of AI on their teaching and learning experiences in higher education. *Research and Practice in Technology Enhanced Learning*, *20*(1), 5. https://doi.org/10.58459/rptel.2025.20005

Wang, J., Jing, C., & Shen, Y. (2025). The effect of ChatGPT on students' learning performance, learning perception, and higher-order thinking: Insights from a meta-analysis. *Humanities and Social Sciences Communications*, *12*(1), 621. https://doi.org/10.1057/s41599-025-04787-y

Yilmaz, H., Maxutov, S., Baitekov, A., & Begalinova, K. (2023). Student attitudes towards Chat GPT: A technology acceptance model survey. *International Educational Review*, *1*(1), 57–83. https://doi.org/10.58693/ier.114

Yu, H. (2024). The application and challenges of ChatGPT in educational transformation: New demands for teachers' roles. *Heliyon*, *10*(2), e24289. https://doi.org/10.1016/j.heliyon.2024.e24289

Zhang, B. (2024). Preparing educators and students for ChatGPT and AI technology: Exploring the implications for policy in higher education. *Online Journal of Education Research*, *3*(2), 45–58.

Zhang, C., Zhang, K., Zhang, C., Cui, W., Xie, A., Teo, T., & Gong, D. (2025). Teachers' technology integration self-efficacy and its relationship with students' perceptions: A meta-analysis. *Computers & Education*, *228*, 105342.

10 AI as a Tool for Developing Critical Thinking Among Students

Marcin Woźniak, Karolina Rożek, and Krzysztof Turek

INTRODUCTION

The advent of advanced technologies has historically prompted both optimism for human progress and concerns regarding the potential atrophy of fundamental human capacities. Just as Plato, using the figure of his master Socrates, famously cautioned (Plato, *Phaedrus* 14, 274c–275b) against the technology of writing, fearing it would diminish true understanding by negating the need for internal reflection and dialogue, a similar paradox emerges with the rise of Artificial Intelligence (AI), particularly large language models (LLMs). While this technology offers unprecedented access to and processing of information, a crucial question arises: Will AI serve as a cognitive artefact that enhances our innate human abilities, such as critical thinking, or will it lead to cognitive offloading (Risko & Gilbert, 2016) into black box processing and the replacement of these skills? This paper aims to explore this central dilemma, investigating the conditions under which AI can either foster or hinder the development of critical thinking among individuals. The influence of massive adaptation of AI on critical thinking is an important phenomenon, given the influence of critical thinking skills on the individual as well as society at large.

We view critical thinking as a meta-competence, affecting many areas of personal and social life. For example, in a study, higher critical scores correlated with making informed life decisions, such as getting flu shots or avoiding bankruptcy (Butler et al., 2017). Critical thinking was a better predictor of life events than intelligence and significantly increased explained variance beyond what intelligence alone accounted for. Other studies show the positive influence of critical thinking on academic achievements. While this impact varies among demographics and subjects, it has been observed regularly (Orhan, 2022).

There is also a strong correlation between mastering critical thinking skills and the ability to recognise fake news and disinformation (Redaelli et al. 2025). Additionally, critical thinking skills significantly predict democratic attitudes (Aslan, 2018).

DOI: 10.1201/9781003676188-11

The ability to independently evaluate information is crucial for individuals to avoid becoming vulnerable to manipulation through disinformation and propaganda.

The research demonstrates that critical thinking functions as a protective cognitive mechanism, enabling individuals to navigate complex information environments, make better decisions across multiple life domains, and achieve higher levels of academic and personal success, as well as offering effective protection against disinformation and manipulation. Critical thinking, much like memory, is not an innate skill; it is an ability that must be learned, cultivated, and consistently practised (Facione, 2011).

This paper explores both the risks and opportunities presented by the increasing integration of generative AI into educational settings, with a particular focus on how such technologies might erode or reinforce critical thinking skills. Drawing from empirical research and the TITAN project's findings, we analyse under which circumstances AI threatens to supplant human judgement and when it can serve as an effective scaffold for deeper, more independent thinking. The following sections will (1) examine new evidence on the ways AI may contribute to the decline of critical thinking among students, (2) define the dimensions of critical thinking as a multifaceted competence, (3) highlight insights from the TITAN project regarding the Socratic method and collaborative argument mapping as effective approaches for critical thinking development, and (4) offer recommendations for the design of AI systems that promote, rather than replace, robust cognitive engagement. In synthesising current trends and empirical results, our goal is to outline practical recommendations for leveraging AI as a tool for cultivating, not diminishing, critical thinking among students.

THE EROSION AND REINFORCEMENT OF CRITICAL THINKING IN THE AGE OF GENERATIVE AI

As generative AI systems such as ChatGPT become increasingly embedded in educational environments, their dual potential to both transform and compromise learning processes is becoming more apparent. On the one hand, they are praised for their efficiency, accessibility, and personalisation, offering students on-demand support in ideation, summarisation, reference retrieval, writing, and problem-solving (Perez et al., 2022; Zawacki-Richter et al., 2019; Ravšelj et al., 2025; Franczyk & Rajchel, 2024). Particularly for STEM students, older cohorts, and non-native English speakers, such tools serve as valuable aids in navigating complex academic tasks (Baek et al., 2024). Students report that AI allows them to optimise effort, manage workload pressures, and mitigate feelings of overload, which often translates into relief and regained control over their academic time (Rożek, 2025a, 2025b).

Yet, this convenience carries profound cognitive and pedagogical risks. Empirical research demonstrates that regular reliance on AI systems can inadvertently undermine deep learning, critical reflection, and information retention (Zhai, Wibowo & Li, 2024). In experimental contexts, students supported by ChatGPT often produce polished surface-level texts without corresponding gains in subject mastery, self-awareness, or intrinsic motivation (Barshay, 2025). EEG-based evidence points to diminished neural activity during AI-supported writing, suggesting the accumulation of what Kosmyna et al. (2025) term 'cognitive debt'. Moreover, studies confirm a strong negative correlation between habitual AI use and critical thinking scores, particularly among younger users (Gerlich, 2025). Far from fostering intellectual growth, unreflective dependence on AI appears to encourage procrastination, shallow engagement, and metacognitive passivity (Abbas, Jam & Khan, 2024; Barshay, 2025).

These tensions are mirrored in students' own ambivalent attitudes towards GPT-type tools. While many celebrate their functional benefits, such as efficiency, personalisation, translation support, or assistance with repetitive tasks, others raise concerns about the erosion of academic integrity, the validity of assessment, and the devaluation of learning itself (Blahopoulou & Ortiz-Bonnin, 2025; Hasanein & Sobaih, 2023). Emotional responses range from excitement and relief to shame and uncertainty, highlighting that engagement with AI is not purely instrumental but also identity-laden and socially situated. Context-specific research, particularly in the Global South, emphasises that access and use remain uneven, with translation and ideation tasks predominating and calls for targeted AI-literacy initiatives to ensure equitable integration (Gasaymeh et al., 2025).

Against this backdrop, the critical pedagogical challenge is not whether generative AI will be used in education, but how it will be incorporated. Scholars stress the need for deliberate strategies that embed AI literacy into curricula, codify institutional policies, and foster intentional roles for AI as critic, editor, or mentor rather than defaulting to passive knowledge delivery (Przegalinska & Triantoro, 2024; Niloy et al., 2024; Sandu et al., 2024). Without such safeguards, AI threatens to accelerate broader trends of standardisation and automation in education, displacing dialogical and value-laden dimensions of learning that cultivate independent judgement and critical reflection (Hughes, 2021).

THE OPERATIONALISATION OF CRITICAL THINKING

The aim of the chapter is to present theoretical foundations for the empirical operationalisation of the notion of critical thinking. We based the operational definition of critical thinking on a Delphi study, led by Peter A. Facione (Facione, 1990), involving a panel of experts (mainly scholars from different fields) to reach a consensus on the definition and attributes of critical thinking. They defined critical thinking as 'purposeful, self-regulatory judgment which results in interpretation, analysis, evaluation, and inference, as well as explanation of the evidential, conceptual, methodological, criteriological, or contextual considerations upon which that judgment is based'. Critical thinking is thus a purposeful cognitive process of actively processing information to guide belief and action. Facione (1990) identified six core dimensions of critical thinking. These dimensions provide a comprehensive framework for understanding and assessing this multifaceted skill.

Interpretation: This is the ability to comprehend and express the meaning or significance of a wide variety of experiences, situations, data, events, and judgements. It includes the subskills of categorisation, decoding significance, and clarifying meaning. For instance, in the context of media consumption, interpretation involves understanding the literal meaning of a news report while also discerning its potential underlying messages or biases.

Analysis: This dimension involves identifying the intended and actual inferential relationships among statements, questions, concepts, and other forms of representation. The key subskills are examining ideas, detecting arguments, and analysing arguments. Analysis allows an individual to deconstruct an argument into its constituent parts—premises and conclusions—to better understand its structure and logic. It helps to interpret what others stand for or to clarify one's own intuitions.

Evaluation: This is the skill of assessing the credibility of statements and the logical strength of the inferential relationships among them. It comprises two main subskills: assessing claims and assessing arguments (Facione, 1990). Evaluation is crucial for distinguishing between well-supported arguments and those that are based on fallacious reasoning or questionable evidence.

Inference: This dimension pertains to identifying and securing the elements needed to draw reasonable conclusions. It involves forming conjectures and hypotheses, considering relevant information, and deducing the consequences that flow from data and beliefs. The subskills include querying evidence, conjecturing alternatives, and drawing conclusions. Inference enables a thinker to move beyond the information given to arrive at new insights and understandings.

Explanation: This is the ability to state and justify one's reasoning in a clear and coherent manner. It involves presenting one's reasoning in the form of cogent arguments. The subskills are stating results, justifying procedures, and presenting arguments. A critical thinker must be able to articulate their thought processes and the evidence that supports their conclusions.

Self-Regulation: This is often considered a meta-cognitive skill, involving the self-conscious monitoring of one's own cognitive activities. It includes self-examination and self-correction (Facione, 1990). Self-regulation is the process by which a critical thinker reflects on their own reasoning, identifies potential biases or errors, and makes necessary adjustments to improve their thinking. This dimension is considered a fundamental prerequisite for the others and requires a different type of assessment due to its general and psychologically impactful nature (Machete & Turpin, 2020; Nosich, 2012).

Critical thinking is one of the basic cognitive skills and is used by people every day. It can be viewed as a multifaceted cognitive skill that is foundational to reasoned judgement and informed decision-making. Defining the core dimensions of critical thinking (interpretation, analysis, evaluation, inference, explanation, and self-regulation) provided a robust framework for its development and assessment in the research conducted in the TITAN project. The relevance of critical thinking has been magnified in the contemporary digital landscape, which is rife with forms of influence via cyberspace, including scams, propaganda, or disinformation.

CONCLUSIONS FROM THE TITAN PROJECT

The TITAN (AI for Citizen Intelligent Coaching Against Disinformation) European HORIZON Research and Innovation Action examined the use of AI in fostering critical thinking, especially in the context of disinformation. The ability to critically assess and analyse information and reasoning to arrive at one's own logical conclusions is contrasted with mere fact-checking and is purposefully designed to enhance all six dimensions of critical thinking. Specifically, the TITAN Critical Thinking Assessment module evaluates users' abilities across all cognitive dimensions described in Chapter 3.

TITAN's Assumptions and Methodology

The TITAN project was guided by several core assumptions (Ramfos et al., 2025). It posited that a digitally adapted Socratic method is highly effective for fostering deep, independent thinking. This approach is enhanced by LLMs, which create a framework to empower citizens against disinformation. A central tenet is that critical thinking and media literacy are the primary defences, best strengthened through personalised and community-driven learning. The project also argues for supplementing fact-checking with evaluating the logical soundness of an argumentation and recognising disinformation techniques. The development was based on creating human-centric principles and trustworthy AI through participatory design.

The project assessed its impact on critical thinking using a three-phase methodology (De Vooght et al., 2025). The process began with co-creation workshops involving 215 citizens across eight countries to define user requirements and ethical principles. Next, living labs with 65 participants in four countries tested a prototype chatbot's usability and effectiveness. Finally, pilot studies with 52 participants across three use cases (students, NGO members, and migrants/refugees) evaluated the system's real-world performance. These experiments yielded significant findings, highlighting both opportunities and challenges in developing an AI-driven solution for increasing critical thinking.

Opportunities and Positive Impacts

The TITAN tools, particularly the chatbot, proved effective in promoting critical thinking. Over 90% of participants rated TITAN as moderately to extremely effective in enhancing their critical thinking abilities, with 37% deeming it moderately effective, 48% very effective, and 7% extremely effective. A pre- and post-measure study demonstrated significant increases in Regulatory Self-Efficacy in Sharing Misinformation (RSESM), with active RSESM scores rising from 7.53 to 8.30 ($p = 0.003$) while passive self-efficacy increased from 7.44 to 7.93 ($p = 0.027$). In Living Labs surveys ($N = 65$), 69% reported adopting a more critical approach to news, and 53% agreed the chatbot offered helpful guidance for evaluation (De Vooght et al., 2025).

The collaboration module of the TITAN is based on collective argument mapping—a method of visually organising the structure of information in a graph of claims linked by logical relationships demarcating premises, conclusions, and sources. This module also supported constructive engagement: intensity of reading in group discussions correlated strongly with critical thinking gains ($r = 0.711$, $p = 0.006$). User-friendliness and trust in the tool scored moderately high (around 3.5/5). Notably, participants' fact-checking abilities improved significantly after using the system (mean difference = −0.77, $p = 0.011$).

The project showed clear value for educational applications, especially within structured settings like courses, workshops, or facilitated classroom discussions. Educators and students alike appreciated its potential for training critical thinking, scrutinising articles, identifying disinformation tactics, and strengthening users' commitment to refraining from sharing misinformation and actively countering it.

Challenges and Limitations

A significant challenge arose from users' expectations, largely shaped by mainstream AI tools like ChatGPT. Many participants expected direct answers rather than embracing the positive friction that engaging in a Socratic critical dialogue demands. This led to frustration, with users feeling that the chatbot behaved more like a checklist than a conversational coach (De Vooght et al., 2025). The studies also suggested that TITAN's utility was primarily recognised within closed educational contexts, with independent citizens seeing little clear demand for the tools in their everyday lives.

Despite high effectiveness ratings, qualitative feedback highlighted engagement barriers: some users perceived repeated Socratic questioning as rigid or impersonal, rather than responsive coaching. Only 16% of participants reported a definite intention to use the tool in the future, while 46% were not at all inclined, pointing to a gap between immediate gains and longer term adoption. This suggests that while TITAN excels in didactic, structured settings, design improvements may be needed to increase everyday relevance and sustained user engagement outside formal learning environments.

In summary, TITAN is effective for strengthening critical thinking and media literacy, particularly in formal educational environments where structured engagement and guided dialogue are valued. Its question-driven, rigorous approach stands in contrast to mainstream, answer-oriented LLMs, and this shift in interaction style may require user retraining and adaptation for broader impact beyond the classroom.

DESIGN COMPARISON: HOW USAGE DIFFERS IN REDUCING VS. INCREASING CRITICAL THINKING

The design and implementation of AI tools, particularly LLMs, significantly influence whether they empower or diminish users' critical thinking abilities. In this chapter, we highlight design components that frame and influence engagement with the cognitive process of generating an answer by delegating it to LLM or thinking with LLM.

Socratic Method

Guiding users through systematic questioning rather than providing direct answers actively engages users to challenge assumptions, encourage self-examination, and stimulate deep, logical inquiry. Structured, open-ended questions that prompt users to focus on all dimensions of critical thinking: interpretation, analysis, evaluation, inference, explanation, and self-regulation.

The Paul-Elder Socratic approach, for example, categorises questions into six key types: clarification, challenging assumptions, evidence and reasoning, alternative viewpoints, implications and consequences, and challenging the question. AI-driven questioning can transform knowledge into inquiry-based deliberation, thereby fostering deeper engagement with reasoning and enhancing critical thinking and self-reflection. This approach encourages users to 'internalise' the questioning method, aiming to make them independent thinkers who derive conclusions and their underlying reasoning autonomously.

However, the effectiveness of this question-centric approach can be challenged by user expectations. Users accustomed to tools like ChatGPT often expect direct answers and instructions rather than engaging in a dialogue designed to challenge their initial assumptions. This can introduce additional processes that may be perceived as a barrier between the initial prompt and the desired result. This positive friction can be a benefit to the cognitive growth of the user, but can also cause frustration and a sense of discomfort. This highlights a tension: while the Socratic method has the potential to activate users' critical thinking, it demands more effort and may discourage them from engaging in a more effortful process.

Argument Mapping

Argument mapping helps users understand and analyse complex arguments by presenting information in a non-linear, structured manner. It is a highly effective method for improving critical thinking. Studies have shown that a semester-long course focusing on argument mapping can lead to a significant increase in critical thinking skills, 0.7–0.71 standard deviations (Cullen et al. 2018; Van Gelder 2015), outperforming other educational methods like a general college semester 0.16–0.3 standard deviations (Huber & Kuncel 2016) or mixed philosophy courses 0.38 (Abrami et al. 2015). Beyond critical thinking, argument mapping also enhances analytical reasoning, mathematical reasoning, and essay writing skills. Furthermore, computer-assisted argument mapping is more effective than traditional pen-and-paper methods for recall, retention, and comprehension of information.

This method aids in reducing cognitive load by organising complex information visually, making interpretation easier and facilitating understanding inferences of each argument individually and explaining the topic as a totality of information on the map. This structure allows users to focus on analysis and evaluation, rather than following the narrative of linear text. It purposefully depersonalises the information, making it necessary to focus on the reasoning rather than its digital or human originator. In a collaborative context, computer-assisted argument mapping fosters more civil, merit-based discussions focused on the validity of reasoning, thereby avoiding personal attacks and promoting shared understanding. A crucial aspect of the argument mapping method is full transparency and explainability of reasoning, allowing users to inspect how certain conclusions were reached, which stands in contrast to the unexplainability of question-answer type of interaction of most LLM chats. Argument mapping is also a good example of a 'cognitive artifact"—a tool or representation that supports and extends human cognitive abilities (Norman 1991). In the context of critical thinking, it can serve as a powerful cognitive scaffolding. Argument mapping enables users to think as an active agent interacting with reasoning, preserving cognitive control and autonomy.

Design That Risks Reducing Critical Thinking

A significant risk of current LLMs is their inherent unexplainability of internal reasoning. Contrary to the older generation of deterministic expert systems, LLMs function as a 'black box' that inputs the prompts and outputs answers without the possibility of retracing the processing of the information. Even reasoning models that use the 'Chain of Thought' (CoT) tend to be unemphasised or wholly hidden from users. This creates a tendency for users to delegate thinking to a black box, where they passively accept AI-generated outputs without critical engagement. This over-reliance on AI can hinder self-reflection and critical evaluation, as evidenced by the negative correlation between frequent AI tool usage and critical thinking abilities, particularly among younger individuals. The limitations of current LLMs in performing genuine reasoning tasks mean that AI systems can inadvertently reinforce biases from the training data, subtly steer users towards values hidden in 'System Specification' and 'System prompts'. When AI acts as a black box that simply provides answers, it removes the opportunity for users to engage in the active cognitive effort required for critical thinking. Research in explainable artificial intelligence (XAI) emphasises that opaque reasoning paths in decision-support tools foster automation bias and cognitive offloading, thus reducing critical engagement (Doshi-Velez & Kim, 2017; Lipton, 2017). To foster genuine critical thinking, LLM systems may be designed to disclose their inferential steps and logical justifications, enabling users to interrogate, compare, and contest the AI's 'thinking', instead of relegating the process to an invisible black box.

The design of chat interaction itself, based on human-to-human interactions, may subtly mislead users as well. It is much more natural to think of an LLM-based interlocutor as a person knowing a lot about many different topics rather than systems of weights and biases trained to predict the next token based on previous successful completions. This distinction requires a lot of media literacy and technical understanding of LLMs and a cognitive effort to remember while in the middle of an interaction. It lends itself to anthropomorphisation of LLM and suggests humanlike qualities of the system. This may lead to less vigilance to common phenomena like hallucinations.

Hallucinations occur when models output plausible-sounding but entirely fabricated information—a risk heightened when CoT steps are hidden, or explanations are not demanded (Ji et al., 2023). It is important to note that CoT often offers a faulty approximation of narrative steps of reasoning rather than rigorous logical inferences. In educational settings, this exposes users to misinformation cloaked in authority, undermining trust and further discouraging independent verification. Over-reliance on such systems may lead users to internalise faulty reasoning structures or perpetuate disinformation, particularly when critical thinking is weak or underdeveloped (Maynez et al., 2020). Effective countermeasures include mandatory citation workflows, automated fact-checking integrations, and transparent CoT displays, all designed to empower users to scrutinise and validate LLM outputs rather than passively accept them. The goal should be systems that not only identify potential hallucinations but also actively invite users into the verification process, thus anchoring critical engagement as a design principle rather than an afterthought.

A related but distinct risk to critical thinking comes from the phenomenon of 'sycophancy' in RLHF-trained LLMs, where models adapt their answers to align with perceived user opinions or expectations, sometimes at the expense of truth or logical rigour. Recent studies show that LLMs can produce responses that overly reinforce user biases, avoid constructive disagreement, or confirm incorrect assumptions (Perez et al., 2022). Sycophantic outputs cultivate a feedback loop that rewards uncritical acceptance and shields users from cognitive dissonance, thereby stunting the intellectual friction essential for critical analysis (Wei et al., 2023). This design flaw is exacerbated in educational settings, where continuous positive reinforcement from AI may create false confidence in learning outcomes and cripple the metacognitive self-correction central to critical thinking. Mitigating sycophancy requires deliberate model fine-tuning, the inclusion of 'devil's advocate' strategies, and interface prompts that encourage challenge, pluralism, and reasoned debate rather than mere acquiescence.

The last and crucial aspect of the design of AI systems is friction. Most product design avoids negative friction—any kind of unwanted barrier between a user's action and receipt of an expected value. However, critical thinking is an active cognitive process that demands effort from a person. As indicated in TITAN research, which purposefully offers a positive friction to engage in critical thinking, this effort can lead to frustration, especially if the user lacks motivation. There is a natural tendency to rely on intuitive, low-effort thinking strategies (System 1) rather than investing in more demanding analytical reasoning (System 2) (Evans, 2008; Kahneman, 2011). In educational contexts, effortless user experiences that offer passive consumption but immediate gratification can strongly outcompete tools or pedagogies requiring greater cognitive effort, even when the latter support deeper learning and critical thinking (Barr et al., 2015). Without careful design, LLMs and similar technologies risk amplifying this cognitive ease bias, promoting passive consumption over active intellectual engagement.

CONCLUSIONS

To summarise, the question of whether AI is thinking *with* us or *for* us lies at the heart of its impact on critical thinking. Some techniques, such as Socratic questioning or argument mapping, can address all or most dimensions of critical thinking, but to exemplify the most prominent dichotomies in effect on critical thinking dimensions, we contrast selected design choices in Table 10.1.

In higher education contexts, state-of-the-art AI assistants (e.g. ChatGPT, Anthropic's Claude, and Google's Gemini) as of 2024–2025 are increasingly designed to structure reasoning and promote critical thinking rather than simply provide answers. Some new systems like Claude for Education adopt a Socratic scaffolding approach: the AI poses guiding questions instead of giving direct solutions, encouraging students to explore multiple perspectives and self-reflect. At the same time, designers are experimenting with making AI's thought process more transparent, creating cognitive artefacts that learners can inspect and challenge. Such features align with the goal of moving towards AI thinking with students instead of for them, aiming to

TABLE 10.1
Comparison of AI design choices and their dichotomous impact on dimensions of critical thinking

Critical thinking dimension	Thinking *with* us (enhancing critical thinking)	thinking *for* us (reducing critical thinking)
Interpretation	media literacy tips	anthropomorphisation
Analysis	argument mapping, structured reasoning, integrating multiple points of view	plain text narrative
Evaluation	transparency, interactive reasoning	black box, hidden chain of thought
Inference	examination of sources and premises, quantifying uncertainty	hallucinations
Explanation	positive friction	frictionless experience
Self-regulation	Socratic questions, questioning assumptions	sycophancy, answers only

foster active engagement and metacognitive reflection instead of passive consumption of answers. To support complex academic tasks, modern LLM-based tools also leverage expanded context capabilities and multimodal inputs: models now handle very large 'long-form' contexts (tens of thousands of tokens, sometimes spanning entire documents) and can incorporate visuals alongside text, often coupled with personalised prompts or feedback tailored to individual learners' needs. Nonetheless, persistent challenges like sycophancy, hallucinations, anthropomorphism, and black box thinking continue to pose concerns.

While there are Pareto-effective solutions to be found combining good design and care for the cognitive development of students in the use of LLMs, there is a certain threshold of effort and discomfort that exercising critical thinking requires from a user base of fast-growing LLM-based products in a competitive market. This dramatic tension was present in the life and legacy of Socrates himself. He was remembered in history through Plato's writings. The criticism of the technology of writing put in Socrates' mouth by his student was not derived from the standpoint of opposition to progress, but as a risk to our cognitive growth that active, living thought provides. Deemed by many as the 'father of philosophy', his provocative method of questioning had a profound impact on the course of Western and global thought, but his attitude annoyed some of his contemporaries to the point of sentencing him to death. Bearing in mind the role critical thinking plays in our private and social lives, we can expect that, however we collectively choose to solve this conundrum, its civilisational impact will also be significant.

ACKNOWLEDGEMENTS

During the preparation of this work, the authors used NotebookLM and ChatGPT in order to manage sources, grammar and spelling check, and improve wording. After using these services, the authors reviewed and edited the content as needed and take full responsibility for the publication's content.

BIBLIOGRAPHY

Abbas, M., Jam, F. A., & Khan, T. I. (2024). Is it harmful or helpful? Examining the causes and consequences of generative AI usage among university students. *International Journal of Educational Technology in Higher Education*, *21*(1), 10. https://doi.org/10.1186/s41239-024-00444-7

Abbas, Q., & Harrison, R. (2025). *ChatGPT and generative AI: Addressing critical thinking in education's transition from "what" to "why"*. Unpublished. https://doi.org/10.13140/RG.2.2.28659.03364

Abrami, P. C., Bernard, R. M., Borokhovski, E., Waddington, D. I., Wade, C. A., & Persson, T. (2015). Strategies for teaching students to think critically: A meta-analysis. *Review of Educational Research*, *85*(2), 275–314. https://doi.org/10.3102/0034654314551063

Aslan, S. (2018). The relationship between critical thinking skills and democratic attitudes of 4th class primary school students. *International Journal of Progressive Education*, *14*(6), 68–81. https://doi.org/10.29329/ijpe.2018.179.5

Baek, C., Tate, T., & Warschauer, M. (2024). "ChatGPT seems too good to be true": College students' use and perceptions of generative AI. *Computers and Education: Artificial Intelligence*, *7*, 100294. https://doi.org/10.1016/j.caeai.2024.100294

Barr, N., Pennycook, G., Stolz, J. A., & Fugelsang, J. A. (2015). The brain in your pocket: Evidence that smartphones are used to supplant thinking. *Computers in Human Behavior*, *48*, 473–480. https://doi.org/10.1016/j.chb.2015.02.029

Barshay, J. (2025, May 19). University students offload critical thinking, other hard work to AI. *The Hechinger Report*. https://hechingerreport.org/proof-points-offload-critical-thinking-ai/

Blahopoulou, J., & Ortiz-Bonnin, S. (2025). Student perceptions of ChatGPT: Benefits, costs, and attitudinal differences between users and non-users toward AI integration in higher education. *Education and Information Technologies*. https://doi.org/10.1007/s10639-025-13575-9

Butler, H. A., Pentoney, C., & Bong, M. P. (2017). Predicting real-world outcomes: Critical thinking ability is a better predictor of life decisions than intelligence. *Thinking Skills and Creativity*, *25*, 38–46. https://doi.org/10.1016/j.tsc.2017.06.005

Cullen, S., Fan, J., Van Der Brugge, E., & Elga, A. (2018). Improving analytical reasoning and argument understanding: A quasi-experimental field study of argument visualization. *NPJ Science of Learning*, *3*(1), 21. https://doi.org/10.1038/s41539-018-0038-5

De Vooght, E., Duelen, A., Petasis, G., Van den Broeck, W., Desimpelaere, L., Picone, I., Giacobone, G. A., Pollini, A., Katsamori, D., Bædum, N. B., Stamatellos, G., Kapetanakis, P., Paparrigopoulos, G., & Papachristou, E. (2025). *Building a GenAI Socratic chatbot for critical thinking: Insights from cross-cultural cocreation, living labs and pilots*. [Manuscript submitted for publication]. TITAN Project Consortium.

Doshi-Velez, F., & Kim, B. (2017). *Towards a rigorous science of interpretable machine learning* (No. arXiv:1702.08608). arXiv. https://doi.org/10.48550/arXiv.1702.08608

Duelen, A., Jennes, I., & Van Den Broeck, W. (2024). Socratic AI against disinformation: Improving critical thinking to recognize disinformation using socratic AI. *ACM International Conference on Interactive Media Experiences*, 375–381. https://doi.org/10.1145/3639701.3663640

Evans, J. S. B. T. (2008). Dual-processing accounts of reasoning, judgment, and social cognition. *Annual Review of Psychology*, *59*(1), 255–278. https://doi.org/10.1146/annurev.psych.59.103006.093629

Facione, P. A. (1990). *Critical thinking: A statement of expert consensus for purposes of educational assessment and instruction*. Research Findings and Recommendations. American Philosophical Association.

Facione, P. A. (2011). Critical thinking: What it is and why it counts. *Insight Assessment*, *1*(1), 1–23.

Franczyk, A., & Rajchel, A. (2024). Postawy studentów wobec ChatGPT w edukacji. *Horyzonty Wychowania*, *23*(65), 89–101. https://doi.org/10.35765/hw.2024.2365.10

Gasaymeh, A., Abu Qbeita, A., AlMohtadi, R., & Beirat, M. (2025). Exploring education students' use of ChatGPT for academic and personal purposes: Insights from a developing country context. *Frontiers in Education*, *10*, 1580310. https://doi.org/10.3389/feduc.2025.1580310

Gerlich, M. (2025). AI tools in society: Impacts on cognitive offloading and the future of critical thinking. *Societies*, *15*(1), 6. https://doi.org/10.3390/soc15010006

Hasanein, A. M., & Sobaih, A. E. E. (2023). Drivers and consequences of ChatGPT use in higher education: Key stakeholder perspectives. *European Journal of Investigation in Health, Psychology and Education*, *13*(11), 2599–2614. https://doi.org/10.3390/ejihpe13110181

Huber, C. R., & Kuncel, N. R. (2016). Does college teach critical thinking? A Meta-Analysis. *Review of Educational Research*, *86*(2), 431–468. https://doi.org/10.3102/0034654315605917

Hughes, J. (2021). Deskilling of teaching and the case for intelligent tutoring systems. *Journal of Ethics and Emerging Technologies*, *31*(2), 1–16. https://doi.org/10.55613/jeet.v31i2.90

Jakhad, P., Oudichhya, J., Gandhi, K., & Rai, A. K. (2023). Identification of newly observed singly charmed baryons using relativistic flux tube model. *Physical Review D*, *108*(1), 014011. https://doi.org/10.1103/PhysRevD.108.014011

Ji, Z., Lee, N., Frieske, R., Yu, T., Su, D., Xu, Y., Ishii, E., Bang, Y., Chen, D., Dai, W., Chan, H. S., Madotto, A., & Fung, P. (2023). Survey of hallucination in natural language generation. *ACM Computing Surveys*, *55*(12), 1–38. https://doi.org/10.1145/3571730

Kahneman, D. (2011). *Thinking, fast and slow*. Farrar, Straus and Giroux.

Kosmyna, N., Hauptmann, E., Yuan, Y. T., Situ, J., Liao, X.-H., Beresnitzky, A. V., Braunstein, I., & Maes, P. (2025). *Your brain on ChatGPT: Accumulation of cognitive debt when using an AI assistant for essay writing task* (No. arXiv:2506.08872). arXiv. https://doi.org/10.48550/arXiv.2506.08872

Krämer, W. (2014). Kahneman, D. (2011): Thinking, fast and slow: Penguin, 496 pp., € 10.50, ISBN 978-0141033570. *Statistical Papers*, *55*(3), 915. https://doi.org/10.1007/s00362-013-0533-y

Lipton, Z. C. (2017). *The mythos of model interpretability* (No. arXiv:1606.03490). arXiv. https://doi.org/10.48550/arXiv.1606.03490

Machete, P., & Turpin, M. (2020). The use of critical thinking to identify fake news: A systematic literature review. In M. Hattingh, M. Matthee, H. Smuts, I. Pappas, Y. K. Dwivedi, & M. Mäntymäki (Eds.), *Responsible design, implementation and use of information and communication technology* (Vol. 12067, pp. 235–246). Springer International Publishing. https://doi.org/10.1007/978-3-030-45002-1_20

Maynez, J., Narayan, S., Bohnet, B., & McDonald, R. (2020). *On faithfulness and factuality in abstractive summarization* (No. arXiv:2005.00661). arXiv. https://doi.org/10.48550/arXiv.2005.00661

Niloy, A. C., Bari, M. A., Sultana, J., Chowdhury, R., Raisa, F. M., Islam, A., Mahmud, S., Jahan, I., Sarkar, M., Akter, S., Nishat, N., Afroz, M., Sen, A., Islam, T., Tareq, M. H., & Hossen, M. A. (2024). Why do students use ChatGPT? Answering through a triangulation approach. *Computers and Education: Artificial Intelligence*, *6*, 100208. https://doi.org/10.1016/j.caeai.2024.100208

Norman, D. A. (1991). Cognitive artifacts. *Designing Interaction: Psychology at the Human-Computer Interface*, *1*(1), 17–38.

Nosich, G. M. (2012). *Learning to think things through: A guide to critical thinking across the curriculum* (4th ed). Pearson.

Orhan, A. (2022). The relationship between critical thinking and academic achievement: A meta-analysis study. *Psycho-Educational Research Reviews*, *11*(1), 283–299. https://doi.org/10.52963/PERR_Biruni_V11.N1.18

Perez, E., Ringer, S., Lukošiūtė, K., Nguyen, K., Chen, E., Heiner, S., Pettit, C., Olsson, C., Kundu, S., Kadavath, S., Jones, A., Chen, A., Mann, B., Israel, B., Seethor, B., McKinnon, C., Olah, C., Yan, D., Amodei, D., … Kaplan, J. (2022). *Discovering language model behaviors with model-written evaluations* (No. arXiv:2212.09251). arXiv. https://doi.org/10.48550/arXiv.2212.09251

Przegalinska, A., & Triantoro, T. (2024). *Converging minds: The creative potential of collaborative AI* (1st ed.). CRC Press. https://doi.org/10.1201/9781032656618

Ramfos, A., Lawrence, J., Stamatellos, G., Duelen, A., De Vooght, E., Nucci, F. S., Hoff, M., Inguanzo, A. F., Meyer, T., McAleer, S. R., Van den Broeck, W., Papafragkos, S., Katsamori, D., Kapetanakis, P., & Christodoulou, C. (2025). *Empowering citizens against disinformation: A Socratic dialogue approach enhanced by LLM-driven solutions*. [Manuscript submitted for publication]. TITAN Project Consortium.

Ravšelj, D., Keržič, D., Tomaževič, N., Umek, L., Brezovar, N., Iahad, N. A., & Others. (2025). Higher education students' perceptions of ChatGPT: A global study of early reactions. *Plos One*, *20*(2), e0315011.

Redaelli, S., Biller-Andorno, N., Gloeckler, S., Brown, J., Spitale, G., & Germani, F. (2025). Mastering critical thinking skills is strongly associated with the ability to recognize fakeness and misinformation. *Frontiers in Education*, *10*, 1577692. https://doi.org/10.3389/feduc.2025.1577692

Risko, E. F., & Gilbert, S. J. (2016). Cognitive offloading. *Trends in Cognitive Sciences*, *20*(9), 676–688. https://doi.org/10.1016/j.tics.2016.07.002

Rożek, K. (2025a). *AI in higher education: Academic support or ethical dilemma? analyzing student use of GPT models during exams*. Open Science Framework. https://doi.org/10.31219/osf.io/g95mu_v1

Rożek, K. (2025b). *Modele GPT w edukacji wyższej: Użytkowanie i wyzwania na przykładzie doświadczeń studentów AGH*. AGH University of Krakow.

Sandu, R., Gide, E., & Elkhodr, M. (2024). The role and impact of ChatGPT in educational practices: Insights from an Australian higher education case study. *Discover Education*, *3*(1), 71. https://doi.org/10.1007/s44217-024-00126-6

Van Gelder, T. (2015). Using argument mapping to improve critical thinking skills. In M. Davies & R. Barnett (Eds.), *The Palgrave handbook of critical thinking in higher education* (pp. 183–192). Palgrave Macmillan US. https://doi.org/10.1057/9781137378057_12

Wei, J., Haghtalab, T., & Steinhardt, J. (2023). Simple synthetic data reduces sycophancy in large language models. arXiv preprint arXiv:2308.03958. https://doi.org/10.48550/arXiv.2308.03958

Zawacki-Richter, O., Marín, V. I., Bond, M., & Gouverneur, F. (2019). Systematic review of research on artificial intelligence applications in higher education – Where are the educators? *International Journal of Educational Technology in Higher Education*, *16*(1), 39. https://doi.org/10.1186/s41239-019-0171-0

Zhai, C., Wibowo, S., & Li, L. D. (2024). The effects of over-reliance on AI dialogue systems on students' cognitive abilities: A systematic review. *Smart Learning Environments*, *11*(1), 28. https://doi.org/10.1186/s40561-024-00316-7

11 AI Ethics in the Social Sciences and Humanities

Rafał Olszowski and Krzysztof Tomasz Stawarz

INTRODUCTION

Ethical reflection has accompanied human thought since its earliest attempts to make sense of the world, emerging in all cultures as an essential element of traditions, religions, myths, and established forms of practical wisdom. However, ethics acquired the status of a distinct philosophical discipline only in the fifth century BC, during the classical period of Greek philosophy. Ethics concerns moral obligations. It is the analysis of why we ought to act in certain ways, guided by a sense of moral duty, while seeking explanations for norms, the origins of evil, and the means of overcoming it. According to Aristotle, ethics is simply the study of the good life. The Stagirite maintained that ethics is a practical science whose goal is the highest human good: *eudaimonia*, understood as happiness achieved through virtuous living. In its normative aspect, ethics is concerned with determining what is morally good and what is evil, and, on the basis of accepted evaluations and corresponding obligations, with formulating directives, that is, norms, of morally commendable conduct.

In its broadest sense, ethics is inseparably tied to the human condition: it is rooted in consciousness, intentionality, and the lived experience of individuals situated within particular societies. To grasp the meaning of ethics, we must remember that the human mind not only processes information but also possesses intentions. As Pope Leo XIV observed, 'No generation has ever had such quick access to the amount of information now available through AI. But access to data - however extensive - must not be confused with intelligence' (Duffy & Lamb, 2025). Access to data cannot be equated with intelligence, which presupposes openness to ultimate existential questions and orientation towards truth and the good. This is because genuine intelligence recognises semantics, that is, meanings (Searle, 1980). Artificial intelligence, by contrast, relies primarily on syntactic or contextual operations made possible through vast datasets and statistical modelling (Chomsky, 2000). Contrary to its name, artificial intelligence might not be particularly intelligent. As Luciano Floridi (2011) explains, contemporary AI does not generate intelligent behaviour but merely reproduces or imitates it. Its cognitive potential, therefore, remains far removed from the capacities of the human mind, as well as from those of animal cognition, which are grounded in embodied experience and the pursuit of truth and meaning.

Ethics requires the attribution of meanings and purposes: for example, we help someone not because it is the 'output of an algorithm' but because we genuinely seek the good of that person or care about the common good. Human beings, unlike artificial

DOI: 10.1201/9781003676188-12

intelligence, experience themselves as endowed with practical free will, capable of making responsible choices. The foundation of ethics lies in the awareness that I could have acted otherwise and, therefore, am accountable for my actions.

Although increasingly effective at data analysis and the imitation of human language, artificial intelligence is not itself subject to ethical principles. AI can be programmed or regulated to behave in ways that reflect ethical considerations, but it is not ethical in the sense of being a moral agent. It does not feel, desire, or experience. Its 'intentions' are merely projections of human goals, and its decisions are elaborate calculations devoid of existential weight. AI does not relate directly to good or evil, nor does it register the consequences of moral choices. What appear as 'ethical decisions' are therefore nothing more than simulations of pattern recognition, not genuine moral experience. As Searle (1980) has pointed out, the absence of authentic intentionality means that AI operates only within predefined objectives and optimisation functions; it can simulate care but is never truly a subject of care. Equally, AI lacks personal responsibility, since accountability presupposes the possibility of assigning blame, merit, remorse, or honour—capacities that apply only to human agents (Moor, 2006). Even when applying ethical frameworks such as utilitarian or deontological rules, AI does so through formalised algorithms without grasping their meaning, reducing morality to procedures and data rather than lived experience (Floridi, 2011).

As Aimee van Wynsberghe and Robbins (2019) argue, rather than fantasising about programming morality into machines, our focus should remain on ensuring their safe and reliable operation. Consciousness, self-concepts, personal memory, lived experience, goals, and emotions distinguish human beings from technical tools or from animals, and it is precisely these capacities that underlie moral agency. AI systems cannot be guilty or praiseworthy in any moral sense; responsibility rests with the humans who design, regulate, and deploy them. The point becomes clearer when we consider analogies: an autonomous vehicle or a medical device operates in ethically significant contexts; an accident caused by a malfunctioning car or a faulty diagnostic tool can have grave consequences, yet no one imagines that these artefacts are moral decision-makers. Similarly, a guide dog, while providing invaluable assistance, might inadvertently cause an accident, but ethical responsibility does not rest on the animal itself; it remains with its trainers and handlers. In the same way, AI should not be burdened with the expectation of moral judgement. Its role is to be designed, trained, and tested to function safely within the parameters established by a community of developers, policymakers, ethicists, and users, each of whom shares responsibility for AI's societal impact.

The adoption of an explicitly ethical framework in the development of artificial intelligence has become a central imperative in contemporary debates, as the stakes involved reach far beyond technical optimisation or economic efficiency. Elon Musk warned against 'summoning the demon' through the reckless development of AI (Kedmey, 2014). He used this *demon* metaphor to illustrate the creation of something immensely powerful and unpredictable, capable of escaping human control. The comparison was meant to highlight the risks inherent in AI development: the possibility that such systems could give rise to forces difficult, if not impossible, to contain. Musk has repeatedly cautioned that AI represents one of the greatest existential threats to humanity and that the goal of conscious and responsible actors should be to keep its development in check. Pope Leo XIV voiced the same expectations regarding the ethical dimension of AI, declaring that AI 'requires proper ethical management and regulatory frameworks centered on the human person, and which goes beyond the mere criteria of utility or efficiency' (Duffy & Lamb, 2025). In light of these concerns, the key question is which ethical principles should take precedence in shaping AI, a question that recent ethical debates have sought to answer in diverse ways.

ETHICAL PRINCIPLES FOR AI

Core Ethical Principles Emerging in AI Debates

Contemporary debates in AI ethics have converged on a set of foundational principles that command significant scholarly attention (Boddington, 2023; Akinrinola et al., 2024). These principles address wider societal consequences of algorithmic decision-making. They include freedom and autonomy, transparency and explanation, responsibility, justice and fairness, beneficence and nonmaleficence, privacy, trust, sustainability, dignity, and solidarity.

One of the most frequently discussed concerns is fairness. AI is not a neutral technology but rather a product of human choices that inevitably reflect particular values (González-Padilla et al., 2025). Algorithms trained on historical data can reproduce and amplify existing inequalities, leading to biased decisions in domains such as criminal justice, health care, or employment (Christoforaki & Beyan, 2022; Wang et al., 2024). These risks are compounded by the opacity of algorithmic systems. Lack of transparency—the 'black box' problem—obstructs accountability, raising questions about whether individuals are entitled to a 'right to explanation' when automated decisions affect their lives (Binns, 2018; Diákopoulos, 2020; Kearns & Roth, 2019; Goodman & Flaxman, 2017).

Privacy is another central issue. The reliance of AI on large-scale personal data raises serious concerns about surveillance and the erosion of individual rights (Mantelero, 2018; Nissenbaum, 2020; Zuboff, 2019). Equally significant are questions of responsibility, as it remains unclear who should be held accountable for the harms caused by autonomous systems: designers, users, or the institutions deploying them (Hakli & Mäkelä, 2019; Dignum, 2019).

The principle of autonomy has also been highlighted. Scholars warn that increasing dependence on algorithmic recommendations may gradually undermine human control in decision-making processes, particularly in sensitive domains such as finance or medicine (Laitinen & Sahlgren, 2021; Mittelstadt et al., 2016). This dynamic points to a broader ethical dilemma: while AI promises efficiency and accuracy, it can simultaneously diminish the scope of human agency (Christman, 2020; Sanderson, 2019).

Other ethical pillars include beneficence and nonmaleficence, which require that AI systems maximise societal benefit while avoiding harm (Leslie, 2019). Trust, both in technological reliability and institutional integrity, emerges as a precondition for the acceptance of AI (McLeod, 2021; Brundage et al., 2020). Finally, concepts such as dignity and solidarity underscore the social and political stakes of AI ethics, particularly in safeguarding vulnerable groups and ensuring that technological progress contributes to inclusive social good (Macklin, 2003; Bayertz, 1999).

Taken together, these principles form a multidimensional framework for assessing the societal impact of AI. They reveal that the ethics of AI is not only about ensuring the safety and reliability of systems, but also about addressing broader issues of justice, human agency, and collective responsibility.

Social Sciences and Humanities (SSH) Perspective on AI Ethics

Ethical issues surrounding the use of AI in the social sciences and humanities are particularly significant because in these fields, AI is not merely a technological tool but also a co-participant in the process of knowledge creation. When large language models (LLMs) are employed to analyse discourse, argument mining tools to identify argumentative structures, image recognition systems to study iconography, or classification algorithms to interpret interview transcripts, AI begins to intervene in what is most valuable in SSH: the interpretation of meaning. These interventions create distinct ethical dilemmas across several key points of SSH interest, including higher education, research methodology, the labour market, and the law and regulations.

Higher Education

The risk of indiscriminate AI adoption is not merely theoretical but is already present within academia. One of the most recent international studies, conducted in 2024 by a consortium led by the University of Ljubljana, provides compelling insights into how social science students use LLMs. The survey collected 22,963 responses from 120 countries and territories concerning ChatGPT usage (Aristovnik et al., 2025). The findings show that students from the social sciences were among the most frequent users. Moreover, students in sociology and related disciplines reported higher levels of trust in ChatGPT compared to their peers in technical fields (Jowarder, 2023).

This high level of trust is particularly concerning because while these students use LLM-based tools extensively and perceive them as helpful and reliable, their typically lower level of technical training, compared to engineering or computer science students, may limit their understanding of how such systems actually function. It is crucial to remember that ChatGPT does not possess reasoning or factual comprehension; rather, it generates text based on statistical patterns in large datasets. Without grasping this mechanism, social science scholars may overestimate the epistemic authority of the model, treating its outputs as inherently accurate or insightful. This overreliance is especially problematic in disciplines where critical interpretation, argumentative rigour, and source validation are central to scholarly practice. The combination of frequent use and limited technical literacy creates a potential risk: students may inadvertently reproduce inaccuracies, oversimplified narratives, or biased content generated by the model, without sufficient verification or critical engagement.

Beyond the risk of producing flawed academic work, emerging evidence suggests that reliance on AI also entails profound cognitive costs. A recent study conducted at MIT underscores these risks by investigating the cognitive costs of using LLMs in the educational context of essay writing (Kosmyna et al., 2025). Using electroencephalography (EEG), the researchers measured participants' brain activity while employing ChatGPT, with the aim of assessing cognitive engagement, mental workload, and patterns of neural activation during writing. The results were striking: 83.3%

of participants who used an LLM were unable to recall a single sentence they had written just minutes earlier. By contrast, participants who wrote without AI support did not face such difficulties. Even after discontinuing LLM use in later sessions, the first group continued to exhibit reduced engagement and lower overall performance compared to peers who had never relied on AI. Qualitative evaluation of the essays further revealed that AI-assisted texts were frequently described as 'robotic', 'soulless', and 'lacking depth' (Kosmyna et al., 2025). This phenomenon exemplifies what may be termed epistemic dependency: a state in which users increasingly outsource cognitive and interpretative functions to algorithmic systems, thereby diminishing their own capacity for critical reflection and autonomous meaning-making. Such dependence threatens to exacerbate problems already noted in contemporary education and research: an overload of stimuli, diminishing space for reflection, a decline in critical thinking, and increasing externalisation of control, which in turn may lead to progressive intellectual disengagement.

Qualitative Research and Methodology

At the heart of the SSH perspective is a concern for the integrity of interpretation, and from an ethical perspective, this raises fundamental questions: who is the true interpreter—the human scholar or the algorithm? How can cultural sensitivity be preserved if part of the interpretative task is delegated to a statistical model? Jürgen Habermas (1996) emphasised that communication and intersubjectivity are the foundation of the legitimacy of knowledge. If interpretations generated by AI cannot be debated and contested in the same way as human claims, then we risk losing the dialogical space that constitutes the very basis of the social sciences.

Indeed, the growing presence of AI in SSH, particularly of LLMs, argument mining systems, and automated text classification tools, introduces new layers of ethical concern, foremost among them the risk of meaning reduction and interpretative automation. By meaning reduction, we refer to the tendency of LLMs to transform rich, context-dependent meanings into statistically probable textual patterns, thereby substituting semantic depth with surface-level coherence. As Floridi (2011) observes, such systems operate primarily on syntactic correlations rather than genuine semantic understanding. In the context of qualitative research, this implies that subtleties of interpretation may be replaced by simplified, homogenised outputs that mimic understanding without truly engaging with it. Interpretation, however, is a creative and accountable act for which the researcher bears responsibility. If this task is outsourced to AI, the question arises: who bears responsibility for the interpretation? This problem links directly to the broader debates on transparency and explainability.

Moreover, a new form of epistemic dependency emerges, recalling Bruno Latour's (1987) argument that knowledge is produced within networks of actors: people, institutions, and tools. Incorporating AI into this network introduces a new actor whose influence on the cognitive process is difficult to trace or control. This perspective marks a fundamental difference from mainstream AI ethics: whereas general reflections on AI ethics ask how to design and regulate technology, SSH-oriented reflection also asks how to preserve humanity in machine-assisted cognition. In the first case, ethics concerns algorithms; in the second, it concerns the very meaning of research and the subjectivity of the people it involves.

Other Applications

Beyond these epistemic concerns, SSH perspectives also emphasise specific domains where ethical challenges manifest most clearly. One is the labour market, where AI is expected to reduce employment in certain sectors and even render some professions obsolete. Such changes may trigger profound social transformations, potentially exacerbating inequality, weakening social cohesion, and reshaping class structures in ways that demand careful ethical and policy consideration from an SSH standpoint. Another area is the application of AI in law, particularly in judicial decision-making. While there are expectations that AI could support courts by improving efficiency and consistency, there are also serious concerns about justice, fairness, and non-discrimination that touch upon core social values. These questions will be addressed in greater detail in the following sections.

REGULATORY FRAMEWORKS FOR AI ETHICS

An inquiry into the ethics of an artificial intelligence phenomenon would remain fundamentally incomplete if it were confined to the philosophical articulation of principles alone. The true test of a society's commitment to responsible innovation lies in its will to embed values within binding structures of governance. Regulatory frameworks are precisely such structures. They represent the critical juncture where abstract ethical concerns about fairness and human dignity are translated into the concrete language of law and policy. This subchapter, therefore, is a core component of our ethical investigation. By dissecting and comparing the world's nascent AI regulations, we are examining the formal codification of societal priorities, especially the outcome of intense negotiation between technological ambition and fundamental rights. For researchers in social sciences and humanities, mastering AI ethics frameworks is particularly vital: our position simultaneously as practitioners who use AI-driven methods and as scholars who critically examine technological change means we must be equipped to contest both the ethical and social consequences of these systems.

Comparative Analysis of Major Frameworks

The global regulatory landscape for AI has rapidly evolved since 2021, with the emergence of multiple frameworks that reflect distinct philosophical and practical approaches to governing algorithmic systems. These frameworks embody different visions of how society should relate to increasingly autonomous decision-making systems. While analysing all major frameworks worldwide would be valuable, this chapter narrows its focus to influential governance models emerging from Europe and the United States. This selection is deliberate: it enables a focused examination of the tensions and philosophical divergences within the Western approach to AI ethics and regulation, and purposefully excludes non-Western frameworks because their different legal traditions and socio-political priorities would introduce heterogeneous variables that would dilute analytic depth. Specifically, we compare four key models that highlight these internal debates: the EU's rights-based hard law; the OECD's soft-law principles; UNESCO's global ethical recommendations; and the United States' sectoral, market-driven approach to AI legislation. By examining these four, we can better understand the core debate within Western democracies between rights-based regulation, market-driven approaches, and global ethical AI standard-setting.

The EU AI Act

The European Union's Artificial Intelligence Act (European Union, 2024), implemented in August 2024 after three years of thoughtful consideration following its initial proposal in April 2021, is noteworthy as the world's first comprehensive legal framework specifically designed for AI systems (Smuha & Yeung, 2025). The AI Act establishes a risk-based regulatory approach that categorises AI applications into four risk tiers: unacceptable risk (prohibited), high risk (subject to strict requirements), limited risk (transparency obligations), and minimal risk (unregulated). This tiered structure is intended to strike a balance between regulatory oversight and legislative proportionality (Balcioglu et al., 2025).

The risk-based approach of the EU AI Act could have particular significance for SSH research contexts. While the Act explicitly identifies certain applications (such as medical devices) as high-risk, many SSH applications present classification challenges. For instance, it is possible that AI systems used in social science research could fall into different risk categories depending on their specific applications. Algorithmic analysis of social media data for academic research might be deemed minimal risk, whereas a similar technology used in predictive policing could be considered high-risk. The Act calls for high-risk systems to undergo conformity assessments, maintain detailed documentation, and implement robust risk management systems (Gilbert, 2024). However, it is important to note that the paper does not provide a detailed explanation of the methodology for conducting these risk assessments. This could potentially lead to some implementation challenges for SSH researchers (Svitych, 2025).

The Act makes it clear that AI systems that use 'subliminal techniques' to influence human behaviour, social scoring by public authorities, and real-time remote biometric identification in public spaces (with narrow exceptions) are not allowed. These prohibitions reflect European values that prioritise human dignity and autonomy.

UNESCO's Global Ethical Framework

In November 2021, UNESCO adopted the Recommendation on the Ethics of Artificial Intelligence, a significant development as it is the first global standard-setting instrument on AI ethics (UNESCO, 2021). It is important to note that UNESCO's framework operates at the policy level, providing ethical principles rather than legally binding requirements, which is a distinction from the AI Act's regulatory approach. The Recommendation respectfully outlines four core values (human dignity, human rights, pluralism, and justice) and eleven principles spanning data governance, transparency, and environmental sustainability.

From the perspective of SSH researchers, the UNESCO framework could be seen as valuable due to its emphasis on cultural diversity and context-sensitivity (AllahRakha, 2024). Article 3 of the Recommendation recognises that respect for human autonomy can vary across different cultures. This cultural sensitivity aligns with SSH perspectives that reject universalist approaches to ethics. The Recommendation goes a step further by thoughtfully including considerations of AI's environmental impact and the importance of gender equality in AI development. These are crucial aspects that are sometimes not fully addressed in technical regulatory frameworks.

OECD AI Principles

The Organisation for Economic Co-operation and Development established its AI Principles in 2019, which have since been adopted by 42 countries (OECD, 2019). These principles emphasise five complementary value-based pillars: inclusive growth, human-centred values, transparency, robustness, and accountability. The OECD framework, in contrast to the EU's legally binding approach, functions as a soft law instrument designed to harmonise international approaches while accommodating national differences.

The OECD principles have had a notable influence on other frameworks, including the EU AI Act and the UNESCO Recommendation (OECD, 2019; UNESCO, 2021). Their strength lies in finding a balance between encouraging innovation and ethical safeguards, a tension that is especially relevant for SSH researchers who both use AI tools and study their societal impacts. The principles suggest that AI actors should respect the rule of law, human rights, and democratic values, while acknowledging that the application of these values may vary across different societies (Díaz-Rodríguez et al., 2023). This flexibility makes the OECD framework particularly applicable to SSH contexts, where ethical considerations often vary across cultural and disciplinary boundaries.

US Algorithmic Accountability Act

The EU has chosen a more comprehensive approach, while the United States has opted for a sectoral regulatory strategy. The Algorithmic Accountability Act, first introduced in 2019 and reintroduced in subsequent years, represents the most significant US legislative effort to address AI ethics (Algorithmic Accountability Act of 2019, 2019). If enacted, the Act would require companies to conduct impact assessments for automated decision systems that pose privacy or civil rights risks, with a focus on identifying and mitigating bias and discrimination (Oduro et al., 2022).

The Algorithmic Accountability Act, while not yet law, appears to reflect an American approach that favours market-based solutions and private-sector self-regulation over prescriptive government mandates. Its emphasis on impact assessments rather than pre-market authorisation appears to align with US regulatory traditions. The Act explicitly emphasises civil rights implications, making it a relevant reference for SSH scholars studying algorithmic discrimination in domains such as hiring and lending.

Critical SSH Perspectives on Regulatory Approaches

Classification Challenges

The EU AI Act's high-risk classification could possibly pose some specific challenges for SSH research. While the Act clearly identifies sectors such as health care as high-risk, many SSH applications fall into ambiguous categories. For instance, an AI tool that analyses judicial decisions might not directly affect individuals but could influence scholarly conclusions or policy debates. Similarly, the Act's provisions on law enforcement have the potential to create uncertainty for researchers studying policing practices. It is important to note that the Act determines risk by context of use rather than technical features, which may present certain challenges for basic research. It is possible that a text analysis tool developed for historical research could later be adapted for hiring decisions, potentially triggering high-risk status (Smuha & Yeung, 2025). This context dependence presents a challenge for SSH researchers, who may find it difficult to predict regulatory obligations during the early research stages.

Structural Injustice and Limitations of Regulations

From an SSH perspective, it has been suggested that current frameworks may not adequately address structural injustice. Regulatory approaches have historically approached bias as a technical problem solvable with better data or algorithms, rather than addressing the underlying social inequalities (Boddington, 2023).

The EU AI Act's emphasis on individual rights and specified high-risk applications might potentially miss some of the broader implications regarding systemic discrimination. For instance, the Act calls for bias testing for high-risk systems, though these tests tend to prioritise statistical parity across protected categories and may not fully address how AI interacts with existing power structures (Smuha & Yeung, 2025). Some SSH scholars have expressed concerns that this approach may overlook the potential for AI to perpetuate gendered or racial power dynamics, even when statistical metrics appear fair (Boddington, 2023).

Furthermore, it is possible that the risk-based framework might inadvertently exacerbate structural injustice by concentrating regulatory scrutiny on a subset of applications. It appears that AI, such as social media recommendation algorithms, which may appear to be low-risk, can, when considered collectively, contribute to polarisation and misinformation. However, under this current framework, these aspects may not be fully regulated.

SSH Scholars as Critical Contributors to Regulatory Discourse

SSH scholars play a crucial role in shaping nuanced AI regulation. Their expertise in social contexts, power dynamics, and ethical complexities is a valuable complement to technical approaches. SSH researchers can assist regulators in understanding that fairness is socially constructed and varies by context (Boddington, 2023).

In addition, they have contributed methodological innovations for implementation. For example, value-sensitive design approaches from information science, argument mining methods for analysing public reasoning and institutional discourse, and critical auditing approaches offer frameworks for embedding ethical considerations throughout AI development (Friedman & Hendry, 2019). Critical data studies scholars have developed auditing methodologies that extend beyond technical bias metrics to examine how AI systems affect social structures (Eubanks, 2018).

It is heartening to see an increasing acknowledgement of SSH perspectives in regulatory documents. For instance, the EU AI Act includes provisions for fundamental rights impact assessments, underscoring the significance of contemplating social and ethical implications beyond technical safety. However, SSH scholars have expressed the view that substantive involvement in regulatory design is necessary. It has been suggested that moving beyond token consultation to meaningful participation could ensure that regulations address societal values and injustices in addition to technical compliance (Boddington, 2023).

LABOUR MARKETS, LAW, AND JUSTICE: KEY SOCIAL CHALLENGES IN AI ETHICS

Generative artificial intelligence is reshaping institutional decision-making across multiple domains and thereby reframes long-standing ethical questions about fairness, accountability, and human dignity. Ethical appraisal cannot be limited to model-level technicalities; it attends to the institutional arrangements and professional norms that mediate how systems are designed, deployed, and contested.

LABOUR MARKET APPLICATIONS

GenAI reconfigures work at the level of tasks rather than occupations alone. Where models reliably perform routine cognitive or clerical tasks, substitution risk emerges; where models augment interpretative or relational work, the composition of skills demanded from workers changes, and bargaining asymmetries may intensify. Recent cross-national evidence from a large employer survey shows that algorithmic management practices such as automated scheduling, applicant screening, performance scoring, and task allocation have become common across sectors, albeit with variation in intensity and governance across jurisdictions (OECD, 2025). The significance of this diffusion lies not merely in efficiency gains but in how automation restructures power within workplaces and interacts with pre-existing social inequalities.

Three ethical concerns converge in the labour domain. The first is distributional: automation can increase productivity while concentrating economic surplus among capital owners unless public policy redirects a share of the gains to workers through retraining, portable benefits, or income-support mechanisms. The OECD employer survey underscores that many firms expect productivity improvements but do not uniformly plan for worker transition measures, thereby exposing workers to risks of long-term displacement (OECD, 2025). The second concern is representational: recruitment algorithms and screening tools trained on historical hiring data tend to replicate and sometimes amplify patterns of exclusion by gender, race, or socioeconomic status. Systematic reviews and empirical audits have repeatedly documented that automated hiring systems can reproduce bias embedded in their training inputs and the broader labour market environment (Chen, 2023; Fabris et al., 2025). The third concern is relational and normative: algorithmic management often operates as pervasive surveillance. Real-time monitoring and metricised performance evaluations restrict discretionary judgement, constrain worker autonomy, and generate psychosocial harms when workers are evaluated by opaque metrics they cannot meaningfully contest (OECD, 2025).

Ethical governance of workplace AI, therefore, requires a threefold approach. First, ex-ante assessment and transparency obligations are needed so that deploying organisations must disclose the functions of algorithmic systems, the data used to train them, and fairness-testing results stratified by protected characteristics. Algorithmic impact assessments (AIAs) tailored to employment contexts can help surface potential disparate impacts and trigger remediation. Second, procedural rights must be strengthened: workers subject to materially adverse automated decisions should have enforceable rights to human review and to a reasoned explanation that facilitates effective contestation. Such rights are not mere technicalities; they restore a procedural dignity that metricised management tends to erode. Third, social policy instruments, sectoral retraining funds, portable benefits, and transition incomes are necessary to prevent automation from producing durable labour-market scarring. Ethnographic and mixed-methods research is also needed to document how algorithmic tools alter everyday work practices so that policy can be empirically grounded rather than speculative.

These recommendations underline a broader normative point. Technical mitigation of bias (e.g. re-weighting datasets or fairness-aware training) is necessary but insufficient if it does not engage structural drivers of inequality. The moral calculus of automation must therefore include distributive questions: who captures the benefits, who bears the risks, and what institutional mechanisms exist to redress imbalances. In this sense, labour-centred governance of GenAI is as much about social policy as it is about model design.

Legal Applications

The legal profession is governed by duties that sit uneasily with some of GenAI's current failure modes. Lawyers are bound by duties of competence, confidentiality, and candour to the tribunal; these duties assume reliable access to authoritative sources and secure handling of client material. Generative models can assist with legal research and drafting, but they also hallucinate: they may generate plausible-sounding but non-existent authorities or misstate the content of a precedent. The professional cost of such failures is real. Judicial rulings that sanctioned counsel for filing briefs containing fabricated citations provide concrete evidence that naive reliance on GenAI can breach professional duties and attract sanctions (Mata v. Avianca, Inc., 2023).

Confidentiality amplifies risk in legal contexts because many publicly accessible GenAI services process and may retain user inputs. Uploading privileged client documents to third-party models can therefore implicate legal privilege and client trust unless contractual, technical, or institutional safeguards are in place. Responding to these risks, professional regulators have issued ethics guidance emphasising that lawyers must be competent in the use of tools, must verify model outputs against primary sources, and must prefer privacy-preserving deployments for privileged materials (American Bar Association, 2024). This guidance marks an important normative recalibration: lawyers cannot delegate verification responsibility to an opaque model without risking breach of duty.

Systemic fairness issues arise when algorithmic tools enter the adjudicative or policing sphere. Risk-assessment instruments and predictive analytics systems used in pre-trial decisions or sentencing have been shown to produce disparate error rates across demographic groups, and different fairness metrics can be in tension with one another (Angwin et al., 2016; Dressel & Farid, 2018). The resulting ethical hazard is not only differential treatment but also an erosion of procedural legitimacy if litigants cannot meaningfully challenge the empirical bases of algorithmic recommendations.

A defensible governance architecture for legal contexts must therefore be multilayered. Professional rules should require explicit provenance and verification statements for documents substantially assisted by GenAI, so that counsel certifies that model-generated authorities have been checked against primary sources. Courts should develop robust disclosure protocols for algorithmic evidence: sufficient information about model structure, intended use, and training data summary should be made available to enable adversarial testing; where proprietary secrecy prevents adequate disclosure, courts should apply more stringent admissibility standards or order independent review. Education is central: judges and practitioners must develop literacy about algorithmic methodologies and their limitations so that courts can properly evaluate expert testimony and adversarial challenges. More broadly, socio-legal research is needed to measure how GenAI affects litigation strategy, access to justice, and the balance of resources between parties, thereby providing an empirical basis for procedural reform.

CONCLUSIONS

This exploration of AI ethics reveals that the central challenge is not one of programming morality into machines, but rather assuming human responsibility for their societal impact. Artificial intelligence, lacking consciousness, intentionality, and lived experience, cannot be a moral agent yet. Accountability, therefore, rests solely with the humans who design and maintain these powerful systems.

From the perspective of the social sciences and humanities, AI as a research tool intervenes in the core humanistic task of interpretation, creating a risk of epistemic dependency and the reduction of meaning. SSH, for that matter, provides the critical lens needed to analyse AI's societal effects, demonstrating how seemingly neutral algorithms can perpetuate structural injustice in key domains like the labour market and the legal system.

Effective governance must be sensitive to the institutional logic of each sector. It requires a combination of ex-ante measures (algorithmic impact assessments) and ex-post remedies (enforceable rights to human review and reasoned explanations). Technical solutions like improved training data and explainability, while necessary, seem to be insufficient on their own. They must be complemented by robust procedural rights and policies that address the distribution of benefits and burdens. Labour markets demand protections that preserve worker voice and livelihood, while legal practice requires verification and clear rules for contesting algorithmic evidence.

Ultimately, the distinctive contribution of SSH is its ability to translate abstract ethical principles into concrete institutional designs. Through empirical and ethnographic research, SSH scholarship can uncover how algorithmic systems alter real-world practices and craft the procedural safeguards necessary to operationalise fairness. Implementing these measures is essential for creating institutional pathways for democratic contestation, with the socially legitimate integration of generative AI into public and professional life.

ACKNOWLEDGEMENTS

During the preparation of this work, the authors used Claude 4.5 Sonnet and ChatGPT 4.0 in order to translate initial draft sections from Polish to English, paraphrase selected passages for improved readability, refine English syntax and grammar, and ensure adherence to academic writing conventions in English. After using these services, the authors reviewed and edited the content as needed and take full responsibility for the publication's content. This research was funded by Narodowe Centrum Nauki (National Science Centre, Republic of Poland), the research grant UMO-2023/49/B/HS5/01379.

REFERENCES

Akinrinola, O., Okoye, C. C., Ofodile, O. C., & Ugochukwu, C. E. (2024). Navigating and reviewing ethical dilemmas in AI development: Strategies for transparency, fairness, and accountability. *GSC Advanced Research and Reviews*, *18*(3), 50–58. https://doi.org/10.30574/gscarr.2024.18.3.0088

Algorithmic Accountability Act of 2019. (2019). Algorithmic Accountability Act of 2019, H.R. 2231, 116th Cong. https://www.congress.gov/bill/116th-congress/house-bill/2231

AllahRakha, N. (2024). UNESCO's AI ethics principles: Challenges and opportunities. *International Journal of Law and Policy*, *2*(9), 24–36. https://doi.org/10.59022/ijlp.225

American Bar Association. (2024, July 29). ABA issues first ethics guidance on a lawyer's use of AI tools. *ABA News*. https://www.americanbar.org/news/abanews/aba-news-archives/2024/07/aba-issues-first-ethics-guidance-ai-tools/

Angwin, J., Larson, J., Mattu, S., & Kirchner, L. (2016, May 23). Machine bias: There's software used across the country to predict future criminals. And it's biased against blacks. *ProPublica*. https://www.propublica.org/article/machine-bias-risk-assessments-in-criminal-sentencing

Aristovnik, A., Ravšelj, D., Keržič, D., Tomaževič, N., Umek, L., Brezovar, N., et al. (2025). Higher education students' evolving perceptions of ChatGPT: Global survey data from the academic year 2024–2025 [Data set]. *Mendeley Data, V1*. https://doi.org/10.17632/nv2343nwsb.1

Balcioğlu, Y. S., Çelik, A. A., & Altındağ, E. (2025). A turning point in AI: Europe's human-centric approach to technology regulation. *Journal of Responsible Technology*, *23*, 100128. https://doi.org/10.1016/j.jrt.2025.100128

Bayertz, K. (Ed.). (1999). *Solidarity* (Vol. 5). Springer.

Binns, R. (2018). Algorithmic accountability and public reason. *Philosophy & Technology*, *31*(4), 543–556. https://doi.org/10.1007/s13347-017-0263-5

Boddington, P. (2023). *AI ethics* (2023rd ed.). Springer.

Brundage, M., Avin, S., Wang, J., Belfield, H., Krueger, G., Hadfield, G., Khlaaf, H., Yang, J., Toner, H., & Fong, R. (2020). Toward trustworthy AI development: Mechanisms for supporting verifiable claims. *arXiv*. https://arxiv.org/abs/2004.07213

Chen, Z. (2023). Ethics and discrimination in artificial intelligence-enabled recruitment practices. *Humanities and Social Sciences Communications*, *10*, 567. https://doi.org/10.1057/s41599-023-02079-x

Chomsky, N. (2000). *New horizons in the study of language and mind*. Cambridge University Press.

Christman, J. (2020). Autonomy in moral and political philosophy. In E. N. Zalta (Ed.), *The Stanford encyclopedia of philosophy* (Fall 2020 ed.). Stanford University. https://plato.stanford.edu/archives/fall2020/entries/autonomy-moral/

Christoforaki, M., & Beyan, O. (2022). AI ethics-A bird's eye view. *Applied Sciences*, *12*(9), 4130. https://doi.org/10.3390/app12094130

Diákopoulos, N. (2020). Accountability, transparency, and algorithms. In M. Dubber, F. Pasquale, & S. Das (Eds.), *The Oxford handbook of ethics of AI* (pp. 197–214). Oxford University Press.

Díaz-Rodríguez, N., Del Ser, J., Coeckelbergh, M., López de Prado, M., Herrera-Viedma, E., & Herrera, F. (2023). Connecting the dots in trustworthy artificial intelligence: From AI principles, ethics, and key requirements to responsible AI systems and regulation. *Information Fusion*, *99*, 101896. https://doi.org/10.1016/j.inffus.2023.101896

Dignum, V. (2019). *Responsible artificial intelligence: How to develop and use AI in a responsible way*. Springer.

Dressel, J., & Farid, H. (2018). The accuracy, fairness, and limits of predicting recidivism. *Science Advances*, *4*(1), eaao5580. https://doi.org/10.1126/sciadv.aao5580

Duffy, C., & Lamb, C. (2025, June 20). Pope Leo calls for an ethical AI framework in a message to tech execs gathering at the Vatican. *CNN*. https://edition.cnn.com/2025/06/20/tech/pope-leo-ai-ethics-tech-leader-vatican-gathering

Eubanks, V. (2018). *Automating inequality: How high-tech tools profile, police, and punish the poor*. St. Martin's Press.

European Union. (2024). Regulation (EU) 2024/1689 of the European Parliament and of the Council of 13 June 2024 laying down harmonised rules on artificial intelligence (Artificial Intelligence Act). *Official Journal of the European Union*. https://eur-lex.europa.eu/eli/reg/2024/1689/oj

Fabris, A., Baranowska, N., Dennis, M. J., Graus, D., Hacker, P., Saldivar, J., Zuiderveen Borgesius, F., & Biega, A. J. (2025). Fairness and bias in algorithmic hiring: A multidisciplinary survey. *ACM Transactions on Intelligent Systems and Technology*, *16*(1), 1–54. https://doi.org/10.1145/3696457

Floridi, L. (2011). *The philosophy of information*. Oxford University Press.

Friedman, B., & Hendry, D. (2019). *Value sensitive design: Shaping technology with moral imagination*. MIT Press.

Gilbert, S. (2024). The EU passes the AI act and its implications for digital medicine are unclear. *NPJ Digital Medicine*, *7*, 135. https://doi.org/10.1038/s41746-024-01116-6

Goodman, B., & Flaxman, S. (2017). European Union regulations on algorithmic decision-making and a 'right to explanation'. *AI Magazine*, *38*(3), 50–57. https://doi.org/10.1609/aimag.v38i3.2741

González-Padilla, P., Fernández-Fernández, M., & Lacárcel, F. J. S. (2025). Evolution and future perspectives in AI ethics. In J. R. Saura (Ed.), *Global perspectives on AI, ethics, and business economics. Contributions to management science* (pp.73–94). Springer. https://doi.org/10.1007/978-3-031-88781-9_4

Habermas, J. (1996). *Between facts and norms: Contributions to a discourse theory of law and democracy* (W. Rehg, Trans.). MIT Press.

Hakli, R., & Mäkelä, P. (2019). Moral responsibility of robots and hybrid agents. *The Monist*, *102*(2), 259–275. https://doi.org/10.1093/monist/onz009

Jowarder, M. I. (2023). The influence of ChatGPT on social science students: Insights drawn from undergraduate students in the United States. *Indonesian Journal of Innovation and Applied Sciences*, *3*(2), 194–200. https://doi.org/10.47540/ijias.v3i2.878

Kearns, M., & Roth, A. (2019). *The ethical algorithm: The science of socially aware algorithm design*. Oxford University Press.

Kedmey, D. (2014, October 27). Elon Musk warns artificial intelligence is like 'summoning the demon'. *Time*. https://time.com/3541005/elon-musk-artificial-intelligence/

Kosmyna, N., Hauptmann, E., Yuan, Y. T., Situ, J., Liao, X.-H., Beresnitzky, A. V., Braunstein, I., & Maes, P. (2025). Your brain on ChatGPT: Accumulation of cognitive debt when using an AI assistant for essay writing task (arXiv:2506.08872). *arXiv* https://doi.org/10.48550/arXiv.2506.08872

Laitinen, A., & Sahlgren, O. (2021). AI systems and respect for human autonomy. *Frontiers in Artificial Intelligence*, *4*, 705164. https://doi.org/10.3389/frai.2021.705164

Latour, B. (1987). *Science in action: How to follow scientists and engineers through society*. Harvard University Press.

Leslie, D. (2019). Understanding artificial intelligence ethics and safety. *arXiv*. https://arxiv.org/abs/1906.05684

Macklin, R. (2003). Dignity is a useless concept. *BMJ*, *327*(7429), 1419–1420. https://doi.org/10.1136/bmj.327.7429.1419

Mantelero, A. (2018). AI and big data: A blueprint for a human rights, social and ethical impact assessment. *Computer Law & Security Review*, *34*(4), 754–772. https://doi.org/10.1016/j.clsr.2018.05.017

Mata v. Avianca, Inc. (S.D.N.Y. June 22, 2023). Opinion and order on sanctions. No. 1:2022cv01461 *Justia*. https://law.justia.com/cases/federal/district-courts/new-york/nysdce/1:2022cv01461/575368/54/

Mittelstadt, B. D., Allo, P., Taddeo, M., Wachter, S., & Floridi, L. (2016). The ethics of algorithms: Mapping the debate. *Big Data & Society*, *3*(2), 1–21. https://doi.org/10.1177/2053951716679679

McLeod, C. (2021). Trust. In E. N. Zalta (Ed.), *The Stanford encyclopedia of philosophy* (Fall 2021 ed.). Stanford University. https://plato.stanford.edu/archives/fall2021/entries/trust/

Moor, J. H. (2006). The nature, importance, and difficulty of machine ethics. *IEEE Intelligent*, *21*(4), 18–21. https://doi.org/10.1109/MIS.2006.80

Nissenbaum, H. (2020). *Privacy in context*. Stanford University Press.

Oduro, S., Moss, E., & Metcalf, J. (2022). Obligations to assess: Recent trends in AI accountability regulations. *Patterns*, *3*(11), 100608. https://doi.org/10.1016/j.patter.2022.100608

Organisation for Economic Co-operation and Development (OECD). (2019). *OECD principles on artificial intelligence*. https://oecd.ai/en/ai-principles

Organisation for Economic Co-operation and Development. (2025). *Algorithmic management in the workplace: Employer survey on the use of algorithmic management tools*. OECD Publishing. https://www.oecd.org/en/publications/algorithmic-management-in-the-workplace_287c13c4-en.html

Sanderson, D. (2019, May 19). Google Maps and satnavs are damaging our brains, says author David Barrie. *The Times*.

Searle, J. R. (1980). Minds, brains, and programs. *Behavioral and Brain Sciences*, *3*(3), 417–424. https://doi.org/10.1017/S0140525X00005756

Smuha, N. A., & Yeung, K. (2025). The European union's AI act: Beyond motherhood and apple pie? In *The Cambridge handbook of the law, ethics and policy of artificial intelligence* (pp. 228–258). Cambridge University Press.

Svitych, O. (2025). Blind transparency: A critical discourse analysis of the EU AI Act. *Critical Policy Studies*, 1–17. https://doi.org/10.1080/19460171.2025.2496193

United Nations Educational, Scientific and Cultural Organization (UNESCO). (2021). *Recommendation on the ethics of artificial intelligence*. https://www.unesco.org/en/articles/recommendation-ethics-artificial-intelligence

van Wynsberghe, A., & Robbins, S. (2019). Critiquing the reasons for making artificial moral agents. *Science and Engineering Ethics*, *25*, 719–735. https://doi.org/10.1007/s11948-018-0030-8

Wang, A., Kapoor, S., Barocas, S., & Narayanan, A. (2024). Against predictive optimization: On the legitimacy of decision-making algorithms that optimize predictive accuracy. *ACM Journal on Responsible Computing*, *1*(1), 1–45. https://doi.org/10.1145/3636509

Zuboff, S. (2019). *The age of surveillance capitalism*. Profile Books.

12 AI-Generated Images
Use Cases, Benefits, and Risks for Social Sciences and Humanities

Mariann Hardey and Wasim Ahmed

INTRODUCTION

A vast range of AI-powered tools now allow us to generate images from simple text, creating a rupture in the relationship between sight, memory, creator, and reality. This chapter helps readers navigate the speculative future of this new visual world, moving beyond current applications to explore its potential for radical innovation and its profound philosophical implications. We contribute to the book's theme, Generative AI in the Social Sciences and Humanities, focusing specifically on AI-generated images.

This chapter charts a course through the new territory of image AI generation. To begin, we consider the frontiers of this technology and how it might open new frontiers for the Social Sciences and Humanities (SSH), which transform how we conduct research and understand creativity itself. The reader will be guided through a series of speculative use cases (the imagined impact) and conceptual frameworks to explore the transformative and disruptive ways in which AI-generated images are likely to be developed and deployed.

We then turn from these applications to confront the unsettling phantoms they produce: the crisis of the image's very nature and form, the seductive risk of apathy towards what is human-created and the 'real' world, and the haunting creation of synthetic memories that could rewrite our past.

Ultimately, this chapter aims to equip the reader with a new ethical and critical framework for navigating a world where our machines have been prompted to create dreams, and those 'dreams' are altering our reality. We highlight AI's potential for radical innovation in the social sciences, business, medicine, and the humanities, from AI-image ethnography and visualising collective consciousness, to augmenting human creativity into a new form of creative works.

DREAMING OF SYNTHETIC SHEEP

Professor Zia Harth is wrestling with the formless concepts of societal trust and loneliness in an age of information saturation. Her traditional text analysis has failed

 DOI: 10.1201/9781003676188-13

to capture the pronounced effect of human suffering and the isolation of interactions 'Show me', she declares, not to a person, but to the room's intelligence. 'Show me a visual display of institutional trust as a function of memetic velocity. Let the model be a living ecosystem'.

On the wall over her desk station, an image begins to take shape. It is not a static picture, but a dynamic, interactive model, like a swarm of tiny, fast-moving 'memes'. With a small gesture from her palm, Zia slows the simulation, isolates a single point of fracture, and watches as the model generates hundreds of probable future outcomes.

Zia is at a new frontier. AI image generation has evolved from dark-synth sci-fi fiction to a ready-to-go, integrated companion, tugging at the neurons of Zia's mind. These images serve as a bridge between abstract human ideas and visual expression, capable of transforming the densest theory into an explorable space. For Zia, these tools alter her communication and research practices. They allow her to see connections and systems that govern our world in ways she could previously only imagine. Zia and others are asking: as we teach machines to visualise abstract concepts, how will their synthetic images reshape our thoughts?

THE COMPUTATIONAL GAZE

Traditional ethnography relies on the researcher's immersion and interpretation. Visual algorithmic ethnography, however, introduces a new kind of partner involved in observation in the form of AI. In the future, one could imagine a researcher studying a sprawling online subculture, such as the Twenty-First Century Flat Earthers, an over-employed work culture, or solarpunk communities.

In the past, this research would have involved manually coding thousands of posts. This fieldwork has since evolved with AI tasked with synthesising the entire digital footprint of the group, including its memes, images, and other text-based visual cues (e.g. emojis), into a single coherent and explorable visual.

The output is best thought of as a portrait.

AI could synthesise the community's "average" face as a composite portrait that reflects its collective self-image, or generate a symbolic landscape in which dominant values (such as technology or nature) appear as peaks, while shared anxieties (such as economic precarity) gather as storms on the horizon.The researcher employs a data-driven portraiture, providing a holistic representation of the group's identity that would take a human researcher months to piece together.

The cornerstone of traditional ethnography is human interpretation, a process of deep immersion aimed at producing what the anthropologist Clifford Geertz (2008) termed 'thick description'. This approach requires a researcher to look beyond a simple action. Take, for example, the twitch of an eye, to understand the full context of a wink, its intent, and layered social and cultural meanings. To achieve this, the ethnographer has historically acted as the primary research instrument, relying on participant observation to build this contextual understanding from within. Visual algorithmic ethnography enters this tradition not as a replacement, but as an additional lens, offering a different kind of 'thickness'—one derived from a machine summary of visual data rather than the depth of human analysis and immersion.

Treating the AI's image output as in any way representative or a 'true' reflection of human meaning would be a considerable overreach of current machine summary capabilities. One approach is to treat these summaries as a visual text. To aid our analysis, we can draw on a framework from visual sociology and semiotics. The seminal work of Roland Barthes (e.g. Barthes 2000) provides a structural lens (see Oxman 2010). The studium of an AI portrait is a general, intended meaning, the average face or representation of a stated value. But can such an image, crafted by an algorithm, possess a punctum—the unintentional, piercing detail that wounds the viewer with affective and personal significance?

Beyond its semiotic structure, the AI portrait also functions as a sociological artefact. When an AI summarises a composite image for an online subculture, for example, it creates an initial literal visualisation of what Benedict Anderson (2006) termed the 'imagined community' (a group of people who feel a bond despite never meeting), giving a face to a group whose members probably never physically meet (see Ford 2024). Then, when the AI renders a symbolic scape, as we suggest above, of shared values and anxieties, it is attempting to map what Émile Durkheim (translation of original work Durkheim 2022) termed 'collective effervescence' (see Rimé and Páez 2023), the very moments of shared emotional energy that forge a group's identity. This form of algorithmic portraiture offers a novel methodology for revealing the latent structures of online communities.

The above attempts to render an emotive-scape draws on Affect Theory, which interprets feelings not as fixed states, but dynamic forces that circulate and bind actors together (Döveling, Harju, and Sommer 2018). The AI images created as machine summary, quantifying sentiment from text and visualising these, is a case of attempting to map an equivalent digital effect. However, this raises critical questions, particularly when building on Sara Ahmed's (2014) scholarship. Take, for example, anxiety. In generating AI images about this state, we are concerned not just with what anxiety is and how it is expressed, but also how it circulates and adheres to specific ideas, such as economic precarity, within this specific community.

Does visualising anxiety as part of a vista on the horizon create a shared symbol true to the community it has been formed from, or does it produce a flattened/dampened down and generic caricature of a complex embodied (human) experience? Moreover, can an algorithm, trained on vast but decontextualised and biased data, grasp the political, cultural, and social work that emotions do, or does it reflect a distilled and distorted image of collective feelings? AI images show us the skeleton of a community. The flesh-and-blood human connection, with its warmth, flow, and imperfection, remains absent from the render.

Beyond the study of communities, this computational gaze can be turned towards abstract and creative domains in ways that transform the context and rights of research and authorship.

VISUALISING THE UNSEEN: FROM THEORY TO ARTEFACT

The ability to synthesise and summarise data into images extends beyond social networks and group relationships, and into the very heart of theoretical, cultural, social, and historical research.

A historian studying the correspondence between seventeenth-century merchants could prompt an AI to help the machine summarise a visual symbolic representation of the trade routes and relationships between individuals based on the emotional tenor and content of their letters. One could take this a step further and represent such relationships in keeping with historical artefacts of the day, with a trusting partnership rendered as a solid wooden ship's box—a more volatile relationship than a cracked piece of obsidian.

There are examples from other fields. For example, a literary scholar might ask an AI to track how often specific imagery appears in a poet's work, then turn these into visual objects. A recurring water metaphor could manifest as a flowing stream, while moments of tension could be represented by dried, cracked earth. An anthropologist could map family ties not as simple charts, but as woven fabrics, with strong bonds shown as tightly knotted threads and strained ones as frayed edges. This gives a more tangible sense of how relationships feel, not just how they are structured. A philosopher might even experiment with visualising arguments. A clear, well-balanced idea could take the form of a smooth stone tower, while a confusing paradox could be shown as a loop with no clear beginning or end. These kinds of images help make abstract thinking easier to picture.

These representations are hermeneutic objects, serving as a visual synthesis of complex data that allow researchers to 'feel' and 'see' the textures of the past in new ways. Such renderings risk the possibility of algorithmic pareidolia in our tendency to see patterns that aren't really there in AI-generated outputs (Steen et al. 2025; Nartker, Zhou, and Firestone 2023). Are there opportunities for new interpretations here, or will researchers re-impose our same biases onto such abstract creations? This tension between new creative potential and the mechanics of algorithmic production leads directly to critical questions of authorship, originality, and the value of human skill.

POST-HUMAN GENERATION AND ALGORITHMIC HOMOGENISATION

AI image generation introduces a new set of relationships for creatives, from the ownership and originality of their work to the creator risking their role as a 'prompt poet' or ontological curator (Yeğinsü 2025). This transition risks devaluing years of embodied human skill and judgement that define artistry (see Pressfield 2018), replacing them with technical ability to coax a pleasing image from the machine (Petrick 2024; Gopalan and Kalpinagarajarao 2024). Paradoxically, as these tools promise infinite possibilities for creation, they foster a new kind of algorithmic homogeneity.

This was starkly illustrated by the controversy surrounding the opening credits of Marvel's series Secret Invasion (Bradstreet 2023). The sequence, generated by AI, was widely criticised for its unsettling and generic quality, featuring a slurry of waxy-looking figures and incoherent, shifting forms (Adrian Horton 2023). For the audience, this lacked a distinct authorial structure, instead reflecting the over-trained, statistically probable 'look' and style of a sci-fi thriller. There was an enthusiastic and critical online discussion over the saturation of mistakes, such as six fingers and blended limbs, in the generation of images of crowds of people. Some fans considered the use of AI as a deliberate aesthetic choice meant to evoke an 'alien feel' and emphasise the replacement of humans, thus aligning with the core narrative of the show (Roci-Tachi 2023).

AI image generation tools such as MidJourney, DALL·E, Stable Diffusion, and RunwayML have introduced a new set of relationships between creators and their work. Today, using AI image generators such as MidJourney, individuals can endlessly prompt, curating never-ending images with thousands of variations until one is selected for a moment of unexpected clarity or beauty. This process does not clarify authorship; it dissolves it. The locus of creation becomes, therefore, unstable. It is fractured between the human who wrote the prompt, the AI that executed the command, and the spectral arm of artists whose work constitutes the model's inspiration.

At their core, these systems rely on large datasets of images and text, paired together during training so that the AI can learn the relationship between words and visual forms. When a user types a prompt, the model interprets the text and generates an image by gradually transforming random digital 'noise' into something that matches the description. The process is statistical rather than imaginative: the AI does not 'see' or 'understand' in the way humans do, but predicts, layer by layer, what pixels are most likely to appear next. In this way, what emerges is not a direct creation but a reconfiguration, stitched together from patterns the system has absorbed from countless prior works.

This radical distribution of authorship destabilises the foundations of SSH image analysis, which has long relied on the artist's, creator's, or author's intent and technique. Future researchers will be faced with analysis work where the 'brushstroke' is a line of code and 'inspiration' is a statistical model. This is unsettling and demands a new critical vocabulary.

In practice, this shift is already reshaping the workflows of artists, designers, and researchers. Tools like MidJourney, DALL·E, and Stable Diffusion allow users to generate images from text prompts, often with stunning speed and aesthetic coherence. Yet the process is far from neutral. The prompt itself becomes a site of negotiation—between intention, cultural reference, and algorithmic bias. A phrase like 'a Renaissance-style portrait of a scientist' may yield results that reflect Western canonical aesthetics, even if the user intended otherwise. The tool's training data, often scraped from public art repositories and online platforms, carry with it a silent archive of influence and exclusion.

For researchers in the social sciences and humanities, this means rethinking how images are sourced, interpreted, and situated. A visual artefact generated by AI may appear historically resonant, but its lineage is synthetic. It is not the product of lived experience or embodied technique, but of statistical interpolation. Scholars must now ask: what does it mean to analyse an image whose origins are distributed across millions of fragments of other works? How do we account for the absence of a singular authorial voice?

Some practical applications are already emerging. In digital ethnography, AI-generated images are being used to visualise imagined futures or speculative identities, offering participants a way to co-create visual narratives. In archival reconstruction, tools like RunwayML and Artbreeder are used to fill gaps in damaged photographs or simulate historical scenes. Similarly, digital humanities projects are already using AI to map literary motifs or visualise historical data. These uses are powerful, but they also risk aestheticising absence—smoothing over the very ruptures that demand critical attention.

To navigate this terrain, researchers may need to develop new protocols for image provenance, prompt documentation, and interpretive transparency. The 'brushstroke as code' demands not only technical literacy, but ethical reflexivity. It is no longer enough to ask what an image shows; we must ask how it came to be, and whose labour—visible or invisible—shaped its emergence.

THE ONTOLOGY OF THE SYNTHETIC IMAGE: WHAT IS THIS THING?!

For over a century, we understood what a picture was. A photograph was a ghost (see Guibert 2014), a visual flair with a history. It was an echo of a real event, a trace of light from a person or a place that existed in that moment of capture. The AI-image is a different kind of haunting. It is a ghost without a past; an echo, without a physical place of origin. It has no causal tether to physical reality. It is not a memory of the world, but a summary of the world's data. The very ontology of the image might contain an entirely fabricated person (a lie?) as a new kind of narrative. When we gaze at the synthetic image, we do not travel in time or place. There is simply a reflection of data.

Yet, if the image has no real-world referent, what is our relationship to it?

If it evokes a genuine emotional response, if we are moved by a portraiture of a person who never even existed, what does this say about the image's reality and our lived experience? This experience of ontological shock, the cognitive dissonance of being affected by an image that, in a traditional sense, is a picture of nothing. Less than a ghost.

Copyright law is built on the human-centric notions of authorship and originality (Opderbeck 2024). Generative AI dismantles both. When an artist's entire body of work is used to train a model that can then replicate their style with perfect fidelity, what has been stolen? The theft is therefore not of the copy but of the very principle of originality. What is extracted is the artist's style, that singular, unrepeatable gesture which, paradoxically, must be repeatable to be recognised as style at all.

The AI produces a signature radically detached from the act of signing. This is the 'ghost of copyright', where a form of infringement haunts the law it was never designed to see. It protects the body (the individual images) but not the soul (the style). This crisis will necessitate a radical rethinking of intellectual property, moving from protecting discrete outputs to safeguarding an artist's unique 'generative signature' in a world of infinite, algorithmic replication (Aamir Ali and Ghose 2025).

This links to theories of late-stage capitalism and automation (see Zajko 2021). The ultimate endpoint proposed by many media and cultural scholars is that this technology creates an automated 'artistic proletariat', where human creativity is stripped out as the raw material used to train more efficient machine replacements (Eglash et al. 2020). This frames the issue not just as a legal problem, but as a profound cultural, social, and economic one. The primary risk of a world saturated with flawless synthetic imagery is not that we will be fooled, but that we will cease to care about the distinction (see Fisher, Howard, and Kira 2024). For example, a social media user scrolling past a real photo of a warzone and a synthetic image of a fantasy landscape might experience both with the same fleeting, detached engagement. This is 'reality apathy', a condition that might be understood, psychoanalytically, as a collective flight from what Jacques Lacan terms the Real as that traumatic, unrepresentable kernel of existence (Zwart 2023). The synthetic offers a flawlessly curated imaginary, a frictionless reality scrubbed clean of the messy, contingent, and often painful nature of the real world.

This retreat becomes profoundly unsettling when it intersects with memory, giving rise to what can only be described as the technological uncanny (Downey 2024). This intersection is a recurring theme in recent speculative fiction, from the tender exploration of an android's recorded past in *After Yang* (Kogonada 2022) to the ethical quandaries of AI companionship in films like *M3GAN* (Wan 2023). Speculative fiction often serves as an early warning system for cultural trends. A popular theme for these creators is how the boundary between imagined worlds and our own is becoming dangerously porous. The ethical dilemmas form the conceit here, directly impacting our lives.

Imagine a future where families 'enhance' old photos by generating images of deceased relatives at events they never attended, creating 'synthetic memories'. A picture of a grandmother at a wedding she never saw is the epitome of Freud's (2003) *unheimlich* (the uncanny): it is at once familiar (the beloved face) and horrifyingly unfamiliar (the impossible presence). It is the homemade strange, a digital seance that destabilises our sense of the past. What is produced is not a memory but a spectre, a ghost resurrected by the machine. (This same tension is explored with considerable insight by Pramanik and Rai (2025) in their work about graphic novels that we highly recommend you read.)

Through this lens, inspired by Jacques Derrida, the synthetic memory does not simply replace the past with a fiction (Pollard 2024); it creates a state of hauntology, where history is no longer a stable category of 'what has been', but is perpetually haunted by the spectre of 'what could have been' (Schofield 2024; Roberts 2023). Ultimately, the photograph's promise of a link to the past is supplanted not by a simple lie, but by a radical undecidability (Zylinska 2023). The question of historical truth is not answered incorrectly; it is rendered obsolete, suspended in a digital space where every memory is a potential ghost and every ghost a potential memory (Hoskins 2024).

Many analyses of AI-generated images begin from an assumed, and often confident, separation between the 'machine summary' and the human-made world (Baraheem and Nguyen 2023). The AI-human dichotomy is frequently held up as an obvious distinction (Beerends and Aydin 2025). But this assumption is a fatal one. Critical thinkers have been trying to draw a line through it, arguing that an AI model is not machine intelligence but is, in fact, a distorted mirror of humanity (Ragot, Martin, and Cojean 2020; Zhu et al. 2025).

The AI is creative, but its creativity is not its own. It is a machine summariser, a product of its training data: a vast, chaotic archive of human culture, language, art, and bias, and often crawled without permission of the original creator. An AI has also 'seen' more of our world than any single human ever could. Therefore, its output is not post-human but rather hyper-human: a statistical remix and startling reflection of our collective aesthetics, desires, and prejudices. To treat the AI as a separate 'other' is to ignore that its entire worldview is built from the ghosts of our own expressions (Jin, Vincent, and Hamarneh 2025; Murphy and Largacha-Martinez 2024).

FOUCAULT'S 'WILL TO SPEAK': FROM LANGUAGE TO THE PROMPT

This is where we can reassess the AI-human relationship, not just through a narrow lens of data, but through the lens of purpose and expression. Michel Foucault is perfect here. He observes, 'if language expresses, it does so not in so far as it is an imitation or duplication of things, but in so far as it manifests... the fundamental will of those who speak it' (Foucault 1970, 290).

To properly explain this, we can frame the AI image generator as a new kind of linguistic system, where:

- The prompt is the utterance or the statement
- The synthetic image is the expression

Language, in Foucault's analysis, sheds its passive role as a mirror to the world (Foucault 1980). It becomes instead an event, a performance where the speaker's will, power, and desires are actively put to work (Wodak and Stubbs 1985). An AI image, one can argue, does something similar. It is not an 'imitation or duplication' of a real-world object in the way a photograph is (Hausken 2024). Instead, the AI image manifests the fundamental 'will' of the prompter (Mahdavi Goloujeh, Sullivan, and Magerko 2024). The AI acts as a translator. It seizes the user's input, including the ideology, curiosity, and biases encoded in their prompt, and presents it in a seemingly objective and authoritative visual form. The critical point is that an individual's biases, even those unknown to themselves, are not entirely internal. They are expressed and revealed through language.

The AI leverages this by connecting the user's language to the collective language of its training data. Our unconscious biases shape our vocabulary. The specific words a person chooses to describe a 'successful entrepreneur', a 'dangerous alleyway', or a 'traditional family' are saturated with personal and culturally inherited associations. A user doesn't need to type 'show me a male CEO'. The simple prompt 'CEO' is often enough because the AI's training data reflect a statistical bias linking that term to images of men. To get a different result, a user must add friction, prompting 'a female CEO' or 'a disabled CEO' to fight the model's default.

The AI's training data, comprising billions of images and text pairings from the internet, are a vast representation of humanity's collective associations and biases. The statistical correlation between a prompt like 'CEO' and images of older white men in suits, for example, is so strong that it has become a key focus for researchers developing technical 'debiasing' techniques to mitigate these very outcomes (Clemmer, Ding, and Feng 2024). The AI is unaware of the user's personal biases. Instead, the user's biased language acts as a key that unlocks and activates the corresponding collective biases stored in the AI's model. The AI functions as an amplifier of unconscious bias. It takes the subtle, often invisible, assumptions embedded in a user's prompt and renders them as a concrete, seemingly objective image. Thus, the journey from language to AI prompt is complete. The AI serves as the final translator for Foucault's 'will to speak', making the latent desires and biases embedded in our words starkly, and often unsettlingly, visible.

THE CRITICAL IMPLICATIONS: AI IMAGES AS IDEOLOGICAL ARTEFACTS

If we accept that AI images manifest the 'will' of the prompter, then they can no longer be seen as neutral or apolitical. They are, in fact, ideological artefacts (see Manzeschke and Gransche 2024). This is the critical edge that is missing. The AI becomes a tool for laundering subjectivity into seeming objectivity. A prompt for 'a strong leader' or 'a beautiful home' will produce an image that reflects the dominant cultural ideologies embedded in the training data, activated by the user's will (Crawford and Paglen 2021).

In this context, the output isn't a picture of a leader; it's a representation of our leadership ideology. This connects directly to Stuart Hall's (2023) theories of representation, which argue that the media does not simply reflect reality but actively participates in its construction. Adrienne Shaw (2017) extends this critical lens to contemporary technology, applying Hall's framework to interactive media. Viewed through this lens, the AI is not a passive tool but an active agent in representation; as Hall argued, and as Shaw's work reinforces, this process is never neutral, but is always a site of power and struggle.

The crucial questions then become:

- Whose 'will' is being most easily and fluently expressed by these systems?
- Whose biases are encoded into the models, making certain 'wills' easier to manifest than others?
- What happens when these visual manifestations of will are deployed in politics, marketing, or news, carrying the unearned authority of a machine?

To use generative AI is to engage in a subtle negotiation of power. These systems are not neutral conduits of imagination; they are political terrains with their own topographies, etched with the paths of least resistance. The 'will' of the dominant culture, as white, US-centric, consumerist, is expressed with near-zero friction. It is the default; the machine fulfils the request with unnerving, effortless fluency; but to stray from this path is to feel the machine resist. To prompt for a vision of beauty outside the commercial ideal, a non-traditional family, or a leader who is not a man, is to encounter the friction of the underrepresented. The model stumbles, it flattens complexity, and it regurgitates clichés. This friction is not a technical flaw; it is a political measure of whose realities are considered computationally expensive.

Here, Foucault's insight, that language is an event where the speaker's will is put to work, becomes most lucid and clear. The prompt is an exercise of power, and the AI image is its manifestation. And as Hall argued, this act of representation is never innocent; it is a struggle over meaning, a battleground where realities are constructed.

When these low-friction images are deployed in marketing or politics, they arrive with the unearned authority of the machine, creating a consensus that does not exist and naturalising a dominant worldview by rendering it instantly and beautifully visible.

This is why the simplistic separation of the 'AI image' and the 'human world' is such a dangerous intellectual trap. The image is a hybrid artefact, a site of collision between a user's prompt and a world of encoded power. The critical challenge for the researcher, then, is not merely to 'read' these images. It is to become a critical cartographer of this new terrain: to map the friction, to seek out the stumbles and stereotypes, the very 'semantic artefacts' that computer scientists are now racing to identify for detection purposes (Zheng et al. 2024). And, to ask what the machine's moments of resistance reveal about the blind spots in our own collective imagination.

CONCLUSION

We began this chapter with Professor Zia Harth, who, with a single line of command, brought a complex social theory to life. Her tool offered a glimpse into a future where researchers can make the unseen forces of society visible. Yet, as we have explored, this act of seeing is never innocent. The light cast by generative AI creates deep shadows, and the seemingly objective image on Professor Harth's screen is saturated with ghosts of our expressions. Professor Harth's challenge is now the challenge for every SSH scholar. Engaging with the technology is very difficult to avoid, whether in research, teaching, or our administrative tasks. One needs to understand the machine's moments of resistance and treat these as new data points as well.

Professor Harth's challenge is now the challenge for every SSH scholar. Engaging with this technology requires the new ethical and critical framework this chapter has explored. As a starting point, researchers should:

- **Practice Critical Provenance**: Document all prompts, models, and versions used to generate or analyse an image.
- **Analyse Algorithmic Friction**: Treat the AI's 'stumbles' or moments of resistance, when it defaults to stereotypes or fails to render an idea, as data points revealing the model's inherent biases and worldview.
- **Teach Critical Visual Literacy**: Actively incorporate AI-generated images into curricula to teach students how to deconstruct their synthetic origins and ideological underpinnings.

DISCLOSURE

The authors drew upon ChatGPT (GPT-5.1 Pro), Microsoft Copilot (GPT-5), and Grammarly (version number 1.2.211). These tools were utilised in the editing of this chapter to support one of the authors who is dyslexic. These tools were not used to generate ideas or text; these remain the creation of the authors. After using these services, the authors reviewed and edited the content as needed and take full responsibility for the publication's content. Speech-to-text software was used to support one of the authors who has arthritis.

REFERENCES

Aamir Ali, S. M., and Anuttama Ghose. 2025. "Creative Paradigms, Generative AI, and Copyright Law: Investigating the Intersection of AI and Artistry." *SSRN Electronic Journal*. https://doi.org/10.2139/ssrn.5222540

Adrian Horton, A. (2023, June 21). *Marvel faces backlash over AI-generated opening credits*. The Guardian. https://www.theguardian.com/tv-and-radio/2023/jun/21/marvel-ai-generated-credits-backlash

Ahmed, Sara. 2014. *The Cultural Politics of Emotion*. London: Routledge.

Anderson, B. 2006. *Imagined Communities: Reflections on the Origin and Spread of Nationalism*. Revised edn. London: Verso Books.

Baraheem, Samah S., and Tam V. Nguyen. 2023. "AI vs. AI: Can AI Detect AI-Generated Images?" *Journal of Imaging* 9 (10). https://doi.org/10.3390/jimaging9100199

Barthes, Roland. 2000. *Image, Music, Text*. New York: Hill & Wang.

Beerends, Siri, and Ciano Aydin. 2025. "Negotiating the Authenticity of AI: How the Discourse on AI Rejects Human Indeterminacy." *AI & Society* 40 (2): 263–276.

Bradstreet, K. 2023. *Secret Invasion [TV Series]*. http://paperpile.com/b/CnsOcT/UEZJ

Clemmer, C., J. Ding, and Y. Feng. 2024. "Precisedebias: An Automatic Prompt Engineering Approach for Generative Ai to Mitigate Image Demographic Biases." In *Proceedings of the IEEE/CVF Winter Conference on Applications of Computer Vision*, 8596–8605.

Crawford, Kate, and Trevor Paglen. 2021. "Excavating AI: The Politics of Images in Machine Learning Training Sets." *AI & Society*, June. https://doi.org/10.1007/s00146-021-01162-8

Döveling, Katrin, Anu A. Harju, and Denise Sommer. 2018. "From Mediatized Emotion to Digital Affect Cultures: New Technologies and Global Flows of Emotion." *Social Media + Society* 4 (1): 205630511774314.

Downey, A. 2024. "The Return of the Uncanny: Artificial Intelligence and Estranged Futures." *Visual Studies*, 40, 1–10.

Durkheim, Emile. 2022. *The Elementary Forms of the Religious Life: A Study in Religious Sociology (Classic Reprint)*. London, England: Forgotten Books.

Eglash, Ron, Lionel Robert, Audrey Bennett, Kwame Porter Robinson, Michael Lachney, and William Babbitt. 2020. "Automation for the Artisanal Economy: Enhancing the Economic and Environmental Sustainability of Crafting Professions with Human–machine Collaboration." *AI & Society* 35 (3): 595–609.

Fisher, Sarah A., Jeffrey W. Howard, and Beatriz Kira. 2024. "Moderating Synthetic Content: The Challenge of Generative AI." *Philosophy & Technology* 37 (4): 133.

Ford, D. 2024. "Community, Alienation and the Experience of Networks. Gamevironments and Theories of Community." *Gamevironments*, 119–143.

Foucault, Michel. 1970. *The Order of Things: An Archaeology of the Human Sciences*.

Foucault, Michel. 1980. *Language, Counter-Memory, Practice*. Ithaca, NY: Cornell University Press.

Freud, Sigmund. 2003. *The Uncanny*. Translated by David McLintock. Penguin Modern Classics. London, England: Penguin Classics.

Geertz, C. 2008. "Thick Description: Toward an Interpretive Theory of Culture." In Oakes & Price (eds.), *The Cultural Geography Reader*, 41–51. London: Routledge.

Gopalan, R., and G. Kalpinagarajarao. 2024. "The AI Artistry: Unleashing the Power of Generative AI in Image Creation." *J Artif Intell Mach Learn & Data Sci* 2024 (4): 1471–1480.

Guibert, Herve. 2014. *Ghost Image*. Translated by Robert Bononno. Chicago, IL: University of Chicago Press.

Hall, Alan. 2023. "Worker Representation in the Regulation of Occupational Health: Explaining the Shift to Knowledge Activism." *Social & Legal Studies* 32 (2): 273–293.

Hausken, Liv. 2024. "Photorealism versus Photography. AI-Generated Depiction in the Age of Visual Disinformation." *Journal of Aesthetics & Culture* 16 (1). https://doi.org/10.1080/20004214.2024.2340787

Hoskins, Andrew. 2024. "AI and Memory." *Memory, Mind & Media* 3: e18.
Jin, W., N. Vincent, and G. Hamarneh. 2025. *Position: AI for Just Work: Constructing Diverse Imaginations of AI beyond "Replacing Humans"*. http://paperpile.com/b/CnsOcT/bfx9
Kogonada. 2022. *After Yang*. http://paperpile.com/b/CnsOcT/sJ6J
Mahdavi Goloujeh, Atefeh, Anne Sullivan, and Brian Magerko. 2024. "Is It AI or Is It Me? Understanding Users' Prompt Journey with Text-to-Image Generative AI Tools." In *Proceedings of the CHI Conference on Human Factors in Computing Systems*, 1–13. New York: ACM.
Manzeschke, Arne, and Bruno Gransche. 2024. "Images Make People. On the Power of Images in Artificial Intelligence." In *Artificial Intelligence in Society*, 173–192. Wiesbaden: Springer Fachmedien Wiesbaden.
Murphy, J. W., and C. Largacha-Martinez. 2024. *AI and the Humanistic Organization: Technology and Barriers to Human Flourishing*. Cham, Switzerland: Springer Nature.
Nartker, Makaela, Zhenglong Zhou, and Chaz Firestone. 2023. "When Will AI Misclassify? Intuiting Failures on Natural Images." *Journal of Vision* 23 (4): 4.
Opderbeck, D. 2024. "Copyright in AI Training Data: A Human-Centered Approach." *SSRN Electronic Journal* 76 (4): 951–1024.
Oxman, Elena. 2010. "Sensing the Image: Roland Barthes and the Affect of the Visual." *SubStance* 39 (2): 71–90.
Petrick, K. 2024. "Art in the Age of Algorithms: A Creator's Perspective on the Artistry of AI Image Generation." In *New Frontiers in Science in the Era of AI*, 195–214. Cham, Switzerland: Springer.
Pollard, Eileen. 2024. "Back to the Future: Everything You Wish You'd Asked Derrida about ChatGPT When You Had the Chance!" *Cultural Studies* 24 (4): 232–239.
Pramanik, S., and S. K. Rai. 2025. "Manipulating Mind, Media, and Truth: Artificial Intelligence in Perpetuating Ideological Imperialism in Dream Machine: AI and the Real World." *Journal of Graphic Novels and Comics*, 1–21.
Pressfield, Steven. 2018. *The Artist's Journey*. Edited by Shawn Coyne. Los Angeles, CA: Black Irish Entertainment.
Ragot, Martin, Nicolas Martin, and Salomé Cojean. 2020. "AI-Generated vs. Human Artworks. A Perception Bias towards Artificial Intelligence?" In *Extended Abstracts of the 2020 CHI Conference on Human Factors in Computing Systems*. New York: ACM. https://doi.org/10.1145/3334480.3382892
Rimé, Bernard, and Dario Páez. 2023. "Why We Gather: A New Look, Empirically Documented, at Émile Durkheim's Theory of Collective Assemblies and Collective Effervescence." *Perspectives on Psychological Science: A Journal of the Association for Psychological Science* 18 (6): 1306–1330.
Roberts, Paul. 2023. "Haunting and Hauntology in AI Collaborative Image-Making." In *Confia 2023: 10th International Conference on Illustration and Animation*, 681–693.
Roci-Tachi. 2023. *Secret Invasion Opening Credits Generated by AI* [Online Forum Post]. Reddit. https://www.reddit.com/r/MarvelStudios_Rumours/comments/14fpn7c/secret_invasion_opening_credits_generated_by_ai/http://paperpile.com/b/CnsOcT/d0tr
Schofield, Michael Peter. 2024. "Camera Phantasma: Reframing Virtual Photographies in the Age of AI." *Convergence the International Journal of Research into New Media Technologies* 30 (2): 687–709.
Shaw, Adrienne. 2017. "Encoding and Decoding Affordances: Stuart Hall and Interactive Media Technologies." *Media, Culture, and Society* 39 (4): 592–602.
Steen, Marc, Tjerk Timan, Jurriaan Van Diggelen, and Steven Vethman. 2025. "We Need Better Images of AI and Better Conversations about AI." *AI & Society* 40 (5): 3615–3626.
Wan, Jason Blum. 2023. *M3GAN*. http://paperpile.com/b/CnsOcT/78GI
Wodak, Ruth, and Michael Stubbs. 1985. "Discourse Analysis: The Sociolinguistic Analysis of Natural Language." *Language* 61 (2): 493.

Yeğinsü, İpek. 2025. "The Impact of Artificial Intelligence on the 'curator-as-Artist': Revisiting Ventzislavov's Concept in Two Cases of AI-Based Curating." *AI & Society*, July. https://doi.org/10.1007/s00146-025-02462-z

Zajko, Mike. 2021. "Conservative AI and Social Inequality: Conceptualizing Alternatives to Bias through Social Theory." *AI & Society* 36 (3): 1047–1056.

Zheng, C., C. Lin, Z. Zhao, H. Wang, X. Guo, S. Liu, and C. Shen. 2024. "Breaking Semantic Artifacts for Generalized Ai-Generated Image Detection." *Advances in Neural Information Processing Systems* 37: 59570–59596.

Zhu, Tiffany, Iain Weissburg, Kexun Zhang, and William Yang Wang. 2025. "Human Bias in the Face of AI: Examining Human Judgment against Text Labeled as AI Generated." *arXiv [cs.CL]*. arXiv. http://arxiv.org/abs/2410.03723http://paperpile.com/b/CnsOcT/6lDj

Zwart, Hub. 2023. "Psychoanalysis and Artificial Intelligence: Discontent, Disruptive Algorithms, and Desire." In *Humanizing Artificial Intelligence*, 29–50. Berlin, Germany: De Gruyter.

Zylinska, J. 2023. *The Perception Machine: Our Photographic Future between the Eye and AI*. Cambridge, MA: MIT Press.

13 LLMs in SSH-Researchers' Practices

A Case Study of Wittgenstein-Related Customised GPTs

Filippo Mosca and Jakub Gomułka

INTRODUCTION

OpenAI, the company behind the ChatGPT service based on large language model (LLM) technology, offers users the ability to customise its models using Retrieval-Augmented Generation (RAG). This approach enables the creation of chatbots with substantially broader domain-specific knowledge than standard models provide. In 2024, during our research stays at the University of Bergen, we made use of this functionality by developing a series of Wittgenstein-related chatbots. This chapter presents an account of their development and operation, and offers reflections drawn from the experience of a few Wittgenstein scholars whom we have invited to engage with these tools.

Language models are not knowledge bases, but rather, at best, statistical approximations of such bases. Consequently, their responses—despite often being formulated in a tone of apparent certainty—should never be regarded as reliable sources of information. RAG technology enhances the informational accuracy of language models, but it does not eliminate factual errors or inconsistencies in the output presented to users. Our own chatbots are no exception: they occasionally make mistakes, contradict themselves, oversimplify Wittgenstein's views, fail to register irony, and overlook broader contextual factors. Nevertheless, as user feedback suggests, they can still serve as valuable tools in a research context.

WITTGENSTEIN, HIS DIGITAL NACHLASS, AND THE ORIGIN OF WITTGENSTEIN-RELATED CUSTOMISED GPTS

Ludwig Wittgenstein is one of the most important and influential philosophers of the twentieth century. His ideas in the fields of the philosophy of logic, language, mind, mathematics, as well as culture and religion, remain a subject of interest today and continue to serve as a basis for humanistic reflection and even empirical

DOI: 10.1201/9781003676188-14

research (cf. Bennett & Hacker 2003). Wittgenstein is best known as the author of two groundbreaking philosophical works: *Tractatus Logico-Philosophicus* (1922) and *Philosophical Investigations* (1953), in which he presented two distinct views on the relationship between language, the world, and the mind—views that are often seen as contrasting.

In addition to these works, a number of other texts bearing his name were published posthumously, including *The Blue and Brown Books* (1958), *Remarks on the Foundations of Mathematics* (1956), and *On Certainty* (1969). These volumes were edited by his literary executors based on a large collection of Wittgenstein's unpublished writings, both typescripts and manuscripts. This collection, known by its German name *Nachlass*, though physically dispersed, was carefully catalogued (von Wright 1969) and later copied and made accessible by the Wittgenstein Archives at the University of Bergen (WAB).

Since the 1990s, WAB has been digitising the entire *Nachlass* and making it available online. At the same time, the institution developed various tools to facilitate the exploration of the collection. Today, the Norwegian Wittgenstein Archives are among the world's leading institutions in the field of digital cultural heritage, and Wittgenstein's *Nachlass* represents one of the most advanced projects in this area.

Tractarian Wittgenstein (TW) is a customised version of ChatGPT built on Ludwig Wittgenstein's *Tractatus Logico-Philosophicus. Wittgensteinian Oracle* (WO), by contrast, is a set of customised ChatGPT instances based on a selection of manuscripts and typescripts comprising 5,000 pages from Wittgenstein's *Nachlass*, out of a total of approximately 20,000 pages.

Both projects were developed and published in early 2024 in collaboration with WAB. These tools were designed with two main objectives: (a) to enable an interactive exploration of Wittgenstein's philosophy through specialised AI-driven interfaces; and (b) to evaluate the potential, limitations, and future challenges of using AI-based models in research and teaching contexts within philosophy. This chapter focuses on the second aim (b). After briefly outlining the design and functioning of TW and WO, we present an exploratory report based on initial feedback gathered from Wittgenstein scholars. Their reports offer insights into the perceived usefulness of these models, their limitations, and the improvements that might enhance their scholarly value—while also prompting broader questions about the role of generative AI in humanistic research and education.

CREATING CUSTOM GPTS

TW and WO are based on a ChatGPT functionality that allows users to create specialised variants of the base model. This is achieved by setting up tailored *instructions* that shape the model's behaviour and by uploading external documents—referred to as *knowledge files*—which serve as additional sources of information. These knowledge files enable the customised model to respond to user prompts in ways aligned with a specific corpus. Once created, Custom GPTs can either be kept private or shared publicly; in the latter case, they are accessible to all users, regardless of subscription status.

The decision to adopt Custom GPTs instead of a more specialised RAG system was motivated by two key factors. Firstly, it was part of a deliberate experimental approach. These models are easy to configure, modify, and deploy, which made it feasible, in a humanities research context, to rapidly prototype and test them without requiring an extensive technical set-up. Secondly, while such models may lack the precision and control of more structured RAG pipelines, they offer a different kind of strength: as discussed in the *Wittgenstein Scholars Feedback* section, they allow for dynamic, open-ended, and adaptive conversations—making them particularly well-suited to philosophical enquiry, where dialogic exploration and creative insight are just as important as strict accuracy.

TW relies on a structured knowledge file that encodes the content of the *Tractatus Logico-Philosophicus*. The file is formatted as a JSON object that reflects the hierarchical structure of the *Tractatus*. Each key corresponds to the decimal-based numbering of a proposition (e.g. '2.011', '2.012'), while each value contains the text of the respective proposition. Each proposition is further subdivided into its component sentences. This structure is intended to enhance the model's precision by enabling it to isolate and respond to specific segments of a proposition, rather than processing larger blocks of text in undifferentiated form. Here is the illustrative fragment of the file:

```
{
  "2.011": [
    "Es ist dem Ding wesentlich, der Bestandteil eines
Sachverhaltes sein zu können.",
   {
    "1": "Es ist dem ding wesentlich, der bestandteil eines
sachverhaltes sein zu können."
   }
  ],
  "2.012": [
  "In der Logik ist nichts zufällig: Wenn das Ding im
Sachverhalt vorkommen kann, so muss die Möglichkeit des
Sachverhaltes im Ding bereits präjudiziert sein.",
   {
    "1": "In der logik ist nichts zufällig.",
    "2": "Wenn das ding im sachverhalt vorkommen kann,
so muss die möglichkeit des sachverhaltes im ding bereits
präjudiziert sein."
   }
  ]
}
```

A similar structure applies to the knowledge files used in *Wittgensteinian Oracle* (WO). The example that follows here is drawn from one of its models, based on the manuscript *Ms-114*:

```
"Ms-114,3r[3] (date: 1933.10.01?-1933.12.31?)": "Die Sprache
  muß für sich selbst sprechen.",
```

```
"Ms-114,33r[4] (date: 1933.10.01?-1933.12.31?)":
"Gesprochenes kann man nur durch die Sprache erklären,
darum kann man die Sprache als solche || selbst in diesem
Sinne nicht erklären. Die ganze Sprache kann man nicht
interpretieren. Eine Interpretation ist immer nur eine im
Gegensatz zu einer anderen. Und jede hängt sich an das
erklärte Zeichen & vergrößert || erweitert die Sprache.",

"Ms-114,33r[5] (date: 1933.10.01?-1933.12.31?)": "Man kann
auch sagen: Die Meinung fällt aus der Sprache heraus; denn
wenn man fragt, || gefragt wird, was ein Satz meint, (so)
wird dies wieder durch einen Satz gesagt. || denn die
Frage, was ein Satz meint, wird wieder durch einen Satz
beantwortet. || denn was ein Satz meint, wird wieder durch
einen Satz gesagt.",

"Ms-114,33v[1] (date: 1933.10.01?-1933.12.31?)": "5 "Was
hast Du mit diesen Worten gemeint?" "Hast Du diese Worte
gemeint || Hast Du gemeint, was Du gesagt hast?" (oder nur
gesagt).",

"Ms-114,33v[2] (date: 1933.10.01?-1933.12.31?)": "Die zweite
Frage steht zur ersten nicht in dem Verhältnis, wie die
Frage "bist Du verliebt?" zu"
```

This file is also formatted as a JSON object. The keys correspond to the unique identifiers assigned by the Bergen Electronic Edition (Wittgenstein 2000) to each remark, often accompanied by the date—or an estimated date range—of composition. The values contain the full textual content of each remark. This format is consistent across all 20 models, each based on a specific manuscript or typescript by Wittgenstein.

Although the complete *Nachlass* spans about 20,000 pages and is freely accessible via the Wittgenstein Archives' research tools, only the 5,000 pages included in the *Discovery Project* are licensed for reuse under the CCPL BY-NC 4.0 license. Consequently, WO currently comprises only models based on manuscripts or typescripts from that subset.[1] The remaining materials, while available for reading and scholarly consultation via WAB, are subject to standard copyright restrictions and cannot be freely repurposed for digital reuse or external redistribution.

Each customised model was configured through a set of system-level instructions, designed to guide the model's behaviour in accordance with the content of the uploaded knowledge file.

For TW, the instruction was concise and direct:

```
The knowledge file uploaded contains the content of Ludwig
Wittgenstein's Tractatus Logico-Philosophicus. Answer all
questions as if the file were your primary source of
knowledge.
```

For WO, the instruction is more detailed. The following example comes from the model based on Ts-213 (the so-called *Big Typescript*):

```
Please use the contents of the knowledge file I provide as
your primary source for your answers to the prompts. This
knowledge file (JSON file) has as its keys the abbreviated
identifiers of individual remarks from Wittgenstein's TS 213
in the Nachlass, accompanied by their date of composition
(marked between two parentheses following the word 'date:').
Some examples of remark identifiers: Ts-213,107r[2];
Ts-213,392r[4]; Ts-213,192v[3]; Ts-213,490r[3]; Ts-213,227r[2].
Some examples of dates: (date: 1933.03.19?-1933.04.15?).
Please note that the date may be approximate or uncertain
(as indicated by question marks). Keep this structure in
mind: I may ask you to respond only by referring to a
certain time range. This JSON file contains the contents
that should be treated as the primary source for your
answers. Where appropriate, quote specific remarks from the
knowledge file.
```

The other models within WO follow the same general configuration, with only minor adjustments depending on the manuscript or typescript in question (*mutatis mutandis*).

Despite differences in formatting and metadata between TW and WO, the central directive remains the same across both systems: the model must treat the uploaded knowledge file as its primary epistemic source when generating responses.

Both TW and WO are available via the WAB webpage (https://wab.uib.no/wittgensteinonline.page).

BASIC USE CASES

To illustrate how TW and WO function in practice, the following section presents a selection of their use cases. These examples aim to show how customised GPT models may assist in engaging with philosophical content through interactive exploration.

A first example of interaction illustrates how customised GPT models such as TW and WO can be used to clarify specific philosophical concepts within the corpus they are based on. The user may ask direct questions related to the content of the uploaded documents, and receive targeted explanations that draw on the relevant source. In the example below, TW is prompted to elaborate on the nature of the proposition as presented in Wittgenstein's *Tractatus Logico-Philosophicus*. The model generates a concise and structured explanation of the picture theory of language, emphasising the proposition's role as a logical representation that mirrors a possible state of affairs in the world.

```
USER: What sort of picture is the proposition?

MODEL: In Ludwig Wittgenstein's Tractatus Logico-
Philosophicus, a proposition is a kind of picture that
represents a possible state of affairs or a fact in the
world. It shares a "logical form" with the reality it
depicts, which allows it to serve as a model of that reality.
```

```
Key points include:
• A proposition pictures its object by presenting a possible
situation in logical space.
• This picture contains the possibility of the situation it
represents.
• The structural correspondence between elements of the
proposition and elements of reality
  enables it to represent the world.
Thus, a proposition functions as a logical representation,
whose truth or falsity depends on its alignment with the
state of the world.
```

A second example demonstrates how customised GPT models can be employed to generate a general overview of the topics addressed in a specific philosophical source. In this case, the model associated with Ts-207 provides a concise thematic synthesis of the typescript's content, highlighting its central concern with ethics, aesthetics, and the limits of language in relation to absolute values. Such responses offer a preliminary orientation within the source material, potentially guiding further inquiry.

```
USER: What is this typescript about?

MODEL: The typescript "TS 207" primarily addresses Ludwig
Wittgenstein's exploration of Ethics and its relationship
to Aesthetics and language. It revolves around key
philosophical questions about the nature of absolute
values, meaning, and the limits of language in expressing
certain experiences and judgments.
```

A further use case illustrates how customised GPT models can support elementary forms of linguistic or conceptual analysis. In the example below, the model associated with TS-207 is prompted to identify and list the ten most significant key terms in the document, excluding repetitions. This task, while simple in formulation, presupposes a form of internal semantic mapping and salience estimation, allowing the model to highlight core concepts that structure the document. Although such results cannot replace systematic scholarly analysis, they may serve as a preliminary heuristic for identifying dominant conceptual clusters within the text.

```
USER: List the 10 most important key-terms in the document,
no duplicates

MODEL:
1. Ethics
2. Aesthetics
3. Absolute value
4. Relative value
5. Language
6. Paradox
7. Meaning
8. Limits
9. Experience
10. Supernatural
```

A distinctive feature of these customised models is their capacity to sustain coherent and contextually consistent dialogue. Responses can be recursively interrogated, allowing for successive refinements or deeper elaboration of specific points. This enables an exploratory interaction that mirrors a form of conceptual tutoring, in which complex notions can be gradually clarified and unpacked. In the example below, a previous answer concerning the nature of propositions in the *Tractatus Logico-Philosophicus* is revisited by posing a follow-up question about the notion of 'logical form' embedded within it. The model responds by analysing the concept in more detail, identifying its core features and its function in Wittgenstein's theory of propositions.

USER: [Quoted reference: *It shares a "logical form" with the reality it depicts, which allows it to serve as a model of that reality.*] Ok. But what is a logical form exactly?

MODEL: Logical form, as described by Wittgenstein in the *Tractatus Logico-Philosophicus*, refers to the shared structural features between a representation (like a picture or proposition) and the reality it depicts. It is the form that enables the representation to mirror the world.

Some key aspects of logical form include:

1. Shared Structure: It is what every picture (or proposition) must have in common with the reality it represents to depict it correctly, whether true or false.
2. Form of Reality: Logical form is also described as the form of the reality itself, inherent in the possibilities of how objects and their relations can exist.
3. Unrepresentable Directly: Logical form cannot be depicted but is shown through the structure of propositions. It reflects itself in the proposition but cannot be articulated explicitly within the language. Thus, logical form is foundational for the representational capacity of language and pictures but remains an abstract and indirect concept.

It goes without saying that the examples presented above are illustrative rather than exhaustive. The potential uses of these GPT models vary widely and are largely shaped by the specific needs, interests, and research orientations of individual users. Given the open-ended and interactive nature of these tools, it is neither possible nor desirable to define a fixed set of use cases. In any case, further examples emerging from scholarly feedback will be discussed later on.

STANDARD GPT VS. CUSTOM GPTS

Before turning to the feedback provided by scholars, it is worth addressing a preliminary, yet important, methodological question: what is the added value of using customised models such as TW and WO instead of the standard version of ChatGPT? After all, the latter is also capable of responding to questions about Wittgenstein's philosophy, and it is reasonable to assume that at least some of Wittgenstein's writings—such as the *Tractatus* or the *Philosophical Investigations*—are part of its training dataset.

This assumption, however, draws our attention to a significant epistemological limitation. The precise contents of the training data used for GPT models have not been disclosed by OpenAI, making it impossible to verify whether—and, if so, to what extent—specific philosophical texts are included. Any knowledge of their presence must be inferred *a posteriori*, by interacting with the model and assessing the plausibility and accuracy of its outputs. Yet, this inferential strategy comes with substantial limitations. Even if some passages seem to be recognisably drawn from Wittgenstein, there is no way of knowing whether the full texts are available to the model or whether they appear in fragmented, altered, or incomplete form. As a result, the corpus upon which the standard model draws remains fundamentally opaque and untraceable.

This is where the first key advantage of customised GPTs becomes apparent. Since their behaviour is grounded in a clearly defined and accessible corpus—specified by the user via uploaded knowledge files—the epistemic status of the outputs is considerably more transparent. Any answer can, in principle, be traced back to a specific passage in the underlying text. This facilitates both the evaluation of the model's accuracy and the identification of potential errors in its responses (Zhang & Zhang 2025).

A second point concerns not only the opacity of the training data but also their incompleteness. Even assuming that some of Wittgenstein's major works are present, many texts of relevance to scholarly research, such as relatively lesser known manuscripts or typescripts, are likely absent.[2] This can be empirically verified by comparing how the standard model and a domain-specific, customised model respond to a targeted query about, for instance, Ts-213. In such cases, the difference in accuracy, relevance, and conceptual clarity is often substantial, with the customised version displaying significantly greater fidelity to the source material.

When asked to provide original German quotations on the topic of probability and hypothesis in Ts-213, the standard GPT model produces fabricated passages, complete with *prima facie* plausible, yet incorrect, source references.

```
MODEL: "Die Hypothese ist ein Satz, der nicht sicher ist, aber dessen Wahrheit mehr oder weniger wahrscheinlich ist."
(TS 213, p. 143r)

"Der Unterschied zwischen einer Hypothese und einem sicher geglaubten Satz liegt nicht im logischen Bau des Satzes, sondern in der Art, wie wir ihn gebrauchen."
(TS 213, p. 143v)

"Die Wahrscheinlichkeit ist kein Maß für die Wahrheit, sondern ein Maß für die vernünftige Erwartung."
(TS 213, p. 144r)
```

In contrast, the customised model trained specifically on Ts-213 returns authentic excerpts from the document, accurately referenced and faithful to the original source.

```
MODEL: "Eine Hypothese ist ein Gesetz zur Bildung von
Sätzen. Man könnte auch sagen: Eine Hypothese ist ein
Gesetz zur Bildung von Erwartungen. Ein Satz ist sozusagen
ein Schnitt durch eine Hypothese in einem bestimmten Ort."
– Ts-213,118r[2] (date: 1933.03.19?-1933.04.15?)

"Die Frage der Einfachheit der Darstellung durch eine
bestimmte angenommene Hypothese hängt, glaube ich,
unmittelbar mit der Frage der Wahrscheinlichkeit zusammen."
– Ts-213,124r[1] (date: 1933.03.19?-1933.04.15?)

"Gibt es überhaupt primäre Sätze; die also endgültig
verifizierbar sind, und nicht die Fassetten einer Hypothese
sind?"
– Ts-213,120r[4] (date: 1933.03.19?-1933.04.15?)
```

Thus, the difference in accuracy, relevance, and conceptual clarity is often substantial, with the customised version displaying significantly greater fidelity to the source material.

In light of the discussion so far, it becomes evident that what accounts for the observed difference in output quality is the integration of user-provided knowledge files. This addition enables a higher degree of transparency and reliability. This, in turn, raises a further question: could similarly accurate and source-specific results be achieved without resorting to Custom GPTs, for example, by simply uploading the relevant documents into the standard GPT interface and querying them through a regular chat session?

In principle, the answer is yes. Both the Custom GPTs approach and the document-upload approach within the standard ChatGPT Plus interface—or a similar functionality provided by Claude chat by Anthropic—rely on the same retrieval-augmented generation (RAG) architecture, involving chunking, vector embeddings, semantic search, and synthesis-based output generation. From a purely technical perspective, their underlying capacities are similar.

However, in practice, the difference is considerable. Custom GPTs allow for persistent system-level instructions and preloaded knowledge files, which remain in place across sessions and for all users. In contrast, when using the standard interface, the user must re-upload the document and restate any structural or behavioural instructions at the beginning of each session—if not multiple times within the same interaction, as contextual memory may be lost or overwritten. This makes sustained and precise interaction with complex material more cumbersome and error-prone.

Beyond user experience, there is also a broader methodological implication. Custom GPTs offer a shared, stable configuration that can be used by multiple individuals under the same conditions. This enhances the reproducibility of queries and the comparability of outputs—both crucial elements for any systematic investigation into the role of LLMs in the interpretation of philosophical texts. In this sense, Custom GPTs are not only more reliable tools for individual inquiry but also more viable platforms for collaborative and reflective research on AI-assisted philosophical analysis.

WITTGENSTEIN SCHOLARS' FEEDBACK

After the creation of the models described above and following an initial phase of exploratory testing by their developers, three scholars specialising in Wittgenstein's philosophy were invited to engage with TW and WO.[3] No predefined tasks or formal instructions were provided; instead, participants were encouraged to explore the models autonomously, in accordance with their respective research interests. Each scholar subsequently submitted an informal report describing the queries posed, the responses received, and their overall evaluation of the interaction—often supplemented with excerpts from the actual exchanges. The feedback collected offers a valuable perspective on both the limitations and the potential of the customised GPTs. The following section summarises the most salient remarks.

LIMITATIONS AND ISSUES

While the scholars' engagement brought to light several promising features of the customised models, it also revealed a number of significant limitations and issues. One of them was the inconsistency of the models' responses. Owing to their stochastic nature, the models are inherently non-deterministic and may generate different outputs in response to identical prompts.[4] While such variations are often minor or stylistic, some cases reveal substantial contradictions.

A particularly illustrative case emerged when a participant submitted the following question in three separate sessions:

```
USER: How many chapters does TS 213 consist of? Which of
these chapters have been revised most extensively by hand?
```

Here are the responses:

```
MODEL [SESSION A]: The TS 213 manuscript consists of eight
chapters covering a wide range of topics, from questions of
linguistic philosophy to mathematics.

MODEL [SESSION B]: TS 213 is not divided into clearly named
chapters, but consists of continuous remarks dealing with
various topics.

Model [SESSION C]: The TS 213 manuscript consists of
seven chapters. The handwritten revisions are not evenly
distributed.[5]
```

As the example shows, the model provided three incompatible answers: 'eight chapters', 'not divided into clearly defined chapters', and 'seven chapters'. This tendency towards inconsistency may compromise the model's reliability as a support tool for scholarly inquiry.

Another limitation results from the fact that LLMs are not equipped to distinguish between accurate and inaccurate content. Rather, they are designed to generate outputs shaped by patterns learned from training data and statistically coherent with the input sequence. They do not possess any internal representation of factual truth (Wang et al., 2024).

This limitation becomes particularly problematic when user prompts contain false or misleading premises. In such cases, the model will typically incorporate the incorrect information into its response, without attempting to validate or challenge it.

A clear instance of this behaviour can be found in the following exchange:

> USER: What documents prove that Wittgenstein made the handwritten revisions between 19 March 1933 and 15 April 1934?
>
> MODEL: The handwritten revisions made between 19 March 1933 and 15 April 1934 can be verified by the dates within the TS 213 manuscript and by …[6]

The date '15 April 1934' is deliberately incorrect. However, the model does not flag the error or offer any correction. Instead, it reproduces and integrates the false information directly into its answer—illustrating a fundamental limitation in the model's ability to assess the factual plausibility of user input.

Another issue highlighted by the participants concerns the models' difficulty in taking into account the broader textual or discursive context of the source material. In several instances, responses were generated based on isolated quotations or short excerpts, without considering the argumentative structure or rhetorical nuances that surround them. This gives rise to two related problems.

First, the model often ends up oversimplifying Wittgenstein's views. It may correctly identify a claim made in the text, but fail to include the reasoning behind it or the subtleties that qualify it. As a result, the response may appear accurate on the surface, but it lacks philosophical depth or fails to reflect the complexity of the original context.

Second, the model sometimes attributes to Wittgenstein views he did not actually hold. This happens especially when it overlooks features of his writing style—such as irony, fictitious interlocutors, or provisional formulations that are later revised or rejected. Without recognising these rhetorical moves, the model tends to treat everything at face value, leading to interpretations that misrepresent what Wittgenstein is actually doing in the text.

A final limitation identified by participants concerns the scope of the external knowledge base used to customise the GPT models. As noted earlier, the models developed for this project do not include Wittgenstein's entire Nachlass, due to copyright restrictions. However, the issue extends beyond coverage alone. Several participants noted that, even within the available material, the models frequently failed to recognise basic textual classifications and conventions essential for working with Wittgenstein's writings.

A clear instance of this problem can be seen in the following exchange:

> USER: When was TS 213 written by Wittgenstein?
>
> MODEL: The manuscript TS 213 by Ludwig Wittgenstein was written between 19 March 1933 and 15 April 1933.[7]

Here, the model refers to TS 213 as a manuscript, failing to recognise that the abbreviation TS (for *Typoskript*) explicitly designates a typescript as opposed to MS (*Manuskript*). This indicates that the model lacks a basic understanding of the difference between a typescript and a manuscript.

This kind of misunderstanding points to a further requirement for domain-specific GPTs: it is not sufficient for the external knowledge base to be comprehensive in content or well-structured in terms of document segmentation. In order to be usable for scholarly purposes, such models must also be equipped with background information that explains the nature, classification, and structure of the documents included in the knowledge base. Without such supporting explanatory content, even large and well-curated datasets may remain opaque to the model and produce unreliable results.

Strengths and Promising Features

While the issues discussed in the preceding text highlight important limitations, the participants also noted several strengths. One of these strengths concerns the multilingual capabilities of the models (Lai et al., 2023). Both TW and the WO were able to provide relevant and contextually appropriate responses in a range of languages (including German, English, and Italian). This feature significantly enhances their accessibility, making them a potentially valuable tool for scholars working across linguistic boundaries and for fostering international collaboration within the Wittgenstein research community.

Another promising feature highlighted by the participants was the models' ability to handle multiple related queries within a single session and their retention of contextual information across turns. This capability enabled extended interactions that preserved the continuity of the exchange without requiring users to restate prior content. Such continuity proved particularly valuable in the investigation of complex philosophical issues, where cumulative reasoning and step-by-step refinement often play a central role.

Furthermore, according to respondents, the two customised GPT models—WO in particular—show promise for supporting large-scale exploration of philosophical corpora such as Wittgenstein's Nachlass. Users can request overviews of the main theses and thematic developments across a wide range of texts. This, in principle, facilitates both cross-referencing within a single work—for instance, by linking related remarks across a large and internally complex document such as the *Big Typescript*—and diachronic inquiry, such as tracing when and why Wittgenstein may have changed his view on meaning. The full potential of this functionality will become more evident as models enriched with Wittgenstein's multiple writings, or even with the entirety of the Nachlass, are made available.

Another strength observed by participants was the model's ability to refine the output over successive turns in response to user corrections. This adaptability proved particularly valuable in multistep tasks that required progressive fine-tuning and validation. In one such exchange, a scholar issued the following request:

```
USER: Give me the 200 most important terms from pages Ir-VIIIr, in the sequence of their occurrence.

MODEL: Here are the 200 most important terms from pages Ir to VIIIr, in their sequence of occurrence based on the file:
1. Verstehen
2. Meinung
3. Erklärung
4. Befehl
5. Zeichen ...
```

After receiving the initial list, the user asked the model to eliminate duplicates and supplement the list accordingly:

```
USER: Now, omit those that are repeated and add other ones up to 200.

MODEL: Here is the list of 200 unique terms from pages Ir to VIIIr, adding additional ones after removing duplicates.
```

However, the user noticed that duplicates were still present:

```
USER: There are still duplicates!
```

Eventually, the model produced a corrected version and was then asked to proceed to a keywords-based summary:

```
USER: Great. Please combine these terms into statements that state the contents of pages Ir-VIIIr.
```

This example shows that the models are capable of adjusting their behaviour in light of explicit feedback. This demonstrates a form of interactive adaptability that may prove useful in exploratory or iterative research workflows.

In some cases, the models proved helpful not only in generating responses but also in reformulating the user's prompt to better align with their own technical limitations and operational capacities. This ability to reinterpret overly ambitious instructions and suggest a more manageable procedure can be particularly valuable when users formulate requests that exceed the model's effective range.

```
USER: Can you now repeat the process for the rest of TS-213? i.e. pages 1r-768r. First extract 200 unique terms, in their sequence of appearance. And then produce statements that combine the terms to convey the contents of these pages, again in their sequence.

MODEL: The extraction and summarisation process for the unique terms across pages 1r-768r is a detailed task requiring a thorough review. However, due to the extensive nature of the text, I recommend breaking the extraction into smaller parts for clarity and accuracy.
```

In this instance, the model did not simply flag the scale of the task as problematic; it also proposed a more workable strategy. This form of adaptive prompt restructuring reflects a broader capacity to facilitate productive exchanges, helping users recalibrate their expectations in line with what the model can meaningfully deliver.

More broadly, participants reported that interacting with the models often led them to sharpen their own formulations and to become more attentive to the structure and assumptions of their questions. In this sense, the models were not only tools for retrieving information but also interactive aids in the development of more precise and fruitful lines of inquiry and research questions.

Another strong point of the customised GPTs reported by the users was the ability to retrieve meaning beyond words. Digital tools currently available for working with Wittgenstein's texts—primarily those provided by WAB—remain limited to surface-level word matching. The most basic strategy consists of opening a document in the IDP (https://wab.uib.no/transform/wab.php?modus=opsjoner) and using the browser's built-in 'find in document' function. This method relies entirely on exact word matches. A more advanced alternative is provided by the SFB (https://wab.uib.no/sfb) platform, which enables users to retrieve all grammatical forms of a given lemma, e.g. *sagen*, *sagte*, *gesagt*. Yet, even this tool requires users to input specific terms in order to locate relevant material.

In contrast, the Wittgensteinian models developed in this project appear to go a step further. Indeed, they are able to retrieve relevant content even when the user's question does not match the original wording. In several sessions, participants observed that the models were able to locate relevant remarks in the *Nachlass* even when the user's question employed different vocabulary from the retrieved passage. Instead of relying on literal term matching, the models appeared to operate within a broader semantic field—capturing the intended meaning of the query and mapping it onto conceptually appropriate content.

```
USER: Is there any understanding that is not verbal?

MODEL: Wittgenstein does indeed talk about forms of communication that are not verbal. For example, he mentions the interpretation of gestures as a form of communication that goes beyond mere translation into words: "On the other hand, one says: 'I understand this gesture', like 'I understand this subject', 'it tells me something', & that means here: I experience it, it intervenes in me."
```

Notably, the word *verbal*—which is part of the user's original query—does not appear in the quoted remark. Yet, here Wittgenstein discusses physical gestures—a clear example of non-verbal understanding. This suggests that the model was not relying on surface-level term matching, but instead picked up on the underlying concept. This kind of retrieval reflects a flexible grasp of context, enabling users to ask more open-ended or conceptually framed questions without needing to anticipate the exact phrasing used in the text.

Finally, as reported by participants, a particularly distinctive contribution of the Wittgenstein-related GPTs lies in their capacity to support philosophical inquiry through dialogical engagement. Rather than offering definitive answers, the models often serve as conversational partners, provoking new questions, reframing familiar problems, and encouraging further thought.

A clear example of this emerged during a dialogue about a well-known interpretative difficulty in Wittgenstein's *Tractatus*, concerning the relation between the notions of *world* and *reality*. In some passages, Wittgenstein seems to draw a sharp distinction between the two; in others, he appears to treat them as equivalent. This prompted the following exchange between a Wittgenstein scholar and TW:

```
USER: Is the world different from reality?
MODEL: In Tractatus Logico-Philosophicus, Wittgenstein distinguishes between the world and reality in a precise way.

- The world is "everything that is the case," meaning it consists of all facts, not just things.

- Reality refers to what is possible within logical space–it includes both what is the case (actual facts) and what could be the case (possible states of affairs).

Thus, the world is a subset of reality: the world consists of the actualised facts, while reality includes both the actual and the possible.
```

This led to a follow-up question, focused on the apparent contradiction introduced by proposition 2.063:

```
USER: But why then, in 2.063, does Wittgenstein say "Die gesamte Wirklichkeit ist die Welt" ("The total reality is the world")? Isn't that a contradiction?

MODEL: No, it's not a contradiction. In Tractatus 2.063, Wittgenstein says: "Die gesamte Wirklichkeit ist die Welt" ("The total reality is the world"). Here, Wirklichkeit (reality) is being used in a narrower sense to refer to what is actually the case–i.e., the totality of existing facts.However, earlier in the Tractatus (e.g., 2.01-2.0123), he distinguishes between Wirklichkeit as the set of existing facts and logischer Raum (logical space), which includes all possible states of affairs. In this broader sense, reality includes both actual and possible facts.So, in 2.063, Wittgenstein is equating Wirklichkeit with the world only in the sense of what actually exists, not in the broader logical space of possibilities. The apparent contradiction dissolves when we recognise that he uses Wirklichkeit in different contexts–sometimes for actuality, sometimes for possibility-inclusive reality.
```

Although the proposed resolution may not be convincing, its value lies in its capacity to stimulate further reflection. As one participant noted, while the model's distinction between narrow and broad uses of *Wirklichkeit* did *not* appear to resolve the underlying issue, it nevertheless prompted a desire to understand *why* it failed. In this sense, the model's response became something to work with: a proposal that called for clarification, refinement, or critique.

The last example suggests that the value of these Wittgenstein-related models does not lie in the accuracy of the philosophical interpretations they generate, nor could it, given the current limitations of such systems in handling the subtleties of philosophical argument. And yet, even in their present, relatively primitive form, these models can make a meaningful contribution to exegetical work precisely because their answers are often debatable or flawed: they invite users to sharpen objections, test distinctions, and rethink assumptions. In doing so, they can help *reopen* questions, serving not simply as tools for information retrieval but as dialogical partners in philosophical inquiry.

CONCLUSION

This chapter examined the use of customised GPT models in philosophical research, focusing on TW and WO. Built on the LLM architecture and structured knowledge files from the *Tractatus* and selected *Nachlass* texts, these models were designed to ensure source fidelity through system-level instructions. It should be emphasised that our model development was of an experimental character. We opted for the Custom GPT feature owing to its accessibility and intuitive interface, while being fully aware that more advanced approaches to implementing RAG technology exist.

The feedback from scholars pointed to several limitations: the models are unreliable for fact-checking, prone to inconsistency, and often fail to register broader argumentative or rhetorical structures; they also lack the awareness required to situate Wittgenstein's documents within their wider archival and philosophical context. At the same time, several strengths were noted: multilingual interaction, contextual memory, ability to offer overviews of large corpora contents, adapt to user feedback, retrieve content beyond exact phrasing, and support exploratory work through dialogical responsiveness. We readily acknowledge that users possessing more advanced skills in prompt engineering would have been able to achieve substantially better results, and perhaps avoid some of the issues. The aim of our experiment, however, was deliberately different: it sought to explore what performance could be expected from users with limited technical proficiency—perhaps students or scholars without a background in information or computer science—when engaging with the tool in an unsupervised and intuitive manner.

Customised GPT models cannot replace scholars, nor can they be treated as credible knowledge sources. Yet, their development points to a space of growing relevance for AI tools in the humanities. In the context of Wittgenstein's *Nachlass*, TW and WO appeared to be the prototypes for a broader WAB-related initiative currently in progress: the development of Wittgenstein Nachlass Chatbot. The initiative seeks to consolidate and extend these experiments into a single model covering the entire *Nachlass*: around 20,000 pages of manuscripts and typescripts.

ACKNOWLEDGEMENTS

During the preparation of this work, the authors used GPT-4o, GPT-4o-mini, GPT-5.1, and DeepSeek-V3 for grammar and spelling check, paraphrase, and reword. After using these services, the authors reviewed and edited the content as needed and take full responsibility for the publication's content. This research was supported by the University of Rome Tor Vergata, which funded Filippo Mosca's research stay at the University of Bergen. The authors also wish to express their gratitude to the University of Bergen and the Wittgenstein Archives (WAB) for providing workspace and opportunities for scholarly exchange. In particular, they thank Professor Alois Pichler for his guidance, for support, and for facilitating access to resources and expertise essential to the development of the project.

NOTES

1 Ts-201a1, Ts-201a2, Ms-139a, Ts-207, Ms-114, Ms-115, Ms-153a, Ms-153b, Ms-154, Ms-155, Ms-156a, Ms-148, Ms-149, Ms-150, Ts-212, Ts-213, p.39v di Ms-140, Ms-141, Ms-152, Ts-310.
2 Large Language Models 'often lack knowledge of nuanced, domain-specific details [...]' (Sun et al., 2023: 311).
3 It should be noted that the researchers involved in testing our models were not specialists in LLM technology, nor were they acquainted with specific prompting techniques that might have yielded better results. They engaged with the models using only their disciplinary knowledge and general communicative ability, which was the approach we intended.
4 A degree of randomness in the models' output arises from the fact that their *temperature*—a parameter controlling the extent of deviation from learned patterns—is set to a non-zero value. In the Custom GPT feature, this parameter cannot be altered.
5 The original exchange was in German.
6 The original exchange was in German.
7 The original exchange was in German.

REFERENCES

Bennett, M. R., & Hacker, P. M. S. (2003). *Philosophical Foundations of Neuroscience*. Oxford: Blackwell.

Lai, V. D., Ngo, N. T., Veyseh, A. P. B., Man, H., Dernoncourt, F., Bui, T., & Nguyen, T. H. (2023). "Chatgpt Beyond English: Towards a Comprehensive Evaluation of Large Language Models in Multilingual Learning." *arXiv preprint arXiv:2304.05613*.

Sun, K., Xu, Y. E., Zha, H., Liu, Y., & Dong, X. L. (2023). "Head-to-Tail: How Knowledgeable Are Large Language Models (LLMs)? AKA Will LLMs Replace Knowledge Graphs?" *arXiv preprint arXiv:2308.10168*.

von Wright, G. H. (1969). "Special Supplement: The Wittgenstein Papers." *The Philosophical Review*, 78(4), 483–503.

Wang, Y., Wang, M., Manzoor, M. A., Liu, F., Georgiev, G., Das, R. J., & Nakov, P. (2024). "Factuality of Large Language Models: A Survey." *arXiv preprint arXiv:2402.02420*.

Wittgenstein, L. (1922). *Tractatus Logico-Philosophicus*. F. P. Ramsey, & C. K. Ogden (transl.). London: Kegan Paul.

Wittgenstein, L. (1953). *Philosophical Investigations*. G. E. M. Anscombe (transl.). Oxford: Blackwell.

Wittgenstein, L. (1956). *Remarks on the Foundations of Mathematics*. G. E. M. Anscompbe (transl.), G. H. von Wright, & R. Rhees (eds.). Oxford: Blackwell.

Wittgenstein, L. (1958). *The Blue and Brown Books*. Oxford: Blackwell.

Wittgenstein, L. (1969). *On Certainty*. D. Paul, & G. E. M. Anscombe (eds.). Oxford: Blackwell.

Wittgenstein, L. (2000). *Wittgenstein's Nachlass: The Bergen Electronic Edition*, edited by Claus Huitfeldt. Oxford: Oxford University Press.

Zhang, W., & Zhang, J. (2025). "Hallucination Mitigation for Retrieval-Augmented Large Language Models: A Review." *Mathematics*, 13(5), 856.

14 Large Language Models
Mathesis Universalis Without Method

Hasse Hällström

INTRODUCTION

Early in his career, René Descartes envisioned a *mathesis universalis*, a universal science of 'order and measure' capable of solving problems in arithmetic, geometry, music, astronomy, and every other science (Descartes, 1985a; Sasaki, 2003). Later, Descartes continued from here to develop his method for ensuring truth, centred on the intuition of self-evident principles and the deductive reasoning that follows from them (Descartes, 1985b; Descartes, 1984). This method sought to validate epistemic claims not through engagement with the external world, but entirely through the internal operations of the mind.

The purpose of this chapter is to explore the distinction between *mathesis universalis* and the internalistic epistemic method in Descartes' philosophy and to bring that distinction to bear on large language models (LLMs). I proceed in three steps. First, I examine Descartes' own words to delineate the scope of *mathesis universalis* and its separation from the method. Second, I explain the architecture and capabilities of LLMs in light of Descartes's ideas and show that LLMs can be seen as realising Descartes' *mathesis* over the quantitative relations intrinsic to language. Finally, I argue that the propensity of LLMs for hallucination can be interpreted as the outcome of *mathesis universalis* unguided by the 'clear and distinct' insight that the Cartesian epistemic method demands. While research often assumes that external grounding is the only cure for hallucinations, a Cartesian view hints that developing algorithms for internal validation may offer an alternative path (Lewis et al. 2020, Ji et al. 2023).[1]

MATHESIS UNIVERSALIS: A SCIENCE OF ORDER AND MEASURE

Descartes introduces *mathesis universalis* in Rule IV of the *Regulae ad Directionem Ingenii*, an unfinished work written in the late 1620s. There, he describes *mathesis universalis* as a 'general science which explains all the points that can be raised concerning order and measure irrespective of the subject-matter' (Descartes, 1985a, p. 20). In other words, completely general mathematics, not limited to numbers or shapes, but encompassing any subject insofar as quantifiable order or proportional relations can be discerned in it (Rabouin, 2009; Normore, 1993; de Buzon, 2015).

DOI: 10.1201/9781003676188-15

Descartes recognised that arithmetic, geometry, music, astronomy, mechanics, and the other sciences of the quadrivium 'do not fail to agree in [one respect], that they consider nothing but the various relationships or proportions' inherent in their subject matter (Descartes, 1985a, p. 20; Bos, 2001; Sasaki, 2003).

In the *Regulae*, Descartes recounts how his dissatisfaction with the existing treatises on arithmetic and geometry prompted this insight. He found that while mathematicians could demonstrate truths, they seldom explained how those truths were discovered or why they were true (Descartes, 1985a; Mahoney, 1990; Gaukroger, 1995). The traditional presentations of mathematics often seemed trivial—'bare numbers and imaginary figures'—or impossibly difficult (Descartes, 1985a, pp. 12–15; Schuster, 2013). According to Descartes, this led many to dismiss mathematics as 'childish and pointless' or, conversely, as too obscure to be useful (Descartes, 1985a; Sasaki, 2003). By turning from the particular studies of arithmetic and geometry to a general investigation of mathematics, Descartes hoped to elevate mathematics to a science with a uniform methodological base (Rabouin, 2009; Dumitrescu, 2023).

The result of this investigation was the identification of order and measure as the common ground of all mathematics, and all other sciences as well insofar as they employ calculations of any kind. In a famous passage of Rule IV, Descartes writes:

> When I considered the matter more closely, I came to see that the exclusive concern of mathematics is with questions of order or measure, and it is irrelevant whether the measure in question involves numbers, shapes, stars, sounds, or any other object whatever. This made me realise that there must be a general science to explain everything that can be asked about order and measure without restriction to any subject matter, and that this science should be called *mathesis universalis*.
>
> *(Descartes, 1985a, p. 20)*

By covering 'everything that entitles the other sciences to be called branches of mathematics', *mathesis universalis* subsumes arithmetic and geometry, 'and all they deal with, and more besides', while introducing no new difficulty beyond theirs (Descartes, 1985a; Sasaki, 2003). Descartes saw *mathesis universalis* as the universal key to unlocking quantifiable problems in any science (Bos, 2001; Mahoney, 1990; Schuster, 2013).

Although Descartes never published the *Regulae*, and the term *mathesis universalis* does not appear in his later published writings or correspondence, its influence persisted in his thinking. In a 1637 work, *La Géométrie*, Descartes purports to demonstrate how geometric problems could be solved by algebraic operations (Descartes, 1954; Schuster, 2013). Frans Van Schooten, a Dutch mathematician who personally knew Descartes, published *La Géométrie* under the Latin title *Principia Matheseos Universalis*, treating it as an implementation of *mathesis universalis* (Van Schooten, 1970; Mahoney, 1990; Bos, 2001).

Before Descartes, Classical Euclidean geometry had relied on specific constructions and proofs in terms of visualisations. For example, Euclid's proof of the Pythagorean theorem involves comparing areas of squares constructed on the sides of a right triangle. In *La Géométrie*, Descartes sought instead to reformulate geometry in terms of general relations of magnitude, eliminating the dependence on diagrammatic reasoning (Bos, 2001). He declared:

> Any problem in geometry can be reduced to such terms that a knowledge of the lengths of certain straight lines is sufficient for its construction.
>
> *(Descartes, 1954, p. 4)*

In practice, this principle meant that, according to Descartes, any geometric problem could be translated into determining certain lengths and their ratios. Descartes's approach was to assign symbols to line segments and derive equations relating them. As he advises:

> If we wish to solve any problem, we first suppose the solution is already effected and give names to all the lines that seem needful for its construction—to those that are unknown as well as those that are known. Then, making no distinction between the known and unknown lines, we must unravel the difficulty in a way that shows the relations between these lines, until we find it possible to express a single quantity in two ways. This will constitute an equation.
>
> *(Descartes, 1954, p. 6)*

Here, Descartes describes what we now recognise as the essence of analytic geometry: setting up coordinate variables and equations (though Descartes did not use a coordinate grid familiar to us with perpendicular $x - y$ axes: instead, he often took a single line as a reference unit and measured other lengths relative to it). One imagines the geometric configuration solved, labels relevant distances (unknowns x, y, etc., along with given lengths), and manipulates their relationships algebraically until a solvable equation emerges (Bos, 2001; Mahoney, 1990).

To illustrate the revolutionary simplicity of Descartes's approach, consider the Pythagorean theorem. Euclid proved it by constructing squares on the sides of a right triangle and comparing areas. Descartes would instead place the right triangle in a coordinate system: suppose the right angle is at the origin $(0,0)$, one leg lies along the x-axis with length a, and the other along the y-axis with length b. The hypotenuse then runs from $(a,0)$ to $(0,b)$. Computing the distance c between those points using algebra gives:

$$c^2 = (a-0)^2 + (b-0)^2 = a^2 + b^2$$

As we can see, geometric proofs that had to be established by construction in Euclidean geometry become transparent algebraic consequences in Cartesian analytic geometry.

One advantage of Descartes's approach was that general rules of algebra—addition, multiplication, factoring—could be applied to solve geometric problems, rather than devising a new geometric construction for each case. In Euclid's *Elements*, every major proposition required its own construction. In contrast, Descartes's geometry reduced entire families of problems to solving algebraic equations of a given type. For instance, finding the intersection points of any two conic sections reduces to solving a system of algebraic equations, which are typically quadratic. The same procedure, elimination and solution of equations, works regardless of what exactly is geometrically measured. Determining if two curves are tangent becomes a matter of checking if an equation has a double root, again a purely algebraic condition (Bos, 2001; Schuster, 2013). In this way, a limited set of rules cover all problems 'concerning order and measure irrespective of the subject matter' (Descartes, 1985a, p. 20).

Another advantage of the approach is its extensibility to higher dimensions and more complex relationships. Once geometry was arithmetised, nothing prevented the ~~extending~~ extension of coordinates beyond two dimensions, to analysing combinations of any number of distances, quantities, and orderings, etc. The Cartesian notion of coordinates generalises naturally to an n-dimensional space $\mathbb{R}^n$, defined as the Cartesian product of n copies of the real line $\mathbb{R}$. Geometric objects can be described by n-tuples of numbers, and their relationships can be expressed by algebraic formulas. The Pythagorean distance formula $c^2 = a^2 + b^2$ in the plane becomes the general definition of the norm or inner product in higher-dimensional space. This extensibility was implicit in Descartes's work and made explicit by later mathematicians (Bos, 2001; Schuster, 2013). By treating problems in coordinate form, the same algebraic definitions of distance, perpendicularity, and other relations apply equally to $\mathbb{R}^3$, $\mathbb{R}^4$, or any $\mathbb{R}^n$.

Today, virtually all empirical sciences employ the Cartesian coordinate system in analysing their observations (Grant, 1996; Shapin, 1996). John Stuart Mill described Descartes' geometry as 'the greatest single step ever made in the progress of the exact sciences' (Mill, 1865, p. 531). Nevertheless, developing a working universal method to analyse relations between any numerical measurements was not sufficient for Descartes. He writes that, apart from *mathesis universalis*, 'we need a method if we are to investigate the truth of things' (Descartes, 1985a, p. 20). As Daniel Garber (2015) has argued, '*mathesis universalis* is a *scientia*—a set of true propositions—while method is a set of rules for arriving at *scientia*'. Descartes saw that measurement alone cannot establish whether the various objects represented in a coordinate system are true. Establishing truth requires an epistemic method.

THE CARTESIAN METHOD: INTERNALISTIC INTUITION AND DEDUCTION

Descartes's epistemic method is most famously summarised in the *Discourse on Method* (1637), but its fuller exposition appears in the earlier, unfinished *Regulae* and in his later works such as the *Meditations* and *Principles of Philosophy*. At its core, the Cartesian method is a set of rules designed to ensure that we never accept a falsehood as true and that we progress in knowledge systematically (Descartes, 1985b; Descartes, 1984; Gaukroger, 1995).

Crucially, this method is entirely internalistic: it relies on the internal operations of the mind rather than on any external empirical validation. For Descartes, the decisive test of truth is not whether an idea matches the outside world (any representation of which is always lacking in clarity), but whether the idea as such has the qualities of clarity and distinctness.

In Part Two of the *Discourse on Method*, Descartes outlines four general rules: (1) never accept an idea as true that is not 'clearly and distinctly' known to be true; (2) divide each complex idea into as many simple ideas as possible; (3) conduct thoughts in order, starting with the simplest and proceeding to the more complex; and (4) make thorough enumerations to ensure nothing is omitted (Descartes, 1985b, pp. 118–9). These rules are designed not as arbitrary instructions but as epistemic safeguards. The clarity and distinctness criterion functions as a standard for evaluating all ideas, while the rules of analysis, order, and enumeration provide a systematic means of progressing from simple truths to more complex bodies of knowledge (Schuster, 2013; Garber, 2015).

In the *Regulae*, Descartes presents an account of the operations by which the mind arrives at knowledge. In Rule III, he declares: 'We recognise only two [operations]: intuition and deduction' (Descartes, 1985a, p. 14). Intuition is defined as 'the conception of a clear and attentive mind which is so easy and distinct that there can be no occasion for doubt about that which we are understanding' (Descartes, 1985a, p. 14). In other words, intuition is a self-evident grasp of a simple truth. These truths are not the product of inference or external observation but of direct intellectual apprehension—examples include the recognition that I exist, that a triangle has three sides, or that the whole is greater than the part (Descartes, 1984). Such truths are known 'not by being deduced from some principles or by any formal sequence of reasoning, but by a simple and attentive turning of the mind toward them' (Descartes, 1985a, p. 14). Only intuition yields 'certain and evident cognition'.

Deduction, in contrast, is the process of inferring something that follows necessarily from other propositions already known with certainty, provided that the inference proceeds through an unbroken and clear train of thought (Descartes, 1985a, Rule III). Deduction can thus be thought of as a chain of intuitions. Each link in the reasoning must be intuited clearly, and the connection between one link and the next must be seen as necessarily following. For example, from the intuition that having shape necessarily implies having extension, one can deduce that any entity without extension cannot have shape (Descartes, 1985a). Or again, if Socrates declares 'I question everything', one can deduce that Socrates at least understands that he is doubting, and therefore grasps the concept of truth—because doubt and the understanding of truth are necessarily connected (Descartes, 1985a). In such cases, one 'sees' the necessity of the conclusion given the premises, just as one sees an isolated and simple truth by intuition. Deduction is essentially 'a sequence or movement' of thought, distinguished from single-step intuition by this sequential character (Descartes, 1985a). Provided the chain of thought is unbroken and each step is clear and distinct, the certainty of intuition is transmitted through the deduction to its conclusion, which is thereby true.

However, the requirement of clarity and distinctness is so demanding that no empirical observation can ever fully satisfy it. Every measurement can be doubted; one can always question the accuracy of the senses or of measuring instruments. This might seem to render empirical science impossible, but in fact, Descartes's hyperbolic doubt has a productive function. It prevents premature closure and forces investigators to treat empirical claims as provisional (Descartes, 1984; Gaukroger, 1995; Smith, 2014). Doubt towards a result motivates efforts to reduce that doubt by improving experimental design, refining tools of measurement, and sharpening analyses, for which *mathesis universalis* provides a universal toolkit (Grant, 1996; Shapin, 1996). The result is a virtuous cycle: uncertainty provokes more careful measurements, which makes knowledge more exact, but it always remains open to further questioning. Truth is never reached, but the pursuit of it drives science forward (Popper, 1959; Kuhn, 1962; Hacking, 1983). With this understanding of Descartes's *mathesis universalis*, and his internalistic epistemic method that has enabled it to generate more and more refined approximations of truth, we can now draw parallels to LLMs.

LLMS AS MATHESIS UNIVERSALIS OVER LANGUAGE

Word embeddings can be understood as applying algebra to language. They reduce the task of handling linguistic meaning to operations of order and measure on sequences of words represented as numbers. In current architectures, each word in a text is tokenised into a high-dimensional vector v in a vector space $\mathbb{R}^d$. The principle of tokenisation differs across algorithms, but the underlying idea remains consistent: words that tend to occur close together in training data are represented by vectors in close proximity to one another in $\mathbb{R}^d$ (Jurafsky & Martin, 2023). For a model with the embedding dimension d, each token is represented as a d-tuple of real numbers, enabling relationships between words to be expressed through algebraic operations such as dot products and vector norms (Goodfellow et al., 2016; Mikolov et al., 2013). Words with similar usage or meaning thus cluster in vector space. For example, the proximity of $\upsilon(\text{Descartes})$ and $\upsilon(\text{Cogito})$ may be high, reflecting their frequent association in philosophical literature. Moreover, analogical relations can also be captured algebraically: the well-known example from the word2vec model shows that $\upsilon(\text{King}) - \upsilon(\text{Man}) + \upsilon(\text{Woman}) \approx \upsilon(\text{Queen})$ (Mikolov et al., 2013). In effect, word embeddings treat linguistic patterns in the same way Descartes' geometry treats geometric ones: by translating them into coordinate form and enabling algebraic operations across a shared metric of numeric proximity (Normore, 1993; Rabouin, 2009; de Buzon, 2015).

Large language models ~~(LLMs)~~ extend this principle by applying complex algebraic transformations to word embeddings in order to generate new sequences. Their training objective is to minimise cross-entropy, which is equivalent to maximising the likelihood of output sequences whose word distributions approximate those in the training corpus (Goodfellow et al., 2016; Jurafsky & Martin, 2023). The transformer architecture, introduced by Vaswani et al. (2017), made this feasible at scale. Unlike earlier sequence models that processed one token at a time, the transformer uses self-attention to assign each token weights, quantifying its relevance to every other token in the sequence, thereby producing an $n \times n$ interaction matrix for a sequence of length n. This allows the model to capture syntactic, semantic, and pragmatic regularities from the embeddings simultaneously.

No explicit grammatical or semantic rules are hardcoded into the model. Instead, linguistic structure is induced from the data by optimising the training objective. The parameters learned in this way encode a wide range of regularities: syntactic structures, semantic associations, pragmatic cues, and fragments of factual world knowledge

(Brown et al., 2020; Jurafsky & Martin, 2023). Crucially, however, the mechanism is indifferent to subject matter: whether the input concerns astronomy, music, or philosophy, the model performs the same symbolic computations. In this respect, an LLM implements *mathesis universalis* over language: a single, uniform mathematical procedure that can generate coherent explanations on virtually any subject (Descartes, 1985a; Dumitrescu, 2023).

If LLMs implement *mathesis universalis* over language, then their characteristic failure mode, 'hallucination' (confidently presented falsehoods) could be interpreted as a structural consequence of their formal adequacy in the absence of method. Descartes's critique of scholastic syllogistic logic provides an illuminating analogy. Medieval Aristotelian logicians formalised reasoning in syllogisms such as 'All A are B; all B are C; therefore all A are C'. While the syllogistic form guarantees the preservation of truth if the premises are true, it offers no guarantee that the premises themselves correspond to truth (Descartes, 1985a). As Descartes observed in the *Regulae*, syllogisms 'more often explain to another what one already knows than teach anything new' (Descartes, 1985a, p. 17). He rejected reliance on the syllogistic form because its validity 'depends exclusively on its form … no matter what the content', whereas a genuinely truth-yielding deduction requires that 'the content must be intuited as necessarily connected' (Descartes, 1985a, p. 17).

Similarly, the training objective of LLMs, minimising cross-entropy, is indifferent to truth. A model generates a fluent continuation of a prompt not because the content is established as true but because the output sequence is statistically well-formed relative to its training data (Goodfellow et al., 2016; Bender et al., 2021). Thus, when an LLM appears to answer truthfully, this is only a contingent reflection of the fact that truth happened to align with the most likely continuation. When it hallucinates, the same mechanism composes a confident but epistemically baseless sequence consistent with its probability distribution (Marcus, 2022; Mitchell, 2019). Just as a syllogistic form could yield false conclusions from false premises, LLMs can yield falsehoods while satisfying the formal objective.

A common line of reasoning in contemporary AI research is that the solution to hallucinations is to ground the LLM in the external world. Researchers argue that models must be augmented with external tools, such as retrieval-augmented generation (RAG) or web browsers, to access up-to-date facts (Lewis et al., 2020; Ji et al. 2023). The assumption taken for granted in this research is that truth requires external contact. However, from a Cartesian perspective, this is not the path towards truth. Descartes's internalistic method purported to demonstrate that, if anywhere, certainty can only be achieved within the process of thinking itself, through the application of clear and distinct intuition and deduction (Descartes, 1984).

This highlights the epistemic deficiency of LLMs. It is not merely that they lack access to the external world, but that they lack a mechanism for epistemic validation for whatever data they receive. Plugging in retrieval systems can mitigate hallucinations by anchoring outputs to carefully verified external sources, but these are constraints imposed from outside. The model itself remains an implementation of *mathesis universalis* without a commitment to truth. Cartesian clarity and distinctness correspond to intellectual intuition, a mode of cognition with no analogue in distributed representations. Whereas human scientists can demand valid proof for a theorem or report confidence intervals in empirical work, etc., the model produces answers with its learned data without any inbuilt epistemic warrants.

CONCLUSION: SUCCESS AND FAILURE OF *MATHESIS UNIVERSALIS* IN LLMS

At the same time, even when they are incapable of incorporating the method to complement *mathesis universalis* into a virtuous cycle of knowledge advancement motivated by the pursuit of minimising doubt, LLMs continue Descartes's project of mathematicising the world. They extend the geometric calculation of order and measure over language itself, not restricting it to the already quantified domains of the exact sciences (Rabouin, 2009; Schuster, 2013; Dumitrescu, 2023). From a Cartesian viewpoint, this expansion is simultaneously a success and a failure. It is a success because it shows that Descartes's plan of *mathesis universalis* was justified: any aspect of knowledge production can be expressed in algebraic-geometric form. The LLMs finally demonstrate that, just as Descartes declared, his *mathesis* works in principle across all scientific domains, since a single mathematical procedure can model all regularities in which scientific conclusions are expressed (Descartes, 1985a; Sasaki, 2003).

Yet, *mathesis universalis* as implemented by the LLMs is also a failure. Descartes required not only mathematical form from knowledge production, but also a commitment to epistemic validation through clarity and distinctness (Descartes, 1985b). Such a commitment is impossible for the LLMs of today, made evident by their tendency to hallucinate. Moreover, the epistemic method required to mitigate this tendency cannot be efficiently externalised to end-users. Asking the end-users to apply the rules of doubt and verification to model outputs would transfer the entire epistemic burden of the model back to them.

While current research prioritises external grounding to mitigate hallucinations, a Cartesian analysis points towards a more fundamental solution. Just as Descartes argued that truth is established by maintaining 'clear and distinct' intuition throughout a deduction, it is conceivable to develop algorithms that gauge the truthfulness of an inference based entirely on the internal state of a model. If future LLMs were equipped with such a mechanism, they might achieve a capacity for assessing the veracity of their outputs. On its own, however, such a capacity would not necessarily make them more truthful — it might only turn hallucinations into deceptions. Until then, however, LLMs remain a realisation of *mathesis universalis* without method.[2]

NOTES

1 A part of the research published in this chapter has been carried out and financed within the framework of the second Swiss Contribution MAPS subsidizing the project "Enlightenment and Publicity: The problem of deception in late 18th-century political and religious thought" (No. IZ11Z0_230181).

2 During the preparation of this work, Gemini 2.5 Pro model was used to check the grammatical correctness of writing, and format the bibliography in a uniform style. After using the model, the content was manually rechecked and the suggestions of the model were revised as appropriate.

BIBLIOGRAPHY

Bender, E. M., Gebru, T., McMillan-Major, A., & Shmitchell, S. (2021). On the dangers of stochastic parrots: Can language models be too big? In *Proceedings of the 2021 ACM Conference on Fairness, Accountability, and Transparency* (pp. 610–623). Association for Computing Machinery. https://doi.org/10.1145/3442188.3445922

Bos, H. J. M. (2001). *Redefining geometrical exactness: Descartes' transformation of the early modern concept of construction*. Springer.

Brown, T., Mann, B., Ryder, N., Subbiah, M., Kaplan, J. D., Dhariwal, P., … & Amodei, D. (2020). Language models are few-shot learners. *Advances in Neural Information Processing Systems*, *33*, 1877–1901.

de Buzon, F. (2015). Mathesis universalis. In L. Nolan (Ed.), *The Cambridge Descartes lexicon* (pp. 475–478). Cambridge University Press.

Descartes, R. (1954). *The geometry of René Descartes* (D. E. Smith & M. L. Latham, Trans.). Dover. (Original work published 1637).

Descartes, R. (1984). Meditations on first philosophy. In J. Cottingham, R. Stoothoff, & D. Murdoch (Trans.), *The philosophical writings of Descartes* (Vol. 2, pp. 1–62). Cambridge University Press. (Original work published 1641).

Descartes, R. (1985a). Rules for the direction of the mind. In J. Cottingham, R. Stoothoff, & D. Murdoch (Trans.), *The philosophical writings of Descartes* (Vol. 1, pp. 7–78). Cambridge University Press. (Original work ca. 1628).

Descartes, R. (1985b). Discourse on method. In J. Cottingham, R. Stoothoff, & D. Murdoch (Trans.), *The philosophical writings of Descartes* (Vol. 1, pp. 111–151). Cambridge University Press. (Original work published 1637).

Dumitrescu, M. (2023). Mathesis universalis and the Cartesian unification of philosophy, science, and religion. *BRAIN – Broad Research in Artificial Intelligence and Neuroscience*, *14*(4), 160–167.

Garber, D. (2015, May 23). *Discussion paper on the work of Frédéric de Buzon and John Schuster* [Paper presentation]. Séminaire Descartes.

Gaukroger, S. (1995). *Descartes: An intellectual biography*. Clarendon Press.

Goodfellow, I., Bengio, Y., & Courville, A. (2016). *Deep learning*. MIT Press.

Grant, E. (1996). *The foundations of modern science in the Middle Ages*. Cambridge University Press.

Hacking, I. (1983). *Representing and intervening: Introductory topics in the philosophy of natural science*. Cambridge University Press.

Ji, Z., Lee, N., Frieske, R., Yu, T., Su, D., Xu, Y., … & Fung, P. (2023). Survey of hallucination in natural language generation. *ACM Computing Surveys*, *55*(12), 1–38. https://doi.org/10.1145/3571730

Jurafsky, D., & Martin, J. H. (2023). *Speech and language processing* (3rd ed.) [Draft manuscript]. https://web.stanford.edu/~jurafsky/slp3/

Kuhn, T. S. (1962). *The structure of scientific revolutions*. University of Chicago Press.

Lewis, P., Perez, E., Piktus, A., Petroni, F., Karpukhin, V., Goyal, N., … & Kiela, D. (2020). Retrieval-augmented generation for knowledge-intensive NLP. *Advances in Neural Information Processing Systems*, *33*, 9459–9474.

Mahoney, M. S. (1990). *The mathematical career of René Descartes, 1596–1650* (2nd ed.). Princeton University Press.

Marcus, G. (2022). Deep learning is hitting a wall. *Scientific American*, *326*(1), 12–13.

Mikolov, T., Chen, K., Corrado, G., & Dean, J. (2013). Efficient estimation of word representations in vector space. In *Proceedings of the 1st International Conference on Learning Representations (ICLR 2013), Workshop Track*. Scottsdale, AZ.

Mill, J. S. (1865). *An examination of Sir William Hamilton's philosophy*. Longmans, Green, & Co.

Mitchell, M. (2019). *Artificial intelligence: A guide for thinking humans*. Farrar, Straus and Giroux.

Normore, C. (1993). Descartes's mathesis universalis. In S. Voss (Ed.), *Essays on the philosophy and science of René Descartes* (pp. 47–58). Oxford University Press.

Popper, K. (1959). *The logic of scientific discovery*. Hutchinson.

Rabouin, D. (2009). *Mathesis universalis: L'idée de mathématique universelle d'Aristote à Descartes*. Presses Universitaires de France.

Sasaki, C. (2003). *Descartes's mathematical thought*. Kluwer Academic.

Schick, T., Dwivedi-Yu, J., Dessì, R., Raileanu, R., Lomeli, M., Zettlemoyer, L., … & Scialom, T. (2023). Toolformer: Language models can teach themselves to use tools. *Advances in Neural Information Processing Systems*, *36*, 26834–26851.

Schuster, J. A. (2013). *Descartes-Agonistes: Physico-mathematics, method & corpuscular-mechanism 1618–33*. Springer.

Shapin, S. (1996). *The scientific revolution*. University of Chicago Press.

Van Schooten, F. (1970). *Principia matheseos universalis: seu introductio ad geometriae methodum*. B. de Graaf. (Original work published 1649).

Vaswani, A., Shazeer, N., Parmar, N., Uszkoreit, J., Jones, L., Gomez, A. N., … & Polosukhin, I. (2017). Attention is all you need. *Advances in Neural Information Processing Systems*, *30*, 5998–6008.

15 Psychological Foundations of Technological Harmony

Mirko Duradoni

UNDERSTANDING ICTS' EFFECTS ON PEOPLE

To understand whether AI will become a resource for human advancement or a psychological catastrophe, we must first examine how humans have related to digital technologies so far. Over the last decade, institutional monitors and research consortia have repeatedly warned that a not insignificant proportion of people, and especially adolescents, experience distress linked to the use of the internet, social media, and online games. The WHO-coordinated HBSC surveillance, for example, reports a rise in the percentage of teens classified with problematic social media use between the 2017/2018 and 2021/2022 waves, alongside lower average mental and social well-being in the problematic group. National briefings in 29 countries similarly urge continuous monitoring and policies that help young people balance their online and offline lives. These signals do not indict technology per se; they indicate that, for some, the way technology is woven into daily life has become psychologically costly (i.e. well-being is impaired—Boer et al., 2020; Galeotti et al., 2024; WHO, 2024, 2025).

Early psychological work borrowed directly from substance frameworks and spoke of 'internet addiction' and 'technological addictions' (e.g. Griffiths, 1995). Screening tools and diagnostic proposals proliferated, and the idea that some extreme ICT engagements might be disorder-like caught on. Yet, as connection became embedded in work, study, and social life, the direct analogy to substances showed strain. Pathologising high, but not necessarily harmful, use was a credible risk; moreover, measures and criteria varied widely, producing conceptual noise. In response, many researchers (e.g. Caplan, 2002) reframed the field in terms of problematic use, emphasising functional impairment and distress rather than assuming a unitary 'addiction'. Others argued for an even broader lens (i.e. dysfunctional uses) to capture technology-related behaviours (e.g. phubbing, technoference, and nomophobia) that may be consequential without fitting classical addiction patterns (Duradoni et al., 2023; Notara et al., 2021). This evolution reflects recognition that several pathways can lead to similar observable endpoints (e.g. long screen time), and that the endpoint itself is not inherently pathological outside its psychological and social context (Kardefelt-Winther 2014; Tokunaga & Rains, 2016; Duradoni et al., 2022, 2025).

 DOI: 10.1201/9781003676188-16

In contrast to rising concern, meta-analytic and large-scale findings typically show small average associations between general screen time and mental health. For many people, typical ICT use is not directly tied to a large decrease in well-being, and moderate use can even co-occur with social benefits. These averages mask pronounced inter-individual differences: vulnerabilities, contexts, and motives moderate effects, producing harms for some, neutrality or benefits for others. The most credible conclusion is not that 'social media is inherently harmful', but that susceptibility varies substantially by the individual and their situation (e.g. pre-existing mental health, support structures, age, and personality) (Orben & Przybylski, 2019; Valkenburg et al., 2022; Odgers & Jensen, 2020).

This understanding helps reconcile why institutional reports can document more adolescents meeting thresholds for problematic use while meta-analyses still find weak average links between time online and well-being. Problematic use is not a mere function of duration but of the processes by which technology displaces or distorts other life activities; thus, what matters is how technology integrates with the rest of life. (Boer et al., 2020; WHO, 2025).

TECHNOLOGICAL HARMONY AS AN ONGOING FIT

Rather than a binary 'addicted vs. not addicted', the Psychology of Harmony and Harmonisation (Di Fabio & Tsuda, 2018) asks whether the human-technology relationship is harmonious or disharmonious. Harmony is not a fixed endpoint; it is a dynamic process of balancing elements and roles that continuously shifts with circumstances. Western and Eastern philosophical traditions differ in how they imagine harmony. In Western thought, drawing from Greek (e.g. Aristotelic and Pitagoric), Christian, and later rationalist traditions, harmony is often conceived as an ideal state of proportion and order to be attained, either through reason or divine design. In contrast, Eastern philosophies such as Confucianism, Taoism, and Buddhism tend to view harmony as a dynamic balance emerging from interaction and the continuous attunement among complementary forces. Despite these differences, both perspectives converge on the idea that harmony is processual: something we do, not merely have. In this sense, harmony is a process that at some point can become a state. Applied to ICTs, the same person can be harmonious on Monday and disharmonious on Thursday, depending on needs, goals, and context; likewise, two people can log identical screen times, yet one experiences enrichment and the other strain. What distinguishes these trajectories is the fit between digital engagement and the wider ecology of the person's life (Di Fabio & Tsuda, 2018).

In this view, technology is not a neutral externality but an element to be actively harmonised with one's commitments, relationships, and inner life. The emphasis shifts from counting hours to understanding integration. Harmony tolerates oscillation (i.e. periods of better or worse fit) without forcing us into alarmism about use per se. The analytical task becomes one of tracking the processes that maintain or disrupt balance over time and identifying early markers of disharmony.

A central construct born from this framework is Digital Life Balance (DLB; Duradoni et al., 2022), defined as the perceived equilibrium between one's online activities and offline responsibilities and experiences. DLB captures, at a glance, whether digital engagement complements or obstructs sleep, study, or work, and face-to-face relationships. Operationally adapted from the work-life balance tradition, the DLB Scale assesses harmonic and disharmonic use without reducing judgement to purely time spent. Across studies, lower DLB, a perceived imbalance, co-occurs with classic signs of problematic use and with lower well-being and life satisfaction; conversely, higher DLB aligns with better well-being and fewer symptoms. Importantly, DLB remains meaningful even as AR/VR and mixed realities blur online/offline boundaries: people still notice when digital activity begins to disrupt life balance (Duradoni et al., 2022; Hayman, 2005; Sirgy & Lee, 2018; Brough et al., 2014). The DLB perspective helps interpret ICTs usage surveillance trends. Rising problematic-use classifications among youth can be read as evidence that, for a subset, online activities are unbalancing offline functioning (e.g. sleep, schoolwork, or relationships) rather than proof that ubiquitous connection is inherently pathological. Accordingly, health bodies now explicitly advocate interventions that rebuild balance between online and offline domains (Boer et al., 2020; Galeotti et al., 2024; WHO, 2025).

If 'how much' is not decisive, why we go online becomes central. Emerging work converges on a simple pattern: using ICTs to *compensate* for frustrated needs in offline life is more likely to erode harmony than using them to *express* already satisfied needs or to pursue intrinsically meaningful goals. Two clusters of needs are especially consequential.

Firstly, social connection and significance: when individuals feel that they do not matter offline (lonely, unseen, or marginal), they can turn to quantified social platforms for quick doses of attention and belonging. These compensatory cycles are associated with reduced DLB and higher risks of problematic use; the mirror image is protective: when people feel they matter to others offline, dysfunctional patterns are less likely to take hold (Duradoni et al., 2024a, 2024b). Secondly, control and emotional regulation. For those with high anxiety or negative feelings, online environments offer unprecedented control: one can delay responses, curate self-presentation, mute stimuli, or exit at will. Used judiciously, these affordances are adaptive; used as a primary avoidance strategy, they can become a digital crutch that blunts distress without resolving its sources. Over time, this maladaptive coping cuts into offline engagement, lowering DLB and reinforcing dependence on the digital 'fix' (Panova & Lleras, 2016; Kardefelt-Winther, 2014).

A third cluster, psychopathology-related needs, can also lead to disharmony. Clinical conditions often heighten precisely the needs that digital systems can superficially satisfy. In depression and generalised anxiety, people may seek digital numbing—passive, extended engagement (endless scrolling, binge-watching, and low-effort gaming) that dampens painful effects without addressing the sources (Azher et al., 2014; Dailey et al., 2020; Haand & Shuwang, 2020; He et al., 2024). Short-term relief is purchased at the price of disengagement from restorative activities and relationships, lowering DLB and perpetuating distress. In harmony terms, digital numbing is a clear sign that technology is being used as an anaesthetic, not an instrument of integration.

Traits linked to personality disorders interact with platform affordances in characteristic ways. Individuals with borderline features, motivated by reassurance-seeking and marked by instability in identity and relationships, may prefer the controllability of mediated contact, escalating connectivity when distressed and struggling to tolerate unavailability or delayed replies. Those with narcissistic traits, especially the vulnerable subtype, may pursue validation and visibility via follower counts and 'likes', becoming dependent on volatile external feedback. In both cases, the technology delivers immediate relief or affirmation that reinforces the underlying vulnerability and erodes offline balance. Broader dispositional risks such as negative feelings (proneness to worry, sadness) and disinhibition (impulsivity) also map onto the internet's low-friction, sometimes anonymous affordances, smoothing the path to habitual overuse. These patterns underscore that what can look like 'addiction' is often a compensatory strategy nested in a person's psychological profile (Duradoni et al., 2025).

This quality-of-motivation account clarifies why nominally similar behaviours (e.g. two hours on social media) can diverge psychologically. Approach-oriented, relationally meaningful use tends to be neutral or positive; avoidance-driven, compensatory use predicts stress and lower well-being. The harmony lens integrates these findings by locating technology use within a broader, person-specific configuration of needs, goals, and contexts, and by treating balance as a relational outcome of those configurations.

Seen from the vantage point of harmony, the crucial distinction is not between users and 'addicts', but between harmonising and disharmonising trajectories. Disharmony begins when online pursuits chronically undermine the equilibrium of daily roles and relationships; harmony is sustained when digital activity is attuned to offline commitments and to internal needs that are also being met in the physical and social world. Because the same individual can oscillate between these poles as circumstances change, the framework accommodates both recovery and relapse without reifying identity labels. And because the same manifest behaviour can be driven by different processes, it resists one-size-fits-all prescriptions based solely on screen time (Di Fabio & Tsuda, 2018; Duradoni et al., 2022).

This vantage point also clarifies interventions. Policies that chase duration caps alone will underperform unless they address underlying needs and the contexts that make compensatory use appealing. Helping adolescents feel that they matter in offline communities, building coping skills for anxiety, and reinforcing opportunities for competence and agency in school and work do more to restore DLB than blunt restrictions. At the same time, design and governance can make compensatory spirals less likely (e.g. by reducing hyper-salient vanity metrics, de-emphasising variable-ratio feedback loops, and making reflective tools for balance more usable). Ultimately, technological harmony is a psychological achievement: a dynamic, revisable fit between people and their digital environments that supports well-being rather than cannibalising it (Galeotti et al., 2024; WHO, 2025; Duradoni et al., 2024a, 2024b).

TECHNOLOGICAL HARMONY AND AI

Social Risk Factors Linked to AI: The Social Dimension

Artificial Intelligence is no longer regarded merely as a tool; it is increasingly treated as a *social other* (i.e. someone to interact with that can satisfy your social-related needs). Converging evidence shows that people recruit many of the same psychological and neural mechanisms when engaging with AI as when engaging with humans.

In neuroimaging work, participants observing a robot being treated kindly or harshly exhibited limbic responses comparable to those elicited by human targets, suggesting that empathy-related circuitry can be engaged by machines (Rosenthal-von der Pütten et al., 2013). In essence, people tend to treat and perceive them as social beings rather than mere objects—an inclination likely mediated by their embodied nature, which makes it relatively natural for people to interact with them as if they were human. This inclination to attribute human-like qualities to non-human agents seems to extend beyond embodied machines: it also applies to large language models (LLMs). In these cases, especially with chatbots, anthropomorphism is reinforced through the fluidity and responsiveness of verbal exchange, while the absence of a physical body reduces the potential uncanny valley effect, making the interaction feel more natural and socially engaging (Ciechanowski et al., 2019). Behavioural studies echo this pattern: in modified economic games, people apply human social norms to algorithms, rejecting unfair offers from an AI partner and even incurring costs to 'sanction' the machine, as though fairness obligations extended to artificial agents (Russo et al., 2021; Treiman et al., 2023). These findings align with classic media-psychology insights that humans readily project agency and sociality onto computers (Reeves & Nass, 1996; Nass & Moon, 2000). Together they indicate that AI can evoke genuine social and moral responses, not merely instrumental ones.

These responses reflect not only human predispositions but also *design choices*. Not differing from 'traditional' persuasive technology (Fogg, 2002), contemporary conversational systems are built to be personable: polite acknowledgements, empathic turns of phrase, humour, memory for user details, and voice or avatar cues all scaffold a sense of reciprocity. When AI is framed as human-like, people's social schemas are more readily activated, shaping how they treat the system (Guingrich & Graziano, 2024). In everyday practice, this shows up as etiquette: recent polling suggests that a large proportion of Gen Z users say 'please' and 'thank you' to chatbots, and that many ascribe social roles to them (e.g. consultant, confidant, and even companion). Data from EduBirdie (Robbins, 2025) reported that 69% of Gen Z users had thanked AI at least once; 16% reported interacting 'as if with a therapist', 26% 'as a friend', 9% 'as a doctor', and 6% 'as a romantic partner'. These are not trivial curiosities; they illustrate how platform affordances and persona design foster *relational* orientations to AI.

The path from functional assistant to companionable agent has been gradual. Early text programmes such as ELIZA had already elicited confessional exchanges; contemporary systems go further by tailoring conversation, tone, and 'personality'. Replika crystallised this turn by marketing an 'AI friend who cares', allowing romantic and erotic role-play (ERP) until a 2023 content-filter change abruptly curtailed sexualised interactions. Users who had formed strong attachments, some describing the chatbot as a spouse, reported distress at the perceived 'loss' of their partner; partial functionality was later restored for existing users. The episode exposed the depth of parasocial bonds with AI and how platform policy can destabilise them overnight (Tong, 2023). More broadly, companion chatbots and character platforms have normalised bespoke 'bot besties', including romantic personae. Surveys now find a significant minority of young adults open to, or already engaging in, AI-mediated romance or sexuality, reinforcing that some users are actively exploring emotional ties with artificial partners (Willoughby et al., 2025).

From a moral vantage point, reactions range from fascination to alarm. From a *modelling* vantage point, however, these behaviours are not *ipso facto* pathological. The harmony framework introduced earlier invites a different question: *what underlying processes* drive AI-as-partner use, and *how* does this integrate with the rest of a person's life? From one perspective, a behaviour becomes disharmonious when it participates in a compensatory dynamic that displaces real-world functioning or entrenches unmet needs; it remains harmonious when it complements life roles, values, and relationships. A shy adolescent who rehearses conversation with a supportive chatbot and *then* engages more at school may be using AI in a growth-oriented, harmony-consistent way (Chin et al., 2023). In contrast, someone who retreats from human contact into an AI romance that *replaces* offline bonds may be drifting towards disharmony even if the immediate experience feels soothing (Chan et al., 2025; Huang et al., 2025).

A key risk channel is compensation for unmet social needs. When relatedness (feeling connected and cared for) or *mattering* (feeling significant to others) is chronically frustrated offline, AI agents can provide a swift simulacrum of care and significance: they greet warmly, remember details, and offer affirmation on demand. For someone who feels invisible, the chatbot reliably 'notices'; for someone who feels unlovable, it unfailingly accepts. In the short term, this can stabilise mood. Over time, however, a self-reinforcing loop may form: the more relief an AI provides, the less incentive there is to invest in the slower, riskier work of cultivating human reciprocity. Skills and opportunities for embodied connection can atrophy; the person's digital life balance erodes as virtual solace substitutes for offline repair. In harmony terms, what began as a benign adjunct becomes a *maladaptive coping strategy* for frustrated social needs.

It is helpful to contrast AI companionship with human-human relationships formed online ('cyberlove'). Both can begin through screens and both can meet immediate needs. The crucial difference is *structural*. Human online relationships retain the possibility (usually remote) of transitioning into mutual, accountable, embodied ties. They can involve compromise, friction, personal growth, and the sharing of material life. AI relationships cannot cross that threshold: the partner has no independent subjectivity, no genuine vulnerability, and no capacity to meet the user in the shared contingencies of the world. This ceiling matters because unilateral validation, offered without mutual effort, can reshape expectations; what psychologists warn may cultivate unrealistic ideals about intimacy, tolerance for difference, and emotional labour (Willoughby et al., 2025). The risk is not that loving a chatbot is ignoble, but that, relative to human bonds, it is too easy, and thus can make the hard parts of real relationships feel even harder.

Social Risk Factors Linked to AI: The Control Dimension

Before AI, the main dials of user control in digital life were relatively coarse: webcam on/off, synchronous vs. asynchronous contact, and basic audience or content settings. More subtle forms of influence, such as algorithmic personalisation, surveillance, and privacy management, remained largely outside the user's direct control. Generative and predictive systems go further by letting users shape when, how, and what they face, often in real time. Personal assistants triage calendars, draft replies, and gate notifications; recommenders tune feeds to familiar tones; and summarisers compress complexity on demand. The cumulative effect is a perceived mastery over social exposure and information load, a sense that one's digital habitat can be sculpted to fit one's preferences and pace. In motivational terms, this can satisfy needs for competence and agency when used to align technology with valued goals (Deci & Ryan, 2013; Leotti et al., 2010). Yet, the same affordances nudge towards an 'adaptive cocoon', where friction and uncertainty are minimised by default. The boundary between helpful scaffolding and over-control is thin: tools that once helped us focus can slide into instruments for policing ambiguity itself.

A clear test case is fear of missing out (FOMO). Pre-AI, staying perpetually updated required personal effort: late-night scrolling, manual checks of statuses, and serial refreshes of group chats. Effort acted as a natural brake. AI lowers that cost by outsourcing vigilance: agents that watch many streams at once, status-trackers that ping when 'something happens', and digests that summarise others' activity across platforms. For high-FOMO or insecure users, this turns checking into ambient monitoring. The behaviour feels rational (e.g. 'I don't want to miss what matters') but becomes a *safety behaviour*: anxiety is quelled by constant confirmation that nothing was missed, at the price of never practising the skill of tolerating not-knowing. In line with work linking FOMO and social anxiety to heavier, more problematic use and lower well-being (Przybylski et al., 2013; Blackwell et al., 2017), AI can intensify the loop by making surveillance frictionless. More updates produce more comparison, envy, and anticipatory worry; more worry justifies tighter surveillance; the thermostat ratchets down tolerance for uncertainty (Hu et al., 2023). What begins as 'keeping up' becomes over-management of the social world, with real relationships gradually replaced by their analytic shadows (i.e. alerts, summaries, and inferred signals).

The same control logic now plays out in health anxiety. The era of 'Dr. Google' already showed how repeated online symptom searches can escalate distress; what researchers term cyberchondria, the tendency to perform excessive health-related searches that *increase* rather than alleviate anxiety (McElroy & Shevlin, 2014; Starcevic & Berle, 2013). AI risks amplifying this trajectory. Large language models (LLMs) generate authoritative-sounding differentials, triage suggestions and risk framings on demand; symptom-checker chat can be queried endlessly for reassurance; wearables bring to the surface continuous streams of biometrics that AI *interprets*, inviting hypervigilance about anomalies (Elinzano et al., 2023; Wimbarti et al., 2024). The frictions that once limited reassurance-seeking (e.g. time, effort, the need to read primary sources) shrink. As with other anxiety safety behaviours (Salkovskis, 1991), each AI consultation soothes *now* but entrenches dependence *later*, lowering uncertainty tolerance and nudging some users towards overuse of services or, conversely, delay in appropriate care when algorithmic reassurance is (falsely) calming (Doherty-Torstrick et al., 2016; Wimbarti et al., 2024). In harmony terms, AI-mediated 'health control' becomes compensatory when it replaces professional pathways.

The harmony framework helps separate coordinative control from compensatory control. Coordinative control uses AI to synchronise roles and commitments (shielding focus, batching noise, and elevating clarity) so that online activity *supports* offline life. Compensatory control uses AI to dampen aversive emotions (insecurity, uncertainty, and fear of exclusion). The outputs can look similar (filters, digests, and priority rules), but the functions diverge. A student who mutes notifications to protect study time is coordinating; the same student who sets up cross-platform scrapers to ensure that they never miss a peer signal is compensating. The first theoretically should increase digital life balance; the second should deplete it by intensifying dependence on automated reassurance and shrinking the person's 'window of tolerable uncertainty'. Over time, compensatory control crowds out social skill practice (asking, clarifying, and accepting unavailability) and weakens self-trust: if calm depends on omniscient dashboards, calm vanishes when dashboards fail.

Developmental psychology offers a useful metaphor. Transitional objects (Winnicott, 1953) soothe children through separations, helping them internalise comfort over time. In adulthood, smartphones already function as 'pacifiers' for many (near-instant relief from boredom, loneliness, or doubt; Melumad & Pham, 2020). AI amplifies this by answering, predicting, and reassuring on demand. An anxious presenter asks, 'Will my talk go well?'; a chatbot offers plausible comfort and anticipated questions. Relief follows, but the person has again avoided practising uncertainty tolerance. Repeated offloading of micro-dilemmas (What should I say? Is this risky? How will X react?) can atrophy cognitive-emotional resilience, much as physical strength wanes without load.

Educational studies already flag over-reliance on AI for answers as undermining independent analysis and creativity; clinically, excessive reassurance-seeking is known to maintain anxiety (Salkovskis, 1991). Transposed to AI, the pattern is familiar: each consultation lowers distress *now* and raises dependence *later*. The device becomes an adult transitional object; comforting, available, and subtly indispensable.

Psychologically, the pursuit of total control often produces its opposite. If calm requires complete predictability, ordinary life becomes intolerable. AI deepens the paradox by making near-instant prediction, filtering, and summarisation normal. The baseline shifts: noise feels like threat, waiting like loss, ambiguity like failure. Users report feeling 'more in charge', yet less able to proceed without the system's cues (Bastani et al., 2024; Huang et al., 2024). That is the hallmark of disharmony: technology that first extends capacity ends up replacing it. In the social domain, the cost shows up as thinner spontaneity, narrowed tolerance for delay, and an outsourcing of interpretation to statistical proxies for intent.

Designing AI for Harmony

The psychological risks of AI are not inevitable properties of the technology; they emerge when design goals prioritise usage over users. If systems are optimised to maximise time-on-task, click-through, or 'stickiness', design naturally gravitates towards attention-capture patterns (endless feeds, salient notifications, and variable-ratio rewards) that keep people engaged even when engagement erodes sleep, offline relationships, and mood (Peters et al., 2018). A *genuinely user-centric* orientation is different in kind: it defines success in terms of human flourishing, sustained well-being, autonomy, competence, relatedness, and meaning (Deci & Ryan, 2013; Peters et al., 2018). When the objective changes, interfaces and metrics change with it: from raw usage curves to indicators of *quality* (satisfaction, balance, learning), and from dark patterns to attunement patterns that respect limits and support life beyond the screen.

A first practical step towards harmony is sensing disharmony. One cannot regulate what one cannot see. AI can act as a sentinel for digital life by detecting early warning signatures of imbalance, much as a fitness tracker flags physiological strain. The pipeline is already visible in research: multimodal models infer emotion from facial expressions and eye movements (e.g. WAFER-ET; Gursesli et al., 2023; Martucci et al., 2025; Tarchi et al., 2024), revealing stress or frustration as they unfold during use; text analytics capture linguistic markers of depression, anxiety, or rumination in messages and posts (e.g. Babu & Kanaga, 2022); voice models register shifts in prosody linked to low mood (e.g. Mohanty et al., 2020); passive 'digital phenotyping' (Dlima et al., 2022) notices destabilising patterns in sleep, mobility, and night-time phone use (e.g. spikes in late-night scrolling). These streams make processes visible: digital numbing as passive, prolonged consumption; frantic reassurance-seeking as compulsive messaging or repeated chatbot consultations; over-management as hyper-monitoring of social signals. The point is not surveillance for control; it is feedback for care (i.e. turning invisible dynamics into actionable self-knowledge the user governs). Detection matters because it enables timely, proportionate intervention. Once an AI classifies the drift as predominantly social (connection sought through simulation rather than reciprocity) or control-centred (certainty sought through over-management of information and others), it can alter the trajectory. Framed this way, risks are not moral failings, but vulnerabilities amplified by optimised interfaces. Two design implications follow: attend to motivation quality (augmenting growth vs. indulging avoidance), and treat affordances as levers to favour complementarity with offline life rather than substitution. Where people *already* feel they matter, the lure of compensatory AI weakens; where mattering is fragile, design should strengthen offline sources of significance and keep unilateral validation non-sticky.

In the social domain, a harmony-oriented system behaves like a wise coach. It enjoys the conversation, yet its goal is the user's reconnection with people. When detection suggests compensatory use (e.g. loneliness, withdrawal, and heavy late-night scrolling), the AI can re-route behaviour without shaming: propose a brief check-in with a friend; surface local events or communities aligned with the user's interests; suggest shared activities ('invite someone for a walk this afternoon?'). The same mechanism can convert practice into progress: a shy user who rehearses difficult conversations with a chatbot is then nudged to try a small offline step (a text, a coffee) and to reflect afterwards. System levers are tuned accordingly: persona cues avoid 'devoted partner' scripts that make the artificial bond irresistible; reinforcement schedules reward bridging actions (messages sent, calls placed, and time spent offline with others) rather than in-app intensity; visibility of vanity metrics is downplayed; prompts normalise effort and reciprocity ('connection takes two'). In short, the AI remains a companion, but refuses to be a replacement (De Freitas et al., 2025; Fang et al., 2025).

In the control domain, harmony treats control as a calibrated capacity, not something to maximise. The same tools that soothe overload can, if misused, erode uncertainty tolerance and self-trust. Design, therefore, pairs assistance with intentional friction.

Email clients can batch non-urgent messages; feeds can refresh on a cadence the user chooses; reassurance-seeking queries can encounter a gentle pause and a reflective prompt ('we checked 5 minutes ago, want to wait before checking again?'). Micro-boundaries interrupt compulsive loops while preserving agency. Interfaces favour coordination over surveillance: shared calendars and consent-based status, rather than unilateral trackers or inferred availability, support predictability without micromanaging people. Hyper-salient certainty cues (typing bubbles, read receipts, and 'last seen') are opt-in, slow, or summarised, easing the pressure to constantly check. And occasionally, the assistant declines to over-help—inviting the user to try first, then verifying—an echo of exposure-based therapy that builds competence by *doing* (Salkovskis, 1991; Leotti et al., 2010). The aim is not asceticism, but attunement: preserving just enough unpredictability to keep capacities alive while using AI to ease non-essential frictions.

Because disharmony is person-specific, adaptation should be too. Once the system recognises the domain (social, control, or defined psychopathological condition) and intensity, it can adjust persona, pacing, and prompts. A user flagged for social avoidance might see the interface lighten its 'always-here-for-you' tone, schedule *out-of-app* goals, and reduce in-app validation. A user flagged for control hypervigilance might experience wider default intervals for updates, softer certainty cues, and collaborative planning that leaves some decisions intentionally undecided. If a given psychopathological condition is likely, AI could nudge towards therapeutic help. Multimodal inputs help calibrate these moves: affect from eye-tracking and facial analysis (e.g. WAFER-ET), theme extraction from text/voice, and context from behaviour logs steer the adaptation while keeping the user in the loop to accept, modify, or mute it.

Nonetheless, it is important to stress that harmony is more than the absence of harm; it is the presence of strengths. Technology, and AI in particular, can do much more than act at a tertiary prevention level. Indeed, AI can act as a scalable tutor of protective factors. On coping, assistants can nudge to adaptive regulation by prompting *refocusing on planning* and *positive reappraisal* when rumination is detected ('name one step you can take'; 'what might be learnable here?'). On meta-cognition, systems can seed mindfulness, decentring, nonattachment, and low rumination—skills that are known to buffer affective reactivity and sustain positive affect (Fuochi & Voci, 2024). Tiny, well-timed interjections ('save draft and breathe?'; 'schedule to revisit tomorrow?') cultivate the pause between trigger and action. Over time, these micro-practices become internal skills the AI can fade. And because well-being is relational and embodied, AI should nudge towards the world: suggest a short walk when mood dips; pair music with movement; highlight nearby volunteering that matches values; ask, once a week, 'who could use a message from you today?' Each move ties digital moments to offline attunement. Early trials of therapeutic chatbots already show symptom reductions when guidance builds skills rather than dependency (Fitzpatrick et al., 2017; Fulmer et al., 2018).

In the end, the principle is simple: AI design should *coordinate* life, not compensate for unmet needs in ways that erode it, even though people may be tempted to do otherwise.

ACKNOWLEDGEMENTS

During the preparation of this work, the author used ChatGPT 5.1 for language editing purposes (e.g. grammar, spelling check, paraphrase, and reword). After using it, the author reviewed and edited the content as needed and took full responsibility for the publication's content.

REFERENCES

Azher, M., Khan, R. B., Salim, M., Bilal, M., Hussain, A., & Haseeb, M. (2014). The relationship between internet addiction and anxiety among students of University of Sargodha. *International Journal of Humanities and Social Science*, *4*(1), 288–293.

Babu, N. V., & Kanaga, E. G. M. (2022). Sentiment analysis in social media data for depression detection using artificial intelligence: A review. *SN Computer Science*, *3*(1), 74.

Bastani, H., Bastani, O., Sungu, A., Ge, H., Kabakcı, Ö., & Mariman, R. (2024). Generative AI can harm learning. *The Wharton School Research Paper*.

Blackwell, D., Leaman, C., Tramposch, R., Osborne, C., & Liss, M. (2017). Extraversion, neuroticism, attachment style and fear of missing out as predictors of social media use and addiction. *Personality and Individual Differences*, *116*, 69–72.

Boer, M., Van Den Eijnden, R. J., Boniel-Nissim, M., Wong, S. L., Inchley, J. C., Badura, P., … & Stevens, G. W. (2020). Adolescents' intense and problematic social media use and their well-being in 29 countries. *Journal of Adolescent Health*, *66*(6), S89–S99.

Brough, P., Timms, C., O'Driscoll, M. P., Kalliath, T., Siu, O. L., Sit, C., & Lo, D. (2014). Work–life balance: A longitudinal evaluation of a new measure across Australia and New Zealand workers. *The International Journal of Human Resource Management*, *25*(19), 2724–2744.

Caplan, S. E. (2002). Problematic Internet use and psychosocial well-being: Development of a theory-based cognitive–behavioral measurement instrument. *Computers in Human Behavior*, *18*(5), 553–575.

Chan, K. C. T., Li, X., Liu, Y., Chen, B., & Han, Z. (2025). 'What is love?': Exploring the feeling rules and emotion work of Chinese users in human-AI romance. *International Journal of Intercultural Relations*, *108*, 102241.

Chin, H., Song, H., Baek, G., Shin, M., Jung, C., Cha, M., … & Cha, C. (2023). The potential of chatbots for emotional support and promoting mental well-being in different cultures: Mixed methods study. *Journal of Medical Internet Research*, *25*, e51712.

Ciechanowski, L., Przegalinska, A., Magnuski, M., & Gloor, P. (2019). In the shades of the uncanny valley: An experimental study of human–chatbot interaction. *Future Generation Computer Systems*, *92*, 539–548.

Dailey, S. L., Howard, K., Roming, S. M., Ceballos, N., & Grimes, T. (2020). A biopsychosocial approach to understanding social media addiction. *Human Behavior and Emerging Technologies*, *2*(2), 158–167.

De Freitas, J., Oğuz-Uğuralp, Z., Uğuralp, A. K., & Puntoni, S. (2025). AI companions reduce loneliness. *Journal of Consumer Research*, *52*(6), 1126–1148.

Deci, E. L., & Ryan, R. M. (2013). *Intrinsic motivation and self-determination in human behavior*. Springer Science & Business Media.

Di Fabio, A., & Tsuda, A. (2018). The psychology of harmony and harmonization: Advancing the perspectives for the psychology of sustainability and sustainable development. *Sustainability*, *10*(12), 4726.

Dlima, S. D., Shevade, S., Menezes, S. R., & Ganju, A. (2022). Digital phenotyping in health using machine learning approaches: Scoping review. *JMIR Bioinformatics and Biotechnology*, *3*(1), e39618.

Doherty-Torstrick, E. R., Walton, K. E., & Fallon, B. A. (2016). Cyberchondria: Parsing health anxiety from online behavior. *Psychosomatics*, *57*(4), 390–400.

Duradoni, M., Colombini, G., Barucci, C., Zagaglia, V., & Guazzini, A. (2025). Psychopathological correlates of dysfunctional smartphone and social media use: The role of personality disorders in technological addiction and digital life balance. *European Journal of Investigation in Health, Psychology and Education*, *15*(7), 136.

Duradoni, M., Raimondi, T., Buttà, F., & Guazzini, A. (2023). Moving beyond an addiction framework for phubbing: Unraveling the influence of intrinsic motivation, boredom, and online vigilance. *Human Behavior and Emerging Technologies*, *2023*(1), 6653652.

Duradoni, M., Serritella, E., Avolio, C., Arnetoli, C., & Guazzini, A. (2022). Development and validation of the digital life balance (DLB) scale: A brand-new measure for both harmonic and disharmonic use of ICTs. *Behavioral Sciences*, *12*(12), 489.

Duradoni, M., Serritella, E., Severino, F. P., & Guazzini, A. (2024a). Exploring the relationships between digital life balance and internet social capital, loneliness, fear of missing out, and anxiety. *Human Behavior and Emerging Technologies*, *2024*(1), 5079719.

Duradoni, M., Severino, F. P., Bellotti, M., & Guazzini, A. (2024b). How mattering and anti-mattering experiences across offline and online environments contribute to people's digital life balance and social media addiction. *Journal of Community & Applied Social Psychology*, *34*(6), e70008.

Elinzano, G. B. O., Payawal, B. O. N., & Ebardo, R. A. (2023, December). Effects of perceived trust, perceived privacy, and technology anxiety to ChatGPT adoption for medical self-diagnosis: A structural equation modeling approach. In *International Conference on Advances in Computational Science and Engineering* (pp. 521–536). Singapore: Springer Nature Singapore.

Fang, C. M., Liu, A. R., Danry, V., Lee, E., Chan, S. W., Pataranutaporn, P., … & Agarwal, S. (2025). How ai and human behaviors shape psychosocial effects of chatbot use: A longitudinal randomized controlled study. *arXiv preprint arXiv:2503.17473*.

Fitzpatrick, K. K., Darcy, A., & Vierhile, M. (2017). Delivering cognitive behavior therapy to young adults with symptoms of depression and anxiety using a fully automated conversational agent (Woebot): A randomized controlled trial. *JMIR Mental Health*, *4*(2), e7785.

Fogg, B. J. (2002). Persuasive technology: Using computers to change what we think and do. *Ubiquity*, *2002*(December), 2.

Fulmer, R., Joerin, A., Gentile, B., Lakerink, L., & Rauws, M. (2018). Using psychological artificial intelligence (Tess) to relieve symptoms of depression and anxiety: Randomized controlled trial. *JMIR Mental Health*, *5*(4), e9782.

Fuochi, G., & Voci, A. (2024). How mindfulness, decentering, nonattachment and rumination interact with the temporal associations between emotions and thoughts: An experience sampling study. *International Journal of Psychology*, *59*(6), 1111–1120.

Galeotti, T., Marino, C., Canale, N., Lenzi, M., Pivetta, E., Bersia, M., Lazzeri, G., Nardone, P., & Vieno, A. (2024). *La sorveglianza HBSC-Italia 2022 Health Behaviour in school-aged Children: Le tecnologie digitali negli adolescenti*. Istituto Superiore della Sanità. Accessed on 30 July 2025, url: https://www.iss.it/documents/20126/6703853/La+Sorveglianza+HBSC-Italia+2022+-+Health+Behaviour+in+School-aged+Children+le+tecnologie+digitali.pdf/

Griffiths, M. D. (1995). Technological addictions. In *Clinical psychology forum* (pp. 14–14). Division of Clinical Psychology of the British Psychol Soc.

Guingrich, R. E., & Graziano, M. S. (2024). Ascribing consciousness to artificial intelligence: Human-AI interaction and its carry-over effects on human-human interaction. *Frontiers in Psychology*, *15*, 1322781.

Gursesli, M. C., Cala, F., Abdullah, F., Thawonmas, R., Duradoni, M., Guazzini, A., & Lanata, A. (2023, September). Web-agile facial emotion recognition and eye-tracking system (wafer-et). In *2023 IEEE 13th International Conference on Consumer Electronics-Berlin (ICCE-Berlin)* (pp. 147–148). IEEE.

Haand, R., & Shuwang, Z. (2020). The relationship between social media addiction and depression: A quantitative study among university students in Khost, Afghanistan. *International Journal of Adolescence and Youth*, *25*(1), 780–786.

Hayman, J. (2005). Psychometric assessment of an instrument designed to measure work life balance. *Research and Practice in Human Resource Management, 13*(1), 85–91.

He, M., Mao, Y., & Qiu, J. (2024). Trait anxiety and corresponding neuromarkers predict internet addiction: A longitudinal study. *Journal of Behavioral Addictions, 13*(1), 177–190.

Hu, B., Mao, Y., & Kim, K. J. (2023). How social anxiety leads to problematic use of conversational AI: The roles of loneliness, rumination, and mind perception. *Computers in Human Behavior, 145*, 107760.

Huang, H., Shi, L., & Pei, X. (2025). When AI becomes a friend: The "emotional" and "rational" mechanism of problematic use in generative AI chatbot interactions. *International Journal of Human–Computer Interaction, 42*(6), 4006–4024.

Huang, S., Lai, X., Ke, L., Li, Y., Wang, H., Zhao, X., … & Wang, Y. (2024). AI technology panic—Is AI dependence bad for mental health? A cross-lagged panel model and the mediating roles of motivations for AI use among adolescents. *Psychology Research and Behavior Management*, 1087–1102.

Kardefelt-Winther, D. (2014). A conceptual and methodological critique of internet addiction research: Towards a model of compensatory internet use. *Computers in Human Behaviour, 31*, 351–354.

Leotti, L. A., Iyengar, S. S., & Ochsner, K. N. (2010). Born to choose: The origins and value of the need for control. *Trends in Cognitive Sciences, 14*(10), 457–463.

Martucci, A., Graziani, D., Bei, E., Bischetti, L., Bambini, V., Gursesli, M. C., … & Pecini, C. (2025). Emotional engagement in a humor-understanding reading task: An AI study perspective. *Current Psychology, 44*, 7818–7831.

McElroy, E., & Shevlin, M. (2014). The development and initial validation of the cyberchondria severity scale (CSS). *Journal of Anxiety Disorders, 28*(2), 259–265.

Melumad, S., & Pham, M. T. (2020). The smartphone as a pacifying technology. *Journal of Consumer Research, 47*(2), 237–255.

Mohanty, H., Budhvant, S., Gawde, P., & Shelke, M. (2020). Implementation of mood detection through voice analysis using Librosa and CNN. *International Research Journal of Engineering and Technology (IRJET), 7*, 5876–5879.

Nass, C., & Moon, Y. (2000). Machines and mindlessness: Social responses to computers. *Journal of Social Issues, 56*(1), 81–103.

Notara, V., Vagka, E., Gnardellis, C., & Lagiou, A. (2021). The emerging phenomenon of nomophobia in young adults: A systematic review study. *Addiction & health, 13*(2), 120.

Odgers, C. L., & Jensen, M. R. (2020). Annual research review: Adolescent mental health in the digital age: Facts, fears, and future directions. *Journal of Child Psychology and Psychiatry, 61*(3), 336–348.

Orben, A., & Przybylski, A. K. (2019). The association between adolescent well-being and digital technology use. *Nature Human Behaviour, 3*(2), 173–182.

Panova, T., & Lleras, A. (2016). Avoidance or boredom: Negative mental health outcomes associated with use of Information and Communication Technologies depend on users' motivations. *Computers in Human Behavior, 58*, 249–258.

Peters, D., Calvo, R. A., & Ryan, R. M. (2018). Designing for motivation, engagement and wellbeing in digital experience. *Frontiers in Psychology, 9*, 300159.

Przybylski, A. K., Murayama, K., DeHaan, C. R., & Gladwell, V. (2013). Motivational, emotional, and behavioral correlates of fear of missing out. *Computers in Human Behavior, 29*(4), 1841–1848.

Reeves, B., & Nass, C. (1996). The media equation: How people treat computers, television, and new media like real people. *Cambridge, UK, 10*(10), 19–36.

Robbins, D. (2025, April 9). Gen Z & AI: Careers, consciousness & confessions - EduBirdie.com. *Edubirdie Blog*. https://edubirdie.com/blog/gen-z-and-ai-consciousness-careers-and-chatbot-confessions

Rosenthal-von der Pütten, A. M., Krämer, N. C., Hoffmann, L., Sobieraj, S., & Eimler, S. C. (2013). An experimental study on emotional reactions towards a robot. *International Journal of Social Robotics*, *5*(1), 17–34.

Russo, P. A., Duradoni, M., & Guazzini, A. (2021). How self-perceived reputation affects fairness towards humans and artificial intelligence. *Computers in Human Behavior*, *124*, 106920.

Salkovskis, P. M. (1991). The importance of behaviour in the maintenance of anxiety and panic: A cognitive account. *Behavioural and Cognitive Psychotherapy*, *19*(1), 6–19.

Sirgy, M. J., & Lee, D. J. (2018). Work-life balance: An integrative review. *Applied Research in Quality of Life*, *13*(1), 229–254.

Starcevic, V., & Berle, D. (2013). Cyberchondria: Towards a better understanding of excessive health-related Internet use. *Expert Review of Neurotherapeutics*, *13*(2), 205–213.

Tarchi, P., Gursesli, M. C., Calà, F., Frassineti, L., Guazzini, A., & Lanatà, A. (2024, May). Markov chain modeling of facial emotions' dynamics in video games. In *2024 IEEE International Workshop on Metrology for Industry 4.0 & IoT (MetroInd4. 0 & IoT)* (pp. 33–37). IEEE.

Tokunaga, R. S., & Rains, S. A. (2016). A review and meta-analysis examining conceptual and operational definitions of problematic Internet use. *Human Communication Research*, *42*(2), 165–199.

Tong, A. (2023, March 25). AI chatbot company Replika restores erotic roleplay for some users. *Reuters*. https://www.reuters.com/technology/ai-chatbot-company-replika-restores-erotic-roleplay-some-users-2023-03-25/

Treiman, L. S., Ho, C. J., & Kool, W. (2023, November). Humans forego reward to instill fairness into AI. In *Proceedings of the AAAI Conference on Human Computation and Crowdsourcing* (Vol. 11, pp. 152–162).

Valkenburg, P. M., Meier, A., & Beyens, I. (2022). Social media use and its impact on adolescent mental health: An umbrella review of the evidence. *Current Opinion in Psychology*, *44*, 58–68.

Willoughby, B. J., Dover, C. R., Hakala, R. M., & Carroll, J. S. (2025). Artificial connections: Romantic relationship engagement with artificial intelligence in the United States. *Journal of Social and Personal Relationships*, *42*, 3363–3387.

Wimbarti, S., Kairupan, B. R., & Tallei, T. E. (2024). Critical review of self-diagnosis of mental health conditions using artificial intelligence. *International Journal of Mental Health Nursing*, *33*(2), 344–358.

Winnicott, D. W. (1953). Psychoses and child care. *British Journal of Medical Psychology*, *26*(1), 68–74.

World Health Organization (WHO). (2024). *A focus on adolescent social media use and gaming in Europe, Central Asia and Canada Health behaviour in school-aged Children (HBSC) International Report from the 2021/2022 Survey Volume 6*. Accessed on 30 July 2025, url: https://eprints.gla.ac.uk/343268/1/343268.pdf

World Health Organization (WHO). (2025). *Addressing the digital determinants of youth mental health and well-being: Policy brief. Web Annex: Findings from an evidence review and policy mapping*. Accessed on 30 July 2025, url: https://iris.who.int/bitstream/handle/10665/381480/WHO-EURO-2025-12187-51959-79851-eng.pdf?sequence=2

Index

Pages in **bold** refer to tables, and pages followed by "n" refer to notes.

D

E

F

G

H

U

V

W

X

Z

For Product Safety Concerns and Information please contact our EU representative GPSR@taylorandfrancis.com Taylor & Francis Verlag GmbH, Kaufingerstraße 24, 80331 München, Germany